The women of Mormondom

Edward W. Tullidge

Alpha Editions

This edition published in 2019

ISBN : 9789353603649

Design and Setting By
Alpha Editions
email - alphaedis@gmail.com

Eliza R. Snow,

THE

WOMEN

OF

MORMONDOM.

By EDWARD W. TULLIDGE.

NEW YORK.

1877.

PREFACE.

Long enough, O women of America, have your Mormon sisters been blasphemed!

From the day that they, in the name and fear of the Lord their God, undertook to "build up Zion," they have been persecuted for righteousness sake: "A people scattered and peeled from the beginning."

The record of their lives is now sent unto you, that you may have an opportunity to judge them in the spirit of righteousness. So shall you be judged by Him whom they have honored, whose glory they have sought, and whose name they have magnified.

Respectfully,

EDWARD W. TULLIDGE.

Salt Lake City, March, 1877.

CONTENTS.

CHAPTER I.

A STRANGE RELIGIOUS EPIC——AN ISRAELITISH TYPE
OF WOMAN IN THE AGE.

An epic of woman! Not in all the ages has there been one like unto it.

Fuller of romance than works of fiction are the lives of the Mormon women. So strange and thrilling is their story,—so rare in its elements of experience,—that neither history nor fable affords a perfect example; yet is it a reality of our own times.

Women with new types of character, antique rather than modern; themes ancient, but transposed to our latter-day experience. Women with their eyes open, and the prophecy of their work and mission in their own utterances, who have dared to enter upon the path of religious empire-founding with as much divine enthusiasm as had the apostles who founded Christendom. Such are the Mormon women,—religious empire-founders, in faith and fact. Never till now did woman essay such an extraordinary character; never before did woman rise to the conception of so supreme a mission in her own person and life.

We can only understand the Mormon sisterhood by introducing them in this cast at the very outset; only comprehend the wonderful story of their lives

by viewing them as apostles, who have heard the
voices of the invisibles commanding them to build
the temples of a new faith.

Let us forget, then, thus early in their story, all
reference to polygamy or monogamy. Rather let us
think of them as apostolic mediums of a new revelation, who at first saw only a dispensation of divine
innovations and manifestations for the age. Let us
view them purely as prophetic women, who undertook to found their half of a new Christian empire,
and we have exactly the conception with which
to start the epic story of the Women of Mormondom.

They had been educated by the Hebrew Bible,
and their minds cast by its influence, long before
they saw the book of Mormon or heard the Mormon prophet. The examples of the ancient apostles were familiar to them, and they had yearned for
the pentecosts of the early days. But most had
they been enchanted by the themes of the old
Jewish prophets, whose writings had inspired them
with faith in the literal renewal of the covenant with
Israel, and the "restitution of all things" of Abrahamic promise. This was the case with nearly all
of the early disciples of Mormonism,—men and
women. They were not as *sinners* converted to
Christianity, but as *disciples* who had been waiting for
the "fullness of the everlasting gospel." Thus had
they been prepared for the new revelation,—an
Israel born unto the promises,—an Israel afterwards
claiming that in a pre-existent state they were the
elect of God. They had also inherited their earnest
religious characters from their fathers and mothers.

The pre-natal influences of generations culminated in the bringing forth of this Mormon Israel.

And here we come to the remarkable fact that the women who, with its apostles and elders, founded Mormondom, were the Puritan daughters of New England, even as were their compeer brothers its sons.

Sons and daughters of the sires and mothers who founded this great nation; sons and daughters of the sires and mothers who fought and inspired the war of the revolution, and gave to this continent a magna charta of religious and political liberty! Their stalwart fathers also wielded the "sword of the Lord" in old England, with Cromwell and his Ironsides, and the self-sacrificing spirit of their pilgrim mothers sustained New England in the heat and burden of the day, while its primeval forests were being cleared, even as these pilgrim Mormons pioneered our nation the farthest West, and converted the great American desert into fruitful fields.

That those who established the Mormon Church are of this illustrious origin we shall abundantly see, in the record of these lives, confirmed by direct genealogical links. Some of their sires were even governors of the British colonies at their very rise: instance the ancestor of Daniel H. Wells, one of the presidents of the Mormon Church, who was none other than the illustrious Thomas Wells, fourth governor of Connecticut; instance the pilgrim forefather of the apostles Orson and Parley Pratt, who came from England to America in 1633, and with the Rev. Thomas Hooker and his congregation pioneered through dense wildernesses, inhabited only by savages and wild beasts, and became the founders of the colony of Hartford, Conn., in June, 1636; instance the Youngs, the Kimballs, the Smiths, the Woodruffs, the Lymans, the Snows, the Carringtons, the Riches, the Hunters, the Huntingtons, the Patridges, the Whitneys, and a host of other early disciples of the Mormon Church. Their ancestors were among the very earliest settlers of the English colonies. There is good reason, indeed, to believe that on board the Mayflower was some of the blood that has been infused into the Mormon Church.

This genealogical record, upon which the Mormon people pride themselves, has a vast meaning, not only in accounting for their empire-founding genius and religious career, but also for their Hebraic types of character and themes of faith. Their genius is in their very blood. They are, as observed, a latter-day Israel,—born inheritors of the promise,—pre-destined apostles, both men and women, of the greater mission of this nation,—the elect of the new covenant of God, which America is destined to unfold to " every nation, kindred, tongue and people." This is not merely an author's fancy; it is an affirm-ation and a prophecy well established in Mormon faith and themes.

If we but truthfully trace the pre-natal expositions of this peculiar people—and the sociologist will at once recognize in this method a very book of revelation on the subject—we shall soon come to look upon these strange Israelitish types and wonders as simply a hereditary culmination in the nineteenth century.

Mormonism, indeed, is not altogether a new faith, nor a fresh inspiration in the world. The facts disclose that its genius has come down to the children, through generations, in the very blood which the invisibles inspired in old England, in the seventeenth century, and which wrought such wonders of God among the nations then. That blood has been speaking in our day with prophet tongue; those wonderful works, wrought in the name of the Lord of Hosts, by the saints of the commonwealth, to establish faith in Israel's God and reverence for His name above all earthly powers, are, in their consummation in America, wrought by these latter-day saints in the same august name and for the same purpose. He shall be honored among the nations; His will done among men; His name praised to the ends of the earth! Such was the affirmation of the saints of the commonwealth of England two hundred and thirty years ago; such the affirmation of the saints raised up to establish the "Kingdom of God" in the nineteenth century. Understand this fully, and the major theme of Mormonism is comprehended. It will have a matchless exemplification in the story of the lives of these single-hearted, simple-minded, but grand women, opening to the reader's view the methods of that ancient genius, even to the establishing of the patriarchal institution and covenant of polygamy.

That America should bring forth a peculiar people, like the Mormons, is as natural as that a mother should bear children in the semblance of the father who begat them. Monstrous, indeed, would it be if, as offspring of the patriarchs and mothers of this nation, America brought forth naught but godless politicians.

CHAPTER II.

THE MOTHER OF THE PROPHET—THE GIFTS OF INSPIRATION AND WORKING OF MIRACLES INHERENT IN HER FAMILY—FRAGMENTS OF HER NARRATIVE.

First among the chosen women of the latter-day dispensation comes the mother of the Prophet, to open this divine drama.

It is one of our most beautiful and suggestive proverbs that "great men have great mothers." This cannot but be peculiarly true of a great prophet whose soul is conceptive of a new dispensation.

Prophecy is of the woman. She endows her offspring with that heaven-born gift.

The father of Joseph was a grand patriarchal type. He was the Abraham of the Church, holding the office of presiding patriarch. To this day he is remembered and spoken of by the early disciples with the profoundest veneration and filial love, and his patriarchal blessings, given to them, are preserved and valued as much as are the patriarchal blessings of Abraham, Isaac and Jacob valued by their own race.

But it is the mother of the Prophet who properly leads in opening the testament of the women of Mormondom. She was a prophetess and seeress born. The gift of prophecy and the power to work miracles also inhered in the family of Lucy Mack, (her maiden name), and the martial spirit which distinguished her son, making him a prophet-general, was quite characteristic of her race. Of her brother, Major Mack, she says :

" My brother was in the city of Detroit in 1812, "the year in which Hull surrendered the territory "to the British crown. My brother, being somewhat "celebrated for his prowess, was selected by General " Hull to take the command of a company as captain. " After a short service in this office he was ordered "to surrender. (Hull's surrender to the British). " At this his indignation was aroused to the highest "pitch. He broke his sword across his knee, and "throwing it into the river, exclaimed that he would "never submit to such a disgraceful compromise "while the blood of an American continued to flow "in his veins."

Lucy Mack's father, Solomon Mack, was a soldier in the American revolution. He entered the army at the age of twenty-one, in the year 1755, and in the glorious struggle of his country for independence he enlisted among the patriots in 1776. With him were his two boys, Jason and Stephen, the latter being the same who afterwards broke his sword and cast it into the river rather than surrender it to the British.

But that which is most interesting here is the seeric gift coupled with the miracle-working power of " Mother Lucy's " race. Hers was a " visionary " family, in the main, while her elder brother, Jason, was a strange evangelist, who wandered about during his lifetime, by sea and land, preaching the gospel

and working miracles. ˙ This Jason even attempted
to establish a body of Christian communists. Of
him she says :

"Jason, my oldest brother, was a studious and
"manly boy. Before he had attained his sixteenth
"year he became what was then called a 'seeker,'
"and believing that by prayer and faith the gifts of
"the gospel, which were enjoyed by the ancient dis-
"ciples of Christ, might be attained, he labored
"almost incessantly to convert others to the same
"faith. He was also of the opinion that God would, at
"some subsequent period, manifest His power, as He
"had anciently done, in signs and wonders. At the
"age of twenty he became a preacher of the gospel."

Then followed a love episode in Jason's life, in
which the young man was betrayed by his rival
while absent in England on business with his father.
The rival gave out that Jason had died in Liverpool,
(being post-master, he had also intercepted their
correspondence,) so that when the latter returned
home he found his betrothed married to his enemy.
The story runs :

"As soon as Jason arrived he repaired imme-
"diately to her father's house. When he got there
"she was gone to her brother's funeral; he went in,
"and seated himself in the same room where he had
"once paid his addresses to her. In a short time
"she came home; when she first saw him she did
"not know him, but when she got a full view of his
"countenance she recognized him, and instantly
"fainted. From this time forward she never recov-
"ered her health, but, lingering for two years, died
"the victim of disappointment.

" Jason remained in the neighborhood a short
"time and then went to sea, but he did not follow
" the sea a great while. He soon left the main, and
" commenced preaching, which he continued until
" his death."

Once or twice during his lifetime Jason visited
his family; at last, after a silence of twenty years,
his brother Solomon received from him the following very evangelistic epistle :

"South Branch of Ormucto,
"Province of New Brunswick,
"June 30, 1835.

" MY DEAR BROTHER SOLOMON: You will, no
doubt, be surprised to hear that I am still alive,
although in an absence of twenty years I have never
written to you before. But I trust you will forgive
me when I tell you that, for most of the twenty
years, I have been so situated that I have had little
or no communication with the lines, and have been
holding meetings, day and night, from place to place ;
besides my mind has been so taken up with the
deplorable situation of the earth, the darkness in
which it lies, that, when my labors did call me near
the lines, I did not realize the opportunity which
presented itself of letting you know where I was.
And, again, I have designed visiting you long since,
and annually have promised myself that the succeeding year I would certainly seek out my relatives,
and enjoy the privilege of one pleasing interview
with them before I passed into the valley and shadow
of death. But last, though not least, let me not
startle you when I say, that, according to my early
adopted principles of the power of faith, the Lord
has, in his exceeding kindness, bestowed upon me
the gift of healing by the prayer of faith, and the
use of such simple means as seem congenial to the

human system ; but my chief reliance is upon Him
who organized us at the first, and can restore at
pleasure that which is disorganized.

"The first of my peculiar success in this way was
twelve years since, and from nearly that date I have
had little rest. In addition to the incessant calls
which I in a short time had, there was the most
overwhelming torrent of opposition poured down
upon me that I ever witnessed. But it pleased God
to take the weak to confound the wisdom of the
wise. I have in the last twelve years seen the
greatest manifestations of the power of God in
healing the sick, that, with all my sanguinity, I ever
hoped or imagined. And when the learned infidel
has declared with sober face, time and again, that
disease had obtained such an ascendency that death
could be resisted no longer, that the victim must
wither beneath his potent arm, I have seen the
almost lifeless clay slowly but surely resuscitated
and revived, till the pallid monster fled so far that
the patient was left in the full bloom of vigorous
health. But it is God that hath done it, and to Him
let all the praise be given.

"I am now compelled to close this epistle, for I
must start immediately on a journey of more than
one hundred miles, to attend a heavy case of sickness; so God be with you all.   Farewell !

"JASON MACK."

"Mother Lucy," in the interesting accounts of her
own and husband's families, tells some charming
stories of visions, dreams, and miracles among them,
indicating the advent of the latter-day power; but
the remarkable visions and mission of her prophet
son claim the ruling place. She says:

"There was a great revival of religion, which ex-
"tended to all the denominations of Christians in

"the surrounding country in which we resided.
" Many of the world's people, becoming concerned
"about the salvation of their souls, came forward
"and presented themselves as seekers after religion.
" Most of them were desirous of uniting with some
"church, but were not decided as to the particular
"faith which they would adopt.　When the numer-
" ous meetings were about breaking up, and the
"candidates and the various leading church mem-
" bers began to consult upon the subject of adopting
"the candidates into some church or churches, as
"the case might be, a dispute arose, and there was
"a great contention among them.

"While these things were going forward, Joseph's
"mind became considerably troubled with regard to
"religion ; and the following extract from his history
"will show, more clearly than I can express, the
"state of his feelings, and the result of his reflec-
"tions on this occasion : "

" I was at this time in my fifteenth year.　My
father's family was proselyted to the Presbyterian
faith, and four of them joined that church, namely,
my mother Lucy, my brothers Hyrum and Samuel
Harrison, and my sister Sophronia.

" During this time of great excitement my mind
was called up to serious reflection and great uneasi-
ness.　*　*　*　*　The Presbyterians were most
decided against the Baptists and Methodists, and
used all their powers of either reason or sophistry
to prove their errors, or at least to make the people
think they were in error.　On the other hand the
Baptists and Methodists, in their turn, were equally
zealous to establish their own tenets and disprove
all others.

" In the midst of this war of words, and tumult

of opinions, I often said to myself, what is to be done? Who, of all these parties, are right? or, are they all wrong together? If any one of them be right, which is it? and how shall I know it?

"While I was laboring under the extreme difficulties caused by the contests of these parties of religionists, I was one day reading the epistle of James, first chapter and fifth verse, which reads, ‘If any of you lack wisdom, let him ask of God, that giveth unto all men liberally, and upbraideth not, and it shall be given him.’ Never did any passage of scripture come with more power to the heart of man than this did at this time to mine. It seemed to enter with great force into every feeling of my heart. I reflected on it again and again, knowing that if any person needed wisdom from God, I did, for how to act I did not know, and, unless I could get more wisdom than I then had, would never know; for the teachers of religion of the different sects understood the same passage so differently, as to destroy all confidence in settling the question by an appeal to the Bible. At length I came to the conclusion that I must either remain in darkness and confusion, or else I must do as James directs—that is, ask of God. I at last came to the determination to ask of God So in accordance with this determination I retired to the woods to make the attempt. It was on the morning of a beautiful clear day, early in the spring of 1820. It was the first time in my life that I had made such an attempt; for amidst all my anxieties I had never as yet made the attempt to pray vocally. After I had retired into the place where I had previously designed to go, having looked around me, and finding myself alone, I knelt down and began to offer up the desires of my heart to God. I had scarcely done so, when immediately I was seized upon by some power which entirely overcame me, and had such astonishing influence over me as to bind my tongue, so that I could not speak. Thick darkness gathered around me, and it seemed to me for a time as if I were doomed to sudden destruction. But exerting all my powers to call upon God to deliver me out of the power of this enemy which had seized upon me, and at the very moment when I was ready to sink into despair, and abandon myself to destruction—not to an imaginary ruin, but to the power of some actual being from the unseen world, who had such a marvelous power as I had never before felt in any being— just at this moment of great alarm, I saw a pillar of light exactly over my head, above the brightness of the sun, which descended gradually until it fell upon me. It no sooner appeared than I found myself delivered from the enemy which held me bound. When the light rested upon me I saw two personages, whose brightness and glory defy all description, standing above me in the air. One of them spake unto me, calling me by name, and said, pointing to the other, ' this is my beloved son, hear him : '

" My object in going to inquire of the Lord, was to know which of all these sects was right, that I might know which to join. No sooner, therefore, did I get possession of myself, so as to be able to speak, than I asked the personages who stood above me in the light, which of all the sects was right— for at this time it had never entered into my heart that all were wrong—and which I should join. I was answered that I should join none of them, for they were all wrong ; and the personage who addressed me said that all their creeds were an abomination in His sight ; that those professors were all corrupt. 'They draw near me with their lips, but their hearts are far from me ; they teach for doctrine the commandments of men, having a form of godliness, but they deny the power thereof.' He again forbade me to join any of them ; and many other

things did he say unto me which I cannot write at
this time. When I came to myself again, I found
myself lying on my back, looking up into heaven."

"From this time until the 21st of September,
" 1823, Joseph continued, as usual, to labor with his
" father, and nothing during this interval occurred of
" very great importance,—though he suffered, as one
" would naturally suppose, every kind of opposition
" and persecution from the different orders of relig-
" ionists.

"On the evening of the 21st of September, he
" retired to his bed in quite a serious and contem-
" plative state of mind. He shortly betook himself
" to prayer and supplication to Almighty God, for
" a manifestation of his standing before Him, and
" while thus engaged he received the following
" vision : "

"While I was thus in the act of calling upon God,
I discovered a light appearing in the room, which
continued to increase until the room was lighter
than at noon-day, when immediately a personage
appeared at my bedside, standing in the air, for his
feet did not touch the floor. He had on a loose
robe of most exquisite whiteness. It was a whiteness beyond anything earthly I had ever seen, nor
do I believe that any earthly thing could be made to
appear so exceedingly white and brilliant. His
hands were naked, and his arms also, a little above
the wrist ; so also were his feet naked, as were his
legs a little above the ankles. His head and neck
were also bare. I could discover that he had no
other clothing on but his robe, as it was open so
that I could see into his bosom. Not only was his
robe exceedingly white, but his whole person was
glorious beyond description, and his countenance

truly like lightning. The room was exceedingly light, but not so very bright as immediately around his person. When I first looked upon him I was afraid, but the fear soon left me. He called me by name, and said unto me that he was a messenger sent from the presence of God to me, and that his name was Moroni; that God had a work for me to do, and that my name should be had for good and evil among all nations, kindreds and tongues; or that it should be both good and evil spoken of among all people. He said there was a book deposited, written upon gold plates, giving an account of the former inhabitants of this continent, and the source from whence they sprung. He also said that the fullness of the everlasting gospel was contained in it, as delivered by the Saviour to the ancient inhabitants. Also, that there were two stones in silver bows, and these stones, fastened to a breastplate, constituted what is called the urim and thummim, deposited with the plates; and the possession and use of these stones were what constituted seers in ancient or former times; and that God had prepared them for the purpose of translating the book. After telling me these things, he commenced quoting the prophecies of the Old Testament. He first quoted a part of the third chapter of Malachi; and he quoted also the fourth or last chapter of the same prophecy, though with a little variation from the way it reads in our Bible. Instead of quoting the first verse as it reads in our books, he quoted it thus: 'For behold the day cometh that shall burn as an oven; and all the proud, yea, and all that do wickedly, shall burn as stubble, for they that come shall burn them, saith the Lord of Hosts, that it shall leave them neither root nor branch.' And again he quoted the fifth verse thus: 'Behold, I will reveal unto you the priesthood by the hand of Elijah the prophet, before the coming of the great and dreadful day of the Lord.' He also quoted the next verse differently: 'And he shall plant in the hearts of the children the promises made to the fathers, and the hearts of the children shall turn to their fathers; if it were not so, the whole earth would be utterly wasted at its coming.' In addition to these, he quoted the eleventh chapter of Isaiah, saying that it was about to be fulfilled. He quoted also the third chapter of Acts, twenty-second and twenty-third verses, precisely as they stand in our New Testament. He said that that prophet was Christ, but the day had not yet come 'when they who would not hear His voice should be cut off from among the people,' but soon would come. He also quoted the second chapter of Joel, from the twenty-eighth verse to the last. He also said that this was not yet fulfilled, but was soon to be. And he further stated the fullness of the Gentiles was soon to come in. He quoted many other passages of scripture, and offered many explanations which cannot be mentioned here. Again, he told me that when I got those plates of which he had spoken (for the time that they should be obtained was not then fulfilled), I should not show them to any person, neither the breast-plate, with the urim and thummim, only to those to whom I should be commanded to show them; if I did I should be destroyed. While he was conversing with me about the plates, the vision was opened to my mind that I could see the place where the plates were deposited, and that so clearly and distinctly that I knew the place again when I visited it.

"After this communication, I saw the light in the room begin to gather immediately around the person of him who had been speaking to me, and it continued to do so until the room was again left dark, except just around him; when instantly I saw, as it were, a conduit open right up into Heaven, and he ascended up until he entirely disappeared, and the room was left as it had been before this heavenly light made its appearance.

"I lay musing on the singularity of the scene, and marveling greatly at what had been told me by this extraordinary messenger, when, in the midst of my meditation, I suddenly discovered that my room was again beginning to get lighted, and, in an instant, as it were, the same heavenly messenger was again by my bedside. He commenced, and again related the very same things which he had done at his first visit, without the least variation, which having done, he informed me of great judgments which were coming upon the earth, with great desolations by famine, sword, and pestilence; and that these grievous judgments would come on the earth in this generation. Having related these things, he again ascended as he had done before."

"When the angel ascended the second time he "left Joseph overwhelmed with astonishment, yet "gave him but a short time to contemplate the "things which he had told him before he made his "reappearance and rehearsed the same things over, "adding a few words of caution and instruction, "thus: That he must beware of covetousness, and "he must not suppose the record was to be brought "forth with the view of getting gain, for this was "not the case, but that it was to bring forth light "and intelligence, which had for a long time been "lost to the world; and that when he went to get "the plates, he must be on his guard, or his mind "would be filled with darkness. The angel then "told him to tell his father all which he had both "seen and heard.

"*   *   *   *   From this time forth, Joseph con-

" tinued to receive instructions from the Lord, and
" we continued to get the children together every
" evening, for the purpose of listening while he gave
" us a relation of the same.   I presume our family
" presented an aspect as singular as any that ever
" lived upon the face of the earth—all seated in a
" circle, father, mother, sons, and daughters, and
" giving the most profound attention to a boy,
" eighteen years of age, who had never read the
" Bible through in his life. He seemed much less
" inclined to the perusal of books than any of the
" rest of our children, but far more given to medi-
" tation and deep study.

    " We were now confirmed in the opinion that God
" was about to bring to light something upon which
" we could stay our minds, or that would give us a
" more perfect knowledge of the plan of salvation
" and the redemption of the human family. This
" caused us greatly to rejoice ; the sweetest union
" and happiness pervaded our house, and tranquillity
" reigned in our midst.

    " During our evening conversations, Joseph would
" occasionally give us some of the most amusing
" recitals that could be imagined. He would de-
" scribe the ancient inhabitants of this continent,
" their dress, mode of traveling, and the animals
" upon which they rode ; their cities, their buildings,
' with every particular ; their mode of warfare ; and
' also their religious worship. This he would do
' with as much ease, seemingly, as if he had spent
' his whole life with them."

    Thus continued the divine and miraculous expe-
rience of the prophetic family until the golden plates

were obtained, the book of Mormon published, and the "Church of Jesus Christ of Latter-day Saints" was established on the 6th of April, 1830.

But all this shall be written in the book of the prophet!

CHAPTER III.

Joseph Smith opened to America a great spiritual dispensation. It was such the Mormon sisterhood received.

A latter-day prophet! A gospel of miracles! Angels visiting the earth again! Pentecosts in the nineteenth century! This was Mormonism.

These themes were peculiarly fascinating to those earnest apostolic women whom we shall introduce to the reader.

Ever must such themes be potent with woman. She has a divine mission always, both to manifest spiritual gifts and to perpetuate spiritual dispensations.

Woman is child of faith. Indeed she is faith. Man is reason. His mood is skepticism. Left alone to *his* apostleship, spiritual missions die, though revealed by a cohort of archangels. Men are too apt to lock again the heavens which the angels have opened, and convert priesthood into priestcraft. It is woman who is the chief architect of a spiritual church.

Joseph Smith was a prophet and seer because his

mother was a prophetess and seeress. Lucy Smith gave birth to the prophetic genius which has wrought out its manifestations so marvelously in the age. Brigham Young, who is a society-builder, also received his rare endowments from his mother. Though differing from Joseph, Brigham has a potent inspiration.

Thus we trace the Mormon genius to these mothers. They gave birth to the great spiritual dispensation which is destined to incarnate a new and universal Christian church.

Until the faith of Latter-day Saints invoked one, there was no Holy Ghost in the world such as the saints of former days would have recognized. Respectable divines, indeed, had long given out that revelation was done away, because no longer needed. The canon of scripture was said to be full. The voice of prophesy was no more to be heard to the end of time.

But the Mormon prophet invoked the Holy Ghost of the ancient Hebrews, and burst the sealed heavens. The Holy Ghost came, and His apostles published the news abroad.

The initial text of Mormonism was precisely that which formed the basis of Peter's colossal sermon on the day of Pentecost:

"And it shall come to pass in the last days, saith "God, I will pour out my spirit upon all flesh; and "your sons and your daughters shall prophesy, and "your young men shall dream dreams;

"And on my servants and on my handmaidens I "will pour out in those days of my spirit; and they "shall prophesy."

Here was a magic gospel for the age! And how greatly was woman in its divine programme!

No sooner was the application made than the prophesy was discovered to be pregnant with its own fulfillment. The experience of the former-day saints became the experience of the "latter-day saints." It was claimed, too, that the supreme fulfillment was reserved for this crowning dispensation. These were emphatically the "last days." It was in the "last days" that God would pour out His spirit upon "*all* flesh." The manifestation of Pentecost was but the foreshadowing of the power of God, to be universally displayed to his glory, and the regeneration of the nations in the "dispensation of the fullness of times."

This gospel of a new dispensation came to America by the administration of angels. But let it not be thought that Joseph Smith alone saw angels. Multitudes received angelic administrations in the early days of the Church; thousands spoke in tongues and prophesied; and visions, dreams and miracles were daily manifestations among the disciples.

The sisters were quite as familiar with angelic visitors as the apostles. They were in fact the best "mediums" of this spiritual work. They were the "cloud of witnesses." Their Pentecosts of spiritual gifts were of frequent occurrence.

The sisters were also apostolic in a priestly sense. They partook of the priesthood equally with the men. They too "held the keys of the administration of angels." Who can doubt it, when faith is the greatest of all keys to unlock the gates of heaven? But "the Church" herself acknowledged woman's

key. There was no Mormon St. Peter in this new
dispensation to arrogate supremacy over woman, on
his solitary pontifical throne. The "Order of Celestial Marriage," not of celestial celibacy, was about
to be revealed to the Church.

Woman also soon became high priestess and prophetess. She was this *officially*. The constitution
of the Church acknowledged her divine mission
to administer for the regeneration of the race.
The genius of a patriarchal priesthood naturally
made her the apostolic help-meet for man. If you
saw her not in the pulpit *teaching* the congregation,
yet was she to be found in the temple, *administering*
for the living and the dead! Even in the holy of
holies she was met. As a high priestess she blessed
with the laying on of hands! As a prophetess she
oracled in holy places! As an endowment giver
she was a Mason, of the Hebraic order, whose Grand
Master is the God of Israel and whose anointer is
the Holy Ghost.

She held the keys of the administration of angels
and of the working of miracles and of the "seal-
ings" pertaining to "the heavens and the earth."
Never before was woman so much as she is in this
Mormon dispensation!

The supreme spiritual character of the "Church
of Jesus Christ of Latter-day Saints" (its proper
name), is well typed in the hymn so often sung by
the saints at their "testimony meetings," and sometimes in their temples. Here is its theme:

> " The spirit of God like a fire is burning,
> The latter-day glory begins to come forth,
> The visions and blessings of old are returning,
> The angels are coming to visit the earth.

Chorus—We'll sing and we'll shout with the armies of heaven—
Hosanna, hosanna to God and the Lamb!
Let glory to them in the highest be given,
Henceforth and forever—amen and amen.

The Lord is extending the saints' understanding,
Restoring their judges and all as at first;
The knowledge and power of God are expanding;
The vail o'er the earth is beginning to burst.

Chorus—We'll sing and we'll shout with the armies of heaven!" etc.

What a strange theme this, forty-seven years ago, before the age of our modern spiritual mediums, when the angels visited only the Latter-day Saints! In that day it would seem the angels only dared to come by stealth, so unpopular was their coming. But the *way* was opened for the angels. What wonder that they have since come in hosts good and bad, and made their advent popular? Millions testify to their advent now; and "modern spiritualism," though of "another source," is a proof of Mormonism more astonishing than prophecy herself.

Yet is all this not more remarkable than the promise which Joseph Smith made to the world in proclaiming his mission. It was the identical promise of Christ: "These signs shall follow them that believe!" These signs meant nothing short of all that extraordinary experience familiar to the Hebrew people and the early-day saints. We have no record that ever this sweeping promise was made before by any one but Jesus Christ. Yet Joseph Smith, filled with a divine assurance, dared to re-affirm it and apply the promise to all nations wherever the gospel of his mission should be preached. The most wonderful of tests is this.

But the test was fulfilled. The signs followed all, and everywhere. Even apostates witness to this much.

There is nothing in modern spiritualism nearly so marvelous as was Mormonism in its rise and progress in America and Great Britain. It has indeed made stir enough in the world. But it had to break the way for coming ages. Revelation was at first a very new and strange theme after the more than Egyptian darkness in which the Christian nations had been for fifty generations. It was the light set upon the hill now; but the darkness comprehended it not. Yet was a spiritual dispensation opened again to the world. Once more was the lost key found. Mormonism was the key; and it was Joseph and his God-fearing disciples who unlocked the heavens. That fact the world will acknowledge in the coming times.

CHAPTER IV.

BIRTH OF THE CHURCH—KIRTLAND AS THE BRIDE,
IN THE CHAMBERS OF THE WILDERNESS—THE
EARLY GATHERING—" MOTHER WHITNEY," AND
ELIZA R. SNOW.

The birth-place of Mormonism was in the State
of New York. There the angels first administered
to the youthful prophet ; there in the " Hill Cumo-
rah," near the village of Palmyra, the plates of the
book of Mormon were revealed by Moroni ; there,
at Manchester, on the 6th of April, 1830, the
"Church of Jesus Christ of Latter-day Saints"
was organized, with six members.

But the divine romance of the sisterhood best
opens at Kirtland. It is the place where this Israelitish drama of our times commenced its first
distinguishing scenes,—the place where the first
Mormon temple was built.

Ohio was the " Great West." Kirtland, the city
of the saints, with its temple, dedicated to the God
of Israel, rose in Ohio.

Not, however, as the New Jerusalem of America,
was Kirtland founded ; but pioneer families, from

New England, had settled in Ohio, who early received the gospel of the Latter-day Church.

Thus Kirtland became an adopted Zion, selected by revelation as a gathering place for the saints; and a little village grew into a city, with a temple.

Among these pioneers were the families of " Mother Whitney," and Eliza R. Snow, and the families of " Father Morley," and Edward Partridge, who became the " first Bishop " of Zion.

Besides these, there were a host of men and women soon numbered among the founders of Mormondom, who were also pioneers in Ohio, Missouri, and Illinois.

There is no feature of the Mormons more interesting than their distinguishing mark as pioneers. In this both their Church and family history have a national significance.

Trace their family migrations from old England to New England in the seventeenth century; from Europe to America in the nineteenth; then follow them as a people in their empire-track from the State of New York, where their Church was born, to Utah and California! It will thus be remarkably illustrated that they and their parents have been pioneering not only America but the world itself to the " Great West " for the last two hundred and fifty years!

As a community the Mormons have been emphatically the Church of pioneers. The sisters have been this equally with the brethren. Their very religion is endowed with the genius of migrating peoples.

So in 1830–31, almost as soon as the Church was

organized, the prophet and the priesthood followed
the disciples to the West, where the star of Messiah
was rising.

As though the bride had been preparing for the
coming ! As though, womanlike, intuitively, she
had gone into the wilderness—the chambers of a
new civilization—to await the bridegroom.

For the time being Kirtland became the Zion of
the West ; for the time being Kirtland among cities
was the bride.

But the illustration is also personal. Woman
herself had gone to the West where the star of Messiah was looming. Daughters of the New Jerusalem
were already in the chamber awaiting the bridegroom.

Early in the century, two had pioneered into the
State of Ohio, who have since been, for a good lifetime, high priestesses of the Mormon temples.
And the voice of prophesy has declared that these
have the sacred blood of Israel in their veins. In
the divine mysticism of their order they are at once
of a kingly and priestly line.

There is a rare consistency in the mysticism of
the Mormon Church. The daughters of the temple are so by right of blood and inheritance They
are discovered by gift of revelation in Him who is
the voice of the Church ; but they inherit from the
fathers and mothers of the temple of the Old Jerusalem.

And so these two of the principal heroines of Mormondom—"Mother Whitney" and "Sister Eliza
R. Snow"—introduced first as the two earliest of
the Church who pioneered to the "Great West,"

before the advent of their prophet, as well as introduced for the divine part which they have played in the marvelous history of their people.

These are high priestesses! These are two rare prophetesses! These have the gifts of revelation and " tongues!" These administer in " holy places " for the living and the dead.

It was about the year of our Lord 1806 that Oliver Snow, a native of Massachusetts, and his wife, R. L. Pettibone Snow, of Connecticut, moved with their children to that section of the State of Ohio bordering on Lake Erie on the north and the State of Pennsylvania on the east, known then as the "Connecticut Western Reserve." They purchased land and settled in Mantua, Portage county.

Eliza R. Snow, who was the second of seven children, four daughters and three sons, one of whom is the accomplished apostle Lorenzo Snow, was born in Becket, Berkshire county, Mass., January 21st, 1804. Her parents were of English descent; their ancestors were among the earliest settlers of New England.

Although a farmer by occupation, Oliver Snow performed much public business, officiating in several responsible positions. His daughter Eliza, being ten years the senior of her eldest brother, so soon as she was competent, was employed as secretary in her father's office.

She was skilled in various kinds of needlework and home manufactures. Two years in succession she drew the prize awarded by the committee on manufactures, at the county fair, for the best manufactured leghorn.

When quite young she commenced writing for publication in various journals, which she continued to do for several years, over assumed signatures,— wishing to be useful as a writer, and yet unknown except by intimate friends.

"During the contest between Greece and Tur- "key," she says, " I watched with deep interest the "events of the war, and after the terrible destruc- "tion of Missolonghi, by the Turks, I wrote an "article entitled 'The Fall of Missolonghi.' Soon " after its publication, the deaths of Adams and Jef- "ferson occurred on the same memorable fourth of " July, and I was requested through the press, to "write their requiem, to which I responded, and "found myself ushered into conspicuity. Subse- "quently I was awarded eight volumes of 'Godey's " Lady's Book,' for a first prize poem published in " one of the journals."

The classical reader will remember how the strug- gle between Greece and Turkey stirred the soul of Byron. That immortal poet was not a saint but he was a great patriot and fled to the help of Greece.

Precisely the same chord that was struck in the chivalrous mind of Lord Byron was struck in the Hebraic soul of Eliza R. Snow. It was the chord of the heroic and the antique.

Our Hebraic heroine is even more sensitive to the heroic and patriotic than to the poetic,—at least she has most self-gratification in lofty and patriotic themes.

" That men are born poets," she continues, "is a " common adage. *I was born a patriot,*—at least a " warm feeling of patriotism inspired my childish

" heart, and mingled in my earliest thoughts, as
" evinced in many of the earliest productions of my
" pen. I can even now recollect how, with beating
" pulse and strong emotion I listened, when but a
" small child, to the tales of the revolution.

" My grandfather on my mother's side, when fight-
" ing for the freedom of our country, was taken
" prisoner by British troops, and confined in a dreary
" cell, and so scantily fed that when his fellow-prisoner
" by his side died from exhaustion, he reported him
" to the jailor as sick in bed, in order to obtain the
" amount of food for both,—keeping him covered in
" their blankets as long as he dared to remain with
" a decaying body.

" This, with many similar narratives of revolu-
" tionary sufferings recounted by my grand-parents,
" so deeply impressed my mind, that as I grew up
" to womanhood I fondly cherished a pride for the
" flag which so proudly waved over the graves of
" my brave and valiant ancestors."

It was the poet's soul of this illustrious Mormon
woman that first enchanted the Church with inspired
song, and her Hebraic faith and life have given
something of their peculiar tone to the entire Mormon people, and especially the sisterhood ; just as
Joseph Smith and Brigham Young gave the types
and institutions to our modern Israel.

Sister Eliza R. Snow was born with more than
the poet's soul. She was a prophetess in her very
nature,—endowed thus by her Creator, before her
birth. Her gifts are of race quality rather than of
mere religious training or growth. They have come
down to her from the ages. From her personal race

indications, as well as from the whole tenor and mission of her life, she would readily be pronounced to be of Hebrew origin. One might very well fancy her to be a descendant of David himself; indeed the Prophet Joseph, in blessing her, pronounced her to be a daughter of Judah's royal house. She understands, nearly to perfection, all of the inner views of the system and faith which she represents. And the celestial relations and action of the great Mormon drama, in other worlds, and in the "eternities past and to come," have constituted her most familiar studies and been in the rehearsals of her daily ministry.

Mother Whitney says:

"I was born the day after Christmas in the first year of the present century, in the quiet, old-fashioned country town of Derby, New Haven County, Conn. My parents' names were Gibson and Polly Smith. The Smiths were among the earliest settlers there, and were widely known. I was the oldest child, and grew up in an atmosphere of love and tenderness My parents were not professors of religion, and according to puritanical ideas were grossly in fault to have me taught dancing; but my father had his own peculiar notions upon the subject, and wished me to possess and enjoy, in connection with a sound education and strict morals, such accomplishments as would fit me to fill, with credit to myself and my training, an honorable position in society. He had no sympathy whatever with any of the priests of that day, and was utterly at variance with their teachings and ministry, notwithstanding he was strenuous on all points of honor, honesty morality and uprightness.

"There is nothing in my early life I remember

with more intense satisfaction than the agreeable companionship of my father. My mother's health was delicate, and with her household affairs, and two younger children, she gave herself up to domestic life, allowing it to absorb her entire interest, and consequently I was more particularly under my father's jurisdiction and influence; our tastes were most congenial, and this geniality and happiness surrounded me with its beneficial influence until I reached my nineteenth year. Nothing in particular occurred to mar the smoothness of my life's current and prosperity, and love beamed upon our home.

"About this time a new epoch in my life created a turning point which unconsciously to us, who were the actors in the drama, caused all my future to be entirely separate and distinct from those with whom I had been reared and nurtured. My father's sister, a spinster, who had money at her own disposal, and who was one of those strong-minded women of whom so much is said in this our day, concluded to emigrate to the great West,—at that time Ohio seemed a fabulous distance from civilization and enlightenment, and going to Ohio then was as great an undertaking as going to China or Japan is at the present day. She entreated my parents to allow me to accompany her, and promised to be as faithful and devoted to me as possible, until they should join us, and that they expected very shortly to do; their confidence in aunt Sarah's ability and self-reliance was unbounded, and so, after much persuasion, they consented to part with me for a short interval of time; but circumstances, over which we mortals have no control, were so overruled that I never saw my beloved mother again. Our journey was a pleasant one; the beautiful scenery through which our route lay had charms indescribable for me, who had never been farther from home than New Haven, in which city I had passed a part of my time, and to me it was nearer a paradise than any other place on earth. The magnificent lakes, rivers, mountains, and romantic forests were all delineations of nature which delighted my imagination.

"We settled a few miles inland from the picturesque Lake Erie, and here in after years, were the saints of God gathered and the everlasting gospel proclaimed. My beloved aunt Sarah was a true friend and instructor to me, and had much influence in maturing my womanly character and developing my home education. She hated the priests of the day, and believed them all deceivers and hypocrites ; her religion consisted in visiting the widow and the fatherless and keeping herself ' unspotted from the world.'

"Shortly after entering my twenty-first year I became acquainted with a young man from Vermont, Newel K. Whitney, who, like myself, had left home and relatives and was determined to carve out a fortune for himself. He had been engaged in trading with the settlers and Indians at Green Bay, Mich., buying furs extensively for the eastern markets. In his travels to and from New York he passed along the charming Lake Erie, and from some unknown influence he concluded to settle and make a permanent home for himself in this region of country ; and then subsequently we met and became acquainted ; and being thoroughly convinced that we were suited to each other, we were married by the Presbyterian minister of that place, the Rev. J. Badger. We prospered in all our efforts to accumulate wealth, so much so, that among our friends it came to be remarked that nothing of Whitney's ever got lost on the lake, and no product of his exportation was ever low in the market ; always ready sales and fair prices. We had neither of us ever made any profession of religion, but contrary to my early education I was naturally religious, and I expressed to my husband a wish that we should unite ourselves to one of the churches, after examining into their principles and deciding for ourselves. Accordingly we united ourselves with the Campbellites, who were then making many converts, and whose principles seemed most in accordance with the scriptures. We continued in this church, which to us was the nearest pattern to our Saviour's teachings, until Parley P. Pratt and another elder preached the everlasting gospel in Kirtland."

CHAPTER V.

And there came one as a "voice crying in the wilderness, prepare ye the way of the Lord!"

Thus ever!

A coming to Israel with "a new and everlasting covenant;" this was the theme of the ancient prophets, now unfolded.

There was the voice crying in the wilderness of Ohio, just before the advent of the latter-day prophet.

The voice was Sidney Rigdon. He was to Joseph Smith as a John the Baptist.

The forerunner made straight the way in the wilderness of the virgin West. He raised up a church of disciples in and around Kirtland. He led those who afterwards became latter-day saints to faith in the promises, and baptized them in water for the remission of sins. But he had not power to baptize them with the Holy Ghost and with fire from heaven. Yet he taught the literal fulfillment of the prophesies concerning the last days, and heralded the advent of the "one greater than I."

"The same is he which baptizeth with the Holy Ghost."

That is ever the "one greater than I," be his name whatever it may.

Joseph Smith baptized with the Holy Ghost. But Sidney knew not that he was heralding Joseph.

And the prophet himself was but as the voice crying in the wilderness of the great dark world: "Prepare ye the way for the second advent of earth's Lord." His mission was also to "make straight in the desert a highway" for the God of Israel; for Israel was going up,—following the angel of the covenant, to the chambers of the mountains.

He came with a great lamp and a great light in those days, dazzling to the eyes of the generation that "crucified" him in its blindness.

Joseph was the sign of Messiah's coming. He unlocked the sealed heavens by faith and "election." He came in "the spirit and power of Elijah." The mantle of Elijah was upon him.

Be it always understood that the coming of Joseph Smith "to restore the covenant to Israel" signifies the near advent of Messiah to reign as King of Israel. Joseph was the Elijah of the last days.

These are the first principles of Mormonism. And to witness of their truth this testament of the sisters is given, with the signs and wonders proceeding from the mission of Him who unlocked the heavens and preached the gospel of new revelations to the world, whose light of revelation had gone out.

But first came the famous Alexander Campbell and his compeer, Sidney Rigdon, to the West with the "lamp." Seekers after truth, whose hearts had been strangely moved by some potent spirit, whose

influence they felt pervading but understood not,
saw the lamp and admired.

Mr. Campbell, of Virginia, was a reformed Baptist. He with Sidney Rigdon, a Mr. Walter Scott,
and some other gifted men, had dissented from the
regular Baptists, from whom they differed much in
doctrine. They preached baptism for the remission
of sins, promised the gift of the Holy Ghost, and
believed in the literal fulfillment of prophesy. They
also had some of the apostolic forms of organization
in their church.

In Ohio they raised up branches. In Kirtland
and the regions round, they made many disciples,
who bore the style of "disciples," though the popular sect-name was "Campbellites." Among them
were Eliza R. Snow, Elizabeth Ann Whitney, and
many more, who afterwards embraced the "fullness
of the everlasting gospel" as restored by the angels
to the Mormon prophet.

But these evangels of a John the Baptist mission
brought not to the West the light of new revelation in their lamp.

These had not yet even heard of the opening of
a new dispensation of revelations. As they came
by the way they had seen no angels with new commissions for the Messiah age. No Moses nor Elijah
had been with them on a mount of transfiguration.
Nor had they entered into the chamber with the
angel of the covenant, bringing a renewal of the
covenant to Israel. This was in the mission of the
"one greater" than they who came after.

They brought the lamp without the light—nothing more. Better *the light* without the evangelical

lamp—better a conscientious intellect than the forms of sectarian godliness without the power.

Without the power to unlock the heavens, and the Elijah faith to call the angels down, there could be no new dispensation—no millennial civilization for the world, to crown the civilization of the ages.

Light came to Sidney Rigdon from the Mormon Elijah, and he comprehended the light; but Alexander Campbell rejected the prophet when his message came; he would have none of his angels. He had been preaching the literal fulfillment of prophesy, but when the covenant was revealed he was not ready. The lamp, not the light, was his admiration. Himself was the lamp; *Joseph had the light from the spirit world*, and the darkness comprehended it not.

Alexander Campbell was a learned and an able man—the very *form of wisdom*, but without the spirit.

Joseph Smith was an unlettered youth. He came not in the polished *form* of wisdom—either divine or human—but in the demonstration of the Holy Ghost, and with signs following the believer.

Mr. Campbell would receive no new revelation from such an one—no everlasting covenant from the new Jerusalem which was waiting to come down, to establish on earth a great spiritual empire, that the King might appear to Zion in his glory, with all his angels and the ancients of days.

The tattered and blood-stained commissions of old Rome were sufficient for the polished divine,—Rome which had made all nations drunk with her spiritual fornications,—Rome which put to death the Son of God when his Israel in blindness rejected him.

Between Rome and Jerusalem there was now the great controversy of the God of Israel. Not the old Jerusalem which had traveled from the east to the west, led by the angel of the covenant, up out of the land of Egypt! The new Jerusalem to the earth then, as she is to-day! Ever will she be the new Jerusalem—ever will " old things " be passing away when " the Lord cometh ! "

And the angel of the west appeared by night to the youth, as he watched in the chamber of his father's house, in a little village in the State of New York. On that charmed night when the invisibles hovered about the earth the angel that stood before him read to the messenger of Messiah the mystic text of his mission :

" *Behold, I will send my messenger, and he shall* " *prepare the way before me; and the Lord, whom ye* " *seek, shall suddenly come to his temple, even the mes-* " *senger of the covenant, whom ye delight in; behold* " *he shall come, saith the Lord of Hosts.*"

CHAPTER VI.

Now there dwelt in Kirtland in those days disciples who feared the Lord.

And they "spake often one to another; and the Lord hearkened and heard it, and a book of remembrance was written before him for them that feared the Lord, and that thought upon his name."

"We had been praying," says mother Whitney, "to know from the Lord how we could obtain the "gift of the Holy Ghost."

"My husband, Newel K. Whitney, and myself, "were Campbellites. We had been baptized for the "remission of our sins, and believed in the laying "on of hands and the gifts of the spirit. But there "was no one with authority to confer the Holy "Ghost upon us. We were seeking to know how "to obtain the spirit and the gifts bestowed upon "the ancient saints.

"Sister Eliza Snow was also a Campbellite. We "were acquainted before the restoration of the gos- "pel to the earth. She, like myself, was seeking for "the fullness of the gospel. She lived at the time "in Mantua.

"One night—it was midnight—as my husband

"and I, in our house at Kirtland, were praying to
"the father to be shown the way, the spirit rested
"upon us and a *cloud* overshadowed the house.

"It was as though we were out of doors. The
"house passed away from our vision. We were not
"conscious of anything but the presence of the spirit
"and the cloud that was over us.

"We were wrapped in the cloud. A solemn awe
"pervaded us. We saw the cloud and we felt the
"spirit of the Lord.

"Then we heard a voice out of the cloud saying:
"'Prepare to receive the word of the Lord, for it
"'is coming!'

"At this we marveled greatly ; but from that mo-
"ment we knew that the word of the Lord was
"coming to Kirtland."

Now this is an Hebraic sign, well known to Israel
after the glory of Israel had departed. It was called
by the sacred people who inherited the covenant
"the daughter of the voice."

Blindness had happened to Israel. The prophets
and the seers the Lord had covered, but the "daughter of the voice" was still left to Israel. From time
to time a few, with the magic blood of the prophets
in them, heard the voice speaking to them out of
the cloud.

Down through the ages the "daughter of the
voice" followed the children of Israel in their dis-
persions. Down through the ages, from time to
time, some of the children of the sacred seed have
heard the voice. This is the tradition of the sons
and daughters of Judah.

It was the "daughter of the voice" that Mother

Whitney and her husband heard, at midnight, in Kirtland, speaking to them out of the cloud. Mother Whitney and her husband were of the seed of Israel (so run their patriarchal blessings); it was their gift and privilege to hear the " voice."

He was coming now, whose right it is to reign. The throne of David was about to be re-set up and given to the lion of the tribe of Judah. The everlasting King of the new Jerusalem was coming down, with the tens of thousands of his saints.

The star of Messiah was traveling from the east to the west The prophet—the messenger of Messiah's covenant—was about to remove farther westward, towards the place where his Lord in due time will commence his reign, which shall extend over all the earth.

This was the meaning of that vision of the " cloud " in Kirtland, at midnight, overshadowing the house of Newel K. Whitney ; this the significance of the " voice " which spoke out of the cloud, saying : " Prepare to receive the word of the Lord, for it is coming !"

The Lord of Hosts was about to make up his jewels for the crown of his appearing ; and there were many of those jewels already in the West.

CHAPTER VII.

The divine narrative leads directly into the personal story of Parley P. Pratt. He it was who first
brought the Mormon mission west. He it was who
presented the Book of Mormon to Sidney Rigdon,
and converted him to the new covenant which Jehovah was making with a latter-day Israel.

Parley P. Pratt was one of the earliest of the new
apostles. By nature he was both poet and prophet.
The soul of prophesy was born in him. In his lifetime he was the Mormon Isaiah. All his writings
were Hebraic. He may have been of Jewish blood.
He certainly possessed the Jewish genius, of the
prophet order.

It would seem that the spirit of this great latter-
day work could not throw its divine charms around
the youthful prophet, who had been raised up to
open a crowning spiritual dispensation, without peculiarly affecting the spiritual minded everywhere
—both men and women.

It is one of the remarkable facts connected with
the rise of Mormonism in the age that, at about the

time Joseph Smith was receiving the administration of angels, thousands both in America and Great Britain were favored with corresponding visions and intuitions. Hence, indeed, its success, which was quite as astonishing as the spiritual work of the early Christians.

One of the first manifestations was that of earnest gospel-seekers having visions of the elders before they came, and recognizing them when they did come bearing the tidings. Many of the sisters, as well as the brethren, can bear witness of this.

This very peculiar experience gave special significance to one of the earliest hymns, sung by the saints, of the angel who "came down from the mansions of glory" with "the fullness of Jesus's gospel," and also the "covenant to gather his people," the refrain of which was,

"O! Israel! O! Israel! in all your abidings,
Prepare for your Lord, when you hear these glad tidings."

An Israel had been prepared in all their "abidings," by visions and signs, like sister Whitney, who heard the voice of the angel, from the cloud, bidding her prepare for the coming word of the Lord. Parley P. Pratt was the elder who fulfilled her vision, and brought the word of the Lord direct from Joseph to Kirtland.

And Parley himself was one of an Israel who had been thus mysteriously prepared for the great latter-day mission, of which he became so marked an apostle.

Before he reached the age of manhood, Parley had in his native State (N. Y.) met with reverses

in fortune so serious as to change the purposes of
his life.

"I resolved," he says, "to bid farewell to the civ-
"ilized world, where I had met with little else but
"disappointment, sorrow and unrewarded toil; and
"where sectarian divisions disgusted, and ignorance
"perplexed me,—and to spend the remainder of my
"days in the solitudes of the great West, among the
"natives of the forest."

In October, 1826, he took leave of his friends and
started westward, coming at length to a small settlement about thirty miles west of Cleveland, in the
State of Ohio. The country was covered with a
dense forest, with only here and there a small
opening made by the settlers, and the surface of the
earth was one vast scene of mud and mire.

Alone, in a land of strangers, without home or
money, and not yet twenty years of age, he became
somewhat discouraged, but concluded to stop for
the winter.

In the spring he resolved to return to his native
State, for there was one at home whom his heart
had long loved and from whom he would not have
been separated, except by misfortune.

But with her, as his wife, he returned to Ohio,
the following year, and made a home on the lands
which he cleared with his own hands.*

Eighteen months thereafter Sidney Rigdon came
into the neighborhood, as a preacher. With this
reformer Parley associated himself in the ministry,
and organized a society of disciples.

* She died in the early persecution of the church, and when Parley was in
prison for the gospel's sake her spirit visited and comforted him.

But Parley was not satisfied with even the ancient *gospel form* without the power.

At the commencement of 1830, the very time the Mormon Church was organized, he felt drawn out in an extraordinary manner to search the prophets, and to pray for an understanding of the same. His prayers were soon answered, even beyond his expectations. The prophesies were opened to his view. He began to understand the things which were about to transpire. The restoration of Israel, the coming of Messiah, and the glory that should follow.

Being now "moved upon by the Holy Ghost" to travel about preaching the gospel "without purse or scrip," in August, 1830, he closed his worldly business and bid adieu to his wilderness home, which he never saw afterwards.

" Arriving at Rochester," he says, " I informed my " wife that, notwithstanding our passage being paid " through the whole distance, yet I must leave the " boat and her to pursue her passage to her friends, " while I would stop awhile in this region. Why, I " did not know; but so it was plainly manifest by " the spirit to me.

" I said to her, we part for a season ; go and visit " our friends in our native place ; I will come soon, " but how soon I know not; for I have a work to do " in this region of country, and what it is, or how " long it will take to perform it, I know not ; but I " will come when it is performed.

" My wife would have objected to this, but she had " seen the hand of God so plainly manifest in his " dealings with me many times, that she dared not " oppose the things manifested to me by his spirit.

"She, therefore, consented; and I accompanied her
"as far as Newark, a small town upwards of one
"hundred miles from Buffalo, and then took leave
"of her, and of the boat.

"It was early in the morning, just at the dawn of
"day; I walked ten miles into the country, and
"stopped to breakfast with a Mr. Wells. I pro-
"posed to preach in the evening. Mr. Wells readily
"accompanied me through the neighborhood to visit
"the people, and circulate the appointment.

"We visited an old Baptist deacon, by the name
"of Hamlin. After hearing of our appointment for
"the evening, he began to tell of a book, a strange
"book, a very strange book, in his possession, which
"had been just published. This book, he said, pur-
"ported to have been originally written on plates,
"either of gold or brass, by a branch of the tribes
"of Israel; and to have been discovered and trans-
"lated by a young man near Palmyra, in the State
"of New York, by the aid of visions, or the ministry
"of angels.

"I inquired of him how or where the book was to
"be obtained. He promised me the perusal of it,
"at his house the next day, if I would call. I felt
"a strange interest in the book.

"Next morning I called at his house, where for
"the first time my eyes beheld the Book of Mor-
"mon,—that book of books—that record which
"reveals the antiquities of the 'new world' back to
"the remotest ages, and which unfolds the destiny
"of its people and the world, for all time to come."

As he read, the spirit of the Lord was upon him,
and he knew and comprehended that the book was

true; whereupon he resolved to visit the young man who was the instrument in bringing forth this "marvelous work."

Accordingly he visited the village of Palmyra, and inquired for the residence of Mr. Joseph Smith, which he found some two or three miles from the village. As he approached the house, at the close of the day, he overtook a man driving some cows, and inquired of him for "Mr. Joseph Smith, the translator of the Book of Mormon." This man was none other than Hyrum, Joseph's brother, who informed him that Joseph then resided in Pennsylvania, some one hundred miles distant. That night Parley was entertained by Hyrum, who explained to him much of the great Israelitish mission just opening to the world.

In the morning he was compelled to take leave of Hyrum, the brother, who at parting presented him with a copy of the Book of Mormon. He had not then completed its perusal, and so after traveling on a few miles he stopped to rest and again commenced to read the book. To his great joy he found that Jesus Christ, in his glorified resurrected body, had appeared to the "remnant of Joseph" on the continent of America, soon after his resurrection and ascension into heaven; and that he also administered, in person, to the ten lost tribes; and that through his personal ministry in these countries his gospel was revealed and written in countries and among nations entirely unknown to the Jewish apostles.

Having rested awhile and perused the sacred book by the roadside, he again walked on.

After fulfilling his appointments, he resolved to preach no more until he had duly received a "commission from on high." So he returned to Hyrum, who journeyed with him some twenty-five miles to the residence of Mr. Whitmer, in Seneca County, who was one of the " witnesses " of the Book of Mormon, and in whose chamber much of the book was translated.

He found the little branch of the church in that place " full of joy, faith, humility and charity."

They rested that night, and on the next day (the 1st of September, 1830), Parley was baptized by Oliver Cowdery, who, with the prophet Joseph, had been ordained "under the hands" of the angel John the Baptist to this ministry,—the same John who baptized Jesus Christ in the River Jordan.

A meeting of these primitive saints was held the same evening, when Parley was confirmed with the gift of the Holy Ghost, and ordained an elder of the church.

Feeling now that he had the true authority to preach, he commenced his new ministry under the authority and power which the angels had conferred. " The Holy Ghost," he says, "came upon me "mightily. I spoke the word of God with power, "reasoning out of the scriptures and the Book "of Mormon. The people were convinced, over- "whelmed with tears, and came forward expressing "their faith, and were baptized."

The mysterious object for which he took leave of his wife was realized, and so he pursued his journey to the land of his fathers, and of his boyhood.

He now commenced his labors in good earnest,

daily addressing crowded audiences; and soon he
baptized his brother Orson, a youth of nineteen,
but to-day a venerable apostle—the Paul of Mormondom.

It was during his labors in these parts, in the
Autumn of 1830, that he saw a very singular and
extraordinary sign in the heavens.

He had been on a visit to the people called Sha-
kers, at New Lebanon, and was returning on foot,
on a beautiful evening of September. The sky was
without a cloud ; the stars shone out beautifully, and
all nature seemed reposing in quiet, as he pursued
his solitary way, wrapt in deep meditations on the
predictions of the holy prophets ; the signs of the
times ; the approaching advent of the Messiah to
reign on the earth, and the important revelations of
the Book of Mormon, when his attention was
aroused by a sudden appearance of a brilliant light
which shone around him "above the brightness of
the sun." He cast his eyes upwards to inquire from
whence the light came, when he perceived a long
chain of light extending in the heavens, very bright
and of a deep fiery red. It at first stood stationary
in a horizontal position ; at length bending in the
centre, the two ends approached each other with a
rapid movement so as to form an exact square. In
this position it again remained stationary for some
time, perhaps a minute, and then again the ends
approached each other with the same rapidity, and
again ceased to move, remaining stationary, for
perhaps a minute, in the form of a compass. It
then commenced a third movement in the same
manner, and closed like the closing of a compass,

the whole forming a straight line like a chain dou-
bled. It again remained stationary a minute, and
then faded away.

"I fell upon my knees in the street," he says, "and
"thanked the Lord for so marvelous a sign of the
"coming of the Son of Man. Some persons may
"smile at this, and say that all these exact move-
"ments were by chance; but for my part I could as
"soon believe that the alphahet would be formed by
"chance and be placed so as to spell my name, as to
"believe that these signs (known only to the wise)
"could be formed and shown forth by chance."

Parley now made his second visit to the prophet,
who had returned from Pennsylvania to his father's
residence in Manchester, near Palmyra, and here
had the pleasure of seeing him for the first time.

It was now October, 1830. A revelation had
been given through the mouth of the prophet in
which elders Oliver Cowdery, Peter Whitmer, Tiber
Peterson and Parley P. Pratt were appointed to go
into the wilderness through the Western States,
and to the Indian Territory.

These elders journeyed until they came to the
spiritual pastorate of Sydney Rigdon, in Ohio. He
received the elders cordially, and Parley presented
his former friend and instructor with the Book of
Mormon, and related to him the history of the same.

"The news of our coming," says Parley, "was
"soon noised abroad, and the news of the discovery
"of the Book of Mormon and the marvelous events
"connected with it. The interest and excitement
"now became general in Kirtland, and in all the
"region round about. The people thronged us

" night and day, insomuch that we had no time for
" rest or retirement. Meetings were convened in
" different neighborhoods, and multitudes came to-
" gether soliciting our attendance ; while thousands
" flocked about us daily, some to be taught, some
" for curiosity, some to obey the gospel, and some
" to dispute or resist it.

" In two or three weeks from our arrival in the
" neighborhood with the news, we had baptized one
" hundred and twenty-seven souls ; and this number
" soon increased to one thousand. The disciples
" were filled with joy and gladness ; while rage and
" lying was abundantly manifested by gainsayers.
" Faith was strong, joy was great, and persecution
" heavy.

" We proceeded to ordain Sidney Rigdon, Isaac
" Morley, John Murdock, Lyman Wight, Edward
" Partridge, and many others to the ministry ; and
" leaving them to take care of the churches, and to
" minister the gospel, we took leave of the saints,
" and continued our journey."

Thus was fulfilled the vision of " Mother Whitney." Kirtland had heard the "word of the Lord."
The angel that spoke from the cloud, at midnight,
in Kirtland, was endowed with the gift of prophesy.
The "daughter of the voice" which followed Israel
down through the ages was potent still—was still
an oracle to the children of the covenant.

CHAPTER VIII.

" You have prayed me here ! Now what do you
want of me ?"

The Master had come !

But who was he ?

Whence came he ?

Good or evil ?

Whose prayers had been answered ?

———

There was in Kirtland a controversy between the
powers of good and evil, for the mastery. Powers
good and evil it would seem to an ordinary discern-
ment. Certainly powers representing two sources.

This was the prime manifestation of the new dispensation. This contention of the invisibles for a
foothold among mortals.

A Mormon iliad! for such it is! It is the epic
of two worlds, in which the invisibles, with mortals,
take their respective parts.

And now it is the dispensation of the fullness of
times ! Now all the powers visible and invisible
contend for the mastery of the earth in the stupen-

dous drama of the last days. This is what Mormonism means.

It is a war of the powers above and below to decide who shall give the next civilization to earth; which power shall incarnate that supreme civilization with its spirit and genius.

S'n ular how exactly this has been repeated since Moses and the magicians of Egypt, and Daniel and the magicians of Babylon, contended.

One had risen up in the august name of Jehovah. Mormonism represents the powers invisible of the Hebrew God.

Shall Jehovah reign in the coming time? Shall he be the Lord God omnipotent? This, in its entirety, is the Mormon problem.

Joseph is the prophet of that stupendous question, to be decided in this grand controversy of the two worlds—this controversy of mortals and immortals!

There are lords many and gods many, but to the prophet and his people there is but one God—Jehovah is his name.

A Mormon iliad, nothing else; and a war of the invisibles—a war of spiritual empires.

That war was once in Kirtland, when the first temple of a new civilization rose, to proclaim the supreme name of the God of Israel.

No sooner had the Church of Latter-day Saints been established in the West than remarkable spiritual manifestations appeared. This was exactly in accordance with the faith and expectations of the disciples; for the promise to them was that these signs should follow the believer.

But there was a power that the saints could not
understand. That it was a power from the invisible
world all readily discerned.

An influence both strange and potent! The
power which was not comprehended was greater,
for the time, in its manifestations, than the spirit
which the disciples better understood.

These spiritual manifestations occurred remarkably at the house of Elder Whitney, where the saints
met often to speak one to the other, and to pray
for the power.

The power had come!

It was in the house which had been overshadowed
by the magic cloud at midnight, out of which the
angel had prophesied of the coming of the word of
the Lord.

The Lord had come!

His word was given. But which Lord? and
whose word? That was the question in that hour
of spiritual controversy.

Similar manifestations were also had in other
branches of the church; and they were given at
those meetings called "testimony meetings." At
these the saints testified one to the other of the
"great work of God in the last days," and magnified the gifts of the spirit. But there were two
kinds of gifts and two kinds of spirits.

Some of these manifestations were very similar
to those of "modern spiritualism." Especially was
this the case with what are styled physical manifestations.

Others read revelations from their hands; holding
them up as a book before them. From this book

they read passages of new scriptures. Books of new revelations had been unsealed.

In letters of light and letters o. gold, writing appeared to their vision, on the hands of these "mediums."

What was singular and confounding to the elders was that many, who could neither read nor write, while under "the influence," uttered beautiful language extemporaneously. At this these "mediums" of the Mormon Church (twenty years before our "modern mediums" were known), would exclaim concerning the "power of God" manifested through them ; challenging the elders, after the spirit had gone out of them, with their own natural inability to utter such wonderful sayings, and do such marvelous things.

As might be expected the majority of these "mediums" were among the sisters. In modern spiritual parlance, they were more "inspirational." Indeed for the manifestation of both powers the sisters have always been the "best mediums" (adopting the descriptive epithet now so popular and suggestive).

And this manifestation of the "two powers" in the church followed the preaching of the Mormon gospel all over the world, especially in America and Great Britain. It was God's spell and the spell of some other spiritual genius.

Where the one power was most manifested, there it was always found that the power from the "other source" was about equally displayed.

So abounding and counterbalancing were these two powers in nearly all the branches of the church in the early rise of Mormonism, in America and

Great Britain, that spiritual manifestations became regarded very generally as fire that could burn as well as bless and build up the work of God.

An early hymn of the dispensation told that "the great prince of darkness was mustering his forces;" that a battle was coming "between the two kingdoms;" that the armies were "gathering round," and that they would "soon in close battle be found."

To this is to be attributed the decline of spiritual gifts in a later period in the Mormon Church, for the "spirits" were poured out so abundantly that the saints began to fear visions, and angels, and prophesy, and the "speaking in tongues."

Thus the sisters, who ever are the "best mediums" of spiritual gifts in the church, have, in latter years, been shorn of their glory. But the gifts still remain with them; and the prophesy is that some day, when there is sufficient wisdom combined with faith, more than the primitive power will be displayed, and the angels will daily walk and talk with the people of God.

But in Kirtland in that day there was the controversy of the invisibles.

———

It was in the beginning of the year 1831 that a sleigh drove into the little town of Kirtland. There were in it a man and his wife with her girl, and a man servant driving.

They seemed to be travelers, and to have come a long distance rather than from a neighboring village; indeed they had come from another State; hundreds of miles from home now; far away in those days for a man to be thus traveling in mid-winter with his wife.

But they were not emigrants; at least seemingly not such; certainly not emigrants of an ordinary kind.

No caravan followed in their wake with merchandise for the western market, nor a train of goods and servants to make a home in a neighboring State.

A solitary sleigh; a man with his wife and two servants; a solitary sleigh, and far from home.

That they were not fugitives was apparent in the manly boldness of the chief personage and the somewhat imperial presence of the woman by his side. This personal air of confidence, and a certain conscious importance, were quite marked in both, especially in the man.

They were two decided personages come West. Some event was in their coming. This much the observer might at once have concluded.

There was thus something of mystery about the solitary sleigh and its occupants.

A chariot with a destiny in it—a very primitive chariot of peace, but a chariot with a charm about it. The driver might have felt akin to the boatman who embarked with the imperial Roman: "Fear not—Cæsar is in thy boat!"

The sleigh wended its course through the streets of Kirtland until it came to the store of Messrs. Gilbert & Whitney, merchants. There it stopped.

Leaping from the primitive vehicle the personage shook himself lightly, as a young lion rising from his restful attitude; for the man possessed a royal strength and a magnificent physique. In age he was scarcely more than twenty-five; young, but with the stamp of one born to command.

Leaving his wife in the sleigh, he walked, with a royal bearing and a wonderfully firm step, straight into the store of Gilbert & Whitney. His bearing could not be other. He planted his foot as one who never turned back—as one destined to make a mark in the great world at his every footfall. He had come to Kirtland as though to possess it.

Going up to the counter where stood the merchant Whitney, he tapped him with hearty affection on the shoulder as he would have done to a long separated brother or a companion of by-gone years. There was the magnetism of love in his very touch. Love was the wondrous charm that the man carried about him..

"Well, Brother Whitney, how do you do?" was his greeting.

"You have the advantage of me," replied Whitney, wondering who his visitor could be. "I could not call you by name."

"I am Joseph, the prophet!"

It was like one of old making himself known to his brethren—"I am Joseph, your brother!"

"Well, what do you want of me?" Joseph asked with a smile; and then with grave solicitude added:

"You have prayed me here, now what do you want of me? The Lord would not let me sleep at nights; but said, up and take your wife to Kirtland!"

An archangel's coming would not have been a greater event to the saints than the coming of Joseph the prophet.

Leaving his store and running across the road to his house, Elder Whitney exclaimed:

"Who do you think was in that sleigh at the store?"

"Well, I don't know," replied Sister Whitney.

"Why, it is Joseph and his wife. Where shall we put them?"

Then came to the mind of Sister Whitney the vision of the cloud that had overshadowed her house at midnight, and the words of the angel who had spoken from the pavilion of his hidden glory. The vision had now to them a meaning and fulfillment indeed. The sister and her husband who had heard the "voice" felt that "the word of the Lord" was to be given to Kirtland in their own dwelling and under the very roof thus hallowed.

One-half of the house was immediately set apart for the prophet and his wife. The sleigh drove up to the door and Joseph entered with Emma—the "elect lady" of the church—and they took up their home in the little city which, with his presence, was now Zion.

It was the controversy of these two powers in the churches in the West which had called Joseph to Kirtland in the opening of the year 1831. The church in the State of New York—its birthplace— had been commanded by revelation to move West, but Joseph hastened ahead with his wife, as we have seen.

He had been troubled at nights in his visions. He had seen Elder Whitney and his wife and the good saints praying for his help. This is how he had known "Brother Whitney" at sight; for Joseph on such occasions saw all things before him as by a map unfolded to his view.

"Up and take your wife to Kirtland," "the Lord" had commanded. And he had come. The church, from the State of New York, followed him the ensuing May.

The master spirit was in Kirtland now. All spirits were subject to him. That was one ruling feature of his apostleship. He held the keys of the dispensation. He commanded and the very invisibles obeyed. *They* also recognized the master spirit. He was only subject to the God of Israel.

"Peace, be still!" the master commanded, and the troubled waters of Kirtland were at peace.

There in the chamber which Sister Whitney consecrated to the prophet the great revelation was given concerning the tests of spirits. There also many of the revelations were given, some of which form part of the book of doctrine and covenants. The chamber was thereafter called the translating room.

Perchance the mystic cloud often overshadowed that house, but the angel of the new covenant could now enter and speak face to face with mortal; for Jehovah's prophet dwelt there. To him the heavens unveiled, and the archangels of celestial spheres appeared in their glory and administered to him.

Wonderful, indeed, if this be true, of which there is a cloud of witnesses; and more wonderful still if hosts of angels, good and bad, have come to earth since that day, converting millions to an age of revelation, unless one like unto Joseph has indeed unlocked the new dispensation with an Elijah's keys of power!

CHAPTER IX.

ELIZA R. SNOW'S EXPERIENCE—GLIMPSES OF THE LIFE
AND CHARACTER OF JOSEPH SMITH—GATHERING
OF THE SAINTS.

"In the autumn of 1829," says Eliza R. Snow,
the high priestess, "the tidings reached my ears
"that God had spoken from the heavens; that he
"had raised up a prophet, and was about to restore
"the fullness of the gospel with all its gifts and
"powers.

"During my brief association with the Campbell-
"ite church, I was deeply interested in the study of
"the ancient prophets, in which I was assisted by
"the erudite Alexander Campbell himself, and Wal-
"ter Scott, whose acquaintance I made,—but more
"particularly by Sidney Rigdon, who was a frequent
"visitor at my father's house.

"But when I heard of the mission of the prophet
"Joseph I was afraid it was not genuine. It was
"just what my soul had hungered for, but I thought
"it was a hoax.

"However, I improved the opportunity and at-
"tended the first meeting within my reach. I lis-
"tened to the testimonials of two of the witnesses
"of the Book of Mormon. Such impressive testi-
"monies I had never before heard. To hear men

" testify that they had seen a holy angel—that they
" had listened to his voice, bearing testimony of the
"work that was ushering in a new dispensation ;
" that the fullness of the gospel was to be restored
" and that they were commanded to go forth and
' declare it, thrilled my inmost soul.

"Yet it must be remembered that when Joseph
" Smith was called to his great mission, more than
" human power was requisite to convince people that
" communication with the invisible world was possi-
"ble. He was scoffed at, ridiculed and persecuted
"for asserting that he had received a revelation ;
" now the world is flooded with revelations.

" Early in the spring of 1835, my eldest sister,
" who, with my mother was baptized in 1831, by the
" prophet, returned home from a visit to the saints
" in Kirtland, and reported of the faith and humility
" of those who had received the gospel as taught
" by Joseph,—the progress of the work, the order
" of the organization of the priesthood and the fre-
"quent manifestations of the power of God.

" The spirit bore witness to me of the truth. I
" felt that I had waited already a little too long to
" see whether the work was going to 'flash in the
"'pan' and go out. But my heart was now fixed;
" and I was baptized on the 5th of April, 1835.
" From that day to this I have not doubted the
" truth of the work.

" In December following I went to Kirtland and
" realized much happiness in the enlarged views and
"rich intelligence that flowed from the fountain of
" eternal truth, through the inspiration of the Most
" High.

" I was present on the memorable event of the
"dedication of the temple, when the mighty power
" of God was displayed, and after its dedication
" enjoyed many refreshing seasons in that holy sanc-
" tuary. Many times have I witnessed manifesta-
"tions of the power of God, in the precious gifts of
"the gospel,—such as speaking in tongues, the in-
" terpretation of tongues, prophesying, healing the
" sick, causing the lame to walk, the blind to see,
"the deaf to hear, and the dumb to speak. Of
" such manifestations in the church I might relate
" many circumstances.

" In the spring I taught a select school for young
"ladies, boarding in the family of the prophet, and
"at the close of the term returned to my father's
" house, where my friends and acquaintances flocked
" around me to inquire about the ‘strange people’
"with whom I was associated. I was exceedingly
" happy in testifying of what I had both seen and
"heard, until the 1st of January, 1837, when I bade
" a final adieu to the home of my youth, to share
" the fortunes of the people of God.

" On my return to Kirtland, by solicitation, I took
" up my residence in the family of the prophet, and
" taught his family school.

" Again I had ample opportunity of judging of his
" daily walk and conversation, and the more I made
"his acquaintance, the more cause I found to ap-
" preciate him in his divine calling. His lips ever
" flowed with instruction and kindness; but, although
" very forgiving, indulgent and affectionate in his
" nature, when his godlike intuition suggested that
" the good of his brethren, or the interests of the

5

" kingdom of God demanded it, no fear of censure,
" no love of approbation, could prevent his severe
" and cutting rebukes.

" His expansive mind grasped the great plan of
" salvation, and solved the mystic problem of man's
" destiny; he was in possession of keys that un-
" locked the past and the future, with its successions
" of eternities; yet in his devotions he was as hum-
" ble as a little child. Three times a day he had
" family worship; and these precious seasons of
" sacred household service, truly seemed a foretaste
" of celestial happiness."

Thus commenced that peculiar and interesting
relationship between the prophet and the inspired
heroine who became his celestial bride, and whose
beautiful ideals have so much glorified celestial
marriage.

There were also others of our Mormon heroines
who had now gathered to the West to build up Zion,
that their " King might appear in his glory." Among
them was that exalted woman—so beloved and honored in the Mormon church—the life-long wife of
Heber C. Kimball. There were also Mary Angel,
and many apostolic women from New England,
who have since stood, for a generation, as pillars
in the latter-day kingdom. We shall meet them
hereafter.

And the saints, as doves flocking to the window
of the ark of the new covenant, gathered to Zion.
They came from the East and the West and the
North and the South.

Soon the glad tidings were conveyed to other
lands. Great Britain "heard the word of the Lord,"

borne there by apostles Heber C. Kimball, Orson Hyde and Willard Richards, and others.

Soon also the saints began to gather from the four quarters of the earth ; and those gatherings have increased until more than a hundred thousand disciples—the majority of them women—have come to America, as their land of promise, to build up thereon the Zion of the last days.

CHAPTER X.

It was "a gathering dispensation." A strange religion indeed, that meant something more than faith and prayers and creeds.

An empire-founding religion, as we have said,— this religion of a latter-day Israel. A religion, in fact, that meant all that the name of " Latter-day Israel" implies. .

The women who did their full half in founding Mormondom, comprehended, as much as did their prototypes who came up out of Egypt, the significance of the name of Israel.

Out of Egypt the seed of promise, to become a peculiar people, a holy nation, with a distinctive God and a distinctive destiny. Out of modern Babylon, to repeat the same Hebraic drama in the latter age.

A Mormon iliad in every view; and the sisters understanding it fully. Indeed perhaps they have best understood it. Their very experience quickened their comprehension.

The cross and the crown of thorns quicken the conception of a crucifixion. The Mormon women have borne the cross and worn the crown of thorns for a full lifetime; not in their religion, but in their experience. Their strange destiny and the divine warfare incarnated in their lives, gave them an experience matchless in its character and unparalleled in its sacrifices.

The sisters understood their religion, and they counted the cost of their divine ambitions.

What that cost has been to these more than Spartan women, we shall find in tragic stories of their lives, fast unfolding in the coming narrative of their gatherings and exterminations.

For the first twenty years of their history the tragedy of the Latter-day Israel was woeful enough to make their guardian angels weep, and black enough in its scenes to satisfy the angriest demons.

This part of the Mormon drama began in 1831 with the removal of the church from the State of New York to Kirtland, Ohio, and to Jackson, and other counties in Missouri ; and it culminated in the martyrdom of the prophet and his brother at Nauvoo, and the exodus to the Rocky Mountains. In all these scenes the sisters have shown themselves matchless heroines.

The following, from an early poem, written by the prophetess, Eliza R. Snow, will finely illustrate the Hebraic character of the Mormon work, and the heroic spirit in which these women entered into the divine action of their lives :

> My heart is fix'd—I know in whom I trust.
> 'Twas not for wealth—'twas not to gather heaps
> Of perishable things—'twas not to twine
> Around my brow a transitory wreath,
> A garland decked with gems of mortal praise,

That I forsook the home of childhood; that
I left the lap of ease—the halo rife
With friendship's richest, soft, and mellow tones;
Affection's fond caresses, and the cup
O'erflowing with the sweets of social life,
With high refinement's golden pearls enrich'd.

Ah, no! A holier purpose fir'd my soul;
A nobler object prompted my pursuit.
Eternal prospects open'd to my view,
And hope celestial in my bosom glow'd.
God, who commanded Abraham to leave
His native country, and to offer up
On the lone altar, where no eye beheld
But that which never sleeps, an only son,
Is still the same; and thousands who have made
A covenant with him by sacrifice,
Are bearing witness to the sacred truth—
Jehovah speaking has reveal'd his will.

The proclamation sounded in my ear—
It reached my heart—I listen'd to the sound—
Counted the cost, and laid my earthly all
Upon the altar, and with purpose fix'd
Unalterably, while the spirit of
Elijah's God within my bosom reigns,
Embrac'd the everlasting covenant,
And am determined now to be a saint,
And number with the tried and faithful ones,
Whose race is measured with their life; whose prize
Is everlasting, and whose happiness
Is God's approval; and to whom 'tis more
Than meat and drink to do his righteous will.

*   *   *   *

Although to be a saint requires
A noble sacrifice—an arduous toil—
A persevering aim; the great reward
Awaiting the grand consummation will
Repay the price, however costly; and
The pathway of the saint the safest path
Will prove; though perilous—for 'tis foretold,
All things that can be shaken, God will shake;
Kingdoms and governments, and institutes,
Both civil and religious, must be tried—
Tried to the core, and sounded to the depth.

Then let me be a saint, and be prepar'd
For the approaching day, which like a snare

Will soon surprise the hypocrite—expose
The rottenness of human schemes—shake off
Oppressive fetters—break the gorgeous reins
Usurpers hold, and lay the pride of man—
The pride of nations, low in dust!

And there was in these gatherings of our latter-
day Israel, like as in this poem, a tremendous meaning. It is of the Hebrew significance and genius
rather than of the Christian; for Christ is now Messiah, King of Israel, and not the Babe of Bethlehem.
Mormondom is no Christian sect, but an Israelitish
nationality, and even woman, the natural prophetess
of the reign of peace, is prophesying of the shaking
of "kingdoms and governments and all human
institutions."

The Mormons from the beginning well digested
the text to the great Hebrew drama, and none better
than the sisters; here it is:

" Now the Lord had said unto Abram, get thee
" out of thy country, and from thy kindred, and from
" thy father's house, unto a land that I will shew
" thee;

" And I will make of thee a great nation, and I
" will bless thee, and make thy name great; and
" thou shalt be a blessing;

" And I will bless them that bless thee, and curse
" him that curseth thee; and in thee shall all fam-
" ilies of the earth be blessed."

And so, for now nearly fifty years, this Mormon
Israel have been getting out of their native countries, and from their kindred, and from their father's
house unto the gathering places that their God has
shown them.

But they have been driven from those gathering

places from time to time; yes, driven farther west. There was the land which God was showing them. At first it was too distant to be seen even by the eye of faith. Too many thousands of miles even for the Spartan heroism of the sisters; too dark a tragedy of expulsions and martyrdoms; and too many years of exoduses and probations. The wrath of the Gentiles drove them where their destiny led them—to the land which God was showing them.

And for the exact reason that the patriarchal Abraham and Sarah were commanded to get out of their country and from their kindred and their father's house, so were the Abrahams and Sarahs of our time commanded by the same God and for the same purpose.

"I will make of thee a great nation." "And I will make my covenant between me and thee, and I will multiply thee exceedingly." "And thou shalt be a father of many nations." "And I will establish my covenant between me and thee and thy seed after thee in their generations, for an everlasting covenant, to be a God unto thee and thy seed after thee."

To fulfill this in the lives of these spiritual sons and daughters of Abraham and Sarah, the gathering dispensation was brought in. These Mormons have gathered from the beginning that they might become the fathers and mothers of a nation, and that through them the promises made to the Abrahamic fathers and mothers might be greatly fulfilled.

This is most literal, and was well understood in the early rise of the church, long before polygamy was known. Yet who cannot now see that in such *a* patriarchal covenant was the very overture of patriarchal marriage—or polygamy.

So in the early days quite a host of the daughters of New England—earnest and purest of women—many of them unmarried, and most of them in the bloom of womanhood—gathered to the virgin West to become the mothers of a nation, and to build temples to the name of a patriarchal God!

CHAPTER XI.

Two thousand years had nearly passed since the
destruction of the temple of Solomon ; three thousand years, nearly, since that temple of the old
Jerusalem was built.

Yet here in America in the nineteenth century,
among the Gentiles, a modern Israel began to rear
temples to the name of the God of Israel! Temples to be reared to his august name in every State
on this vast continent! Thus runs the Mormon
prophesy.

All America, the New Jerusalem of the last days!
All America for the God of Israel! What a conception! Yet these daughters of Zion perfectly
understood it nearly fifty years ago.

Joseph was indeed a sublime and daring oracle.
Such a conception grasped even before he laid the
foundation stone of a Zion—that all America is to
be the New Jerusalem of the world and of the
future—was worthy to make him the prophet of
America.

Zion was not a county in Missouri, a city in Ohio or Illinois; nor is she now a mere embryo State in the Rocky Mountains.

Kirtland was but a "stake of Zion" where the first temple rose. Jackson county is the enchanted spot where the "centre stake" of Zion is to be planted, and the grand temple reared, by-and-by. Nauvoo with its temple was another stake. Utah also is but a stake. Here we have already the temple of St. George, and in Salt Lake City a temple is being built which will be a Masonic unique to this continent.

Perchance it will stand in the coming time scarcely less a monument to the name of its builder—Brigham Young—than the temple of Old Jerusalem has been to the name of Solomon.

But all America is the world's New Jerusalem!

With this cardinal conception crowding the soul of the Mormon prophet, inspired by the very archangels of Israel, what a vast Abrahamic drama opened to the view of the saints in Kirtland when the first temple lifted its sacred tower to the skies!

The archangels of Israel had come down to fulfill on earth the grand Abrahamic programme. The two worlds—the visible and the invisible—were quickly engaging in the divine action, to consummate, in this "dispensation of the fullness of times," the promises made unto the fathers.

And all America for the God of Israel.

There is method in Mormonism—method infinite. Mormonism is Masonic. The God of Israel is a covenant maker; the crown of the covenant is the temple.

But woman must not be lost to view in our admiration of the prophet's conceptions.

How stands woman in the grand temple economy, as she loomed up in her mission, from the house of the Lord in Kirtland?

The apostles and elders laid the foundations, raised the arches, and put on the cap stone; but it was woman that did the "inner work of the temple."

George A. Smith hauled the first load of rock; Heber C. Kimball worked as an operative mason, and Brigham Young as a painter and glazier in the house; but the sisters wrought on the "veils of the temple."

Sister Polly Angel, wife of Truman O. Angel, the church architect, relates that she and a band of sisters were working on the "veils," one day, when the prophet and Sidney Rigdon came in.

"Well, sisters," observed Joseph, "you are always "on hand. The sisters are always first and fore-"most in all good works. Mary was first at the "resurrection; and the sisters now are the first to "work on the inside of the temple."

'Tis but a simple incident, but full of significance. It showed Joseph's instinctive appreciation of woman and her mission. Her place was *inside* the temple, and he was about to put her there,—a high priestess of Jehovah, to whose name he was building temples. And wonderfully suggestive was his prompting, that woman was the first witness of the resurrection.

Once again woman had become an oracle of a new dispensation and a new civilization. She can only properly be this when a temple economy comes round in the unfolding of the ages. She can only be a legitimate oracle *in* the temple.

When she dares to play the oracle, without her divine mission and anointing, she is accounted in society as a witch, a fortune-teller, a medium, who divines for hire and sells the gift of the invisibles for money.

But in the temple woman is a sacred and sublime oracle. She is a prophetess and a high priestess. Inside the temple she cannot but be as near the invisibles as man—nearer indeed, from her finer nature, inside the mystic veil, the emblems of which she has worked upon with her own hands.

Of old the oracle had a priestly royalty. The story of Alexander the Great and the oracle of Delphi is famous. The conqueror demanded speech from the oracle concerning his destiny. The oracle was a woman; and womanlike she refused to utter the voice of destiny at the imperious bidding of a mortal. But Alexander knew that woman was inspired—that he held in his grip the incarnated spirit of the temple, and he essayed to drag her to the holy ground where speech was given.

" He is invincible !" exclaimed the oracle, in wrath.

" The oracle speaks !" cried Alexander, in exultation.

The prophetess was provoked to an utterance; woman forced to obey the stronger will of man; but it was woman's inspired voice that sent Alexander through the world a conquering destiny.

And the prophet of Mormondom knew that woman is, by the gifts of God and nature, an inspired being. If she was this in the temples of

Egypt and Greece, more abundantly is she this in the temples of Israel. In them woman is the medium of Jehovah.. This is what the divine scheme of the Mormon prophet has made her to this age; and she began her great mission to the world in the temple at Kirtland.

But this temple-building of the Mormons has a vaster meaning than the temples of Egypt, the oracles of Greece, or the cathedrals of the Romish Church.

It is the vast Hebrew iliad, begun with Abraham and brought down through the ages, in a race still preserved with more than its original quality and fibre; and in a God who is raising up unto Abraham a mystical seed of promise, a latter-day Israel.

Jehovah is a covenant-maker. "And I will make with Israel a new and everlasting covenant," is the text that Joseph and Brigham have been working upon. Hence this temple building in America, to fulfill and glorify the new covenant of Israel.

The first covenant was made with Abraham and the patriarchs *in the East*. The greater and the everlasting covenant will restore the kingdom to Israel. That covenant has been made *in the West*, with these veritable children of Abraham. God has raised up children unto Abraham to fulfill the promises made to him. This is Mormonism.

The West is the future world. Yet how shall there be the new civilization without its distinctive temples? Certainly there shall be no Abrahamic dispensation and covenant unless symbolized by temples raised to the name of the God of Israel!

All America, then, is Zion!

A hundred temples lifting their towers to the skies in the world's New Jerusalem. Temples built to the name of the God of Israel.

Mark this august wonder of the age; the Mormons build not temples to the name of Jesus, but to the name of Jehovah—not to the Son, but to the Father.

The Hebrew symbol is not the cross, but the sceptre. The Hebrews know nothing of the cross. It is the symbol of heathenism, whence Rome received her signs and her worship. Rome adopted the cross and she has borne it as her mark. She never reared her cathedrals to the name of the God of Israel, nor has she taught the nations to fear his name. Nor has she prophesied of the New Jerusalem of the last days, which must supersede Rome and give the millennial civilization to the world.

The reign of Messiah! Temples to the Most High God! The sceptre, not the cross!

There is a grand Masonic consistency in the divine scheme of the Mormon prophet, and the sisters began to comprehend the infinite themes of their religion when they worked in the temple at Kirtland, and beheld in the service the glory of Israel's God.

CHAPTER XII.

The erection of the Kirtland temple was a leading characteristic of the work of the last dispensation.

It was commenced in June, 1833, under the immediate direction of the Almighty, through his servant, Joseph Smith, whom he had called in his boyhood, like Samuel of old, to introduce the fullness of the everlasting gospel.

At that time the saints were few in number, and most of them very poor; and, had it not been for the assurance that God had spoken, and had commanded that a house should be built to his name, of which he not only revealed the form, but also designated the dimensions, an attempt towards building that temple, under the then existing circumstances, would have been, by all concerned, pronounced preposterous.

Although many sections of the world abounded with mosques, churches, synagogues and cathedrals, built professedly for worship, this was the first instance, for the lapse of many centuries, of God having given a pattern, from the heavens, and manifested by direct revelation how the edifice should be constructed, in order that he might accept and acknowledge it as his own. This knowledge inspired the saints to almost superhuman efforts, while through faith and union they acquired strength. In comparison with eastern churches and cathedrals, this temple is not large, but in view of the amount of available means possessed, a calculation of the cost, at the lowest possible figures, would have staggered the faith of any but Latter-day saints; and it now stands as a monumental pillar.

Its dimensions are eighty by fifty-nine feet; the walls fifty feet high, and the tower one hundred and ten feet. The two main halls are fifty-five by sixty-five feet, in the inner court. The building has four vestries in front, and five rooms in the attic, which were devoted to literature, and for meetings of the various quorums of the priesthood.

There was a peculiarity in the arrangement of the inner court which made it more than ordinarily impressive—so much so that a sense of sacred awe seemed to rest upon all who entered; not only the saints, but strangers also manifested a high degree of reverential feeling. Four pulpits stood, one above another, in the centre of the building, from north to south, both on the east and west ends; those on the west for the presiding officers of the Melchisidec priesthood, and those on the east for the Aaronic; and each of these pulpits was separated by curtains of white painted canvas, which were let down and drawn up at pleasure. In front of each of these two rows of pulpits, was a sacrament table, for the administration of that sacred ordinance. In each corner of the court was an elevated pew for the singers—the choir being distributed into four compartments. In addition to the pulpit curtains, were others, intersecting at right angles, which divided the main ground-floor hall into four equal sections—giving to each one-half of one set of pulpits.

From the day the ground was broken for laying the foundation for the temple, until its dedication on the 27th of March, 1836, the work was vigorously prosecuted.

With very little capital except brain, bone and sinew, combined with unwavering trust in God, men, women, and even children, worked with their might; while the brethren labored in their departments, the sisters were actively engaged in boarding and clothing workmen not otherwise provided for—all living as abstemiously as possible so that every cent might be appropriated to the grand object, while their energies were stimulated by the prospect of participating in the blessing of a house built by the direction of the Most High and accepted by him.

The dedication was looked forward to with intense interest ; and when the day arrived (Sunday, March 27th, 1836), a dense multitude assembled— the temple was filled to its utmost, and when the ushers were compelled to close the doors, the outside congregation was nearly if not quite as large as that within.

Four hundred and sixteen elders, including prophets and apostles, with the first great prophets of the last dispensation at their head, were present— men who had been " called of God as was Aaron," and clothed with the holy priesthood; many of them having just returned from missions, on which they had gone forth like the ancient disciples, "without purse or scrip," now to feast for a little season on the sweet spirit of love and union, in the midst of those who had "tasted of the powers of the world to come."

'At the hour appointed, the assembly was seated, the Melchisidec and Aaronic priesthoods being arranged as follows: West end of the house, Presidents Frederick G. Williams, Joseph Smith, Sr., and William W. Phelps, occupied the first pulpit for the Melchisidec priesthood; Presidents Joseph Smith, Jr., Hyrum Smith and Sidney Rigdon, the second; Presidents David Whitmer, Oliver Cowdry and John Whitmer, the third; the fourth pulpit was occupied by the president of the high-priest's quorum and his councilors, and two choristers. The twelve apostles were on the right, in the highest three seats; the president of the elders, his two councilors and clerk in the seat directly below the twelve. The High Council of Kirtland, consisting of twelve, were on the left, on the first three seats. The fourth seat, and next below the High Council, was occupied by Warren A. Cowdry and Warren Parrish, who officiated as scribes.

In the east end of the house, the Bishop of Kirtland—Newel K. Whitney—and his councilors occupied the first pulpit for the Aaronic priesthood; the Bishop of Zion—Edward Partridge—and his councilors, the second; the President of the priests and his councilors, the third; the President of the teachers, and his councilors, and one chorister, the fourth;

the High Council of Zion, consisting of twelve councilors, on the right; the President of the deacons, and his councilors, in the next seat below them, and the seven presidents of the seventies, on the left.

At nine o'clock, President Sidney Rigdon commenced the services of that great and memorable day, by reading the ninety-sixth and twenty-fourth Psalms; "Ere long the vail will be rent in twain," etc., was sung by the choir, and after President Rigdon had addressed the throne of grace in fervent prayer, "O happy souls who pray," etc., was sung. President Rigdon then read the eighteenth, nineteenth, and twentieth verses of the eighteenth chapter of Matthew, and spoke more particularly from the last-named verse, continuing his eloquent, logical and sublime discourse for two and a half hours. At one point, as he reviewed the toils and privations of those who had labored in rearing the walls of that sacred edifice, he drew tears from many eyes, saying, there were those who had wet those walls with their tears, when, in the silent shades of the night, they were praying to the God of heaven to protect them, and stay the unhallowed hands of ruthless spoilers, who had uttered a prophesy, when the foundation was laid, that the walls should never be erected.

In reference to his main subject, the speaker assumed that in the days of the Saviour there were synagogues where the Jews worshipped God; and in addition to those, the splendid temple in Jerusalem; yet when, on a certain occasion, one proposed to follow him, withersoever he went, though heir of all things, he cried out in bitterness of soul, " The "foxes have holes, and the birds of the air have "nests, but the Son of Man hath not where to lay his "head." From this the speaker drew the conclusion that the Most High did not put his name there, neither did he accept the worship of those who paid their vows and adorations there. This was evident from the fact that they did not receive the Saviour, but thrust him from them, saying, "Away with him! Crucify him! Crucify him!" It was therefore evident that his spirit did not dwell in them. They were the degenerate sons of noble sires, but they had long since slain the prophets and seers, through whom the Lord had revealed himself to the children of men. They were not led by revelation. This, said the speaker, was the grand difficulty—their unbelief in present revelation. He then clearly demonstrated the fact that diversity of, and contradictory opinions did, and would prevail among people not led by present revelation; which forcibly applies to the various religious sects of our own day; and inasmuch as they manifest the same spirit, they must be under the same condemnation with those who were coeval with the Saviour.

He admitted there were many houses—many sufficiently large, built for the worship of God, but not one, except this, on the face of the whole earth, that was built by divine revelation; and were it not for this, the dear Redeemer might, in this day of science, intelligence and religion, say to those who would follow him, "The foxes have holes, the birds of the "air have nests, but the Son of Man hath not where "to lay his head."

After the close of his discourse, President Rigdon presented for an expression of their faith and confidence, Joseph Smith, Jr., as prophet, seer and revelator, to the various quorums, and the whole congregation of saints, and a simultaneous rising up followed, in token of unanimous confidence, and covenant to uphold him as such, by their faith and prayers.

The morning services were concluded by the choir singing, "Now let us rejoice in the day of salvation," etc. During an intermission of twenty minutes, the congregation remained seated, and the afternoon services opened by singing, "This earth was once a garden place," etc. President Joseph Smith, Jr., addressed the assembly for a few moments, and then presented the first presidency of the church as prophets, seers, and revelators, and called upon all who felt to acknowledge them as such, to manifest it by rising up. All arose. He then presented the twelve apostles who were present, as prophets, seers, and revelators, and special witnesses to all the earth, holding the keys of the kingdom of God, to unlock it, or cause it to be done among them ; to which all assented by rising to their feet. He then presented the other quorums in their order, and the vote was unanimous in every instance.

He then prophesied to all, that inasmuch as they would uphold these men in their several stations (alluding to the different quorums in the church), the Lord would bless them, "yea, in the name of "Christ, the blessings of heaven shall be yours; "and when the Lord's anointed shall go forth to "proclaim the word, bearing testimony to this gen-

"eration, if they receive it they shall be blest ; but
"if not, the judgments of God will follow close upon
"them, until that city or that house which rejects
"them, shall be left desolate."

The hymn commencing with " How pleased and
blest was I," was sung, and the following dedicatory
prayer offered by the prophet, Joseph Smith :

"Thanks be to thy name, O Lord God of Israel,
who keepest covenant and showest mercy unto thy
servants who walk uprightly before thee, with all
their hearts ; thou who hast commanded thy servants to build a house to thy name in this place.
And now thou beholdest, O Lord, that thy servants
have done according to thy commandment. And
now we ask thee, Holy Father, in the name of Jesus
Christ, the son of thy bosom, in whose name alone
salvation can be administered to the children of
men, we ask thee, O Lord, to accept of this house,
the workmanship of the hands of us, thy servants,
which thou didst command us to build; for thou
knowest that we have done this work through great
tribulation ; and out of our poverty we have given
of our substance, to build a house to thy name, that
the Son of Man might have a place to manifest himself to his people. And as thou hast said in a revelation, given to us, calling us thy friends, saying,
'call your solemn assembly, as I have commanded
you ; and as all have not faith, seek ye diligently,
and teach one another words of wisdom ; yea, seek
ye out of the best books, words of wisdom ; seek
learning even by study, and also by faith. Organize
yourselves ; prepare every needful thing, and establish a house, even a house of prayer, a house of
fasting, a house of faith, a house of learning, a house
of glory, a house of order, a house of God. That
your incomings may be in the name of the Lord,
that your outgoings may be in the name of the Lord,

that all your salutations may be in the name of the
Lord, with uplifted hands to the Most High.'

"And now, Holy Father, we ask thee to assist us,
thy people, with thy grace, in calling our solemn
assembly, that it may be done to thy honor, and to
thy divine acceptance. And in a manner that we
may be found worthy in thy sight, to secure a fulfillment of the promises which thou hast made unto
us, thy people, in the revelations given unto us ; that
thy glory may rest down upon thy people, and upon
this thy house, which we now dedicate to thee, that
it may be sanctified and consecrated to be holy, and
that thy holy presence may be continually in this
house, and that all people who shall enter upon the
threshold of the Lord's house may feel thy power,
and feel constrained to acknowledge that thou hast
sanctified it, and that it is thy house, a place of thy
holiness. And do thou grant, Holy Father, that all
those who shall worship in this house, may be taught
words of wisdom out of the best books, and that
they may seek learning even by study, and also by
faith, as thou hast said ; and that they may grow up
in thee, and receive a fullness of the Holy Ghost
and be organized according to thy laws, and be prepared to obtain every needful thing ; and that this
house may be a house of prayer, a house of fasting,
a house of faith, a house of glory and of God, even
thy house ; that all the incomings of thy people,
into this house, may be in the name of the Lord ;
that all the outgoings from this house may be in the
name of the Lord ; and that all their salutations
may be in the name of the Lord, with holy hands,
uplifted to the Most High ; and that no unclean
thing shall be permitted to come into thy house to
pollute it ; and when thy people transgress, any
of them, they may speedily repent, and return unto
thee, and find favor in thy sight, and be restored to
the blessings which thou hast ordained to be poured
out upon those who shall reverence thee in thy

house. And we ask thee, Holy Father, that thy servants may go forth from this house, armed with thy power, and thy name may be upon them, and thy glory be round about them, and thine angels have charge over them; and from this place they may bear exceedingly great and glorious tidings, in truth, unto the ends of the earth, that they may know that this is thy work, and that thou hast put forth thy hand, to fulfill that which thou hast spoken by the mouths of the prophets, concerning the last days. We ask thee, Holy Father, to establish the people that shall worship and honorably hold a name and standing in this thy house, to all generations, and for eternity, that no weapon formed against them shall prosper; that he who diggeth a pit for them shall fall into the same himself; that no combination of wickedness shall have power to rise up and prevail over thy people upon whom thy name shall be put in this house; and if any people shall rise against this people, that thy anger be kindled against them, and if they shall smite this people thou wilt smite them, thou wilt fight for thy people as thou didst in the day of battle, that they may be delivered from the hands of all their enemies.

" We ask thee, Holy Father, to confound, and astonish, and to bring to shame and confusion, all those who have spread lying reports abroad, over the world, against thy servant, or servants, if they will not repent when the everlasting gospel shall be proclaimed in their ears, and that all their works may be brought to naught, and be swept away by the hail, and by the judgments which thou wilt send upon them in thy anger, that there may be an end to lyings and slanders against thy people; for thou knowest, O Lord, that thy servants have been innocent before thee in bearing record of thy name, for which they have suffered these things; therefore we plead before thee a full and complete deliverance from under this yoke; break it off, O Lord; break it off from the necks of thy servants, by thy power, that we may rise up in the midst of this generation and do thy work.

"O Jehovah, have mercy on this people, and as all men sin, forgive the transgressions of thy people, and let them be blotted out forever. Let the anointing of thy ministers be sealed upon them with power from on high ; let it be fulfilled upon them as upon those on the day of pentecost; let the gift of tongues be poured out upon thy people, even cloven tongues as of fire, and the interpretation thereof, and let thy house be filled,. as with a rushing mighty wind, with thy glory. Put upon thy servants the testimony of the covenant, that when they go out and proclaim thy word, they may seal up the law, and prepare the hearts of thy saints for all those judgments thou art about to send, in thy wrath, upon the inhabitants of the earth, because of their transgressions; that thy people may not faint in the day of trouble. And whatsoever city thy servants shall enter, and the people of that city receive their testimony, let thy peace and thy salvation be upon that city, that they may gather out of that city the righteous, that they may come forth to Zion, or to her stakes, the places of thy appointment, with songs of everlasting joy; and until this be accomplished, let not thy judgments fall upon this city. And whatsoever city thy servants shall enter, and the people of that city receive not the testimony of thy servants, and thy servants warn them to save themselves from this untoward generation, let it be upon that city according to that which thou hast spoken by the mouths of thy prophets; but deliver thou, O Jehovah, we beseech thee, thy servants from their hands, and cleanse them from their blood. O Lord, we delight not in the destruction of our fellow men ! Their souls are precious before thee; but thy word must be fulfilled; help thy servants to say, with thy grace assisting them, thy will be done, O Lord, and not

ours. We know that thou hast spoken by the
mouth of thy prophets terrible things concerning
the wicked, in the last days—that thou wilt pour out
thy judgments without measure; therefore, O Lord,
deliver thy people from the calamity of the wicked;
enable thy servants to seal up the law, and bind up
the testimony, that they may be prepared against
the day of burning. We ask thee, Holy Father, to
remember those who have been driven (by the inhabitants of Jackson county, Missouri), from the
lands of their inheritance, and break off, O Lord,
this yoke of affliction that has been put upon them.
Thou knowest, O Lord, that they have been greatly
oppressed and afflicted by wicked men, and our
hearts flow out with sorrow, because of their grievous burdens. O Lord, how long wilt thou suffer
this people to bear this affliction, and the cries of
their innocent ones to ascend up in thine ears, and
their blood come up in testimony before thee, and
not make a display of thy testimony in their behalf?
Have mercy, O Lord, upon that wicked mob, who
have driven thy people, that they may cease to spoil,
that they may repent of their sins, if repentance is
to be found; but if they will not, make bare thine
arm, O Lord, and redeem that which thou didst
appoint a Zion unto thy people.

" And if it cannot be otherwise, that the cause of
thy people may not fail before thee, may thine anger
be kindled, and thine indignation fall upon them,
that they may be wasted away, both root and branch,
from under heaven; but inasmuch as they will repent, thou art gracious and merciful, and wilt turn
away thy wrath, when thou lookest upon the face of
thine anointed. Have mercy, O Lord, upon all the
nations of the earth; have mercy upon the rulers of
our land; may those principles which were so honorably and nobly defended, viz.: the constitution of
our land, by our fathers, be established forever.
Remember the kings, the princes, the nobles, and

the great ones of the earth, and all people, and the
churches, all the poor, the needy and afflicted ones of
the earth, that their hearts may be softened, when thy
servants shall go out from thy house, O Jehovah,
to bear testimony of thy name, that their prejudices
may give way before the truth, and thy people may
obtain favor in the sight of all, that all the ends of
the earth may know that we thy servants have heard
thy voice, and that thou hast sent us ; that from all
these, thy servants, the sons of Jacob, may gather
out the righteous to build a holy city to thy name,
as thou hast commanded them. We ask thee to
appoint unto Zion other stakes, besides this one
which thou hast appointed, that the gathering of thy
people may roll on in great power and majesty, that
thy work may be cut short in righteousness. Now
these words, O Lord, we have spoken before thee,
concerning the revelations and commandments
which thou hast given unto us, who are identified
with the Gentiles ; but thou knowest that thou hast
a great love for the children of Jacob, who have
been scattered upon the mountains, for a long time,
in a cloudy and dark day ; we therefore ask thee to
have mercy upon the children of Jacob, that Jerusalem, from this hour, may begin to be redeemed,
and the yoke of bondage begin to be broken off
from the house of David, and the children of Judah
may begin to return to the lands which thou didst
give to Abraham, their father ; and cause that the
remnants of Jacob, who have been cursed and smit-
ten, because of their transgressions, be converted
from their wild and savage condition, to the fullness
of the everlasting gospel, that they may lay down
their weapons of bloodshed, and cease their rebel-
lions ; and may all the scattered remnants of Israel,
who have been driven to the ends of the earth,
come to a knowledge of the truth, believe in the
Messiah, and be redeemed from oppression, and
rejoice before thee. O Lord, remember thy servant,

Joseph Smith, Jr., and all his afflictions and persecutions, how he has covenanted with Jehovah, and
vowed to thee, O mighty God of Jacob, and the
commandments which thou hast given unto him,
and that he hath sincerely striven to do thy will.
Have mercy, O Lord, upon his wife and children,
that they may be exalted in thy presence, and preserved by thy fostering hand ; have mercy upon all
their immediate connections, that their prejudices
may be broken up, and swept away as with a flood,
that they may be converted and redeemed with
Israel, and know that thou art God. Remember,
O Lord, the presidents, even all the presidents of
thy church, that thy right hand may exalt them,
with all their families, and their immediate connections, that their names may be perpetuated, and
had in everlasting remembrance, from generation
to generation. Remember all thy church, O Lord,
with all their families, and all their immediate
connections, with all their sick and afflicted ones,
with all the poor and meek of the earth, that
the kingdom which thou hast set up without
hands, may become a great mountain, and fill
the whole earth ; that thy church may come forth
out of the wilderness of darkness, and shine forth
fair as the moon, clear as the sun, and terrible
as an army with banners, and be adorned as a
bride for that day when thou shalt unveil the
heavens, and cause the mountains to flow down at
thy presence, and the valleys to be exalted, the
rough places made smooth ; that thy glory may fill
the earth, that when the trump shall sound for the
dead, we shall be caught up in the cloud to meet
thee, that we may ever be with the Lord, that our
garments may be pure, that we may be clothed upon
with robes of righteousness, with palms in our hands,
and crowns of glory upon our heads, and reap eternal joy for all our sufferings.

" O Lord God Almighty, hear us in these petitions, and answer us from heaven, thy holy habitation, where thou sittest enthroned, with glory, honor, power, majesty, might, dominion, truth, justice, judgment, mercy, and an infinity of fullness, from everlasting to everlasting.   O hear, O hear, O hear us, O Lord, and answer these petitions, and accept the dedication of this house unto thee, the work of our hands, which we have built unto thy name !   And also this church, to put upon it thy name ; and help us by the power of thy spirit, that we may mingle our voices with those bright shining seraphs around thy throne, with acclamations of praise, singing hosanna to God and the Lamb ; and let these thine anointed ones be clothed with salvation, and thy saints shout aloud for joy.   Amen, and amen."

The choir then sang, " The spirit of God like a fire is burning," etc., after which the Lord's supper was administered to the whole assembly.   Then President Joseph Smith bore testimony of his mission and of the ministration of angels, and, after testimonials and exhortations by other elders, he blest the congregation in the name of the Lord.

Thus ended the ceremonies of the dedication of the first temple built by special command of the Most High, in this dispensation.

One striking feature of the ceremonies, was the grand shout of hosanna, which was given by the whole assembly, in standing position, with uplifted hands.   The form of the shout is as follows : " Hosanna—hosanna—hosanna—to God and the Lamb—amen—amen, and amen."   The foregoing was deliberately and emphatically pronounced, and three times repeated, and with such power as seemed almost sufficient to raise the roof from the building.

A singular incident in connection with this shout

may be discredited by some, but it is verily true. A notice had been circulated that children in arms would not be admitted at the dedication of the temple. A sister who had come a long distance with her babe, six weeks old, having, on her arrival, heard of the above requisition, went to the patriarch Joseph Smith, Sr., in great distress, saying that she knew no one with whom she could leave her infant; and to be deprived of the privilege of attending the dedication seemed more than she could endure. The ever generous and kind-hearted father volunteered to take the responsibility on himself, and told her to take her child, at the same time giving the mother a promise that her babe should make no disturbance ; and the promise was verified. But when the congregation shouted hosanna, that babe joined in the shout. As marvelous as that incident may appear to many, it is not more so than other occurrences on that occasion.

The ceremonies of that dedication may be rehearsed, but no mortal language can describe the heavenly manifestations of that memorable day. Angels appeared to some, while a sense of divine presence was realized by all present, and each heart was filled with "joy inexpressible and full of glory."

CHAPTER XIII.

Concerning affairs at Kirtland subsequent to the
dedication of the temple, and people and incidents
of those times, Eliza R. Snow continues: With
the restoration of the fullness of the gospel came
also the ancient order of patriarchal blessings.
Each father, holding the priesthood, stands as a
patriarch, at the head of his family, with invested
right and power to bless his household, and to pre-
dict concerning the future, on the heads of his children, as did Jacob of old.

Inasmuch as many fathers have died without
having conferred those blessings, God, in the order
of his kingdom, has made provisions to supply the
deficiency, by choosing men to officiate as patriarchs,
whose province it is to bless the fatherless. Joseph
Smith, Sr., was ordained to this office, and held the
position of first patriarch in the church. He was
also, by appointment, president of the Kirtland
stake of Zion, consequently the first presiding officer
in all general meetings for worship.

A few words descriptive of this noble man may

not be deemed amiss in this connection. Of a fine physique, he was more than ordinarily prepossessing in personal appearance. His kind, affable, dignified and unassuming manner naturally inspired strangers with feelings of love and reverence. To me he was the veritable personification of my idea of the ancient Father Abraham.

In his decisions he was strictly just; what can be said of very few, may be truly said of him, in judging between man and man : his judgment could not be biased by either personal advantage, sympathy, or affection. Such a man was worthy of being the father of the first prophet of the last dispensation ; while his amiable and affectionate consort, Mother Lucy Smith, was as worthy of being the mother. Of her faith, faithfulness and untiring efforts in labors of love and duty, until she was broken down by the weight of years and sorrow, too much cannot be said.

I was present, on the 17th of May, when a messenger arrived and informed the prophet Joseph that his grandmother, Mary Duty Smith, had arrived at Fairport, on her way to Kirtland, and wished him to come for her. The messenger stated that she said she had asked the Lord that she might live to see her children and grandchildren once more. The prophet responded with earnestness, " I wish she had set the time longer." I pondered in silence over this remark, thinking there might be more meaning in the expression than the words indicated, which was proven by the result, for she only lived a few days after her arrival. She was in the ninety-fourth year of her age—in appearance not over

seventy-five. She had not been baptized, on account
of the opposition of her oldest son, Jesse, who was
a bitter enemy to the work. She said to Mother
Lucy Smith, " I am going to have your Joseph baptize me, and my Joseph (the patriarch) bless me."

Her husband, Israel Smith, died in St. Lawrence
county, New York, after having received the Book
of Mormon, and read it nearly through. He had,
long before, predicted that a prophet would be raised
up in his family, and was satisfied that his grandson
was that prophet. The venerable widow was also
well assured of the fact.

The next day after her arrival at the house of the
prophet, where she was welcomed with every manifestation of kindness and affection, her children,
grandchildren and great-grandchildren—all who
were residents of Kirtland, and two of her sons,
who arrived with her—came together to enjoy with
her a social family meeting; and a happy one it
was—a season of pure reciprocal conviviality, in
which her buoyancy of spirit greatly augmented the
general joy. Let the reader imagine for a moment
this aged matron, surrounded by her four sons,
Joseph, Asael, Silas and John, all of them, as well
as several of her grandsons, upwards of six feet in
height, with a score of great-grandchildren of various sizes intermixed ; surely the sight was not an
uninteresting one. To her it was very exciting—
too much so for her years. Feverish symptoms,
which were apparent on the following day, indicated
that her nervous system had been overtaxed. She
took her bed, and survived but a few days. I was
with her, and saw her calmly fall asleep. About ten

minutes before she expired, she saw a group of angels
in the room; and pointing towards them she exclaimed, "O, how beautiful! but they do not speak."
It would seem that they were waiting to escort her
spirit to its bright abode.

But to return to the temple. After its dedication,
the "Kirtland High School" was taught in the attic
story, by H. M. Hawes, professor of Greek and
Latin. The school numbered from one hundred
and thirty to one hundred and forty students, divided
into three departments—the classics, where only
languages were taught; the English department,
where mathematics, common arithmetic, geography,
English grammar, reading and writing were taught;
and the juvenile department. The two last were
under assistant instructors. The school was commenced in November, 1836, and the progress of the
several classes, on examinations before trustees of
the school, parents and guardians, was found to be
of the highest order.

Not only did the Almighty manifest his acceptance of that house, at its dedication, but an abiding
holy heavenly influence was realized; and many
extraordinary manifestations of his power were
experienced on subsequent occasions. Not only
were angels often seen within, but a pillar of light
was several times seen resting down upon the
roof.

Besides being devoted to general meetings for
worship and the celebration of the Lord's Supper
every first day of the week, the temple was occupied
by crowded assemblies on the first Thursday in each
month, that day being observed strictly, by the

Latter-day Saints, as a day of fasting and prayer. These, called fast-meetings, were hallowed and interesting beyond the power of language to describe. Many, many were the pentecostal seasons of the outpouring of the spirit of God on those days, manifesting the gifts of the gospel and the power of healing, prophesying, speaking in tongues, the interpretation of tongues, etc. I have there seen the lame man, on being administered to, throw aside his crutches and walk home perfectly healed; and not only were the lame made to walk, but the blind to see, the deaf to hear, the dumb to speak, and evil spirits to depart.

On those fast days, the curtains, or veils, mentioned in a preceding chapter, which intersected at right angles, were dropped, dividing the house into four equal parts. Each of these sections had a presiding officer, and the meeting in each section was conducted as though no other were in the building, which afforded opportunity for four persons to occupy the same time. These meetings commenced early in the day and continued without intermission till four P. M. One hour previous to dismissal, the veils were drawn up and the four congregations brought together, and the people who, in the forepart of the day were instructed to spend much of the time in prayer, and to speak, sing and pray, mostly in our own language, lest a spirit of enthusiasm should creep in, were permitted, after the curtains were drawn, to speak or sing in tongues, prophesy, pray, interpret tongues, exhort or preach, however they might feel moved upon to do. Then the united faith of the saints brought them into close fellowship with the spirits of the just, and earth and heaven seemed in close proximity.

On fast days, Father Smith's constant practice was to repair to the temple very early, and offer up his prayers before sunrise, and there await the coming of the people; and so strictly disciplined himself in the observance of fasting, as not even to wet his lips with water until after the dismissal of the meeting at four P. M. One morning, when he opened meeting, he prayed fervently that the spirit of the Most High might be poured out as it was at Jerusalem, on the day of pentecost—that it might come "like a mighty rushing wind." It was not long before it did come, to the astonishment of all, and filled the house. It appeared as though the old gentleman had forgotten what he had prayed for. When it came, he was greatly surprised, and exclaimed, "What! is the house on fire?"

While the faithful saints were enjoying those supernal privileges, "the accuser of the brethren" did not sleep. Apostasy, with its poisonous fangs, crept into the hearts of some who but a few months before were in quorum meetings, when heavenly hosts appeared; and where, in all humility of soul, they united with their brethren in sublime shouts of hosanna to God and the Lamb. And now, full of pride and self-conceit, they join hands with our enemies and take the lead in mobocracy against the work which they had advocated with all the energies of their souls.

What a strange and fearful metamorphosis! How suddenly people become debased when, having grieved away the spirit of God, the opposite takes possession of their hearts! We read that angels have fallen, and that one of our Saviour's chosen twelve was Judas, the traitor. Inasmuch as the same causes produce the same effects in all ages, it is no wonder that Joseph Smith, in introducing the same principles, should have to suffer what was to the philosophic Paul the greatest of all trials—that among false brethren.

Illegal, vexatious lawsuits, one after another, were successively instituted, and the leading officers of the church dragged into court, creating great annoyance and expenditure. This not being sufficient to satisfy the greed of persecution, the lives of some of the brethren were sought, and they left Kirtland, and sought safety in the West.

At this time my father was residing one mile south of the temple. About twelve o'clock one bitter cold night he was startled by a knock at the door, and who should enter but Father Smith, the patriarch! A State's warrant had been served on him for an alleged crime, and the officer in whose custody he was placed, although an enemy to the church, knowing the old gentleman to be innocent, had preconcerted a stratagem by which he had been let down from a window in the room to which he had taken him, ostensibly for private consultation, but purposely to set him at liberty, having previously prepared a way by which he could reach the ground uninjured. He also told him where to go for safety, directing him to my father's house. The officer returned to the court-room as though Father Smith followed in the rear, when, on a sudden, he looked back, and not seeing his prisoner, he hurried back to the private room, examining every point, and returned in great apparent amazement and confusion, declaring that the prisoner had gone in an unaccountable manner, saying, ludicrously, "This, gentlemen, is another Mormon miracle." No vigorous search was made—all must have been convinced that the proceedings were as unjust as illegal. To return to my father's house: We were proud of our guest, and all of the family took pleasure in anticipating and supplying his wants. He remained with us two weeks, and in the meantime settled up all his business matters, and, having been joined by his youngest son, Don Carlos, and five other brethren, whose lives had been threatened, he bade a final adieu to Kirtland, at one hour past midnight, on the 21st of December, 1837. The night was intensely cold, but, as they had no conveyance except one horse, they had sufficient walking exercise to prevent freezing. They found a few Latter-day Saints in a southern county of Ohio, where they stayed till spring, when they left for Missouri.

The pressure of opposition increased, and before spring the prophet and his brother Hyrum had to leave; and, in the spring and summer of 1838, the most of the church followed; leaving our homes, and our sacred, beautiful temple, the sanctuary of the Lord God of Hosts.

CHAPTER XIV.

AN ILLUSTRIOUS MORMON WOMAN—THE FIRST WIFE
OF THE IMMORTAL HEBER C. KIMBALL—OPENING
CHAPTER OF HER AUTOBIOGRAPHY—HER WON-
DERFUL VISION—AN ARMY OF ANGELS SEEN IN
THE HEAVENS.

One of the very queens of Mormondom, and a
woman beloved by the whole church, during her
long eventful lifetime, was the late Vilate Kimball.
To-day she sleeps by the side of her great husband,
for Heber C. Kimball was one of the world's remarkable men. He soon followed her to the grave;
a beautiful example she of the true love existing
between two kindred souls notwithstanding polygamy. Her sainted memory is enshrined in the
hearts of her people, and ever will be as long as the
record of the sisters endures.

"My maiden name," she says, in her autobiography, "was Vilate Murray. I am the youngest
"daughter of Roswell and Susannah Murray. I
"was born in Florida, Montgomery county, New
"York, June 1st, 1806. I was married to Heber
"Chase Kimball November 7, 1822, having lived
"until that time with my parents in Victor, Ontario
"county.

" After marriage my husband settled in Mendon,
" Monroe county. Here we resided until we gath-
" ered in Kirtland in the fall of 1833.

" About three weeks before we heard of the latter-
" day work we were baptized into the Baptist
" Church.

" Five elders of the Church of Latter-day Saints
" came to the town of Victor, which was five miles
" from Mendon, and stopped at the house of Phineas
" Young, the brother of Brigham. Their names
" were Eleazer Miller, Elial Strong, Alpheus Gifford,
" Enos Curtis and Daniel Bowen.

" Hearing of these men, curiosity prompted Mr.
" Kimball to go and see them. Then for the first
" time he heard the fullness of the everlasting gospel
" and was convinced of its truth. Brigham Young
" was with him.

" At their meetings Brigham and Heber saw the
" manifestations of the spirit and heard the gift of
" speaking and singing in tongues. They were con-
" strained by the spirit to bear testimony to the
" truth, and when they did this the power of God
" rested upon them.

" Desiring to hear more of the saints, in January,
" 1832, Heber took his horses and sleigh and started
" for Columbia, Bradford county, Penn., a distance
" of one hundred and twenty-five miles. Brigham
" and Phineas Young and their wives went with him.

" They stayed with the church about six days, saw
" the power of God manifested and heard the gift of
" tongues, and then returned rejoicing, bearing tes-
" timony to the people by the way. They were not
" baptized, however, until the following spring.

"Brigham was baptized on Sunday, April 14th,
"1832, by Eleazer Miller, and Heber C. Kimball
"was baptized the next day.

"Just two weeks from that time I was baptized
"by Joseph Young, with several others.

"The Holy Ghost fell upon Heber so greatly,
"that he said it was like a consuming fire. He felt
"as though he was clothed in his right mind and
"sat at the feet of Jesus; but the people called him
"crazy. He continued thus for months, till it seemed
"his flesh would consume away. The Scriptures
"were unfolded to his mind in such a wonderful
"manner by the spirit of revelation that he said it
"seemed he had formerly been familiar with them.

"Brigham Young and his wife Miriam, with their
"two little girls, Elizabeth and Vilate, were at the
"time living at our house; but soon after her bap-
"tism Miriam died. In her expiring moments, she
"clapped her hands and praised the Lord, and called
"on all around to help her praise him; and when
"her voice was too weak to be heard, her lips and
"hands were seen moving until she expired.

"This was another testimony to them of the pow-
"erful effect of the everlasting gospel, showing that
"we shall not die, but will sleep and come forth in
"the resurrection and rejoice with her in the flesh.

"Her little girls sister Miriam left to my care, and
"I did all I could to be a mother to her little ones
"to the period of our gathering to Kirtland, and
"the marriage of Brigham to Miss Mary Ann
"Angell.

"The glorious death of sister Miriam caused us
"to rejoice in the midst of affliction. But enemies

"exulted over our loss and threw many obstacles in
"the way of our gathering with the saints.

" To my husband's great surprise some of the
"neighbors issued attachments against his goods;
"yet he was not indebted to any of them to the
"value of five cents, while there were some hundreds
"of dollars due to him. However, he left his own
"debts uncollected, settled their unjust claims, and
"gathered to Kirtland with the saints about the last
"of September, 1832, in company with Brigham
"Young.

" Here I will relate a marvelous incident, of date
"previous to our entering the church.

" On the night of the 22d of September, 1827,
"while living in the town of Mendon, after we re-
"tired to bed, John P. Green, who was then a trav-
"eling Reformed Methodist preacher, living within
"one hundred steps of our house, came and called
"my husband to come out and see the sight in the
"heavens. Heber awoke me, and Sister Fanny
"Young (sister of Brigham), who was living with
"us, and we all went out of doors.

" It was one of the most beautiful starlight nights,
"so clear we could see to pick up a pin. We looked
"to the eastern horizon, and beheld a white smoke
"arise towards the heavens. As it ascended, it
"formed into a belt, and made a noise like the rush-
"ing wind, and continued southwest, forming a reg-
"ular bow, dipping in the western horizon.

" After the bow had formed, it began to widen
"out, growing transparent, of a bluish cast. It grew
"wide enough to contain twelve men abreast. In
"this bow an army moved, commencing from the

"east and marching to the west. They continued
"moving until they reached the western horizon.
"They moved in platoons, and walked so close the
"rear ranks trod in the steps of their file leaders, until
"the whole bow was literally crowded with soldiers.

"We could distictly see the muskets, bayonets
"and knapsacks of the men, who wore caps and
"feathers like those used by the American soldiers
"in the last war with Great Britain. We also saw
"their officers with their swords and equipage, and
"heard the clashing and jingling of their instruments
"of war, and could discern the form and features
"of the men. The most profound order existed
"throughout the entire army. When the foremost
"man stepped, every man stepped at the same time.
"We could *hear* their steps.

"When the front rank reached the western hori-
"zon, a battle ensued, as we could hear the report
"of the arms, and the rush.

"None can judge of our feelings as we beheld
"this army of spirits as plainly as ever armies of
"men were seen in the flesh. Every hair of our
"heads seemed alive.

"We gazed upon this scenery for *hours*, until it
"began to disappear.

"After we became acquainted with Mormonism,
"we learned that this took place the same evening
"that Joseph Smith received the records of the Book
"of Mormon from the angel Moroni, who had held
"those records in his possession.

"Father Young, and John P. Green's wife (Brig-
"ham's sister Rhoda), were also witnesses of this
"marvelous scene.

" Frightened at what we saw, I said, Father Young,
"what does all this mean ? He answered, Why it is
"one of the signs of the coming of the Son of Man.

"The next night a similar scene was beheld in
"the west, by the neighbors, representing armies of
"men engaged in battle.

" After our gathering to Kirtland the church was
"in a state of poverty and distress. It appeared
"almost impossible that the commandment to build
"the temple could be fulfilled, the revelation requir-
"ing it to be erected by a certain period.

" The enemies were raging, threatening destruc-
"tion upon the saints; the brethren were under
"guard night and day to preserve the prophet's life,
"and the mobs in Missouri were driving our people
"from Jackson county.

" In this crisis the 'Camp of Zion' was organized
"to go to the defence of the saints in Jackson, Heber
"being one of the little army. On the 5th of May,
"1834, they started. It was truly a solemn morning
"on which my husband parted from his wife, chil-
"dren and friends, not knowing that we should ever
"meet again in the flesh. On the 26th of July,
"however, the brethren returned from their expe-
"dition.

" The saints now labored night and day to build
"the house of the Lord, the sisters knitting and
"spinning to clothe those who labored upon it.

" When the quorum of the twelve apostles was
"called, my husband was chosen one of them, and
"soon he was out with the rest of the apostles
"preaching the gospel of the last days; but they
"returned on the 27th of the following September

" " and found their families and friends enjoying good
" health and prosperity.

" The temple was finished and dedicated on the
" 27th of March, 1836. It was a season of great
" rejoicing, indeed, to the saints, and great and mar-
" velous were the manifestations and power in the
" Lord's house. Here I will relate a vision of the
" prophet concerning the twelve apostles of this dis-
" pensation, for whose welfare his anxiety had been
" very great.

" He saw the twelve going forth, and they appeared
" to be in a far distant land; after some time they
" unexpectedly met together, apparently in great
" tribulation, their clothes all ragged, and their knees
" and feet sore. They formed into a circle, and all
" stood with their eyes fixed on the ground. The
" Saviour appeared and stood in their midst and
" wept over them, and wanted to show himself to
" them, but they did not discover him.

" He saw until they had accomplished their work
" and arrived at the gate of the celestial city. There
" Father Adam stood and opened the gate to them,
" and as they entered he embraced them one by one,
" and kissed them. He then led them to the throne
" of God, and then the Saviour embraced each of
" them in the presence of God. He saw that they
" all had beautiful heads of hair and all looked alike.
" The impression this vision left on Brother Joseph's
" mind was of so acute a nature, that he never could
" refrain from weeping while rehearsing it.

" On the 10th of May, 1836, my husband again
" went East on a mission, and I made a visit to my
" friends in Victor, where Heber and I met, and after

"spending a few days, returned to Ohio, journeying
"to Buffalo, where a magistrate came forward and
"paid five dollars for our passage to Fairport.

"The passengers were chiefly Swiss emigrants.
"After sitting and hearing them some time, the spirit
"of the Lord came upon my husband so that he
"was enabled to preach to them in their own lan-
"guage, though of himself he knew not a word of
"their language. They seemed much pleased, and
"treated him with great kindness.

"We returned to Kirtland to find a spirit of
"speculation in the church, and apostacy growing
"among some of the apostles and leading elders.
"These were perilous times indeed.

"In the midst of this my husband was called on
"his mission to Great Britain, this being the first
"foreign mission.

"One day while Heber was seated in the front
"stand in the Kirtland temple, the prophet Joseph
"opened the door and came and whispered in his
"ear, 'Brother Heber, the spirit of the Lord has
"whispered to me, let my servant Heber go to
"England and proclaim the gospel, and open the
"door of salvation.'"

Here we may digress a moment from Sister
Vilate's story, to illustrate the view of the apostles
"opening the door of salvation to the nations," and
preaching the gospel in foreign lands without purse
or scrip.

At a later period the Mormon apostles and elders
have deemed it as nothing to take missions to foreign lands, but in 1837, before the age of railroads
and steamships had fairly come, going to Great

Britain on mission was very like embarking for another world ; and the apostolic proposition to gather a people from foreign lands and many nations to form a latter-day Israel, and with these disciples to build up a Zion on this continent, was in seeming the maddest undertaking possible in human events. This marvelous scheme of the Mormon prophet, with many others equally bold and strangely uncommon for modern times, shall be fully treated in the book of his own life, but it is proper to throw into prominence the wondrous apostolic picture of Heber C. Kimball " opening the door of salvation to the nations that sat in darkness ;" and for the gathering of an Israel from every people and from every tongue. Relative to this, by far the greatest event in his life, Heber says, in his family journals :

" The idea of being appointed to such an impor-
"tant mission was almost more than I could bear
"up under. I felt my weakness and was nearly
"ready to sink under it, but the moment I under-
"stood the will of my heavenly Father, I felt a
"determination to go at all hazards, believing that
"he would support me by his almighty power, and
"although my family were dear to me, and I should
"have to leave them almost destitute, I felt that the
"cause of truth, the gospel of Christ, outweighed
"every other consideration. At this time many fal-
"tered in their faith, some of the twelve were in
"rebellion against the prophet of God. John
"Boynton said to me, if you are such a d—d fool
"as to go at the call of the fallen prophet, I will not
"help you a dime, and if you are cast on Van Die-
"man's Land I will not make an effort to help you.

"Lyman E. Johnson said he did not want me to go
"on my mission, but if I was determined to go, he
"would help me all he could; he took his cloak from
"off his back and put it on mine. Brother Sidney
"Rigdon, Joseph Smith, Sr., Brigham Young, Newel
"K. Whitney and others said go and do as the pro-
"phet has told you and you shall prosper and be
"blessed with power to do a glorious work. Hyrum,
"seeing the condition of the church, when he talked
"about my mission wept like a little child; he was con-
"tinually blessing and encouraging me, and pouring
"out his soul in prophesies upon my head; he said go
"and you shall prosper as not many have prospered."

"A short time previous to my husband's starting,"
continues Sister Vilate, "he was prostrated on his
"bed from a stitch in his back, which suddenly seized
"him while chopping and drawing wood for his
"family, so that he could not stir a limb without
"exclaiming, from the severeness of the pain. Joseph
"Smith hearing of it came to see him, bringing
"Oliver Cowdery and Bishop Partridge with him.
"They prayed for and blessed him, Joseph being
"mouth, beseeching God to raise him up, &c. He
"then took him by the right hand and said, 'Brother
"Heber, I take you by your right hand, in the name
"of Jesus Christ of Nazareth, and by virtue of the
"holy priesthood vested in me, I command you, in
"the name of Jesus Christ, to rise, and be thou
"made whole.' He arose from his bed, put on his
"clothes, and started with them, and went up to the
"temple, and felt no more of the pain afterwards.

"At length the day for the departure of my hus-
"band arrived. It was June 13th, 1837. He was

8

"in the midst of his family, blessing them, when
" Brother R. B. Thompson, who was to accompany
"him two or three hundred miles, came in to ascer-
"tain when Heber would start. Brother Thompson,
"in after years, writing an account in Heber's jour-
"nal of his first mission to Great Britain, in its pre-
"face thus describes that solemn family scene : ' The
"door being partly open I entered and felt struck
"with the sight which presented itself to my view.
"I would have retired, thinking I was intruding, but
"I felt riveted to the spot. The father was pouring
"out his soul to

> That God who rules on high,
> Who all the earth surveys;
> That rides upon the stormy sky,
> And calms the roaring seas,

" that he would grant unto him a prosperous voy-
"age across the mighty ocean, and make him useful
"wherever his lot should be cast, and that he who
"careth for the sparrows, and feedeth the young
"ravens when they cry, would supply the wants of
"his wife and little ones in his absence. He then,
"like the patriarchs, and by virtue of his office, laid
"his hands upon their heads individually, leaving a
"father's blessing upon them, and commending them
"to the care and protection of God, while he should
"be engaged preaching the gospel in foreign lands.
"While thus engaged his voice was almost lost in
"the sobs of those around, who tried in vain to
"suppress them. The idea of being separated from
"their protector and father for so long a time, was
"indeed painful. He proceeded, but his heart was
"too much affected to do so regularly ; his emotions

" were great, and he was obliged to stop at intervals,
" while the big tears rolled down his cheeks, an
" index to the feelings which reigned in his bosom.
" My heart was not stout enough to refrain; in spite
" of myself I wept and mingled my tears with theirs
" at the same time. I felt thankful that I had the priv-
" ilege of contemplating such a scene. I realized that
" nothing could induce that man to tear himself from
" so affectionate a family group—from his partner and
" children who were so dear to him—but a sense of
" duty and love to God and attachment to his cause.'

" At nine o'clock in the morning of this never-to-
" be-forgotten-day," continues Sister Vilate, " Heber
" bade adieu to his brethren and friends and started
" without purse or scrip to preach the gospel in
" a foreign land. He was accompanied by myself and
" children, and some of the brethren and sisters, to
" Fairport. Sister Mary Fielding, who became after-
" wards the wife of Hyrum Smith, gave him five
" dollars, with which Heber paid the passage of him-
" self and Brother Hyde to Buffalo. They were also
" accompanied by her and Brother Thompson and
" his wife (Mary Fielding's sister), who were going
" on a mission to Canada. Heber himself was ac-
" companied to Great Britain by Elders Orson Hyde,
" Willard Richards, J. Goodson and J. Russell, and
" Priest Joseph Fielding."

Here, for the present, we must leave Brother
Heber to prosecute his important mission, and this
illustrious woman to act her part alone as an apostle's wife, while we introduce others of the sisters,
and follow the church through its scenes of persecution and removal from Missouri to Illinois.

CHAPTER XV.

Towards the close of October, 1838, several small
detachments of migrants from Ohio entered the
State of Missouri. They were of the refugees from
Kirtland. Their destinations were the counties of
Caldwell and Davies, where the saints had located
in that State.

Haun's Mill, in Caldwell county, was soon to
become the scene of one of the darkest tragedies
on record.

The mill was owned by a Mormon brother whose
name it bore, and in the neighborhood some Mormon families had settled.

To Haun's Mill came the doomed refugees.

They had been met on their entrance into the
State of Missouri by armed mobs. Governor Boggs
had just issued his order to exterminate the entire
Mormon community.

The coming of the refugees into the inhospitable
State could not have been more ill-timed, though
when they left Kirtland they expected to find a
brotherhood in Far West.

" Halt !" commanded the leader of a band of well-mounted and well-armed mobocrats, who charged down upon them as they journeyed on their way.

" If you proceed any farther west," said the captain, " you will be instantly shot."

" Wherefore?" inquired the pilgrims.

" You are d—d Mormons !"

" We are law-abiding Americans, and have given no cause of offence."

" You are d—d Mormons. That's offence enough. " Within ten days every Mormon must be out of " Missouri, or men, women and children will be shot " down indiscriminately. No mercy will be shown. " It is the order of the Governor that you should " all be exterminated ; and by G—d you will be."

In consternation the refugees retreated, and gathered at Haun's Mill.

It was Sunday, October 26. The Mormons were holding a council and deliberating upon the best course to pursue to defend themselves against the mob that was collecting in the neighborhood, under the command of a Colonel Jennings, or Livingston, and threatening them with house-burning and killing.

Joseph Young, the brother of Brigham, was in the council. He had arrived at the mill that day, with his family, retreating from the mob.

The decision of the council was that the neighborhood of Haun's Mill should put itself in an attitude of defence. Accordingly about twenty-eight of the brethren armed themselves and prepared to resist an attack.

But the same evening the mob sent one of their

number to enter into a treaty with the Mormons at
the mill. The treaty was accepted on the condition
of mutual forbearance, and that each party should
exert its influence to prevent any further hostilities.

At this time, however, there was another mob
collecting at William Mann's, on Grand River, so
that the brethren remained under arms over Mon-
day, the 29th, which passed without attack from any
quarter.

" On Tuesday, the 30th," says Joseph Young, " that
" bloody tragedy was enacted, the scenes of which I
" shall never forget.

" More than three-fourths of the day had passed
" in tranquillity, as smiling as the preceding one. I
" think there was no individual of our company that
" was apprised of the sudden and awful fate which
" hung over our heads like an overwhelming torrent,
" and which was to change the prospects, the feel-
" ings and sympathies of about thirty families.

" The banks of Shoal Creek, on either side, teemed
" with children sporting and playing, while their
" mothers were engaged in domestic employments.
" Fathers or husbands were either on guard about
" the mills or other property, or employed in gath-
" ering crops for winter consumption. The weather
" was very pleasant, the sun shone clearly, and all
" was tranquil, and no one expressed any apprehen-
" sion of the awful crisis that was near us—even at
" our doors.

" It was about four o'clock P. M., while sitting in
" my cabin, with my babe in my arms, and my wife
" standing by my side, the door being open, I cast
" my eyes on the opposite bank of Shoal Creek, and

" saw a large body of armed men on horses directing
" their course towards the mills with all possible
" speed. As they advanced through the scattering
" trees that bordered the prairie, they seemed to
" form themselves into a three-square position, form-
" ing a vanguard in front. At this moment David
" Evans, seeing the superiority of their numbers
" (there being two hundred and forty of them, ac-
" cording to their own account), gave a signal and
" cried for peace. This not being heeded, they con-
" tinued to advance, and their leader, a man named
" Comstock, fired a gun, which was followed by a
" solemn pause of about ten or twelve seconds, when
" all at once they discharged about one hundred
" rifles, aiming at a blacksmith's shop, into which
" our friends had fled for safety. They then charged
" up to the shop, the crevices of which, between the
" logs, were sufficiently large to enable them to aim
" directly at the bodies of those who had there fled for
" refuge from the fire of their murderers. There were
" several families tented in the rear of the shop,
" whose lives were exposed, and amid showers of
" bullets these fled to the woods in different direc-
" tions.

" After standing and gazing at this bloody scene
" for a few minutes, and finding myself in the utter-
" most danger, the bullets having reached the house
" where I was living, I committed my family to the
" protection of heaven ; and leaving the house on
" the opposite side, I took a path which led up the
" hill, following in the trail of three of my brethren
" that had fled from the shop.

" While ascending the hill we were discovered by

"the mob, who fired at us, and continued so to do
"till we reached the summit. In descending the
"hill I secreted myself in a thicket of bushes, where
"I lay till 8 o'clock in the evening. At this time I
"heard a voice calling my name in an undertone.
"I immediately left the thicket and went to the
"house of Benjamin Lewis, where I found my family—
"who had fled there in safety—and two of my
"friends, mortally wounded, one of whom died be-
"fore morning. Here we passed the painful night
"in deep and awful reflections upon the scenes of
"the preceding evening.

"After daylight appeared some four or five men,
"with myself, who had escaped with our lives from
"this horrid massacre, repaired as soon as possible
"to the mills to learn the condition of our friends
"whose fate we had but too truly anticipated.

"When we arrived at the house of Mr. Haun, we
"found Mr. Merrick's body lying in the rear of the
"house, and Mr. McBride's in front, literally man-
"gled from head to foot. We were informed by
"Miss Rebecca Judd, who was an eye-witness, that
"he was shot with his own gun after he had given it
"up, and then cut to pieces with a corn-cutter by a
"man named Rogers, of Davies county, who kept a
"ferry on Grand River, and who afterwards repeat-
"edly boasted of this same barbarity. Mr. York's
"body we found in the house. After viewing these
"corpses we immediately went to the blacksmith's
"shop, where we found nine of our friends, eight
"of whom were already dead—the other, Mr. Cox,
"of Indiana, in the agonies of death, who soon
"expired."

But to sister Amanda Smith must be given the principal thread of this tragedy, for around her centres the terrible interest of the Haun's Mill massacre, which even to-day rises before her in all the horrors of an occurring scene. She says :

" We sold our beautiful home in Kirtland for a " song, and traveled all summer to Missouri—our " teams poor, and with hardly enough to keep body " and soul together.

" We arrived in Caldwell county, near Haun's " Mill, nine wagons of us in company. Two days " before we arrived we were taken prisoners by an " armed mob that had demanded every bit of am-" munition and every weapon we had. We surren-" dered all. They knew it, for they searched our " wagons.

" A few miles more brought us to Haun's Mill, " where that awful scene of murder was enacted. " My husband pitched his tent by a blacksmith's " shop.

" Brother David Evans made a treaty with the " mob that they would not molest us. He came " just before the massacre and called the company " together and they knelt in prayer.

" I sat in my tent. Looking up I suddenly saw " the mob coming—the same that took away our " weapons. They came like so many demons or " wild Indians.

" Before I could get to the blacksmith's shop door " to alarm the brethren, who were at prayers, the " bullets were whistling amongst them.

" I seized my two little girls and escaped across " the mill-pond on a slab-walk. Another sister fled

"with me. Yet though we were women, with ten-
"der children, in flight for our lives, the demons
"poured volley after volley to kill us.

" A number of bullets entered my clothes, but I
"was not wounded. The sister, however, who was
"with me, cried out that she was hit. We had just
"reached the trunk of a fallen tree, over which I
"urged her, bidding her to shelter there where the
"bullets could not reach her, while I continued my
"flight to some bottom land.

" When the firing had ceased I went back to the
"scene of the massacre, for there were my husband
"and three sons, of whose fate I as yet knew
"nothing.

" As I returned I found the sister in a pool of
"blood where she had fainted, but she was only shot
"through the hand. Farther on was lying dead
"Brother McBride, an aged white-haired revolu-
"tionary soldier. His murderer had literally cut him
"to pieces with an old corn-cutter. His hands had
"been split down when he raised them in supplication
"for mercy. Then the monster cleft open his head
"with the same weapon, and the veteran who had
"fought for his country, in the glorious days of the
"past, was numbered with the martyrs.

" Passing on I came to a scene more terrible still
"to the mother and wife. Emerging from the black-
"smith shop was my eldest son, bearing on his
"shoulders his little brother Alma.

"'Oh! my Alma is dead!' I cried, in anguish.

"'N), mother; I think Alma is not dead. But
"father and brother Sardius are killed!'

"What an answer was this to appal me! My

" husband and son murdered; another little son
" seemingly mortally wounded; and perhaps before
" the dreadful night should pass the murderers would
" return and complete their work!

" But I could not weep then. The fountain of
" tears was dry; the heart overburdened with its
" calamity, and all the mother's sense absorbed in
" its anxiety for the precious boy which God alone
" could save by his miraculous aid.

" The entire hip joint of my wounded boy had
" been shot away. Flesh, hip bone, joint and all had
" been ploughed out from the muzzle of the gun
" which the ruffian placed to the child's hip through
" the logs of the shop and deliberately fired.

" We laid little Alma on a bed in our tent and I
" examined the wound. It was a ghastly sight. I
" knew not what to do. It was night now.

" There were none left from that terrible scene,
" throughout that long, dark night, but about half a
" dozen bereaved and lamenting women, and the
" children. Eighteen or nineteen, all grown men
" excepting my murdered boy and another about
" the same age, were dead or dying; several more
" of the men were wounded, hiding away, whose
" groans through the night too well disclosed their
" hiding places, while the rest of the men had fled,
" at the moment of the massacre, to save their lives.

" The women were sobbing, in the greatest an-
" guish of spirit; the children were crying loudly
" with fear and grief at the loss of fathers and
" brothers; the dogs howled over their dead mas-
" ters and the cattle were terrified with the scent of
" the blood of the murdered.

"Yet was I there, all that long, dreadful night,
"with my dead and my wounded, and none but God
"as our physician and help.

"Oh my Heavenly Father, I cried, what shall I
"do? Thou seest my poor wounded boy and know-
"est my inexperience. Oh Heavenly Father direct
"me what to do!

"And then I was directed as by a voice speaking
"to me.

"The ashes of our fire was still smouldering. We
"had been burning the bark of the shag-bark hickory.
"I was directed to take those ashes and make a lye
"and put a cloth saturated with it right into the
"wound. It hurt, but little Alma was too near dead
"to heed it much. Again and again I saturated the
"cloth and put it into the hole from which the hip-
"joint had been ploughed, and each time mashed
"flesh and splinters of bone came away with the
"cloth ; and the wound became as white as chicken's
"flesh.

"Having done as directed I again prayed to the
"Lord and was again instructed as distinctly as
"though a physician had been standing by speaking
"to me.

"Near by was a slippery-elm tree. From this I
"was told to make a slippery-elm poultice and fill
"the wound with it.

"My eldest boy was sent to get the slippery-elm
"from the roots, the poultice was made, and the
"wound, which took fully a quarter of a yard of
"linen to cover, so large was it, was properly dressed.

"It was then I found vent to my feelings in tears,
"and resigned myself to the anguish of the hour.

" And all that night we, a few poor, stricken women,
" were thus left there with our dead and wounded.
" All through the night we heard the groans of the
" dying.   Once in the dark we crawled over the heap
" of dead in the blacksmith's shop to try to help or
" soothe the sufferers' wants; once we followed the
" cries of a wounded brother who hid in some bushes
" from the murderers, and relieved him all we could.

" It has passed from my memory whether he was
" dead in the morning or whether he recovered.

" Next morning brother Joseph Young came to
" the scene of the massacre.

" ' What shall be done with the dead ?' he inquired,
" in horror and deep trouble.

" There was not time to bury them, for the mob
" was coming on us.   Neither were there left men to
" dig the graves.   All the men excepting the two or
" three who had so narrowly escaped were dead or
" wounded.   It had been no battle, but a massacre
" indeed.

" ' Do anything, Brother Joseph,' I said, ' rather
" than leave their bodies to the fiends who have
" killed them.'

" There was a deep dry well close by.   Into this
" the bodies had to be hurried, eighteen or nineteen
" in number.

" No funeral service could be performed, nor
" could they be buried with customary decency.   The
" lives of those who in terror performed the last
" duty to the dead were in jeopardy.   Every moment
" we expected to be fired upon by the fiends who we
" supposed were lying in ambush waiting the first
" opportunity to dispatch the remaining few who

" had escaped the slaughter of the preceding day.
" So in the hurry and terror of the moment some
" were thrown into the well head downwards and
" some feet downwards.

" But when it came to the burial of my murdered
" boy Sardius, Brother Joseph Young, who was
" assisting to carry him on a board to the well, laid
" down the corpse and declared that he could not
" throw that boy into this horrible grave.

" All the way on the journey, that summer, Joseph
" had played with the interesting lad who had been
" so cruelly murdered. It was too much for one
" whose nature was so tender as Uncle Joseph's, and
" whose sympathies by this time were quite over-
" wrought. He could not perform that last office.
" My murdered son was left unburied.

" ' Oh ! they have left my Sardius unburied in the
" sun,' I cried, and ran and got a sheet and covered
" his body.

" There he lay until the next day, and then I, his
" mother, assisted by his elder brother, had to throw
" him into the well. Straw and earth were thrown
" into this rude vault to cover the dead.

" Among the wounded who recovered were Isaac
" Laney, Nathaniel K. Knight, Mr. Yokum, two
" brothers by the name of Myers, Tarlton Lewis,
" Mr. Haun and several others, besides Miss Mary
" Stedwell, who was shot through the hand while
" fleeing with me, and who fainting, fell over the log
" into which the mob shot upwards of twenty balls.

" The crawling of my boys under the bellows in
" the blacksmith's shop where the tragedy occurred,
" is an incident familiar to all our people. Alma's

"hip was shot away while thus hiding. Sardius was
"discovered after the massacre by the monsters who
"came in to despoil the bodies. The eldest, Willard,
"was not discovered. In cold blood, one Glaze, of
"Carroll county, presented a rifle near the head of
"Sardius and literally blew off the upper part of it,
"leaving the skull empty and dry while the brains
"and hair of the murdered boy were scattered
"around and on the walls.

" At this one of the men, more merciful than the
" rest, observed :

"'It was a d—d shame to kill those little boys.'

" ' D—n the difference !' retorted the other ; 'nits
"make lice !'

" My son who escaped, also says that the mobo-
"crat William Mann took from my husband's feet,
"before he was dead, a pair of new boots. From
"his hiding place, the boy saw the ruffian drag his
"father across the shop in the act of pulling off his
"boot.

" 'Oh ! you hurt me !' groaned my husband. But
"the murderer dragged him back again, pulling off
"the other boot; 'and there,' says the boy, 'my
"father fell over dead.'

" Afterwards this William Mann showed the boots
"on his own feet, in Far West, saying : ' Here is a
"pair of boots that I pulled off before the d—d
"Mormon was done kicking !'

" The murderer Glaze also boasted over the coun-
"try, as a heroic deed, the blowing off the head of
"my young son.

" But to return to Alma, and how the Lord helped
"me to save his life.

" I removed the wounded boy to a house, some
" distance off, the next day, and dressed his hip ; the
" Lord directing me as before.   I was reminded that
" in my husband's trunk there was a bottle of bal-
" sam. This I poured into the wound, greatly sooth-
" ing Alma's pain.

" ' Alma, my child,' I said, 'you believe that the
" Lord made your hip ?'

" ' Yes, mother.'

" ' Well, the Lord can make something there in the
" place of your hip, don't you believe he can, Alma ?'

" ' Do you think that the Lord can, mother ?' in-
" quired the child, in his simplicity.

" ' Yes, my son,' I replied, ' he has shown it all to
" me in a vision.'

" Then I laid him comfortably on his face, and
" said : ' Now you lay like that, and don't move, and
" the Lord will make you another hip.'

" So Alma laid on his face for five weeks, until he
" was entirely recovered—a flexible gristle having
" grown in place of the missing joint and socket,
" which remains to this day a marvel to physicians.

" On the day that he walked again I was out of
" the house fetching a bucket of water, when I heard
" screams from the children. Running back, in
" affright, I entered, and there was Alma on the
" floor, dancing around, and the children screaming
" in astonishment and joy.

" It is now nearly forty years ago, but Alma has
" never been the least crippled during his life, and
" he has traveled quite a long period of the time as
" a missionary of the gospel and a living miracle of
" the power of God.

" I cannot leave the tragic story without relating
" some incidents of those five weeks when I was a
" prisoner with my wounded boy in Missouri, near
" the scene of the massacre, unable to obey the
" order of extermination.

" All the Mormons in the neighborhood had fled
" out of the State, excepting a few families of the
" bereaved women and children who had gathered
" at the house of Brother David Evans, two miles
" from the scene of the massacre. To this house
" Alma had been carried after that fatal night.

" In our utter desolation, what could we women
" do but pray? Prayer was our only source of com-
" fort; our Heavenly Father our only helper. None
" but he could save and deliver us.

" One day a mobber came from the mill with the
" captain's fiat :

" ' The captain says if you women don't stop your
" d—d praying he will send down a posse and kill
" every d—d one of you !'

" And he might as well have done it, as to stop
" us poor women praying in that hour of our great
" calamity.

" Our prayers were hushed in terror. We dared
" not let our voices be heard in the house in suppli-
" cation. I could pray in my bed or in silence, but
" I could not live thus long. This godless silence
" was more intolerable than had been that night of
" the massacre.

" I could bear it no longer. I pined to hear once
" more my own voice in petition to my Heavenly
" Father.

" I stole down into a corn-field, and crawled into

9

"a 'stout of corn.' It was as the temple of the Lord
"to me at that moment. I prayed aloud and most
"fervently.

"When I emerged from the corn a voice spoke
"to me. It was a voice as plain as I ever heard one.
"It was no silent, strong impression of the spirit,
"but a *voice*, repeating a verse of the saint's hymn:

> "That soul who on Jesus hath leaned for repose,
> I cannot, I will not desert to its foes;
> That soul, though all hell should endeavor to shake,
> I'll never, no never, no never forsake!

"From that moment I had no more fear. I felt
"that nothing could hurt me. Soon after this the
"mob sent us word that unless we were all out of
"the State by a certain day we should be killed.

"The day came, and at evening came fifty armed
"men to execute the sentence.

"I met them at the door. They demanded of
"me why I was not gone? I bade them enter and
"see their own work. They crowded into my room
"and I showed them my wounded boy. They came,
"party after party, until all had seen my excuse.
"Then they quarreled among themselves and came
"near fighting.

"At last they went away, all but two. These I
"thought were detailed to kill us. Then the two
"returned.

"'Madam,' said one, 'have you any meat in the
"house?'

"'No,' was my reply.

"'Could you dress a fat hog if one was laid at
"your door?'

"'I think we could!' was my answer

" And then they went and caught a fat hog from
" a herd which had belonged to a now exiled brother,
"killed it and dragged it to my door, and departed.

" These men, who had come to murder us, left on
" the threshold of our door a meat offering to atone
" for their repented intention.

" Yet even when my son was well I could not
" leave the State, now accursed indeed to the saints.

" The mob had taken my horses, as they had the
" drove of horses, and the beeves, and the hogs, and
" wagons, and the tents, of the murdered and ex-
" iled.

" So I went down into Davies county (ten miles)
" to Captain Comstock, and demanded of him my
" horses. There was one of them in his yard. He
" said I could have it if I paid five dollars for its
" keep. I told him I had no money.

" I did not fear the captain of the mob, for I had
" the Lord's promise that nothing should hurt me.
" But his wife swore that the mobbers were fools for
" not killing the women and children as well as the
" men—declaring that we would 'breed up a pack
" ten times worse than the first.'

" I left without the captain's permission to take
" my horse, or giving pay for its keep; but I went
" into his yard and took it, and returned to our
" refuge unmolested.

" Learning that my other horse was at the mill, I
" next yoked up a pair of steers to a sled and went
" and demanded it also.

" Comstock was there at the mill. He gave me
" the horse, and then asked if I had any flour.

" ' No; we have had none for weeks.'

" He then gave me about fifty pounds of flour
" and some beef, and filled a can with honey.

" But the mill, and the slaughtered beeves which
" hung plentifully on its walls, and the stock of flour
" and honey, and abundant spoil besides, had all be-
" longed to the murdered or exiled saints.

" Yet was I thus providentially, by the very mur-
" derers and mobocrats themselves, helped out of
" the State of Missouri.

" The Lord had kept his word.   The soul who on
" Jesus had leaned for succor had not been forsaken
" even in this terrible hour of massacre, and in that
" infamous extermination of the Mormons from Mis-
" souri in the years 1838-39.

" One incident more, as a fitting close.

" Over that rude grave—that well—where the
" nineteen martyrs slept, where my murdered hus-
" band and boy were entombed, the mobbers of
" Missouri, with an exquisite fiendishness, which no
" savages could have conceived, had constructed a
" rude privy.   This they constantly used, with a de-
" light which demons might have envied, if demons
" are more wicked and horribly beastly than were
" they.

" Thus ends my chapter of the Haun's Mill mas-
" sacre, to rise in judgment against them !"

CHAPTER XVI.

But the iliad of Mormondom was now in Far
West.

Haun's Mill massacre was merely a tragic episode;
a huge tragedy in itself, it is true, such as civilized
times scarcely ever present, yet merely an episode of
this strange religious iliad of America and the nineteenth century.

The capital of Mormondom was now the city of
Far West, in Missouri.

There was Joseph the prophet. There was Brigham Young—his St. Peter—who by this time fairly
held the keys of the latter-day kingdom. There
were the apostles. There were two armies marshaled—the army of the Lord and the army of
Satan. And these were veritable hosts, of flesh and
blood, equipped and marshaled in a religious crusade—not merely spiritual powers contending.

" On the 4th of July, 1838," writes Apostle Parley
Pratt, "thousands of the citizens who belonged to
"the church of the saints assembled at the city of

"Far West, the county seat of Caldwell, in order to
"celebrate our nation's birth.

"We erected a tall standard, on which was hoisted
"our national colors, the stars and stripes, and the
"bold eagle of American liberty. Under its waving
"folds we laid the corner-stone of a temple of God,
"and dedicated the land and ourselves and families
"to him who had preserved us in all our troubles.

"An address was then delivered by Sidney
"Rigdon, in which was portrayed in lively colors
"the oppression which we had suffered at the hands
"of our enemies.

"We then and there declared our constitutional
"rights as American citizens, and manifested our
"determination to resist, with our utmost endeavors,
"from that time forth, all oppression, and to main-
"tain our rights and freedom, according to the holy
"principles of liberty as guaranteed to every person
"by the constitution and laws of our country.

"This declaration was received with shouts of
"hosanna to God and the Lamb, and with many
"long cheers by the assembled thousands, who were
"determined to yield their rights no more unless
"compelled by superior power."

Very proper, too were such resolutions of these
sons and daughters of sires and mothers who were
among the pilgrim founders of this nation, and
among the heroes and heroines of the Revolution.

But Missouri could not endure this temple-building to the God of Israel, nor these mighty shouts
of hosanna to his name; while the all-prevailing
faith of the sisters brought more of the angels down
from the New Jerusalem than earth just then was

prepared to receive. In popular words, this form-idable gathering of a modern Israel and this city building within its borders loomed up to Missouri as the rising of a Mormon empire.

Soon the State was alive with mobs determined on the extermination of the saints; soon those mobs numbered ten thousand armed men; soon also were they converted into a State army, officered by generals and major-generals, with the governor as the commander-in-chief of a boldly avowed religious crusade, with rival priests as its "inspiring demons."

One feature, all worthy of note, in this Hebraic drama of Mormondom, is that while modern Israel was ever in the action inspired by archangels of the new covenant, the anti-Mormon crusade was as constantly inspired by sectarian priests at war with a dispensation of angels.

Even the mobber, Captain Comstock, who was bold enough to perpetrate a Haun's Mill massacre, was in consternation over the magic prayers of a few stricken women who honored the God of Israel in the hour of direst calamity.

Thus throughout Missouri. And so the exterminating order of Governor Boggs prevailed like the edict of a second Nebuchadnezzar.

There was a *Mormon war* in the State. So it was styled.

Mobs were abroad, painted like Indian warriors, committing murder, robbery, burning the homesteads of the saints, and spreading desolation.

Next, one thousand men were ordered into service by the Governor, under the command of Major-

General Atchison and Brigadier-Generals Park and Doniphan.

This force marched against the saints in several counties. A Presbyterian priest, Rev. Sashel Woods, was its chaplain. He said prayers in the camp, morning and evening. 'Twas a godly service in an ungodly crusade, but the Rev. Sashel Woods was equal to it. The Philistines drove modern Israel before them, and their priest prayed Jehovah out of countenance.

In Far West a thousand men of our Mormon Israel flew to arms, and in Davies county several hundred men assembled for defence. Colonel David Patten, an apostle, with his company put to flight some of the mob; but the crusaders in general drove the saints from settlement after settlement.

Hundreds of men, women and children fled from their homes to the cities and strongholds of their people. From Davies county and the frontiers of Caldwell the refugees daily poured into the city of Far West. Lands and crops were abandoned to the enemy. The citizens in the capital of the saints were constantly under arms. Men slept in their clothes, with arms by their side, ready to muster at a given signal at any hour of the night.

A company under Colonel Patten went out to meet the enemy across the prairies, a distance of twelve miles, to stop the murder and spoliation of a settlement of their people. Parley Pratt was one of the posse.

"The night was dark," he says; "the distant plains "far and wide were illuminated by blazing fires; "immense columns of smoke were seen rising in

"awful majesty, as if the world was on fire. This
"scene, added to the silence of midnight, the rumb-
"ling sound of the tramping steeds over the hard
"and dried surface of the plain, the clanking of
"swords in their scabbards, the occasional gleam of
"bright armor in the flickering firelight, the gloom
"of surrounding darkness, and the unknown destiny
"of the expedition, or even of the people who sent
"it forth, all combined to impress the mind with
"deep and solemn thoughts."

At dawn of day they met the enemy in ambush
in the wilderness. The enemy opened fire, mortally
wounding a brother named O'Banyon. Soon the
brethren charged the enemy in his camp; several
fell upon both sides, among whom was the brave
apostle, David Patten; but the foemen flung
themselves into a stream and escaped on the
opposite shore, while the wilderness resounded
with the watchword of the heroes, "*God and Liberty.*"

Six of the brethren were wounded, and one left
dead on the ground.

The heroes returned to Far West. Among those
who came out to meet them was the wife of the
dying apostle, Patten.

"O God! O my husband!" she exclaimed, bursting into tears.

The wounds were dressed. David was still able
to speak, but he died that evening in the triumphs
of faith.

"I had rather die," he said, "than live to see it
"thus in my country!"

The young O'Banyon also died about the same

time. They were buried together under military honors ; a whole people in tears followed them to their grave.

David Patten was the first of the modern apostles who found a martyr's grave. He is said to have been a great and good man, who chose to lay down his life for the cause of truth and right.

Not long now ere Governor Boggs found the opportunity for the grand expulsion of the entire Mormon community—from twelve to fifteen thousand souls. He issued an order for some ten thousand troops to be mustered into service and marched to the field against the Mormons, giving the command to General Clark. His order was expressly to *exterminate* the Mormons, or drive them from the State.

The army of extermination marched upon the city of Far West.

The little Mormon host, about five hundred strong, marched out upon the plains on the south of the city, and formed in order of battle. Its line of infantry extended near half a mile ; a small company of horse was posted on the right wing on a commanding eminence, and another in the rear of the main body extended as a reserve.

The army of extermination halted and formed along the borders of a stream called Goose Creek ; and both sides sent out white flags, which met between the armies.

" We want three persons out of the city before we massacre the rest !" was the voice of the white flag from the governor's army.

Small need this, for the flag of mercy ! But it was

as good as the mercy of Haun's Mill, which was given on the very same day.

That night Major-General Lucas encamped near the city. The brethren continued under arms, and spent the night throwing up temporary breastworks. They were determined to defend their homes, wives and children to the last. Both armies were considerably reinforced during the night, the army of extermination being reinforced with the monsters from the Haun's Mill massacre.

But the prophet and brethren were on the next day betrayed by the traitor Colonel George M. Hinkle, who was in command of the defence of Far West.

Joseph was now a prisoner of war; Parley and others were prisoners also; Brigham was at Far West, but even he could not save the prophet and the saints from this formidable army, nor lessen the blow which a traitor had dealt. The treachery of Colonel Hinkle had, however, perhaps saved the lives of hundreds of women and children, and prevented brave men from fighting in a just cause.

It was November, now, and Major-General Clark was also at Far West with *his* army of extermination. No book of the persecutions could be properly written without his speech to the Mormons, especially a book of the sisters, whom it so much concerned:

" GENTLEMEN: You, whose names are not on this list, will now have the privilege of going to your fields to obtain grain for your families—wood, etc. Those that compose the list will go hence to prison, to be tried, and receive the due demerits of their

crimes. But you are now at liberty, all but such as
charges may hereafter be preferred against. It now
devolves upon you to fulfill the treaty that you have
entered into—the leading items of which I now lay
before you.

"The first of these items you have already complied with—which is, that you deliver up your leading men to be tried according to law. Second, that
you deliver up your arms—this has been attended
to. The third is, that you sign over your property
to defray the expenses of the war; this you have
also done. Another thing yet remains for you to
comply with; that is: that you leave the State
forthwith; and, whatever your feeling concerning
this affair, whatever your innocence, it is nothing to
me. General Lucas, who is equal in authority with
me, has made this treaty with you. I am determined
to see it executed.

"The orders of the Governor to me, were, that
you should be exterminated, and not allowed to remain in the State. And had your leaders not been
given up, and the treaty complied with, before this
you and your families would have been destroyed
and your houses in ashes.

"There is a discretionary power resting in my
hands, which I shall try to exercise for a season. I
did not say that you must go now, but you must
not think of stopping here another season, or of
putting in crops; for the moment you do, the citizens will be upon you. I am determined to see the
Governor's orders fulfilled, but shall not come upon
you immediately. Do not think that I shall act as
I have done any more; but if I have to come again
because the treaty which you have made is not
complied with, you need not expect any mercy, but
extermination; for I am determined that the Governor's order shall be executed.

"As for your leaders, do not think, do not imagine
for a moment, do not let it enter your minds that

they will be delivered, or that you will see their faces again, for their fate is fixed, their die is cast, their doom is sealed.

"I am sorry, gentlemen, to see so great a number of apparently intelligent men found in the situation that you are. And, oh! that I could invoke the spirit of the unknown God to rest upon you, and deliver you from that awful chain of superstition, and liberate you from those fetters of fanaticism with which you are bound. I would advise you to scatter abroad and never again organize with bishops, presidents, etc., lest you excite the jealousies of the people, and subject yourselves to the same calamities that have now come upon you.

"You have always been the aggressors; you have brought upon yourselves these difficulties by being disaffected, and not being subject to rule; and my advice is, that you become as other citizens, lest by a recurrence of these events you bring upon yourselves inevitable ruin."

CHAPTER XVII.

EPISODES OF THE PERSECUTIONS — CONTINUATION OF ELIZA R. SNOW'S NARRATIVE—BATHSHEBA W. SMITH'S STORY—LOUISA F. WELLS INTRODUCED TO THE READER—EXPERIENCE OF ABIGAIL LEONARD—MARGARET FOUTZ.

The prophet and his brother Hyrum were in prison and in chains in Missouri; Sidney Rigdon, Parley Pratt and others were also in prison and in chains, for the gospel's sake.

The St. Peter of Mormondom was engaged in removing the saints from Missouri to Illinois. He had made a covenant with them that none of the faithful should be left. Faithfully he kept that covenant. It was then, in fact, that Brigham rose as a great leader of a people, giving promise of what he has been since the martyrdom of the prophet.

While Joseph is in chains, and Brigham is accomplishing the exodus from Missouri, the sisters shall relate some episodes of those days.

Sister Snow, continuing the thread of her narrative already given, says:

In Kirtland the persecution increased until many had to flee for their lives, and in the spring of 1838,

in company with my father, mother, three brothers,
one sister and her two daughters, I left Kirtland,
and arrived in Far West, Caldwell county, Mo., on
the 16th of July, where I stopped at the house of
Sidney Rigdon, with my brother Lorenzo, who was
very sick, while the rest of the family went farther,
and settled in Adam-Ondi-Ahman, in Davies county.
In two weeks, my brother being sufficiently recovered, my father sent for us and we joined the family
group.   My father purchased the premises of two
of the "old settlers," and paid their demands in full.
I mention this, because subsequent events proved
that, at the time of the purchase, although those
men ostensibly were our warm friends, they had, in
. connection with others of the same stripe, concocted
plans to mob and drive us from our newly acquired
homes, and repossess them.   In this brief biographi-
cal sketch, I shall not attempt a review of the scenes
that followed.   Sufficient to say, while we were busy
in making preparations for the approaching winter,
to our great surprise, those neighbors fled from the
place, as if driven by a mob, leaving their clocks
ticking, dishes spread for their meal, coffee-pots
boiling, etc., etc., and, as they went, spread the report
in every direction that the " Mormons " had driven
them from their homes, arousing the inhabitants of
the surrounding country, which resulted in the disgraceful, notorious "exterminating order" from the
Governor of the State ; in accordance therewith, we
left Davies county for that of Caldwell, preparatory
to fulfilling the injunction of leaving the State
" before grass grows " in the spring.
   The clemency of our law-abiding, citizen-expelling

Governor allowed us ten days to leave our county, and, till the expiration of that term, a posse of militia was to guard us against mobs; but it would be very difficult to tell which was better, the militia or the mob—nothing was too mean for the militia to perform—no property was safe within the reach of those men.

One morning, while we were hard at work, preparing for our exit, the former occupant of our house entered, and in an impudent and arrogant manner inquired how soon we should be out of it. My American blood warmed to the temperature of an insulted, free-born citizen, as I looked at him, and thought, poor man, you little think with whom you have to deal—God lives! He certainly overruled in that instance, for those wicked men never got possession of that property, although my father sacrificed it to American mobocracy.

In assisting widows and others who required help, my father's time was so occupied that we did not start until the morning of the 10th, and last day of the allotted grace. The weather was very cold and the ground covered with snow. After assisting in the arrangements for the journey, and shivering with cold, in order to warm my aching feet, I walked until the teams overtook me. In the mean time, I met one of the so-called militia, who accosted me with, "Well, I think this will cure you of your faith!" Looking him steadily in the eye, I replied, " No, sir; it will take more than *this* to cure me of my faith." His countenance suddenly fell, and he responded, "I must confess, you are a better soldier than I am." I passed on, thinking that, unless he was above the average of his fellows in that section, I was not highly complimented by his confession. It is true our hardships and privations were sufficient to have disheartened any but the saints of the living God—those who were prompted by higher than earthly motives, and trusting in the arm of Jehovah.

We were two days on our way to Far West, and stopped over night at what was called the Half-way House, a log building perhaps twenty feet square, with the chinkings between the logs, minus—they probably having been burned for firewood—the owner of the house, Brother Littlefield, having left with his family to escape being robbed; and the north wind had free ingress through the openings, wide enough for cats to crawl through. This had been the lodging place of the hundreds who had preceded us, and on the present occasion proved the almost shelterless shelter of seventy-five or eighty souls. To say lodging, would be a hoax, although places were allotted to a few aged and feeble, to lie down, while the rest of us either sat or stood, or both, all night. My sister and I managed so that mother lay down, and we sat by (on the floor, of course), to prevent her being trampled on, for the crowd was such that people were hardly responsible for their movements.

It was past the middle of December, and the cold was so intense that, in spite of well packing, our food was frozen hard, bread and all, and although a blazing fire was burning on one side of the room, we could not get to it to thaw our suppers, and had to resort to the next expediency, which was this:

The boys milked, and while one strained the milk, another held the pan (for there was no chance for putting anything down); then, while one held a bowl of the warm milk, another would, as expeditiously as possible, thinly slice the frozen bread into it, and thus we managed for supper. In the morning, we were less crowded, as some started very early, and we toasted our bread and thawed our meat before the fire. But, withal, that was a very merry night. None but saints can be happy under every circumstance. About twenty feet from the house was a shed, in the centre of which the brethren built a roaring fire, around which some of them stood and sang songs and hymns all night, while others parched corn and roasted frosted potatoes, etc. Not a complaint was heard—all were cheerful, and judging from appearances, strangers would have taken us to be pleasure excursionists rather than a band of gubernatorial exiles.

After the mobbing commenced, although my father had purchased, and had on hand, plenty of wheat, he could get none ground, and we were under the necessity of grating corn for our bread on graters made of tin-pails and stove-pipe. I will here insert a few extracts from a long poem I wrote while in Davies county, as follows :

'Twas autumn—Summer's melting breath was gone,
And Winter's gelid blast was stealing on;
To meet its dread approach, with anxious care
The houseless saints were struggling to prepare;
When round about a desperate mob arose,
Like tigers waking from a night's repose;
They came like hordes from nether shades let loose—
Men without hearts, just fit for Satan's use!
With wild, demoniac rage they sallied forth,

Resolved to drive the saints of God from earth.
Hemm'd in by foes—deprived the use of mill,
Necessity inspires their patient skill;
Tin-pails and stove-pipe, from their service torn,
Are changed to graters to prepare the corn,
That Nature's wants may barely be supplied—
They ask no treat, no luxury beside.
But, where their shelter? Winter hastens fast;
Can tents and wagons stem this northern blast?

The scene presented in the city of Far West, as we stopped over night on our way to our temporary location, was too important to be omitted, and too sad to narrate. Joseph Smith, and many other prominent men, had been dragged to prison. Their families, having been plundered, were nearly or quite destitute—some living on parched corn, others on boiled wheat; and desolation seemed inscribed on everything but the hearts of the faithful saints. In the midst of affliction, they trusted in God.

After spending the remainder of the winter in the vicinity of Far West, on the 5th of March, 1839, leaving much of our property behind, we started for Illinois.

From the commencement of hostilities against us, in the State of Missouri, till our expulsion, no sympathy in our behalf was ever, to my knowledge, expressed by any of the former citizens, with one single exception, and that was so strikingly in contrast with the morbid state of feeling generally manifested that it made a deep impression on my mind, and I think it worthy of record. I will here relate the circumstance. It occurred on our outward journey.

After a night of rain which turned to snow and covered the ground in the morning, we thawed our tent, which was stiffly frozen, by holding and turning it alternately before a blazing fire until it could be folded for packing ; and, all things put in order, while we all shook with the cold, we started on. As the sun mounted upwards, the snow melted, and increased the depth of the mud with which the road before us had been amply stocked, and rendered travel almost impossible. The teams were puffing, and the wagons dragging so heavily that we were all on foot, tugging along as best we could, when an elderly gentleman, on horseback, overtook us, and, after riding alongside for some time, apparently absorbed in deep thought, as he (after inquiring who we were) watched the women and girls, men and boys, teams and wagons, slowly wending our way up a long hill, *en route* from our only earthly homes, and, not knowing where we should find one, he said emphatically, " If I were in your places, I should want the Governor of the State hitched at the head of my teams." I afterwards remarked to my father that I had not heard as sensible a speech from a stranger since entering the State. I never saw that gentleman afterwards, but have from that time cherished a filial respect for him, and fancy I see his resemblance in the portrait of Sir Von Humboldt, now hanging on the wall before me.

We arrived in Quincy, Ill., where many of the exiled saints had preceded us, and all were received with generous hospitality.

My father moved to one of the northern counties. I stopped in Quincy, and, while there, wrote for the press, "An Appeal to the Citizens of the United States," "An Address to the Citizens of Quincy," and several other articles, for which I received some very flattering encomiums, with solicitations for effusions, which, probably, were elicited by the fact that they were from the pen of a " Mormon girl."

From Quincy, my sister, her two daughters and I, went to Lima, Hancock county, where we found a temporary home under the roof of an old veteran of the Revolution, who, with his family, treated us with much kindness, although, through ignorance of the character of the saints, their feelings were like gall towards them as a people, which we knew to be the result of misrepresentation. It was very annoying to our feelings to hear bitter aspersions against those whom we knew to be the best people on earth ; but, occupying, as we did, an upper room with a slight flooring between us and those below, we were obliged to hear. Frequently, after our host had traduced our people, of whom he knew nothing, he would suddenly change his tone and boast of the "noble women " he had in his house; " no better women ever lived," etc., which he would have said of the Mormon people generally, had he known them as well. We were pilgrims, and for the time being had to submit to circumstances. Almost anything is preferable to dependence—with these people we would earn our support at the tailoring business, thanks to my mother's industrial training, for which I even now bless her dear memory.

In May the saints commenced gathering in Commerce (afterwards Nauvoo), and on the 16th of July I left our kind host and hostess, much to their regret, Elder Rigdon having sent for me to teach his family school in Commerce, and, although I regretted to

part with my sister, I was truly thankful to be again
associated with the body of the church, with those
whose minds, freed from the fetters of sectarian
creeds, and man-made theology, launch forth in the
divine path of investigation into the glorious fields
of celestial knowledge and intelligence.

———

Concerning these times, Sister Bathsheba W.
Smith says: "When I was in my sixteenth year,
"some Latter-day Saint elders visited our neigh-
"borhood. I heard them preach and believed what
"they taught; I believed the Book of Mormon to
"be a divine record, and that Joseph Smith was a
"prophet of God. I knew by the spirit of the Lord,
"which I received in answer to prayer, that these
"things were true. On the 21st of August, 1837, I
"was baptized into the Church of Jesus Christ of
"Latter-day Saints, by Elder Samuel James, in
"Jones' Run, on the farm and near the residence of
"Augustus Burgess, and was confirmed by Elder
"Francis G. Bishop. The spirit of the Lord rested
"upon me, and I knew that he accepted of me as a
"member in his kingdom. My mother was baptized
"this same day. My sister Sarah, next older than
"me, was baptized three days previously. My father,
"and my two oldest sisters, Matilda and Nancy,
"together with their husbands, Col. John S. Martin
"and Josiah W. Fleming, were baptized into the
"same church soon afterwards. My uncle, Jacob
"Bigler, and his family had been baptized a few
"weeks before. A part of my first experience as a

"member of the church was, that most of my young
"acquaintances and companions began to ridicule
"us. The spirit of gathering with the saints in
"Missouri came upon me, and I became very anx-
"ious indeed to go there that fall with my sister
"Nancy and family, as they had sold out and were
"getting ready to go. I was told I could not go
"This caused me to retire to bed one night feeling
"very sorrowful. While pondering upon what had
"been said to me about not going, a voice said to
"me, 'Weep not, you will go this fall.' I was satis-
"fied and comforted. The next morning I felt con-
"tented and happy, on observing which my sister
"Sarah said, 'You have got over feeling badly about
"not going to Zion this fall, have you ?' I quietly,
"but firmly, replied, 'I am going—you will see.'

  "My brother, Jacob G. Bigler, having gone to
"Far West, Mo., joined the church there and bought
"a farm for my father, and then returned. About
"this time my father sold his farm in West Virginia,
"and fitted out my mother, my brother, and my
"sister Sarah, Melissa and myself, and we started
"for Far West, in company with my two brothers-
"in-law and my uncle and their families. Father
"stayed to settle up his business, intending to join
"us at Far West in the spring, bringing with him,
"by water, farming implements, house furniture, etc.
"On our journey the young folks of our party had
"much enjoyment ; it seemed so novel and romantic
"to travel in wagons over hill and dale, through
"dense forests and over extensive prairies, and occa-
"sionally passing through towns and cities, and
"camping in tents at night. On arriving in Missouri

"we found the State preparing to wage war against
"the Latter-day Saints. The nearer we got to our
"destination, the more hostile the people were. As
"we were traveling along, numbers of men would
"sometimes gather around our wagons and stop us.
"They would inquire who we were, where we were
"from, and where we were going to. On receiving
"answers to their questions, they would debate
"among themselves whether to let us go or not;
"their debate would result generally in a statement
"to the effect of, 'As you are Virginians, we will let
"you go on, but we believe you will soon return, for
"you will quickly become convinced of your folly.'
"Just before we crossed Grand River, we camped
"over night with a company of Eastern saints. We
"had a meeting, and rejoiced together. In the
"morning it was thought best for the companies to
"separate and cross the river by two different fer-
"ries, as this arrangement would enable all to cross
"in less time. Our company arrived at Far West
"in safety. But not so with the other company;
"they were overtaken at Haun's Mill by an armed
"mob—nineteen were killed, many others were
"wounded, and some of them maimed for life.

"Three nights after we had arrived at the farm
"which my brother had bought, and which was four
"miles south of the city of Far West, word came
"that a mob was gathering on Crooked River, and
"a call was made for men to go out in command of
"Captain David W. Patten, for the purpose of trying
"to stop the depredations of the men, who were
"whipping and otherwise maltreating our brethren,
"and who were destroying and burning property.

"Captain Patten's company went, and a battle
"ensued. Some of the Latter-day Saints were
"killed, and several were wounded. I saw Brother
"James Hendrix, one of the wounded, as he was
"being carried home; he was entirely helpless and
"nearly speechless. Soon afterwards Captain David
"W. Patten, who was one of the twelve apostles,
"was brought wounded into the house where we
"were. I heard him bear testimony to the truth of
"Mormonism. He exhorted his wife and all present
"to abide in the faith. His wife asked him if he
"had anything against any one. He answered, 'No.'
"Elder Heber C. Kimball asked him if he would
"remember him when he got home. He said he
"would. Soon after this he died, without a struggle.

" In this State I saw thousands of mobbers arrayed
"against the saints, and I heard their shouts and
"savage yells when our prophet Joseph and his
"brethren were taken into their camp. I saw much,
"very much, of the sufferings that were brought
"upon our people by those lawless men. The saints
"were forced to sign away their property, and to
"agree to leave the State before it was time to put
"in spring crops. In these distressing times, the
"spirit of the Lord was with us to comfort and sus-
"tain us, and we had a sure testimony that we were
"being persecuted for the gospel's sake, and that
"the Lord was angry with none save those who
"acknowledged not his hand in all things.

" My father had to lose what he had paid on his
"farm; and in February, 1839, in the depth of win-
"ter, our family, and thousands of the saints, were
"on the way to the State of Illinois. On this jour-

"ney I walked many a mile, to let some poor sick
"or weary soul ride. At night we would meet
"around the camp-fire and take pleasure in singing
"the songs of Zion, trusting in the Lord that all
"would yet be well, and that Zion would eventually
"be redeemed.

"In the spring, father joined us at Quincy, Ill.
"We also had the joy of having our prophet, Joseph
"Smith, and his brethren, restored to us from their
"imprisonment in Missouri. Many, however, had
"died from want and exposure during our journey.
"I was sick for a long time with ague and fever,
"during which time my father was taken severely
"sick, and died after suffering seven weeks. It was
"the first sickness that either of us ever had.

"In the spring of 1840 our family moved to
"Nauvoo, in Illinois. Here I continued my punc-
"tuality in attending meetings, had many opportu-
"nities of hearing Joseph Smith preach, and tried
"to profit by his instructions, and received many
"testimonials to the truth of the doctrines he taught.
"Meetings were held out of doors in pleasant
"weather, and in private houses when it was unfa-
"vorable. I was present at the laying of the corner-
"stones of the foundation of the Nauvoo temple,
"and had become acquainted with the prophet
"Joseph and his family.

"On the 25th of July, 1841, I was united in holy
"marriage to George Albert Smith, the then
"youngest member of the quorum of the twelve
"apostles, and first cousin of the prophet (Elder
"Don Carlos Smith officiating at our marriage).
"My husband was born June 26th, 1817, at Potsdam,

"St. Lawrence county, N. Y.   When I became ac-
"quainted with him in Virginia, in 1837, he was the
"junior member of the first quorum of seventy.   On
"the 26th day of June, 1838, he was ordained a
"member of the High Council of Adam-Ondi-
"Ahman, Davies county, Missouri.   Just about the
"break of day, on the 26th of April, 1839, while
"kneeling on the corner-stone of the foundation of
"the Lord's house in the city of Far West, Cald-
"well county, Missouri, he was ordained one of the
"twelve apostles.   Two days after we were married,
"we started, carpet bag in hand, to go to his father's,
"who lived at Zarahemla, Iowa Territory, about a
"mile from the Mississippi.   There we found a feast
"prepared for us, in partaking of which my hus-
"band's father, John Smith, drank our health, pro-
"nouncing the blessings of Abraham, Isaac and
"Jacob upon us.   I did not understand the import
"of this blessing as well then as I do now."

————

Here we meet another of these Spartan women
of Mormondom in the person of Louisa F. Wells,
the senior wife of Lieutenant-General Daniel H.
Wells.

In July, 1837, her father, Absalom Free, who had
embraced Mormonism in Fayetteville, St. Clair
county, Ill., in the year 1835, emigrated with his
family to Caldwell county, Mo.

In Caldwell, Brother Free purchased a farm and
built a good house. He was of the well-to-do farmer
class.   With his ample means he soon collected a

fine farming outfit, and before him was the promise of great prosperity.

The saints had been driven out of Jackson county, and mobs were ravaging in Davies county, but there was peace in Caldwell until the Fourth of July, in 1838, when the anti-Mormons, who were waiting and watching for a pretext, took occasion, from some remarks made by Elder Sidney Rigdon, in a commemorative speech at the celebration, to commence a crusade against the city of Far West.

When the father of Louisa joined the organization for defence of the city of Far West, he left a sick son at home, with the women folks of his own and five other families, who had gathered there. These were left to defend their homes.

Louisa and her sister Emeline, with their cousin, Eliza Free, stood guard, on a ridge near the house, for three weeks, night and day, to warn the families of the approach of the mob. This sister Emeline is the same who was afterwards so well known in Utah as the wife of Brigham Young.

While thus standing guard, one day, the girls saw a troop of horsemen near, marching with a red flag and the beating of drums. They had with them a prisoner, on foot, whom they were thus triumphantly marching to their camp. They were a troop of the mob. The prisoner was grandfather Andrew Free, though at the time the sisters knew it not.

It was almost night. The horsemen made direct for their camp with their "prisoner of war," whom they had taken, not in arms, for he was aged, yet was he a soldier of the cross, ready to die for his faith.

Already had the veteran disciple been doomed by his captors. He was to be shot; one escape only had they reserved for him.

Before the mob tribunal stood the old man, calm and upright in his integrity, and resolved in his faith. No one was near to succor him. He stood alone, face to face with death, with those stern, cruel men, whose class had shown so little mercy in Missouri, massacring men, women and children, at Haun's Mill, and elsewhere about the same time.

Then the captain and his band demanded of the old man that he should swear there and then to renounce Jo. Smith and his d—d religion, or they would shoot him on the spot.

Drawing himself up with a lofty mien, and the invincible courage that the Mormons have always shown in their persecutions, the veteran answered: " I have not long to live. At the worst you cannot "deprive me of many days. I will never betray or "deny my faith which I know to be of God. Here "is my breast, shoot away, I am ready to die for my "religion!"

At this he bared his bosom and calmly waited for the mob to fire.

But the band was abashed at his fearless bearing and answer. For a time the captain and his men consulted, and then they told their prisoner that they had decided to give him till the morning to reconsider whether he would retract his faith or die.

Morning came. Again the old man was before the tribunal, fearless in the cause of his religion as he had been the previous night. Again came from him a similar answer, and then he looked for death, indeed, the next moment.

But he had conquered his captors, and the leader declared, with an oath : "Any man who can be so d—d true to any d—d religion, deserves to live !"

Thereupon the mob released the heroic disciple of Mormonism, and he returned to his home in safety.

During the three weeks the girls stood on guard, their father, who was desirous to get tidings of his sick son, came frequently to a thicket of underbrush, where the girls would bring his food and communicate with him concerning affairs at the house.

One evening during this season of guard duty, the girls discovered five armed men approaching. Running to the house, they gave the alarm. In a few moments every woman and child of the six families were hiding in the neighboring corn-field, excepting Louisa, her mother and her sick brother.

"Mother," said the boy, "you and Louisa run and "hide. The mob will be sure to kill me. They "will see how tall I am by the bed-clothes, and will "think I am a man. You and sister Louisa escape "or they will kill you too."

But the mother resolved to share the fate of her son, unless she could protect him by her presence, and soften the hearts of savage mobocrats by a mother's prayers for mercy; but she bade her daughter fly with the baby. Louisa, however, also determined to stay to defend both her brother and her mother. So they armed themselves—the mother with an axe, and Louisa with a formidable pair of old-fashioned fire-tongs, and stationed themselves at either door.

But it turned out that the men were a squad of friends, whom the father had sent to inquire after his family; yet the incident illustrates those days of universal terror for the Mormons in the State of Missouri. Worse, even, than the horrors of ordinary war must it have been, when thus women, children and the sick, when not a Mormon man was present to provoke the mob to bloodshed, looked for massacre upon massacre as daily scenes which all in turn might expect to overtake them.

After the fall of the city of Far West, it being decided that the Mormons should make a grand exodus from Missouri in the spring, Mr. Free determined to anticipate it. Gathering up what property he could save from the sacrifice, he started with his family for Illinois, abandoning the beautiful farm he had purchased and paid for, along with the improvements he had made.

In their flight to Illinois they were frequently overtaken and threatened by mobs, but fortunately escaped personal violence, as it was evident they were hastening from the inhospitable State. But the inhumanity of the Missourians in those times is well illustrated in the following incident:

Along with Brother Free's party were William Duncan and Solomon Allen, whose feet were so badly frozen one day that they were unable to proceed. At every house on the route the exiles called, soliciting permission to shelter and care for the disabled men; but at every place they were turned away, until at last, at eleven o'clock at night, they were graciously permitted to occupy some negro quarters. The grace, however, of Missouri was redeemed by a codicil that "No d—d Mormon should stop among white folks!"

This was mercy, indeed, for Missouri, and it is written in the book of remembrance.

The party stopped and occupied the negro quarters, nursing the men during the night, and so far restored them that they were enabled to go on the next day.

Arriving at the Mississippi river, above St. Charles, it was found that the ice was running so fiercely that it was well-nigh impossible to cross, but the mobbers insisted that they should cross at once.

The crossing was made on a scow ferry-boat, common in those times; and as the boat was near being swamped in the current, to add to the horror of the incident, it was seriously proposed by the boatmen to throw some of the "d—d Mormons overboard," to lighten the load! The proposition, however, was abandoned, and the party landed safely on the opposite shore.

Having escaped all the perils of that flight from Missouri, Father Free and his family made their home in the more hospitable State of Illinois, where the Mormons for a season found their "second Zion."

Here we leave "Sister Louisa" for awhile, to meet her again in the grand exodus of her people from "civilization."

———

The following experience of Abigail Leonard, a venerable and respected lady, now in her eighty-second year of life, will also be of interest in this connection. She says:

"In 1829 Eleazer Miller came to my house, for "the purpose of holding up to us the light of the "gospel, and to teach us the necessity of a change "of heart. He did not teach creedism, for he did "not believe therein. That night was a sleepless "one to me, for all night long I saw before me our "Saviour nailed to the cross. I had not yet re-"ceived remission of my sins, and, in consequence "thereof, was much distressed. These feelings con-"tinued for several days, till one day, while walking "alone in the street, I received the light of the "spirit.

"Not long after this, several associated Metho-"dists stopped at our house, and in the morning, "while I was preparing breakfast, they were con-"versing upon the subject of church matters, and "the best places for church organization. From the "jottings of their conversation, which I caught from "time to time, I saw that they cared more for the "fleece than the flock. The Bible lay on the table "near by, and as I passed I occasionally read a few "words until I was impressed with the question: "'What is it that separates two Christians?'

"For two or three weeks this question was con-"stantly on my mind, and I read the Bible and "prayed that this question might be answered to me.

"One morning I took my Bible and went to the "woods, when I fell upon my knees, and exclaimed: "'Now, Lord, I pray for the answer of this question, "and I shall *never* rise till you reveal to me what it "is that separates two Christians.' Immediately a "vision passed before my eyes, and the different "sects passed one after another by me, and a voice

"called to me, saying : ' These are built up for gain.'
" Then, beyond, I could see a great light, and a voice
" from above called out: ' I shall raise up a people,
" whom I shall delight to own and bless.' I was
" then fully satisfied, and returned to the house.

" Not long after this a meeting was held at our
" house, during which every one was invited to
" speak ; and when opportunity presented, I arose
" and said : ' To-day I come out from all names, sects
" and parties, and take upon myself the name of
" Christ, resolved to wear it to the end of my days.'

" For several days afterward, many people came
" from different denominations and endeavored to
" persuade me to join their respective churches. At
" length the associated Methodists sent their pre-
" siding elder to our house to preach, in the hope
" that I might be converted. While the elder was
" discoursing I beheld a vision in which I saw a
" great multitude of people in the distance, and over
" their heads hung a thick, dark cloud. Now and
" then one of the multitude would struggle, and rise
" up through the gloomy cloud ; but the moment his
" head rose into the light above, the minister would
" strike him a blow, which would compel him to
" retire ; and I said in my heart, ' They will never
" serve *me* so.'

" Not long after this, I heard of the ' Book of
" Mormon,' and when a few of us were gathered at
" a neighbor's we asked that we might have manifes-
" tations in proof of the truth and divine origin of
" this book, although we had not yet seen it. Our
" neighbor, a lady, was quite sick and in much dis-
" tress. It was asked that she be healed, and imme-

"diately her pain ceased, and health was restored. "Brother Bowen defiantly asked that he might be "slain, and in an instant he was prostrated upon the "floor. I requested that I might know of the truth "of this book, by the gift and power of the Holy "Ghost, and I immediately felt its presence. Then, "when the Book of Mormon came, we were ready "to receive it and its truths. The brethren gathered "at our house to read it, and such days of rejoicing "and thanksgiving I never saw before nor since. We "were now ready for baptism, and on or about the "20th of August, 1831, were baptized.

"When we heard of the 'gathering,' we were "ready for that also, and began preparations for the "journey. On the 3d of July, 1832, we started for "Jackson county, Mo., where we arrived some time "in the latter part of December of the same year.

"Here we lived in peace, and enjoyed the bless-"ings of our religion till the spring of 1833, when "the mob came upon us, and shed its terror in our "midst. The first attack was made upon Indepen-"dence, about twelve miles from our place. The "printing press was destroyed, and the type scat-"tered in the streets. Other buildings, and their "furniture, were destroyed; and Bishop Partridge "was tarred and feathered. Next, we heard that the "enemy had attacked our brethren in the woods "about six miles distant. Then my husband was "called upon to go and assist his brethren. He "arrived on the field in the heat of the battle, and "received fourteen bullet-holes in his garments, but "received no wounds, save two very slight marks, "one on the hip, the other on the arm.

" The mob was defeated, and my husband returned
"home for food. I gave it him, and bade him
"secrete himself immediately. He did so, and none
"too soon; for scarcely was he hidden, when the
"mob appeared. As soon as my husband was
"secreted I took my children and went to a neigh-
"bor's house, where the sisters were gathering for
"safety. About this time Sister Parley Pratt was
"being helped from a sick bed to this place of se-
"curity, and the mob, seeing the sisters laboring to
"carry her, gave their assistance and carried her in.
"The mob then searched for fire-arms, but could
"find none.

"The brethren and the mob formed a treaty
"about this time, in which we agreed to abandon the
"country by a specified time. Immediately our
"people commenced moving across the Missouri
"river, into Clay county. The people of Clay
"county becoming alarmed at our numbers, and
"incited to malice by the people of Jackson county,
"cut away the boat before all our people had
"crossed, and thus compelled our family with some
"others to remain in Jackson county. There were
"nine families in all. And the mob came and drove
"us out into the prairie before the bayonet. It was
"in the cold, cheerless month of November, and
"our first night's camp was made the thirteenth of
"that month, so wide-famed as the night of falling
"stars. The next day we continued our journey,
"over cold, frozen, barren prairie ground, many of
"our party barefoot and stockingless, feet and legs
"bleeding. Mine was the only family whose feet
"were clothed, and that day, while alone, I asked

"the Lord what I should do, and his answer was:
"'Divide among the sufferers, and thou shalt be
"repaid four-fold!' I then gave till I had given
"more than fifteen pairs of stockings. In three and
"a half days from the time of starting, we arrived
"at a grove of timber, near a small stream, where
"we encamped for the winter. From the time of
"our arrival till the following February we lived
"like saints.

"For awhile our men were permitted to return
"to the settlements in Jackson county, and haul
"away the provisions which they had left behind;
"but at last they would neither sell to us nor allow
"us any longer to return for our own provisions left
"behind.

"A meeting was held, and it was decided that but
"one thing was left to do, which was to return to
"Jackson county, to the place we had recently left
"from compulsion. This we did, and on the even-
"ing of February 20, 1834, soon after our arrival in
"the old deserted place, we had been to meeting
"and returned. It was about eleven o'clock at
"night, while we were comfortably seated around a
"blazing fire, built in an old-fashioned Dutch fire-
"place, when some one on going out discovered a
"crowd of men at a little distance from the house,
"on the hill. This alarmed the children, who ran
"out, leaving the door open. In a moment or two
"five armed men pushed their way into the house
"and presented their guns to my husband's breast,
"and demanded, 'Are you a Mormon?' My husband
"replied: 'I profess to belong to the Church of
"Christ.' They then asked if he had any arms, and

"on being told that he had not, one of them said:
"' Now, d—n you, walk out doors !' My husband
"was standing up, and did not move.

"Seeing that he would not go, one of them laid
"down his gun, clutched a chair, and dealt a fierce
"blow at my husband's head; but fortunately the
"chair struck a beam overhead, which turned and
"partially stopped the force of the blow, and it fell
"upon the side of his head and shoulder with too
"little force to bring him down, yet enough to smash
"the chair in pieces upon the hearth. The fiend
"then caught another chair, with which he succeeded
"in knocking my husband down beneath the stair-
"way. They then struck him several blows with a
"chair-post, upon the head, cutting four long gashes
"in the scalp. The infuriated men then took him
"by the feet and dragged him from the room. They
"raised him to his feet, and one of them, grasping
"a large boulder, hurled it with full force at his
"head ; but he dropped his head enough to let the
"stone pass over, and it went against the house like
"a cannon ball. Several of them threw him into
"the air, and brought him, with all their might, at
"full length upon the ground. When he fell, one
"of them sprang upon his breast, and stamping with
"all his might, broke two of his ribs.

"They then turned him upon his side, and with
"a chair-post dealt him many severe blows upon the
"thigh, which were heard at a distance of one hun-
"dred and twenty rods. Next they tore off his coat
"and shirt, and proceeded to whip him with their
"gun-sticks. I had been by my husband during this
"whole affray, and one of the mob seeing me, cried

"out: 'Take that woman in the house, or she will
"overpower every devil of you!' Four of them pre-
"sented their guns to my breast, and jumping off
"the ground with rage, uttering the most tremen-
"dous oaths, they commanded me to go into the
"house. This order I did not obey, but hastened
"to my husband's assistance, taking stick after stick
"from them, till I must have thrown away twenty.

"By this time my husband felt that he could hold
"out no longer, and raising his hands toward heaven,
"asking the Lord to receive his spirit, he fell to the
"ground, helpless. Every hand was stayed, and I
"asked a sister who was in the house to assist me
"to carry him in doors.

"We carried him in, and after washing his face
"and making him as comfortable as possible, I went
"forth into the mob, and reasoned with them, tell-
"ing them that my husband had never harmed one
"of them, nor raised his arm in defence against
"them. They then went calmly away, but next
"day circulated a report that they had killed one
"Mormon.

"After the mob had gone, I sent for the elder,
"and he, with two or three of the brethren, came
"and administered to my husband, and he was
"instantly healed. The gashes on his head grew
"together without leaving a scar, and he went to
"bed comfortable. In the morning I combed the
"coagulated blood out of his hair, and he was so
"well that he went with me to meeting that same
"day.

"The mob immediately held a meeting and in-
"formed us that we were to have only three days to

" leave in, and if we were not off by that time the
" whole party would be massacred. We accordingly
" prepared to leave, and by the time appointed were
" on our way to Clay county. Soon after our arrival
" in Clay county, the 'Camp of Zion' came, and
" located about twenty miles from us. The cholera
" broke out in the camp, and many died. Three of
" the party started to where we lived, but two died
" on the way, leaving Mr. Martin Harris to accom-
" plish the journey alone. The first thing, when he
" saw me, he exclaimed: 'Sister Leonard, I came
" to your house to save my life.' For eight days my
" husband and I worked with him before he began
" to show signs of recovery, scarcely lying down to
" take our rest. While Mr. Harris was lying sick,
" the prophet Joseph Smith came, with eleven
" others, to visit him. This was the first time I
" had ever seen the prophet.

    " The prophet advised us to scatter out over the
" county, and not congregate too much together, so
" that the people would have no cause for alarm.

    " While we were yet living in this place, the ague
" came upon my family, and my husband lay sick for
" five months, and the children for three. During
" the whole time I procured my own wood, and
" never asked any one for assistance. On the re-
" covery of my husband he bought a beautiful little
" farm near by, where we lived long enough to raise
" one crop, when the mob again came against us,
" and we were compelled to move into Caldwell
" county.

    " When we arrived there we moved into a log
" cabin, without door, window, or fireplace, where

" my husband left the children and me, and returned
" to Clay county, for some of the brethren who were
" left behind. During his absence a heavy snow-
" storm came, and we were without wood or fire.
" My little boy and I, by turns, cut wood enough to
" keep us warm till my husband returned.

" Here my husband entered eighty acres of land,
" and subsequently bought an additional twenty
" acres. Here, too, we stayed long enough to raise
" one crop, and then moved to Nauvoo, Hancock
" county, Illinois.

" As soon as we were located, we were all seized
" with sickness, and scarcely had I recovered, when
" there came into our midst some brethren from Eng-
" land, who were homeless, and our people took them
" in with their own families. One of the families we
" took to live with us. The woman was sick, and
" we sent for the elders to heal her, but their en-
" deavors were not successful, and I told the husband
" of the sick woman that but one thing was left to
" be done, which was to send for the sisters. The
" sisters came, washed, anointed, and administered
" to her. The patient's extremities were cold, her
" eyes set, a spot in the back apparently mortified,
" and every indication that death was upon her.
" But before the sisters had ceased to administer,
" the blood went coursing through her system, and
" to her extremities, and she was sensibly better.
" Before night her appetite returned, and became
" almost insatiable, so much so at least that, after I
" had given her to eat all I dared, she became quite
" angry because I would not give her more. In
" three days she sat up and had her hair combed,
" and soon recovered."

The following portion of Margaret Foutz's narrative will also be of interest in this connection. She says:

"I am the daughter of David and Mary Munn, "and was born December 11th, 1801, in Franklin "county, Pa. I was married to Jacob Foutz, July "22d, 1822. In the year 1827 we emigrated to "Richland county, Ohio. After living here a few "years, an elder by the name of David Evans came "into the neighborhood, preaching the gospel of "Jesus Christ, commonly called Mormonism. We "united ourselves with the church, being baptized "by Brother Evans, in the year 1834. Subsequently "we took our departure for Missouri, to gather with "the saints. We purchased some land, to make a "permanent home, on Crooked River, where a small "branch of the church was organized, David Evans "being the president. We enjoyed ourselves ex-"ceedingly well, and everything seemed to prosper; "but the spirit of persecution soon began to make "itself manifest. Falsehoods were circulated about "the Mormon population that were settling about "that region, and there soon began to be signs of "trouble. The brethren, in order to protect their "families, organized themselves together.

"Threats being made by the mob to destroy a "mill belonging to Brother Haun, it was considered "best to have a few men continually at the mill to "protect it. One day Brother Evans went and had "an interview with a Mr. Comstock, said to be the "head man of the mob. All things were amicably "adjusted. Brother Evans then went to inform the "brethren (my husband being among them) that all

"was well. This was about the middle of the after-
"noon, when Brother Evans returned from Mr.
"Comstock's. On a sudden, without any warning
"whatever, sixty or seventy men, with blackened
"faces, came riding their horses at full speed. The
"brethren ran, for protection, into an old blacksmith
"shop, they being without arms. The mob rode up
"to the shop, and without any explanation or ap-
"parent cause, began a wholesale butchery, by firing
"round after round through the cracks between the
"logs of the shop. I was at home with my family
"of five little children, and could hear the firing. In
"a moment I knew the mob was upon us. Soon a
"runner came, telling the women and children to
"hasten into the timber and secrete themselves,
"which we did, without taking anything to keep us
"warm ; and had we been fleeing from the scalping
"knife of the Indian we would not have made
"greater haste. And as we ran from house to house,
"gathering as we went, we finally numbered about
"forty or fifty women and children. We ran about
"three miles into the woods, and there huddled to-
"gether, spreading what few blankets or shawls we
"chanced to have on the ground for the children ;
"and here we remained until two o'clock the next
"morning, before we heard anything of the result of
"the firing at the mill. Who can imagine our feel-
"ings during this dreadful suspense? And when the
"news did come, oh ! what terrible news ! Fathers,
"brothers and sons, inhumanly butchered ! We
"now took up the line of march for home. Alas!
"what a home ! Who would we find there? And
"now, with our minds full of the most fearful fore-

" bodings, we retraced those three long, dreary miles.
" As we were returning I saw a brother, Myers, who
" had been shot through his body.   In that dreadful
" state he crawled on his hands and knees, about
" two miles, to his home.

" After I arrived at my house with my children, I
" hastily made a fire to warm them, and then started
" for the mill, about one mile distant.   My children
" would not remain at home, saying, ' If father and
" mother are going to be killed, we want to be with
" them.'   It was about seven o'clock in the morning
" when we arrived at the mill.   In the first house I
" came to there were three dead men.   One, a
" Brother McBride, I was told was a survivor of the
" Revolution.   He was a terrible sight to behold,
" having been cut and chopped, and horribly man-
" gled, with a corn-cutter.

" I hurried on, looking for my husband.   I found
" him in an old house, covered with some rubbish.
" (The mob had taken the bedding and clothing
" from all the houses near the mill).   My husband
" had been shot in the thigh.   I rendered him all
" the assistance I could, but it was evening before I
" could get him home.   I saw thirteen more dead
" bodies at the shop, and witnessed the beginning of
" the burial, which consisted in throwing the bodies
" into an old, dry well.   So great was the fear of the
" men that the mob would return and kill what few
" of them there were left, that they threw the bodies
" in, head first or feet first, as the case might be.
" When they had thrown in three, my heart sick-
" ened, and I turned fainting away.

" At the moment of the massacre, my husband

" and another brother drew some of the dead bodies
" on themselves, and pretended to be dead also, by
" so doing saving their lives. While in this situation
" they heard what the ruffians said after the firing
" was over. Two little boys, who had not been hit,
" begged for their lives; but with horrible oaths
" they put the muzzles of their guns to the chil-
" dren's heads, and blew their brains out.

   "Oh! what a change one short day had brought!
" Here were my friends, dead and dying; one in
" particular asked me to give him relief by taking a
" hammer and knocking his brains out, so great was
" his agony. And we knew not what moment our
" enemies would be upon us again. And all this, not
" because we had broken any law—on the contrary,
" it was a part of our religion to keep the laws of
" the land. In the evening Brother Evans got a
" team and conveyed my husband to his house, car-
" ried him in, and placed him on a bed. I then had
" to attend him, alone, without any doctor or any
" one to tell me what to do. Six days afterwards I,
" with my husband's assistance, extracted the bullet,
" it being buried deep in the thick part of the thigh,
" and flattened like a knife. During the first ten
" days, mobbers, with blackened faces, came every
" day, cursing and swearing like demons from the
" pit, and declaring that they would 'kill that d—d
" old Mormon preacher.' At times like these, when
" human nature quailed, I felt the power of God
" upon me to that degree that I could stand before
" them fearless; and although a woman, and alone,
" those demons in human shape had to succumb;
" for there was a power with me that they knew not

"of. During these days of mobocratic violence I
"would sometimes hide my husband in the house,
"and sometimes in the woods, covering him with
"leaves. And thus was I constantly harassed, until
"the mob finally left us, with the understanding that
"we should leave in the spring. About the middle
"of February we started for Quincy, Ill. Arriving
"there, we tarried for a short time, and thence
"moved to Nauvoo."

CHAPTER XVIII.

JOSEPH SMITH'S DARING ANSWER TO THE LORD—
WOMAN, THROUGH MORMONISM, RESTORED TO HER
TRUE POSITION—THE THEMES OF MORMONISM.

What potent faith had come into the world that a people should thus live and die by it?

Show us this new temple of theology in which the sisters had worshipped.

Open the book of themes which constitute the grand system of Mormonism.

———

The disciples of the prophet believed in the Book of Mormon; but nearly all their themes, and that vast system of theology which Joseph conceived, as the crowning religion for a world, were derived from the Hebrew Bible, the New Testament of Christ, and modern revelation.

New revelation is the signature of Mormonism.

The themes begin with Abraham, rather than with Christ; but they go back to Adam, and to the long "eternities" ere this world was.

Before Adam, was Mormonism!

There are the *generations of worlds.* The Genesis of the Gods was before the Genesis of Man.

The Genesis of the Gods is the first book of the Mormon iliad.

" Then the Lord answered Job out of the whirl-wind, and said, ' Who is this that darkeneth counsel by words without knowledge ? Gird up now thy loins like a man ; for I will demand of thee, and answer thou me.

" ' Where wast thou when I laid the foundations of the earth ? Declare if thou hast understanding.

" ' Who hath laid the measures thereof, if thou knowest ? Or who hath stretched the line upon it ?

" ' Whereupon are the foundations thereof fasten-ed ? Or who laid the corner-stone thereof :

" ' When the morning stars sang together, and all the sons of God shouted for joy ?'

Brother Job, where wast thou ? Joseph answered the Lord when the Masonic question of the Gods was put to him :

" Father, I was with *thee;* one of the 'morning "stars' then ; one of the archangels of thy presence."

'Twas a divinely bold answer. But Joseph *was* divinely daring.

The genius of Mormonism had come down from the empyrean ; it hesitated not to assert its origin among the Gods.

This is no fanciful treatment—no mere flight to the realm of ideals. The Mormons have literally answered the Lord, their Father, the question which he put to their brother, Job, and have made that answer a part of their theology.

But where was woman "when the morning stars "sang together, and the sons of God shouted for "joy?"

Where was Zion ? Where the bride ? Where was woman ?

" Not yet created ; taken afterwards from the rib "of Adam; of the earth, not of heaven; created for " Adam's glory, that he might rule over her."

So said not Joseph.

It was the young East who thus declared. The aged West had kept the book of remembrance.

Joseph was gifted with wonderful memories of the "eternities past." He had not forgotten woman. He knew Eve, and he remembered Zion. He restored woman to her place among the Gods, where her primeval Genesis is written.

Woman was among the morning stars, when they sang together for joy, at the laying of the foundations of the earth.

When the sons of God thrice gave their Masonic shouts of hosanna, the daughters of God lifted up their voices with their brothers ; and the hallelujahs to the Lord God Omnipotent, were rendered sweeter and diviner by woman leading the theme.

In the temples, both of the heavens and the earth, woman is found. She is there in her character of Eve, and in her character of Zion. The one is the type of earth, the other the type of heaven ; the one the mystical name of the mortal, the other of the celestial, woman.

The Mormon prophet rectified the divine drama. Man is nowhere where woman is not. Mormonism has restored woman to her pinnacle.

Presently woman herself shall sing of her divine origin. A high priestess of the faith shall interpret the themes of herself and of her Father-and-Mother God!

At the very moment when the learned divines of

Christendom were glorying that this little earth was the "be-all and the end-all" of creation, the prophet of Mormondom was teaching the sisters in the temple at Kirtland that there has been an eternal chain of creations coming down from the generations of the Gods—worlds and systems and universes. At the time these lights of the Gentiles were pointing to the star-fretted vault of immensity as so many illuminations—lamps hung out by the Creator, six thousand years ago, to light this little earth through her probation—the prophet of Israel was teaching his people that the starry hosts were worlds and suns and universes, some of which had being millions of ages before this earth had physical form.

Morever, so vast is the divine scheme, and stupendous the works of creations, that the prophet introduced the expressive word *eternities.* The eternities are the times of creations.

This earth is but an atom in the immensities of creations. Innumerable worlds have been peopled with "living souls" of the order of mankind; innumerable worlds have passed through their probations; innumerable worlds have been redeemed, resurrected, and celestialized.

Hell-loving apostles of the sects were sending ninety-nine hundredths of this poor, young, forlorn earth to the bottomless pit. The Mormon prophet was finding out grand old universes, in exaltation with scarcely the necessity of losing a soul.

The spirit of Mormonism is universal salvation. Those who are not saved in one glory, may be saved in another.

There are the "glory of the sun," and the "glory "of the moon," and the "glory of the stars."

The children of Israel belong to the glory of the sun. They kept their first estate. They are nobly trying to keep their second estate on probation. Let the devotion, the faith, the divine heroism of the Mormon sisters, witness this.

"Adam is our Father and God. He is the God "of the earth."

So says Brigham Young.

Adam is the great archangel of this creation. He is Michael. He is the Ancient of Days. He is the father of our elder brother, Jesus Christ—the father of him who shall also come as Messiah to reign. He is the father of the spirits as well as the tabernacles of the sons and daughters of man. Adam!

Michael is one of the grand mystical names in the works of creations, redemptions, and resurrections. Jehovah is the second and the higher name. Eloheim—signifying the Gods—is the first name of the celestial trinity.

Michael was a celestial, resurrected being, of another world.

"In the beginning" the Gods created the heavens and the earths.

In their councils they said, let us make man in our own image. So, in the likeness of the Fathers, and the Mothers—the Gods—created they man— male and female.

When this earth was prepared for mankind, Michael, as Adam, came down. He brought with him one of his wives, and he called her name Eve.

Adam and Eve are the names of the fathers and mothers of worlds.

Adam was not made out of a lump of clay, as we make a brick, nor was Eve taken as a rib—a bone— from his side. They came by generation. But woman, as the wife or mate of man, was a rib of man. She was taken from his side, in their glorified world, and brought by him to earth to be the mother of a race.

These were father and mother of a world of spirits who had been born to them in heaven. These spirits had been waiting for the grand period of their probation, when they should have bodies or tabernacles, so that they might become, in the resurrection, like Gods.

When this earth had become an abode for man- kind, with its Garden of Eden, then it was that the morning stars sang together, and the sons and daughters of God shouted for joy. They were coming down to earth.

The children of the sun, at least, knew what the grand scheme of the everlasting Fathers and the everlasting Mothers meant, and they, both sons and daughters, shouted for joy. The temple of the eternities shook with their hosannas, and trembled with divine emotions.

The father and mother were at length in their Garden of Eden. They came on purpose to fall. They fell " that man might be; and man is, that he "might have joy." They ate of the tree of mortal life, partook of the elements of this earth that they might again become mortal for their children's sake. They fell that another world might have a proba- tion, redemption and resurrection.

The grand patriarchal economy, with Adam, as a resurrected being, who brought his wife Eve from another world, has been very finely elaborated, by Brigham, from the patriarchal genesis which Joseph conceived.

Perchance the scientist might hesitate to accept the Mormon ideals of the genesis of mortals and immortals, but Joseph and Brigham have very much improved on the Mosaic genesis of man. It is certainly not scientific to make Adam as a model adobe; the race has come by generation. The genesis of a hundred worlds of his family, since his day, does not suggest brickyards of mortality. The patriarchal economy of Mormonism is at least an improvement, and is decidedly epic in all its constructions and ideals.

A grand patriarchal line, then, down from the "eternities;" generations of worlds and generations of Gods; all one universal family.

The Gods are the fathers and the mothers, and the brothers and the sisters, of the saints.

Divine ambitions here; a daring genius to thus conceive; a lifting up of man and woman to the very plane of the celestials, while yet on earth.

Now for the father and the children of the covenant.

With Abraham begins the covenant of Israel. The Mormons are a Latter-day Israel.

God made a covenant with Abraham, for Abraham was worthy to be the grand patriarch of a world, under Adam. Like Jesus, he had a pre-existence.

He was "in the beginning" with God; an archangel in the Father's presence; one not less noble than his elder brother and captain of salvation ; the patriarch, through whose line Messiah was ordained to come into the world.

Abraham was the elect of God before the foundation of this earth. In him and his seed were all the promises—all the covenants—and all the divine empires. In them was the kingdom of Messiah to consummate the object and vast purposes of earth's creation.

He is the father of the faithful and the friend of God. In him and his seed all the nations of the earth shall be blessed. He shall become the father of many nations. His seed shall be as the sand on the sea-shore.

In Abraham many nations have already been blessed. He and his seed have given Bible and civilization to Christendom. From his loins came Jesus—from him will come Messiah.

Abraham and his seed have done much for the world, but they will do a hundred fold more. Their genius, their prophets, and their covenants, will leaven and circumscribe all civilization.

Jehovah is the God of Israel—the covenant people. There is none like him in all the earth. There are Lords many, and Gods many, but unto Israel there is but one God.

Between Jehovah and Abraham there are the everlasting covenants. The divine epic is between Abraham and his God.

Mormonism is now that divine epic.

This grand patriarch may be said to be a grand Mormon ; or, better told, the Mormons are a very proper Israel, whom the patriarch acknowledges as his children, chosen to fulfill the covenants in connection with the Jews.

Jehovah never made any covenants outside of Israel. The Gentiles are made partakers, by adoption into the Abrahamic family.

All is of election and predestination. There is but very little free-grace; just enough grace to give the Gentiles room to enter into the family of Israel, that the promise may be fulfilled that in Israel all the nations of the earth shall be blessed.

In ancient times Jehovah made his people a nation, that his name might be glorified. He established his throne in David, by an everlasting covenant; but the throne and sceptre were taken from Israel, no more to be, until he comes whose right it is to reign. Messiah is that one. He is coming to restore the kingdom to Israel.

The earth and mankind were created that they might have a probation; and a probation, that a millennial reign of peace and righteousness may consummate the divine plan and purposes.

Righteousness and justice must be established upon the earth in the last days, or nations must perish utterly.

In the last days God shall set up a kingdom upon the earth, which shall never be destroyed. It will break into pieces all other kingdoms and empires, and stand forever. It will be given to the saints of the Most High, and they will possess it. The Mormons are the saints of the Most High.

That kingdom has already been set up, by the administration of angels to Joseph Smith. This is the burden of Mormonism. It was for that the saints were driven from Missouri and Illinois; that for which they made their exodus to the Rocky Mountains; that for which the sisters have borne the cross for half a century.

Now also in the present age is to be fulfilled the vision of Daniel; here it is:

" I beheld till thrones were cast down, and the Ancient of Days (Adam) did sit, whose garments were white as snow, and the hair of his head like the pure wool; his throne was like the fiery flame, and his wheels as burning fire.

" A fiery stream issued and came forth from before him; thousands ministered unto him, and ten thousand times ten thousand stood before him; the judgment was set, and the books were opened.

  *   *   *   *   *   *

" I saw in the night visions, and, behold, one like the Son of Man came with the clouds of heaven, and came to the Ancient of Days, and they brought him near before him.

" And there was given him dominion and glory, and a kingdom, that all people, nations and languages, should serve him; his dominion is an everlasting dominion, which shall not pass away, and his kingdom that which shall not be destroyed.

  *   *   *   *   *   *

" But the saints of the Most High shall take the kingdom, and possess the kingdom forever, even forever and ever. *   *   *   *

" I beheld, and the same horn made war with the saints, and prevailed against them.

" Until the Ancient of Days came, and judgment was given to the saints of the Most High; and the time came that the saints possessed the kingdom.

  *   *   *   *   *   *

" And the kingdom and dominion, and the greatness of the kingdom under the whole heaven, shall be given to the saints of the Most High, whose kingdom is an everlasting kingdom, and all dominions shall serve and obey him."

Here is the imperial drama of Mormonism which the saints have applied most literally, and sought to work out in America; or, rather the God of Israel has purposed to fulfill his wondrous scheme, in them, and multiply them until they shall be an empire of God-fearing men and women—ten thousand times ten thousand saints.

No wonder that Missouri drove the saints—no wonder that the sisters, with such views, have risen to such sublime heroism and been inspired with such exalted faith. Scarcely to be wondered at even that they have been strong enough to bear their crosses throughout eventful lives, which have no parallel in history. With a matchless might of spirit, and divine ambitions, inspired by such a theology, literally applied in the action of their lives, they have risen to the superhuman.

Comprehend this Hebraic religion of the sisters, and it can thus be comprehended somewhat how they have borne the cross of polygamy, with more than the courage of martyrs at the stake.

We are coming to polygamy, by-and-by, to let these braver than Spartan women speak for themselves, upon their own special subject; but polygamy was not established until years after the saints were driven from Missouri.

We are but opening these views of Hebraic faith and religion. The themes will return frequently in their proper places. But let the sisters most reveal themselves in their expositions, episodes, and testimonies.

Thus, here, the high priestess of Mormondom, with her beautiful themes of our God-Father and our God-Mother!

CHAPTER XIX.

Joseph endowed the church with the genesis of a grand theology, and Brigham has reared the colossal fabric of a new civilization; but woman herself must sing of her celestial origin, and her relationship to the majesty of creation.

Inspired by the mystic memories of the past, Eliza R. Snow has made popular in the worship of the saints a knowledge of the grand family, in our *primeval spirit-home.* The following gem, which opens the first volume of her poems, will give at once a rare view of the spiritual type of the high priestess of the Mormon Church, and of the divine drama of Mormonism itself. It is entitled, " Invocation ; or, the Eternal Father and Mother ·

> O ! my Father, thou that dwellest
> In the high and holy place;
> When shall I regain thy presence,
> And again behold thy face ?
>
> In thy glorious habitation,
> Did my spirit once reside ?
> In my first primeval childhood,
> Was I nurtured by thy side ?

For a wise and glorious purpose,
  Thou hast placed me here on earth;
And withheld the recollection
  Of my former friends and birth.

Yet oft-times a secret something,
  Whisper'd, " You're a stranger here;"
And I felt that I had wandered
  From a more exalted sphere.

I had learned to call thee Father,
  Through thy spirit from on high;
But until the key of knowledge
  Was restored, I knew not why.

In the heavens are parents single?
  No; the thought makes reason stare;
Truth is reason; truth eternal,
  Tells me I've a Mother there.

When I leave this frail existence—
  When I lay this mortal by,
Father, Mother, may I meet you
  In your royal court on high?

Then at length, when I've completed
  All you sent me forth to do,
With your mutual approbation,
  Let me come and dwell with you.

A divine drama set to song. And as it is but a choral dramatization, in the simple hymn form, of the celestial themes revealed through Joseph Smith, it will strikingly illustrate the vast system of Mormon theology, which links the heavens and the earths.

It is well remembered what an ecstacy filled the minds of the transcendental Christians of America, when the voice of Theodore Parker, bursting into the fervor of a new revelation, addressed, in prayer, our Father and Mother in heaven!

An archangel proclamation that!

Henceforth shall the mother half of creation be worshipped with that of the God-Father; and in that worship woman, by the very association of ideas, shall be exalted in the coming civilization.

Wonderful revelation, Brother Theodore; worthy thy glorious intellect! Quite as wonderful that it was not universal long before thy day!

But it will be strange news to many that years before Theodore Parker breathed that theme in public prayer, the Mormon people sang their hymn of invocation to the Father and Mother in heaven, given them by the Hebraic pen of Eliza R. Snow.

And in this connection it will be proper to relate the fact that a Mormon woman once lived as a servant in the house of Theodore Parker. With a disciple's pardonable cunning she was in the habit of leaving Mormon books in the way of her master. It is not unlikely that the great transcendentalist had read the Mormon poetess' hymn to "Our Father-and-Mother God!"

And perhaps it will appear still more strange to the reader, who may have been told that woman in the Mormon scheme ranked low—almost to the barbarian scale—to learn that the revelation of the Father and Mother of creation, given through the Mormon prophet, and set to song by a kindred spirit, is the basic idea of the whole Mormon theology.

The hymn of invocation not only treats our God parents in this grand primeval sense, but the poetess weaves around their parental centre the divine drama of the pre-existence of worlds.

This celestial theme was early revealed to the church by the prophet, and for now nearly forty years the hymn of invocation has been familiar in the meetings of the saints.

A marvel indeed is this, that at the time modern Christians, and even "philosophers," were treating this little earth, with its six thousand years of mortal history, as the sum of the intelligent universe— to which was added this life's sequel, with the gloom of hell prevailing—the Mormon people, in their very household talk, conversed and sang of an endless succession of worlds.

They talked of their own pre-existing lives. They came into the divine action ages ago, played their parts in a primeval state, and played them well. Hence were they the first fruits of the gospel. They scarcely limited their pre-existing lives to a beginning, or compassed their events, recorded in other worlds, in a finite story. Down through the cycles of all eternity they had come, and they were now entabernacled spirits passing through a mortal probation.

It was of such a theme that " Sister Eliza " sang; and with such a theme her hymn of invocation to our Father and Mother in heaven soon made the saints familiar in every land.

Let us somewhat further expound the theme of this hymn, which our poetess could not fully embody in the simple form of verse.

God the Father and God the Mother stand, in the grand pre-existing view, as the origin and centre of the spirits of all the generations of mortals who had been entabernacled on this earth.

First and noblest of this great family was Jesus Christ, who was the elder brother, in spirit, of the whole human race. These constituted a world-family of pre-existing souls.

Brightest among these spirits, and nearest in the circle to our Father and Mother in heaven (the Father being Adam), were Seth, Enoch, Noah and Abraham, Moses, David, and Jesus Christ—indeed that glorious cohort of men and women, whose lives have left immortal records in the world's history. Among these the Mormon faith would rank Joseph Smith, Brigham Young, and their compeers.

In that primeval spirit-state, these were also associated with a divine sisterhood. One can easily imagine the inspired authoress of the hymn on pre-existence, to have been a bright angel among this sister throng. Her hymn is as a memory of that primeval life, and her invocation is as the soul's yearning for the Father and Mother in whose courts she was reared, and near whose side her spirit was nurtured.

These are the sons and daughters of Adam—the Ancient of Days—the Father and God of the whole human family. These are the sons and daughters of Michael, who is Adam, the father of the spirits of all our race.

These are the sons and daughters of Eve, the Mother of a world.

What a practical Unitarianism is this! The Christ is not dragged from his heavenly estate, to be mere mortal, but mortals are lifted up to his celestial plane. He is still the God-Man; but he is one among many brethren who are also God-Men.

Moreover, Jesus is one of a grand order of Saviours. Every world has its distinctive Saviour, and every dispensation its Christ.

There is a glorious Masonic scheme among the Gods. The everlasting orders come down to us with their mystic and official names. The heavens and the earths have a grand leveling; not by pulling down celestial spheres, but by the lifting up of mortal spheres.

Perchance the skeptic and the strict scientist who measures by the cold logic of facts, but rises not to the logic of ideas, might not accept this literal preexisting view, yet it must be confessed that it is a lifting up of the idealities of man's origin. Man is the offspring of the Gods. This is the supreme conception which gives to religion its very soul. Unless man's divinity comes in somewhere, religion is the wretchedest humbug that ever deluded mortals.

Priestcraft, indeed, then, from the beginning to the end—from the Alpha to the Omega of theologic craft, there is nothing divine.

But the sublime and most primitive conception of Mormonism is, that man in his essential being is divine, that he is the offspring of God—that God is indeed his Father.

And woman? for she is the theme now.

Woman is heiress of the Gods. She is joint heir with her elder brother, Jesus the Christ; but she inherits from her God-Father and her God-Mother. Jesus is the "beloved" of that Father and Mother— their well-tried Son, chosen to work out the salvation and exaltation of the whole human family.

And shall it not be said then that the subject *rises* from the God-Father to the God-Mother? Surely it is a rising in the sense of the culmination of the divine idea. The God-Father is not robbed of his everlasting glory by this maternal completion of himself. It is an expansion both of deity and humanity.

They twain are one God!

The supreme Unitarian conception is here; the God-Father and the God-Mother! The grand unity of God is in them—in the divine Fatherhood and the divine Motherhood—the very beginning and consummation of creation. Not in the God-Father and the God-Son can the unity of the heavens and the earths be worked out; neither with any logic of facts nor of idealities. In them the Masonic trinities; in the everlasting Fathers and the everlasting Mothers the unities of creations.

Our Mother in heaven is decidedly a new revelation, as beautiful and delicate to the masculine sense of the race as it is just and exalting to the feminine. It is the woman's own revelation. Not even did Jesus proclaim to the world the revelation of our Mother in heaven—co-existent and co-equal with the eternal Father. This was left, among the unrevealed truths, to the present age, when it would seem the woman is destined by Providence to become very much the oracle of a new and peculiar civilization.

The oracle of this last grand truth of woman's divinity and of her eternal Mother as the partner with the Father in the creation of worlds, is none other than the Mormon Church. It was revealed in the glorious theology of Joseph, and established

13

by Brigham in the vast patriarchal system which he
has made firm as the foundations of the earth, by
proclaiming Adam as our Father and God. The
Father is first in name and order, but the Mother
is with him—these twain, one from the beginning.

Then came our Hebraic poetess with her hymn
of invocation, and woman herself brought the per-
fected idea of deity into the forms of praise and
worship. Is not this exalting woman to her sphere
beyond all precedent?

Let it be marked that the Roman Catholic idea
of the Mother of God is wonderfully lower than the
Mormon idea. The Church of Rome only brings
the maternal conception, linked with deity, in Christ,
and that too in quite the inferior sense. It is not
primitive—it is the exception; it begins and ends
with the Virgin Mary. A question indeed whether
it elevates womanhood and motherhood. The ordinary idea is rather the more exalted; for that
always, in a sense, makes the mother superior to the
son. The proverb that great mothers conceive great
sons has really more poetry in it than the Roman
Catholic doctrine that Mary was the Mother of God.

The Mormon Church is the oracle of the grandest
conception of womanhood and motherhood. And
from her we have it as a revelation to the world, and
not a mere thought of a transcendental preacher—
a glorious Theodore Parker flashing a celestial ray
upon the best intellects of the age.

Excepting the Lord's prayer, there is not in the
English language the peer of this Mormon invocation; and strange to say the invocation is this time
given to the Church through woman—the prophetess and high priestess of the faith.

CHAPTER XX.

THE TRINITY OF MOTHERHOOD—EVE, SARAH, AND ZION—THE MORMON THEORY CONCERNING OUR FIRST PARENTS.

A trinity of Mothers!

The celestial Masonry of Womanhood!

The other half of the grand patriarchal economy of the heavens and the earths!

The book of patriarchal theology is full of new conceptions. Like the star-bespangled heavens—like the eternities which it mantles—is that wondrous theology!

New to the world, but old as the universe. 'Tis the everlasting book of immortals, unsealed to mortal view, by these Mormon prophets.

A trinity of Mothers—Eve the Mother of a world; Sarah the Mother of the covenant; Zion the Mother of celestial sons and daughters—the Mother of the new creation of Messiah's reign, which shall give to earth the crown of her glory and the cup of joy after all her ages of travail.

Still tracing down the divine themes of Joseph; still faithfully following the methods of that vast patriarchal economy which shall be the base of a new order of society and of the temple of a new civilization.

When Brigham Young proclaimed to the nations that Adam was our Father and God, and Eve, his partner, the Mother of a world—both in a mortal and a celestial sense—he made the most important revelation ever oracled to the race since the days of Adam himself.

This grand patriarchal revelation is the very keystone of the "new creation" of the heavens and the earth. It gives new meaning to the whole system of theology—as much new meaning to the economy of salvation as to the economy of creation. By the understanding of the works of the Father, the works of the Son are illumined.

The revelation was the "Let there be light" again pronounced. "And there was light!"

"And God created man in his own image; in the image of God created he him; male and female created he them.

"And God blessed them; and God said unto them, be fruitful, and multiply, and replenish the earth, and subdue it."

Here is the very object of man and woman's creation exposed in the primitive command. The first words of their genesis are, "Be fruitful and multiply."

So far, it is of but trifling moment *how* our "first "parents" were created; whether like a brick, with the spittle of the Creator and the dust of the earth, or by the more intelligible method of generation. The prime object of man and woman's creation was for the *purposes of creation.*

"Be fruitful, and multiply and replenish the earth, "and subdue it," by countless millions of your offspring.

Thus opened creation, and the womb of everlasting motherhood throbbed with divine ecstacy.

It is the divine command still.   All other may be dark as a fable, of the genesis of the race, but this is not dark.   Motherhood to this hour leaps for joy at this word of God, " Be fruitful ; " and motherhood is sanctified as by the holiest sacrament of nature.

We shall prefer Brigham's expounding of the dark passages of Genesis.

Our first parents were not made up like mortal bricks. They came to be the Mother and the Father of a new creation of souls.

We say Mother now, first, for we are tracing this everlasting theme of motherhood, in the Mormon economy, without which nothing of the woman part of the divine scheme can be known—next to nothing of patriarchal marriage, to which we are traveling, be expounded.

Eve—immortal Eve—came down to earth to become the Mother of a race.

How become the Mother of a world of mortals except by herself again becoming mortal ?   How become mortal only by transgressing the laws of immortality ?   How only by "eating of the forbid-"den fruit"—by partaking of the elements of a mortal earth, in which the seed of death was everywhere scattered ?

All orthodox theologians believe Adam and Eve to have been at first immortal, and all acknowledge the great command, " Be fruitful and multiply."

That they were not about to become the parents of a world of immortals is evident, for they were on a mortal earth.   That the earth was mortal all nature here to-day shows. The earth was to be subdued by teeming millions of mankind—the dying earth actually eaten, in a sense, a score of times, by the children of these grand parents.

The fall is simple. Our immortal parents came down to fall; came down to transgress the laws of immortality; came down to give birth to mortal tabernacles for a world of spirits.

The " forbidden tree," says Brigham, contained in its fruit the elements of death, or the elements of mortality. By eating of it, blood was again infused into the tabernacles of beings who had become immortal. The basis of mortal generation is blood. Without blood no mortal can be born. Even could immortals have been conceived on earth, the trees of life had made but the paradise of a few; but a mortal world was the object of creation then.

Eve, then, came down to be the Mother of a world.

Glorious Mother, capable of dying at the very beginning to give life to her offspring, that through mortality the eternal life of the Gods might be given to her sons and daughters.

Motherhood the same from the beginning even to the end! The love of motherhood passing all understanding! Thus read our Mormon sisters the fall of their Mother.

And the serpent tempted the woman with the forbidden fruit.

Did woman hesitate a moment then? Did motherhood refuse the cup for her own sake, or did she, with infinite love, take it and drink for her children's sake? The Mother had plunged down, from the

pinnacle of her celestial throne, to earth, to taste
of death that her children might have everlasting
life.

What! should Eve ask Adam to partake of the
elements of death first, in such a sacrament! 'Twould
have outraged motherhood!

Eve partook of that supper of the Lord's death
first. She ate of that body and drank of that blood.

Be it to Adam's eternal *credit* that he stood by
and let our Mother—our ever blessed Mother Eve—
partake of the sacrifice before himself. Adam followed the Mother's example, for he was great and
grand—a Father worthy indeed of a world. He
was wise, too ; for the *blood of life* is the stream of
mortality.

What a psalm of everlasting praise to woman,
that Eve fell first!

A Goddess came down from her mansions of glory
to bring the spirits of her children down after her,
in their myriads of branches and their hundreds of
generations!

She was again a mortal Mother now. The first
person in the trinity of Mothers.

The Mormon sisterhood take up their themes of
religion with their Mother Eve, and consent with
her, at the very threshold of the temple, to bear the
cross. Eve is ever with her daughters in the temple
of the Lord their God.

The Mormon daughters of Eve have also in this
eleventh hour come down to earth, like her, to
magnify the divine office of motherhood. She came
down from her resurrected, they from their spirit,
estate. Here, with her, in the divine providence of

maternity, they begin to ascend the ladder to heaven, and to their exaltation in the courts of their Father and Mother God.

Who shall number the blasphemies of the sectarian churches against our first grand parents? Ten thousand priests of the serpent have thundered anathemas upon the head of "accursed Adam." Appalling, oftentimes, their pious rage. And Eve— the holiest, grandest of Mothers—has been made a very by-word to offset the frailties of the most wicked and abandoned.

Very different is Mormon theology! The Mormons exalt the grand parents of our race. Not even is the name of Christ more sacred to them than the names of Adam and Eve. It was to them the poetess and high priestess addressed her hymn of invocation; and Brigham's proclamation that Adam is our Father and God is like a hallelujah chorus to their everlasting names. The very earth shall yet take it up; all the sons and daughters of Adam and Eve shall yet shout it for joy, to the ends of the earth, in every tongue!

Eve stands, then, first—the God-Mother in the maternal trinity of this earth. Soon we shall meet Sarah, the Mother of the covenant, and in her daughters comprehend something of patriarchal marriage—"Mormon polygamy." But leave we awhile these themes of woman, and return to the personal thread of the sisters' lives.

CHAPTER XXI.

Who are these thus pursued as by the demons
that ever haunt a great destiny?

As observed in the opening chapter, they are the
sons and daughters of the Pilgrim sires and mothers
who founded this nation; sons and daughters of
the patriots who fought the battles of independence
and won for these United States a transcendent
destiny.

Here meet we two of the grand-nieces of Samuel
Huntington, one of the signers of the Declaration
of Independence, Governor of Connecticut, and
President of Congress.

Zina Diantha Huntington has long been known
and honored as one of the most illustrious women
of the Church. She was not only sealed to the
prophet Joseph in their sacred covenant of celestial
marriage, but after his martyrdom she was sealed to
Brigham Young as one of Joseph's wives. For
over a quarter of a century she has been known as

Zina D. Young—being mother to one of Brigham's daughters. In her mission of usefulness she has stood side by side with Sister Eliza R. Snow, and her life has been that of one of the most noble and saintly of women. Thus is she introduced to mark her honored standing among the sisterhood. Of her ancestral record she says:

"My father's family is directly descended from "Simon Huntington, the 'Puritan immigrant,' who "sailed for America in 1633. He died on the sea, "but left three sons and his widow, Margaret. The "church records of Roxbury, Mass., contain the "earliest record of the Huntington name known in "New England, and is in the handwriting of Rev. "John Elliot himself, the pastor of that ancient "church. This is the record: 'Margaret Hunting-"ton, widow, came in 1633. Her husband died by "the way, of the small-pox. She brought — children "with her.'

"Tradition says that Simon, the Puritan emi-"grant, sailed for this country to escape the perse-"cutions to which non-conformists were subjected, "during the high-handed administrations of Laud "and the first Charles. Tradition also declares him "to have been beyond doubt an Englishman. The "Rev. E. B. Huntington, in his genealogical memoir "of the Huntington family in this country, observes: "'The character of his immediate descendants is "perhaps in proof of both statements; they were "thoroughly English in their feelings, affinities, and "language; and that they were as thoroughly relig-"ious, their names and official connection with the "early churches in this country abundantly attest'

" Of one of my great-grandfathers the Huntington
" family memoir records thus: ' John, born in Nor-
" wich, March 15th, 1666, married December 9th,
" 1686, Abigal, daughter of Samuel Lathrop, who
" was born in May, 1667. Her father moved to
" Norwich from New London, to which place he
" had gone from Scituate, Mass., in 1648. He was
" the son of the Rev. John Lathrop, who, for non-
" conformity, being a preacher in the First Con-
" gregational Church organized in London, was
" imprisoned for two years, and who, on being re-
" leased in 1634, came to this country, and became
" the first minister of Scituate.'

" The Lathrops, from which my branch of the
" family was direct, also married with the other
" branches of the Huntingtons, making us kin of
" both sides, and my sister, Prescindia Lathrop
" Huntington, bears the family name of generations.

" My grandfather, Wm. Huntington, was born
" September 19th, 1757; married, February 13th,
" 1783, Prescindia Lathrop, and was one of the first
" settlers in the Black River Valley, in Northern
" New York. He resided at Watertown. He mar-
" ried for his second wife his first wife's sister, Alvira
" Lathrop Dresser. He died May 11th, 1842. The
" following is an obituary notice found in one of the
" Watertown papers :

" ' At his residence, on the 11th inst., Wm. Hunt-
" ington, in the eighty-fifth year of his age. Mr.
" Huntington was one of our oldest and most re-
" spected inhabitants. He was a native of Tolland,
" Conn., and for three or four years served in the
" army of the Revolution. In the year 1784 he emi-
" grated to New Hampshire, where he resided till the

"year 1804, when he removed to Watertown. He
"was for many years a member and an officer of the
"Presbyterian Church.'

"Before his death, however, my grandfather was
"baptized into the Church of Jesus Christ of Latter-
"day Saints. He always spoke of Samuel Hunt-
"ington, the signer of the Declaration of Indepen-
"dence, as his Uncle Samuel."

This genealogical record is given to illustrate the
numerous Puritan and Revolutionary relations of
the leading families of the Mormon people, and to
emphasize the unparalleled outrage of the repeated
exile of such descendants—exiles at last from American civilization. How exact has been the resemblance of their history to that of their Pilgrim
fathers and mothers!

But the decided connection of the Huntingtons
with the Mormon people was in William Huntington, the father of sisters Zina and Prescindia, who
for many years was a presiding High Priest of the
Church, being a member of the High Council.

This Wm. Huntington was also a patriot, and
served in the war with Great Britain, in 1812.

The sisters Zina and Prescindia, with their brothers, were raised fourteen miles east of Sackett's
Harbor, where the last battle was fought between
the British and Americans, in that war; so that the
Revolutionary history of their country formed a
peculiarly interesting theme to the "young folks"
of the Huntington family. Indeed their brother,
Dimock, at the period of the exodus of the Mormons from Nauvoo, had so much of the blood of
the patriots in his veins that he at once enlisted in

the service of his country in the war with Mexico—
being a soldier in the famous Mormon battalion.

Prescindia Lathrop Huntington, the eldest of
these two illustrious sisters, was born in Watertown,
Jefferson county, N. Y., September 7th, 1810, and
was her mother's fourth child; Zina Diantha was
born at the same place, January 31st, 1821.

Prescindia is a woman of very strong character;
and her life has been marked with great decision
and self-reliance, both in thought and purpose. She
was also endowed with a large, inspired mind—the
gifts of prophesy, speaking in tongues, and the
power to heal and comfort the sick, being quite pre-
eminent in her apostolic life. In appearance she is
the very counterpart of the Eliza Huntington whose
likeness is published in the book of the Huntington
family. A mother in Israel is Sister Prescindia, and
the type of one of the Puritan mothers in the olden
time. She was sealed to Joseph Smith, and for
many years was one of the wives of the famous
Heber C. Kimball.

Mother Huntington was also an exemplary saint.
She died a victim of the persecutions, when the
saints were driven from Missouri, and deserves to
be enshrined as a martyr among her people. Her
name was Zina Baker, born May 2d, 1786, in Plain-
field, Cheshire county, N. H., and married to Wm.
Huntington, December 28, 1806. Her father was
one of the first physicians in New Hampshire, and
her mother, Diantha Dimock, was descended from
the noble family of Dymocks, whose representatives
held the hereditary knight-championship of England—instance Sir Edward Dymock, Queen Elizabeth's champion.

Mother Huntington was a woman of great faith.
"She believed that God would hear and answer
"prayer in behalf of the sick. The gift of healing
"was with her before the gospel was restored in its
"fullness."

Thus testify her daughters of their mother, whose
spirit of faith was also instilled into their own
hearts, preparing them to receive the gospel of a
great spiritual dispensation, and for that apostolic
calling among the sick, to which their useful lives
have been greatly devoted.

Father and Mother Huntington had both been
strict Presbyterians; but about the time of the
organization of the Latter-day Church he withdrew
from the congregation, which had become divided
over church forms, and commenced an earnest
examination of the Scriptures for himself. To his
astonishment he discovered that there was no
church extant, to his knowledge, according to the
ancient pattern, with apostles and prophets, nor any
possessing the gifts and powers of the ancient gospel. For the next three years he was as a watcher
for the coming of an apostolic mission, when one
day Elder Joseph Wakefield brought to his house
the Book of Mormon. Soon his family embraced
the Latter-day faith, rejoicing in the Lord. Himself and wife, and his son Dimock and his wife, with
"Zina D.," then only a maiden, were the first of the
family baptized. Zina was baptized by Hyrum
Smith, in Watertown, August 1st, 1835.

Prescindia at that time was living with her husband at Loraine, a little village eighteen miles from
her native place, when her mother, in the summer

of 1835, brought to her the Book of Mormon and her first intelligence of the Mormon prophet. She gathered to Kirtland in May, 1836, and was baptized on the 6th of the following June, and was confirmed by Oliver Cowdry.

In Kirtland," she says, " we enjoyed many very "great blessings, and often saw the power of God "manifested. On one occasion I saw angels clothed "in white walking upon the temple. It was during "one of our monthly fast meetings, when the saints "were in the temple worshipping. A little girl "came to my door and in wonder called me out, "exclaiming, ' The meeting is on the top of the "meeting house !' I went to the door, and there I "saw on the temple angels clothed in white covering "the roof from end to end. They seemed to be "walking to and fro; they appeared and disap- "peared. The third time they appeared and dis- "appeared before I realized that they were not "mortal men. Each time in a moment they vanished, "and their reappearance was the same. This was "in broad daylight, in the afternoon. A number of "the children in Kirtland saw the same.

"When the brethren and sisters came home in "the evening, they told of the power of God mani- "fested in the temple that day, and of the prophe- "sying and speaking in tongues. It was also said, "in the interpretation of tongues, ' That the angels "were resting down upon the house.'

"At another fast meeting I was in the temple "with my sister Zina. The whole of the congrega- "tion were on their knees, praying vocally, for such "was the custom at the close of these meetings

"when Father Smith presided; yet there was no
"confusion; the voices of the congregation mingled
"softly together. While the congregation was thus
"praying, we both heard, from one corner of the
"room above our heads, a choir of angels singing
"most beautifully. They were invisible to us, but
"myriads of angelic voices seemed to be united in
"singing some song of Zion, and their sweet har-
"mony filled the temple of God.

  " We were also in the temple at the pentecost.
" In the morning Father Smith prayed for a pente-
"cost, in opening the meeting. That day the power
"of God rested mightily upon the saints. There
"was poured out upon us abundantly the spirit of
"revelation, prophesy and tongues. The Holy
"Ghost filled the house; and along in the afternoon
"a noise was heard. It was the sound of a mighty
"rushing wind. But at first the congregation was
"startled, not knowing what it was. To many it
"seemed as though the roof was all in flames.
"Father Smith exclaimed, 'Is the house on fire!'

  "'Do you not remember your prayer this morn-
"ing, Father Smith?' inquired a brother.

  " Then the patriarch, clasping his hands, exclaim-
"ed, 'The spirit of God, like a mighty rushing
"wind!'

  "At another time a cousin of ours came to visit
"us at Kirtland. She wanted to go to one of the
"saints' fast meetings, to hear some one sing or
"speak in tongues, but she said she expected to
"have a hearty laugh.

  "Accordingly we went with our cousin to the
"meeting, during which a Brother McCarter rose

"and sang a song of Zion in tongues; I arose and
"sang simultaneously with him the same tune and
"words, beginning and ending each verse in perfect
"unison, without varying a word. It was just as
"though we had sung it together a thousand times.

"After we came out of meeting, our cousin ob-
"served, 'Instead of laughing, I never felt so solemn
"in my life.'"

The family of Huntingtons removed with the
saints from Kirtland to Far West, and passed
through the scenes of the expulsion from Missouri.
In this their experience was very similar to the narratives of the other sisters already given; but Sister
Prescindia's visit to the prophet, in Liberty jail,
must have special notice. She says:

"In the month of February, 1839, my father, with
"Heber C. Kimball, and Alanson Ripley, came and
"stayed over night with us, on their way to visit the
"prophet and brethren in Liberty jail. I was invited
"to go with them.

"When we arrived at the jail we found a heavy
"guard outside and inside the door. We were
"watched very closely, lest we should leave tools to
"help the prisoners escape.

"I took dinner with the brethren in prison; they
"were much pleased to see the faces of true friends;
"but I cannot describe my feelings on seeing that
"man of God there confined in such a trying time
"for the saints, when his counsel was so much
"needed. And we were obliged to leave them in
"that horrid prison, surrounded by a wicked mob.

"While in prison, the brethren were presented
"with human flesh to eat. My brother, Wm. Hunt-

14

"ington, tasted before the word could be passed
"from Joseph to him. It was the flesh of a colored
"man.

"After my second visit to the prison, with Fred-
"erick G. Williams, the prophet addressed to me
"the following letter:

                    "' LIBERTY JAIL, March 15th, 1839.
"' DEAR SISTER:
    "' My heart rejoiced at the friendship you mani-
"fested in requesting to have conversation with us;
"but the jailer is a very jealous man, for fear some
"one will have tools for us to get out with. He is
"under the eye of the mob continually, and his life
"is at stake if he grants us any privilege. He will
"not let us converse with any one alone.

    "' O what a joy it would be for us to see our
"friends. It would have gladdened my heart to
"have had the privilege of conversing with you;
"but the hand of tyranny is upon us; but thanks
"be to God, it cannot last always ; and he that sit-
"teth in the heavens will laugh at their calamity and
"mock when their fear cometh.

    "' We feel, dear sister, that our bondage is not of
"long duration. I trust that I shall have the chance
"to give such instructions as have been communi-
"cated to us, before long; and as you wanted some
"instruction from us, and also to give us some infor-
"mation, and administer consolation to us, and to
"find out what is best for you to do, I think that
"many of the brethren, if they will be pretty still,
"can stay in this country until the indignation is
"over and passed. But I think it will be better for
"Brother Buell to leave and go with the rest of the
"brethren, if he keeps the faith, and at any rate, for
"thus speaketh the spirit concerning him. I want
"him and you to know that I am your true friend.

    "' I was glad to see you. No tongue can tell what

"inexpressible joy it gives a man to see the face of
"one who has been a friend, after having been in-
"closed in the walls of a prison for five months. It
"seems to me my heart will always be more tender
"after this than ever it was before.

" ' My heart bleeds continually when I contem-
"plate the distress of the Church. O that I could
"be with them ; I would not shrink at toil and hard-
"ship to render them comfort and consolation. I
"want the blessing once more to lift my voice in the
"midst of the saints. I would pour out my soul to
"God for their instruction. It has been the plan of
"the devil to hamper and distress me from the begin-
"ning, to keep me from explaining myself to them,
"and I never have had opportunity to give them
"the plan that God has revealed to me. Many have
"run without being sent, crying, ' Tidings, my Lord,'
"and have caused injury to the Church, giving the
"adversary more power over them that walk by
"sight and not by faith. Our trouble will only give
"us that knowledge to understand the mind of the
"ancients. For my part I think I never could have
"felt as I now do if I had not suffered the wrongs
"which I have suffered. All things shall work to-
"gether for good to them that love God.

" ' Beloved sister, we see that perilous times have
"truly come, and the things which we have so long
"expected have at last begun to usher in; but when
"you see the fig tree begin to put forth its leaves,
"you may know that the summer is nigh at hand.
"There will be a short work on the earth; it has
"now commenced. I suppose there will soon be
"perplexity all over the earth. Do not let our
"hearts faint when these things come upon us, for
"they must come or the word cannot be fulfilled. I
"know that something will soon take place to stir
"up this generation to see what they have been
"doing, and that their fathers have inherited lies,

"and they have been led captive by the devil to no
"profit. But they know not what they do. Do not
"have any feeling of enmity towards any son or
"daughter of Adam. I believe I shall be let out of
"their hands some way or other, and shall see good
"days. We cannot do anything, only stand still
"and see the salvation of God. He must do his
"own work or it must fall to the ground. We must
"not take it in our hands to avenge our wrongs.
"'Vengeance is mine, saith the Lord; I will repay.'
"I have no fears; I shall stand unto death, God
"being my helper.

"'I wanted to communicate something, and I
"wrote this. Write to us if you can.

&c.,

"'J. SMITH, JR.'"

This letter to Sister Prescindia, which has never
before been published, gives an excellent example
of the spirit and style of the prophet. It will be
read with interest, even by the anti-Mormon. Himself in prison, and his people even at that moment
passing through their expulsion, what passages for
admiration are these :

"Do not have any feelings of enmity towards any
"son or daughter of Adam." "They know not
"what they do!" "We must not take it in our
"hands to avenge our wrongs. Vengeance is mine,
"saith the Lord; I will repay." "I have no fears;
"I shall stand unto death, God being my helper!"

Like his divine Master this; "Father, forgive
"them; they know not what they do!" A great
heart, indeed, had Joseph, and a spirit exalted with
noble aims and purposes.

When Sister Prescindia returned to Far West,

her father and mother, with her sister Zina, had
started in the exodus of the saints from Missouri
to Illinois. She says :

"I never saw my mother again. I felt alone on
"the earth, with no one to comfort me, excepting
"my little son, George, for my husband had become
"a bitter apostate, and I could not speak in favor of
"the Church in his presence. There was by this
"time not one true saint in the State of Missouri,
"to my knowledge."

Sister Zina says : " On the 18th of April, 1839, I
"left Far West, with my father, mother, and two
"younger brothers, and arrived at Quincy, Ill., on
"the 25th of April, and from thence to Commerce,
"afterwards called Nauvoo, which we reached on
"the 14th of May.

" Joseph, the prophet, had just escaped from prison
"in Missouri, and the saints were gathering to
" Nauvoo. My brother Dimock was also in Illinois,
"living at Judge Cleveland's.

" On the 24th of June my dear mother was taken
"sick with a congestive chill. About three hours
"afterwards she called me to her bedside and said :

"' Zina, my time has come to die. You will live
"many years ; but O, how lonesome father will be.
"I am not afraid to die. All I dread is the mortal
"suffering. I shall come forth triumphant when the
" Saviour comes with the just to meet the saints on
"the earth.'

" The next morning I was taken sick ; and in a
"few days my father and brother Oliver were also
"prostrate. My youngest brother, John, twelve
"years of age, was the only one left that could give

"us a drink of water; but the prophet sent his
"adopted daughter to assist us in our affliction, and
"saw to our being taken care of, as well as circum-
"stances would permit—for there were hundreds,
"lying in tents and wagons, who needed care as
"much as we. Once Joseph came himself and made
"us tea with his own hands, and comforted the sick
"and dying.

"Early in the morning of the 8th of July, 1839,
"just before the sun had risen, the spirit of my
"blessed mother took its flight, without her moving
"a muscle, or even the quiver of the lip.

"Only two of the family could follow the remains
"to their resting place. O, who can tell the an-
"guish of the hearts of the survivors, who knew
"not whose turn it would be to follow next?

"Thus died my martyred mother! The prophet
"Joseph often said that the saints who died in the
"persecutions were as much martyrs of the Church
"as was the apostle David Patten, who was killed
"in the defence of the saints, or those who were
"massacred at Haun's Mill. And my beloved
"mother was one of the many bright martyrs of
"the Church in those dark and terrible days of per-
"secution."

CHAPTER XXII.

WOMAN'S WORK IN CANADA AND GREAT BRITAIN—
HEBER C. KIMBALL'S PROPHESY—PARLEY P. PRATT'S
SUCCESSFUL MISSION TO CANADA—A BLIND WOMAN
MIRACULOUSLY HEALED—DISTINGUISHED WOMEN
OF THAT PERIOD.

By this time (1840, the period of the founding of
Nauvoo), the Church has had a remarkable history
in Canada and Great Britain. To these missions
we must now go for some of our representative
women, and also to extend our view of Mormonism
throughout the world.

Brigham Young was the first of the elders who
took Mormonism into Canada, soon after his entrance into the Church. There he raised up several
branches, and gathered a few families to Kirtland;
but it was not until the apostle Parley P. Pratt took
his successful and almost romantic mission to
Canada, that Mormonism flourished in the British
Province, and from there spread over to Great
Britain, like an apostolic wave.

Presently we shall see that the romance of Mormonism has centred around the sisters abroad as
well as at home. Frequently we shall see them the
characters which first come to view; the first pre-

pared for the great spiritual work of the age; the
first to receive the elders with their tidings of the
advent of a prophet and the administration of angels,
after the long night of spiritual darkness, and centuries of angelic silence; and were it possible to
trace their every footstep in the wonderful work
abroad, we should find that the sisters have been
effective missionaries of the Church, and that, in
some sections, they have been instrumental in
making more disciples than even the elders.

Here is the opening of the story of Parley P.
Pratt's mission to Canada, in which a woman immediately comes to the foreground in a famous prophesy:

"It was now April" (1836). "I had retired to
"rest," says he, "one evening, at an early hour, and
"was pondering my future course, when there came
"a knock at the door. I arose and opened it, when
"Heber C. Kimball and others entered my house,
"and being filled with the spirit of prophesy, they
"blessed me and my wife, and prophesied as follows:
"'Brother Parley, thy wife shall be healed from this
"hour, and shall bear a son, and his name shall be
"Parley; and he shall be a chosen instrument in the
"hands of the Lord to inherit the priesthood and
"to walk in the steps of his father. He shall do a
"great work in the earth in ministering the word
"and teaching the children of men. Arise, there-
"fore, and go forth in the ministry, nothing doubt-
"ing. Take no thought for your debts, nor the
"necessaries of life, for the Lord will supply you
"with abundant means for all things.

"'Thou shalt go to Upper Canada, even to the

"city of Toronto, the capital, and there thou shalt
" find a people prepared for the fullness of the gos-
" pel, and they shall receive thee, and thou shalt
" organize the Church among them, and it shall
" spread thence into the regions round about, and
" many shall be brought to the knowledge of the
" truth, and shall be filled with joy ; and from the
" things growing out of this mission, shall the full-
" ness of the gospel spread into England, and cause
" a great work to be done in that land.'

" This prophesy was the more marvelous, because
" being married near ten years we had never had
" any children ; and for near six years my wife had
" been consumptive, and had been considered incur-
" able. However, we called to mind the faith of
" Abraham of old, and judging Him faithful who
" had promised, we took courage.

" I now began in earnest to prepare for the mis-
" sion, and in a few days all was ready. Taking an
" affectionate leave of my wife, mother and friends,
" I started for Canada, in company with a Brother
" Nickerson, who kindly offered to bear expenses."

Away to Canada with Parley. We halt with him
in the neighborhood of Hamilton. He is an entire
stranger in the British Province, and without money.
He knows not what to do. His narrative thus continues :

" The spirit seemed to whisper to me to try the
" Lord, and see if anything was too hard for him,
" that I might know and trust him under all circum-
" stances. I retired to a secret place in a forest, and
" prayed to the Lord for money to enable me to
" cross the lake. I then entered Hamilton, and

"commenced to chat with some of the people. I
"had not tarried many minutes before I was accosted
"by a stranger, who inquired my name and where I
"was going. He also asked me if I did not want
"some money. I said yes. He then gave me ten
"dollars, and a letter of introduction to John Tay-
"lor, of Toronto, where I arrived the same evening.
"Mrs. Taylor received me kindly, and went for
"her husband, who was busy in his mechanic shop.
"To them I made known my errand to the city, but
"received little direct encouragement. I took tea
"with them, and then sought lodgings at a public
"house."

Already had he met in Canada a woman destined
to bear a representative name in the history of her
people, for she is none other than the wife of the
afterwards famous apostle John Taylor. She is the
first to receive him into her house; and the apostolic story still continues the woman in the foreground :

"In the morning," he says, "I commenced a
"regular visit to each of the clergy of the place,
"introducing myself and my errand. I was abso-
"lutely refused hospitality, and denied the oppor-
"tunity of preaching in any of their houses or
"congregations. Rather an unpromising beginning,
"thought I, considering the prophesies on my head
"concerning Toronto. However, nothing daunted, I
"applied to the sheriff for the use of the court-house,
"and then to the authorities for a public room in the
"market-place; but with no better success. What
"could I do more ? I had exhausted my influence
"and power without effect. I now repaired to a

"pine grove just out of the town, and, kneeling
"down, called on the Lord, bearing testimony of my
"unsuccessful exertions; my inability to open the
"way; at the same time asking him in the name
"of Jesus to open an effectual door for his servant
"to fulfill his mission in that place.

"I then arose and again entered the town, and
"going to the house of John Taylor, had placed my
"hand on my baggage to depart from a place where
"I could do no good, when a few inquiries on the
"part of Mr. Taylor, inspired by a degree of curi-
"osity or of anxiety, caused a few moments' delay,
"during which a lady by the name of Walton entered
"the house, and, being an acquaintance of Mrs.
"Taylor, was soon engaged in conversation with her
"in an adjoining room. I overheard the following:

"'Mrs. Walton, I am glad to see you; there is a
"gentleman here from the United States who says
"the Lord sent him to this city to preach the gos-
"pel. He has applied in vain to the clergy and to
"the various authorities for opportunity to fulfill his
"mission, and is now about to leave the place. He
"may be a man of God; I am sorry to have him
"depart.'

"'Indeed!' said the lady; 'well, I now understand
"the feelings and spirit which brought me to your
"house at this time. I have been busy over the
"wash-tub and too weary to take a walk; but I felt
"impressed to walk out. I then thought I would
"make a call on my sister, the other side of town;
"but passing your door, the spirit bade me go in;
"but I said to myself, I will go in when I return; but
"the spirit said, go in now. I accordingly came in,

"and I am thankful that I did so. Tell the stranger "he is welcome to my house. I am a widow; but I "have a spare room and bed, and food in plenty. " He shall have a home at my house, and two large "rooms to preach in just when he pleases. Tell "him I will send my son John over to pilot him to "my house, while I go and gather my relatives and " friends to come in this very evening and hear him "talk; for I feel by the spirit that he is a man sent "by the Lord with a message which will do us "good.'

" The evening found me quietly seated at her "house," says Parley, " in the midst of a number of "listeners, who were seated around a large work "table in her parlor, and deeply interested in con- "versation like the following :

"'Mr. Pratt, we have for some years been anx- "iously looking for some providential event which "would gather the sheep into one fold ; build up the "true Church as in days of old, and prepare the "humble followers of the Lamb, now scattered and "divided, to receive their coming Lord when he "shall descend to reign on the earth. As soon as " Mrs. Taylor spoke of you I felt assured, as by a "strange and unaccountable presentiment, that you "were a messenger, with important tidings on these "subjects; and I was constrained to invite you here; "and now we are all here anxiously waiting to hear "your words.'

" 'Well, Mrs. Walton, I will frankly relate to you "and your friends the particulars of my message and "the nature of my commission. A young man in "the State of New York, whose name is Joseph

"Smith, was visited by an angel of God, and, after
'several visions and much instruction, was enabled
"to obtain an ancient record, written by men of old
"on the American continent, and containing the
"history, prophesies and gospel in plainness, as re-
"vealed to them by Jesus and his messengers. This
"same Joseph Smith and others, were also commis-
"sioned by the angels in these visions, and ordained
"to the apostleship, with authority to organize a
"church, to administer the ordinances, and to ordain
"others, and thus cause the full, plain gospel in its
"purity, to be preached in all the world.

"'By these apostles thus commissioned, I have
"been ordained as an apostle, and sent forth by the
"word of prophesy to minister the baptism of
"repentance for remission of sins, in the name of
"Jesus Christ; and to administer the gift of the
"Holy Ghost, to heal the sick, to comfort the
"mourner, bind up the broken in heart, and proclaim
"the acceptable year of the Lord.

"'I was also directed to this city by the spirit of
"the Lord, with a promise that I should find a peo-
"ple here prepared to receive the gospel, and should
"organize them in the same. But when I came and
"was rejected by all parties, I was about to leave
"the city; but the Lord sent you, a widow, to receive
"me, as I was about to depart; and thus I was pro-
"vided for like Elijah of old. And now I bless your
"house, and all your family and kindred, in his
"name. Your sins shall be forgiven you; you shall
"understand and obey the gospel, and be filled with
"the Holy Ghost; for so great faith have I never
"seen in any of my country.'

"'Well, Mr. Pratt, this is precisely the message "we were waiting for; we believe your words and "are desirous to be baptized.'

"'It is your duty and privilege,' said I; 'but wait "yet a little while till I have an opportunity to teach "others, with whom you are religiously connected, "and invite them to partake with you of the same "blessings.'"

Next comes a great miracle—the opening of the eyes of the blind—which seems to have created quite a sensation in Canada; and still the woman is the subject. The apostle continues:

"After conversing with these interesting persons "till a late hour, we retired to rest. Next day Mrs. "Walton requested me to call on a friend of hers, "who was also a widow in deep affliction, being to-"tally blind with inflammation in the eyes; she had "suffered extreme pain for several months, and had "also been reduced to want, having four little chil-"dren to support. She had lost her husband, of "cholera, two years before, and had sustained her-"self and family by teaching school until deprived "of sight, since which, she had been dependent "on the Methodist society; herself and children "being then a public charge. Mrs. Walton sent her "little daughter of twelve years old to show me the "way. I called on the poor blind widow and help-"less orphans, and found them in a dark and gloomy "apartment, rendered more so by having every "ray of light obscured to prevent its painful effects "on her eyes. I related to her the circumstances of "my mission, and she believed the same. I laid my "hands upon her in the name of Jesus Christ, and

"said unto her, 'Your eyes shall be well from this
"very hour.' She threw off her bandages—opened
"her house to the light—dressed herself, and walk-
"ing with open eyes, came to the meeting that
"same evening at Sister Walton's, with eyes as well
"and as bright as any other persons.

"The Methodist society were now relieved of
"their burthen in the person of this widow and four
"orphans. This remarkable miracle was soon noised
"abroad, and the poor woman's house was thronged
"from all parts of the city and country with visitors;
"all curious to witness for themselves, and to inquire
"of her how her eyes were healed.

"'How did the man heal your eyes?' 'What did
"he do?—tell us,' were questions so oft repeated
"that the woman, wearied of replying, came to me
"for advice to know what she should do. I advised
"her to tell them that the Lord had healed her, and
"to give him the glory, and let that suffice. But
"still they teased her for particulars. 'What did
"this man do?' 'How were your eyes opened and
"made well?'

"'He laid his hands upon my head in the name
"of Jesus Christ, and rebuked the inflammation,
"and commanded them to be made whole and re-
"stored to sight; and it was instantly done.'

"'Well, give God the glory; for, as to this man,
"it is well known that he is an impostor, a follower of
"Joseph Smith, the false prophet.'

"'Whether he be an impostor or not, I know not;
"but this much I know, whereas I was blind, now
"I see! Can an impostor open the eyes of the
"blind?'"

The widow Walton was baptized, with all her
household; John Taylor and his wife, also; and
John soon became an able assistant in the ministry.

And here we meet two more representative
women—sisters—whose family were destined to
figure historically in the church. The narative of
Parley continues:

"The work soon spread into the country and en-
"larged its operations in all that region; many were
"gathered into the Church, and were filled with
"faith and love, and with the holy spirit, and the
"Lord confirmed the word with signs following.
"My first visit to the country was about nine miles
"from Toronto, among a settlement of farmers, by
"one of whom I had sent an appointment beforehand.
"John Taylor accompanied me. We called at a
"Mr. Joseph Fielding's, an acquaintance and friend
"of Mr. Taylor's. This man had two sisters, young
"ladies, who seeing us coming ran from their house
"to one of the neighboring houses, lest they should
"give welcome, or give countenance to 'Mormon-
"ism.' Mr. Fielding stayed, and as we entered the
"house he said he was sorry we had come; he had
"opposed our holding meeting in the neighborhood;
"and, so great was the prejudice, that the Methodist
"meeting house was closed against us, and the min-
"ister refused, on Sunday, to give out the appoint-
"ment sent by the farmer.

"'Ah!' said I, 'why do they oppose Mormonism?'
"'I don't know,' said he, 'but the name has such a
"contemptible sound; and, another thing, we do not
"want a new revelation, or a new religion contrary
"to the Bible.' 'Oh,' said I, 'if that is all we shall

"soon remove your prejudices. Come, call home
"your sisters, and let's have some supper. Did you
"say the appointment was not given out?' 'I said,
"sir, that it was not given out in the meeting house,
"nor by the minister; but the farmer by whom you
"sent it agreed to have it at his house.' 'Come, then,
"send for your sisters, we will take supper with you,
"and all go over to meeting together. If you and
"your sisters will agree to this, I will agree to preach
"the old Bible gospel, and leave out all new reve-
"lations which are opposed to it.'

"The honest man consented. The young ladies
"came home, got us a good supper, and all went to
"meeting. The house was crowded; I preached,
"and the people wished to hear more. The meet-
"ing house was opened for further meetings, and in
"a few days we baptized Brother Joseph Fielding
"and his two amiable and intelligent sisters, for such
"they proved to be in an eminent degree. We also
"baptized many others in that neighborhood, and
"organized a branch of the church, for the people
"there drank in truth as water, and loved it as they
"loved life."

Arriving at home the apostle Parley met continued examples of the fulfillment of prophesy. Sister
Pratt is now the interesting character who takes the
foreground. He says:

"I found my wife had been healed of her seven
"years' illness from the time Brother Kimball had
"ministered unto her, and I began to realize more
"fully that every word of his blessing and prophesy
"upon my head would surely come to pass."

"After a pleasant visit with the saints," he con-

tinues, " I took my wife with me and returned again
"to Toronto, in June, 1836. The work I had com-
"menced was still spreading its influence, and the
" saints were still increasing in faith and love, in joy
"and in good works. There were visions, prophe-
"syings, speaking in tongues and healings, as well
"as the casting out of devils and unclean spirits."

The work inaugurated by Parley P. Pratt seemed
to have achieved a signal triumph almost from the
very beginning. Indeed all had come to pass according to the prophesy of Heber C. Kimball, even
not excepting the promised son and heir, who was
born March 25th, 1837. But with this event came
the mortal end of Parley's estimable wife. She
lived just long enough to accomplish her destiny;
and when the child was dressed, and she had looked
upon it and embraced it, she passed away.

The following personal description and tribute of
the poet apostle to the memory of his mate is too
full of love and distinctively Mormon ideality to be
lost:

" She was tall, of a slender frame, her face of an
" oval form, eyes large and of a dark color, her fore-
" head lofty, clear complexion, hair black, smooth
"and glossy. She was of a mild and affectionate
" disposition and full of energy, perseverance, in-
" dustry and cheerfulness, when not borne down
" with sickness. In order, neatness and refinement
" of taste and habit she might be said to excel. She
" was an affectionate and dutiful wife, an exemplary
" saint, and, through much tribulation, she has gone
" to the world of spirits to meet a glorious resur-
" rection and an immortal crown and kingdom.

" Farewell, my dear Thankful, thou wife of my
" youth, and mother of my first born ; the beginning
" of my strength—farewell. Yet a few more linger-
" ing years of sorrow, pain and toil, and I shall be
" with thee, and clasp thee to my bosom, and thou
"shalt sit down on my throne, as a queen and
" priestess unto thy Lord, arrayed in white robes of
" dazzling splendor, and decked with precious stones
" and gold, while thy queen sisters shall minister
" before thee and bless thee, and thy sons and
" daughters innumerable shall call thee blessed, and
" hold thy name in everlasting remembrance."

The interesting story which Parley tells of the
visit of the spirit of his wife to him, while he was
lying, a prisoner for the gospel's sake, in a dark,
cold and filthy dungeon in Richmond, Ray county,
Missouri, will be to the foregoing a charming sequel.
While tortured with the gloom and discomforts of
his prison, and most of all with the inactivity of his
life of constraint, and earnestly wondering, and
praying to know, if he should ever be free again to
enjoy the society of friends and to preach the gospel, the following was shown to him, which we will
tell in his own language :

" After some days of prayer and fasting," says he,
" and seeking the Lord on the subject, I one evening
" retired to my bed in my lonely chamber at an early
" hour, and while the other prisoners and the guard
" were chatting and beguiling the lonesome hours
" in the upper part of the prison, I lay in silence,
" seeking and expecting an answer to my prayer,
" when suddenly I seemed carried away in the spirit,
" and no longer sensible to outward objects with

"which I was surrounded. A heaven of peace and
"calmness pervaded my bosom ; a personage from
"the world of spirits stood before me with a smile
"of compassion in every look, and pity mingled
"with the tenderest love and sympathy in every
"expression of the countenance. A soft hand seemed
"placed within my own, and a glowing cheek was
"laid in tenderness and warmth upon mine. A
"well-known voice saluted me, which I readily recog-
"nized as that of the wife of my youth, who had
"then for nearly two years been sweetly sleeping
"where the wicked cease from troubling and the
"weary are at rest. I was made to realize that she
"was sent to commune with me, and to answer my
"question.

"Knowing this, I said to her, in a most earnest
"and inquiring tone : ' Shall I ever be at liberty again
"in this life, and enjoy the society of my family and
"the saints, and preach the gospel, as I have done ?'
"She answered definitely and unhesitatingly : ' Yes !'
"I then recollected that I had agreed to be satisfied
"with the knowledge of that one fact, but now I
"wanted more.

"Said I : ' Can you tell me how, or by what means,
"or when, I shall escape ?' She replied : ' That thing
"is not made known to me yet.' I instantly felt that
"I had gone beyond my agreement and my faith in
"asking this last question, and that I must be con-
"tented at present with the answer to the first.

"Her gentle spirit then saluted me and withdrew.
"I came to myself. The noise of the guards again
"grated on my ears, but heaven and hope were in
"my soul.

"Next morning I related the whole circumstance
"of my vision to my two fellow-prisoners, who
"rejoiced exceedingly. This may seem to some like
"an idle dream, or a romance of the imagination;
"but to me it was, and always will be, a reality, both
"as it regards what I then experienced and the ful-
"fillment afterwards."

The famous escape from Richmond jail forms one
of the romantic chapters of Mormon history, but it
belongs rather to the acts of the apostles than to
the lives of the sisters.

CHAPTER XXIII.

Among the early fruits of the Canadian mission, perhaps the name of no other lady stands more conspicuous for good works and faithful ministrations, than that of Mrs. Mary I. Horne. It will, therefore, be eminently proper to introduce her at this time to the reader, and give a brief sketch of her early career. From her own journals we quote as follows:

"I was born on the 20th of November, 1818, in "the town of Rainham, county of Kent, England. " I am the daughter of Stephen and Mary Ann Hales, "and am the eldest daughter of a large family. My "parents were honest, industrious people; and when' "very young I was taught to pray, to be honest and "truthful, to be kind to my associates, and to do "good to all around me. My father was of the "Methodist faith, but my mother attended the "Church of England. As I was religiously inclined, "I attended the Methodist Church with my father,

" who was faithful in the performance of his religious
" duties, although he never became a very enthusi-
" astic Methodist.

" In the year 1832, when I was in my thirteenth
" year, there was great excitement in the town where
" I lived, over the favorable reports that were sent
" from Van Dieman's Land, and the great induce-
" ments held out to those who would go to that
" country. My father and mother caught the spirit
" of going, and began to make preparations for
" leaving England. Before arrangements had been
" completed for us to go, however, letters were re-
" ceived from Upper Canada, picturing, in glowing
" terms, the advantages of that country. My father
" changed his mind immediately and made arrange-
" ments to emigrate to the town of York, afterwards
" called Toronto. Accordingly, on the 16th day of
" April, 1832, our family, consisting of my parents,
" five sons, myself and a younger sister, bade adieu
" to England. We had a tedious voyage of six
" weeks across the ocean, and my mother was sick
" during the entire voyage. During the passage
" across there were three deaths on board—one of
" the three being my brother Elias, whom we sor-
" rowfully consigned to a watery grave.

" Our ship anchored at Quebec in May, and after
" a tedious passage up the St. Lawrence by steamer,
" we landed in safety at the town of York, June 16th,
" thankful that we were at our journey's end. Here
" we were in a strange land, and to our dismay we
" found that the cholera was raging fearfully in that
" region ; but through all of those trying scenes the
" Lord preserved us in health.

"In the spring of 1833 we removed into the
'country about eight miles, to a place located in the
"township of York, and in the spring of 1834 I
"attended a Methodist camp-meeting in that neigh-
"borhood, where I formed the acquaintance of Mr.
"Joseph Horne, who is now my husband.

"The most of the time for the next two years I
"lived in service in the city of Toronto, going once
"in three months to visit my parents.

"On the 9th day of May, 1836, I was married to
"Mr. Horne. He owned a farm about one mile from
"my father's house, and I removed to his residence
"soon after our marriage. I now felt that I was
"settled in life; and, although I had not been used
"to farm work, I milked cows, fed pigs and chickens,
"and made myself at home in my new situation,
"seeking to make my home pleasant for my hus-
"band, and working to advance his interests.

"About the first of June, of that year, report
"came to us that a man professing to be sent of God
"to preach to the people would hold a meeting
"about a mile from our house. My husband decided
"that we should go and hear him. We accordingly
"went, and there first heard Elder Orson Pratt.
"We were very much pleased with his sermon.
"Another meeting was appointed for the following
"week, and Elder Pratt told us that business called
"him away, but his brother, Parley P. Pratt, would
"be with us and preach in his stead. I invited my
"father to go with us to hear him, and the appointed
"evening found all of his family at the 'Mormon'
"meeting. Elder Pratt told us that God was an un-
"changable being—the same yesterday, to-day, and

"forever—and taught us the gospel in its purity;
"then showed from the Bible that the gospel was
"the same in all ages of the world; but man had
"wandered from God and the true gospel, and that
"the Lord had sent an angel to Joseph Smith,
"restoring to him the pure gospel with its gifts and
"blessings. My father was so delighted with the
"sermon that he left the Methodist Church and at-
"tended the 'Mormon meetings' altogether; and in a
"short time every member of his family had received
"and obeyed the gospel. This made quite a stir
"among the Methodists. One of the class-leaders
"came to converse with us, and used every argument
"he could to convince us that Mormonism was
"false, but without avail. 'Well,' said he, finally,
"'there are none but children and fools who join
"them,' and left us to our fate. In July (1836) I
"was baptized by Orson Hyde, and ever after that
"our house was open for meetings, and became a
"home for many of the elders.

"The following from Brother Parley P. Pratt's
"autobiography, is a truthful statement of a circum-
"stance which occurred in the fall of that year, and
"to which I can bear witness, as it was of my own
"personal observation, the lady in question being a
"neighbor of ours. He says:

"'Now, there was living in that neighborhood a
"young man and his wife, named Whitney; he was
"a blacksmith by trade; their residence was perhaps
"a mile or more from Mr. Lamphere's, where I held
"my semi-monthly meetings. His wife was taken
"down very suddenly about that time with a strange
"affliction. She would be prostrated by some power

"invisible to those about her, and suffer an agony
"of distress indescribable. She often cried out that
"she could see two devils in human form, who were
"thus operating upon her, and that she could hear
"them talk ; but, as the bystanders could not see
"them, but only see the effects, they did not know
"what to think or how to understand.

"'She would have one of these spells once in
"about twenty-four hours, and when it had passed
"she would lie in bed so lame, bruised, sore, and
"helpless that she could not rise alone, or even sit
"up, for some weeks. All this time she had to have
"watchers both night and day, and sometimes four
"and five at a time, insomuch that the neighbors
"were worn out and weary with watching. Mr.
"Whitney sent word for me two or three times, or
"left word for me to call next time I visited the neigh-
"borhood. This, however, I had neglected to do,
"owing to the extreme pressure of labors upon me
"in so large a circuit of meetings—indeed I had not
"a moment to spare. At last, as I came round on
"the circuit again, the woman, who had often re-
"quested to see the man of God, that he might
"minister to her relief, declared she would see him
"anyhow, for she knew she could be healed if she
"could but get sight of him. In her agony she
"sprang from her bed, cleared herself from her
"frightened husband and others, who were trying to
"hold her, and ran for Mr. Lamphere's, where I was
"then holding meeting. At first, to use her own
"words, she felt very weak, and nearly fainted, but
"her strength came to her, and increased at every step
"till she reached the meeting. Her friends were all

" astonished, and in alarm, lest she should die in the
" attempt, tried to pursue her, and they several times
" laid hold of her and tried to force or persuade her
" back. ' No,' said she, ' let me see the man of God;
" I can but die, and I cannot endure such affliction
" any longer.' On she came, until at last they gave
" up, and said, ' Let her go, perhaps it will be accord-
" ing to her faith.' So she came, and when the thing
" was explained the eyes of the whole multitude
" were upon her. I ceased to preach, and, stepping
" to her in the presence of the whole meeting, I laid
" my hands upon her and said, ' Sister, be of good
" cheer, thy sins are forgiven, thy faith hath made
" thee whole; and, in the name of Jesus Christ, I
" rebuke the devils and unclean spirits, and com-
" mand them to trouble thee no more.' She returned
" home well, went about her housekeeping, and
" remained well from that time forth.'

" In the latter part of the summer of 1837," continues Mrs. Horne, " I had the great pleasure of
" being introduced to, and entertaining, the beloved
" prophet, Joseph Smith, with Sidney Rigdon and
" T. B. Marsh. I said to myself, ' O Lord, I thank
" thee for granting the desire of my girlish heart, in
" permitting me to associate with prophets and apos-
" tles.' On shaking hands with Joseph Smith, I
" received the holy spirit in such great abundance
" that I felt it thrill my whole system, from the
" crown of my head to the soles of my feet. I
" thought I had never beheld so lovely a counte-
" nance. Nobility and goodness were in every
" feature.

" The saints in Kirtland removed in the following

"spring to Missouri. We started from Canada in
"March, 1838, with a small company of saints. The
"roads were very bad, as the frost was coming out
"of the ground, consequently I had to drive the
"team during a great portion of the journey, while
"my husband walked.

"On arriving at Huntsville, one hundred miles
"from Far West, we found several families of saints,
"and tarried a short time with them. There I was in-
"troduced to the parents of the prophet, and also to
"his cousin, George A. Smith. At a meeting held
"in that place I received a patriarchal blessing from
"Joseph Smith, Sr. He told me that I had to pass
"through a great deal of sickness, sorrow and tribu-
"lation, but 'the Lord will bring you through six
"troubles, and in the seventh he will not leave you;'
"all of which has verily been fulfilled."

Mrs. Horne, with her husband and family, reached
Far West in August of that year, and received their
full share of the privations incident to the settlement of that city, and also a full share of exposure,
sickness and peril incident to the expulsion of the
saints from Missouri. Finally thereafter they gathered to Nauvoo; and there for the present let us
leave them—promising the reader that Mrs. Horne
shall again come to the front when we treat of the
wonderful missionary efforts of the Mormon women
in Utah.

CHAPTER XXIV.

MORMONISM CARRIED TO GREAT BRITAIN—"TRUTH
WILL PREVAIL"—THE REV. MR. FIELDING—FIRST
BAPTISM IN ENGLAND—FIRST WOMAN BAPTIZED—
STORY OF MISS JEANNETTA RICHARDS — FIRST
BRANCH OF THE CHURCH IN FOREIGN LANDS
ORGANIZED AT THE HOUSE OF ANN DAWSON—
FIRST CHILD BORN INTO THE CHURCH IN ENG-
LAND — ROMANTIC SEQUEL — VILATE KIMBALL
AGAIN.

The voice of prophesy was no longer hushed;
the heavens were no longer sealed; the Almighty
really spoke to these prophets and apostles of the
latter days; their words were strangely, sometimes
romantically, fulfilled; the genius of Mormonism
was alike potent at home and abroad.

"Thou shalt go to Upper Canada, even to the
"city of Toronto, and there thou shalt find a people
"prepared for the fullness of the gospel, and they
"shall receive thee;" the prophet Heber had oracled
over the head of a fellow laborer, "and from the
"things growing out of this mission shall the full-
"ness of the gospel spread into England and cause
"a great work to be done in that land."

One part of this prophesy the reader has seen

exactly fulfilled in the mission of Parley P. Pratt to Canada, enlivened with some very interesting episodes. It falls upon Heber himself—the father of the British mission—to fulfill, with the brethren who accompany him, the supreme part of the prophesy referring to Great Britain.

It will be remembered from the sketch of Vilate Kimball, that Mary Fielding gave to Heber five dollars to help him on his journey, and that she with her sister and her sister's husband, Elder R. B. Thompson, were on their way to Canada to engage in the second mission to that Province, while Heber, Orson Hyde, Willard Richards, and Joseph Fielding, with several other brethren from Canada, pursued their course to England.

It was July 1st, 1837, when these elders embarked on board the ship *Garrick*, bound for Liverpool, which they reached on the 20th of the same month.

On their arrival in that foreign land the three principal elders—Heber, Orson and Willard—had not as much as one farthing in their possession, yet were they destined to accomplish marvelous results ere their return to America.

Having remained two days in Liverpool, these elders were directed by the spirit to go to Preston, a flourishing English town in Lancashire, to plant the standard of their Church.

It generally came to pass that some singular incident occurred in all of the initial movements of these elders, opening their way before them, or omening their success. So now, the people of Preston were celebrating a grand national occasion. Queen Victoria, a few days previously (July 17th), had ascended the throne. A fitting event this to notice in a woman's book. The "Woman's Age" dawned, not only upon England, but, it would seem, upon all of the civilized world.

A general election was being held throughout the realm in consequence of the ascension of the Queen. The populace were parading the streets of Preston, bands were playing, and flags flying.

In the midst of this universal joy the elders alighted from the coach, and just at that moment a flag was unfurled over their heads, from the hotel, bearing this motto in gold letters: " Truth is mighty "and will prevail !" It was as a prophesy to these elders, as if to welcome their coming, and they lifted up their voices and shouted, "Glory be to "God, truth will prevail !" By the way, this flag proclaimed the rise of the temperance movement in England.

That night Heber and his compeers were entertained by the Rev. James Fielding, the brother of the sisters Fielding. Already was the other half of the prophesy uttered over the head of Parley being fulfilled—that the gospel should spread from Canada into England, "and cause a great work to be done " in that land."

Previously to this the Rev. James Fielding had received letters from his brother Joseph, and his sisters, who had, as we have seen, embraced Mormonism in Canada ; and these letters, burdened with the tidings of the advent of the prophet of America and the administration of angels in our own times, he read to his congregation. He also exhorted his flock to pray fervently that the Lord would send over to

England his apostles, and solemnly adjured them to receive their message when they should come bearing their glad tidings. Thus in England, as in Canada, a people were " prepared " according to the prophesy.

On Sunday morning, the day after their arrival in Preston, the elders went to Vauxhall Chapel to hear the Rev. James Fielding preach. At the close of his discourse he gave out that in the afternoon and evening meetings ministers from America would preach in his chapel.

The news spread rapidly in the town, and in a few hours quite a sensation was abroad among the inhabitants, who flocked to the chapel at the appointed times, some out of curiosity, others from a genuine interest. Both in the afternoon and evening the chapel was crowded, and the apostles preached their opening sermons, Heber C. Kimball being the first of them who bore his testimony to " Mormonism " in foreign lands.

. On the following Wednesday Vauxhall Chapel was again crowded, when Elder Orson Hyde preached, and Willard Richards bore testimony; and the Holy Ghost, we are told, powerfully accompanied the word on the occasion.

Only a few days had passed since the elders arrived on the shores of Great Britain, yet " a " number believed and began to praise God and " rejoice exceedingly."

The Rev. Mr. Fielding, however, saw now the consequence of all this. He was in danger of losing his entire flock. Many were resolving to be baptized into the Church of Latter-day Saints. A continuation of this result for a few weeks signified the entire dissolution of his own church. He was in consternation at the prospect. Trembling, it is said, as if suddenly stricken with the palsy, he presented himself before the elders on the morning appointed for the baptism of a number of his former disciples, and forbade the baptism. Of course this was in vain. He had met the inevitable.

On Sunday, July 30th, just one month from the time the elders embarked at New York, the eventful scene occurred in Preston, of the baptism in the River Ribble of the nine first converts to Mormonism in foreign lands. They were

George D. Watt,	Ann Elizabeth Walmesley,
Thomas Walmesley,	George Wate,
Miles Hodgen,	Mary Ann Brown,
Henry Billsburg,	——— Miller,

Ann Dawson.

A public ceremony of baptism in the open air was such a novel event in England at that time, when religious innovations were so rare, that seven or eight thousand persons assembled on the banks of the river to witness the scene. It is said that this was the first time baptism by immersion was ever thus administered in England, though at a later period several sects of Baptists arose who immersed openly in the rivers and for the remission of sins. Such scenes were picturesque, and some of the " new lights" seem to have delighted in them for their religious sensation, just as the Methodists did in their camp meetings.

The first woman whose name is recorded in the list of the baptized of the Mormon Church in

England is Sister Ann Elizabeth Walmesley; and
her case presents the first miracle of the Church in
foreign lands. Here is the incident as related by
Heber C. Kimball:

"I had visited Thomas Walmesley, whose wife
"was sick of the consumption, and had been so for
"several years. She was reduced to skin and bone—
"a mere skeleton—and was given up by the doctors
"to die. I preached the gospel to her, and promised
"her in the name of the Lord Jesus Christ that if she
"would believe, repent and be baptized, she should
"be healed of her sickness. She was carried to the
"water, and after her baptism began to mend, and
"at her confirmation she was blessed and her dis-
"ease rebuked, when she immediately recovered,
"and in less than one week after, she was attending
"to her household duties."

This incident will be the more interesting to the
reader from the fact that to-day (forty years after
the miracle) Sister Walmesley is living at Bloom-
ington, Bear Lake Valley, Oneida county, Idaho.

Next came quite an evangelical episode, introducing, with a touch of romance, Miss Jennetta
Richards.

This young lady was the daughter of a minister,
of the independent order, who resided at Walkerfold, about fifteen miles from Preston. She was not
only personally interesting and intelligent, but, from
the influence she possessed over her father and his
congregation, coupled with the fact that the most
classical of the apostles "fell in love" with her, she
appears to have been a maiden of considerable
character. She was a proper person to be the

heroine of the British mission, and her conversion was very important in its results, as will be seen in the following incidents, related by Heber:

It was several days after the public baptism in Preston. "Miss Jennetta Richards," says the apos-tle, "came to the house of Thomas Walmesley, with "whom she was acquainted. Calling in to see them "at the time she was there, I was introduced to her, "and we immediately entered into conversation on "the subject of the gospel. I found her very intel-"ligent. She seemed very desirous to hear the "things I had to teach and to understand the "doctrines of the gospel. I informed her of my "appointment to preach that evening, and invited "her to attend. She did so; and likewise the even-"ing following. After attending these two services "she was fully convinced of the truth.

"Friday morning, 4th, she sent for me, desiring "to be baptized, which request I cheerfully complied "with, in the River Ribble, and confirmed her at "the water side, Elder Hyde assisting. This was "the first confirmation in England. The following "day she started for home, and wept as she was "about to leave us. I said to her, 'Sister, be of "good cheer, for the Lord will soften the heart of "thy father, that I will yet have the privilege of "preaching in his chapel, and it shall result in a "great opening to preach the gospel in that region.' "I exhorted her to pray and be humble. She re-"quested me to pray for her, and gave me some "encouragement to expect that her father would "open his chapel for me to preach in. I then has-"tened to my brethren, told them of the circum-

"stances and the result of my visit with the young
"lady, and called upon them to unite with me in
"prayer that the Lord would soften the heart of her
"father, that he might be induced to open his chapel
"for us to preach in."

On the third Sabbath after the arrival of the
elders in England, they met at the house of Sister
Ann Dawson, when twenty-seven members were
confirmed and the first branch of the Church was
organized in foreign lands. In the forepart of the
ensuing week Heber received a letter from Miss
Jennetta Richards, and an invitation from her father
to come to Walkerfold and preach in his chapel.
The invitation was accepted, and Heber met with
great success in laying the gospel before the congregation of Mr. Richards; so successful was he
indeed that the reverend gentleman was forced to
shut his chapel doors in order to prevent a complete
stampede of his flock.

This evangelical success is crowned with an interesting incident between Jennetta and Elder Willard
Richards. Willard, who had been on a mission to
Bedford early in January, 1838, visited his brethren
at Preston; and then, he says:

" I took a tour through the branches, and preached.
" While walking in Thornly I plucked a snowdrop,
"far through the hedge, and carried it to James
" Mercer's and hung it up in his kitchen. Soon
" after Jennetta Richards came into the room, and I
" walked with her and Alice Parker to Ribchester,
" and attended meeting with Brothers Kimball and
" Hyde, at Brother Clark's.

" While walking with these sisters, I remarked,

" ' Richards is a good name ; I never want to change
" it ; do you, Jennetta ?' ' No ; I do not,' was her
" reply, 'and I think I never will.'".

The following note in his diary of the same year,
furnishes the sequel :

" September 24, 1839, I married Jennetta Richards,
" daughter of the Rev. John Richards, independent
" minister at Walkerfold, Chaidgley, Lancashire.
" Most truly do I praise my Heavenly Father for
" his great kindness in providing me a partner ac-
" cording to his promise. I receive her from the
" Lord, and hold her at his disposal. I pray that
" he may bless us forever. Amen ! "

Passing from Sister Jennetta Richards, we now
introduce the first child born in the British mission.
It is a female child. She is also the first infant
blessed in England; and the incidents of her birth
and blessing are both pretty and novel, especially
when coupled with the sequel of her womanhood.
Heber thus tells the initial part of her story :

" She was the daughter of James and Nancy
" Smithies, formerly Nancy Knowles. After she
" was born her parents wanted to take her to the
" church to be sprinkled, or christened, as they call
" it. I used every kind of persuasion to convince
" them of their folly—it being contrary to the Scrip-
" tures and the will of God; the parents wept bit-
" terly, and it seemed as though I could not prevail
" on them to omit it. I wanted to know of them
" why they were so tenacious. The answer was, ' If
" she dies she cannot have a burial in the church-
" yard.' I said to them, ' Brother and Sister Smithies,
" I say unto you in the name of Israel's God, she

"shall not die on this land, for she shall live until
"she becomes a mother in Israel, and I say it in the
"name of Jesus Christ, and by virtue of the holy
"priesthood vested in me.' That silenced them, and
"when she was two weeks old they presented the
"child to me; I took it in my arms and blessed it,
"that it should live to become a mother in Israel.
"She was the first child blessed in that country, and
"the first born unto them."

The child lived, and fulfilled the prophesy that
she should become a "mother in Israel." Her birth
was destined to glorify Heber's own kingdom, for
she, twenty years afterwards, became his last wife,
and is now the mother of four of his children.

The gospel spread rapidly during the first mission
of the elders in England. In eight months two
thousand were baptized, and the "signs followed the
"believers." We shall meet some of the British
converts hereafter, and read the testimonies of the
sisters concerning the great spiritual work of Mormonism in their native land.

Heber, and Orson Hyde, returned to America,
leaving the British mission in charge of Joseph
Fielding, with Willard Richards and William Clayton as councilors. Here the apostolic thread connects with the wife and family of Heber, who have
been left to the care of Providence and the brotherly and sisterly love of the saints during this
immortal mission to Great Britain. His daughter
Helen, in her journal, says:

"In the absence of my father the Lord was true
"to his promise. My father's prayer, that he had
"made upon the heads of his wife and little ones

"whom he had left poor and destitute, was answered.
"Kind friends came forward to cheer and comfort
"them, and administer to their wants.

"Soon after my father's return to Kirtland he
"commenced making preparations to move his
"family to Missouri, where Brother Joseph Smith
"and a majority of the church authorities and nearly
"all of the members had gone. About the first of
"July he commenced the journey with his family,
"accompanied by Brother Orson Hyde and others,
"and arrived in Far West on the 25th of July, when
"he had a happy meeting with Joseph, Hyrum,
"Sidney, and others of the twelve, and numbers of
"his friends and brethren, some of whom were
"affected to tears when they took him by the hand.
"During our journey from Kirtland, the weather
"being very warm, we suffered very much, and were
"much reduced by sickness. Father continued quite
"feeble for a considerable length of time. Joseph
"requested him to preach to the saints, saying, 'It
"will revive their spirits and do them good if you
"will give them a history of your mission;' which he
"did, although he was scarcely able to stand. It
"cheered their hearts and many of the elders were
"stirred up to diligence.

"Soon after our arrival Bishop Partridge gave
"father a lot, and also sufficient timber to build a
"house. While it was being erected we lived in a
"place eight by eleven feet and four feet high at the
"eaves, which had been built for a cow. The breth-
"ren were remarkably kind, and contributed to our
"necessities. Brother Charles Hubbard made my
"father a present of forty acres of land; another

"brother gave him a cow. But about the last of
"August, after he had labored hard and nearly fin-
"ished his house, he was obliged to abandon it to
"the mob, who again commenced to persecute the
"saints."

The history of those persecutions, and the exodus
of the saints, is already sufficiently told. Suffice it
to say that Sister Vilate nobly bore her part in those
trying scenes, while Heber, with Brigham and the
rest of the twelve, kept their covenant—never to
rest a moment until the last faithful saint was delivered from that State, and the feet of the whole
people planted firmly, in peace and safety, in a new
gathering place.

CHAPTER XXV.

SKETCH OF THE SISTERS MARY AND MERCY R. FIELD-
ING—THE FIELDINGS A SEMI-APOSTOLIC FAMILY—
THEIR IMPORTANT INSTRUMENTALITY IN OPENING
THE BRITISH MISSION—MARY FIELDING MARRIES
HYRUM SMITH — HER TRIALS AND SUFFERINGS
WHILE HER HUSBAND IS IN PRISON—TESTIMONY
OF HER SISTER MERCY—MARY'S LETTER TO HER
BROTHER IN ENGLAND.

Already has the name of Mary Fielding become
quite historical to the reader, but she is now to be
introduced in her still more representative character
as wife of the patriarch and martyr Hyrum, and as
mother of the apostle Joseph F. Smith.

This much-respected lady was born July 21st,
1801, at Honidon, Bedfordshire, England. She was
the daughter of John and Rachel Fielding, and was
the eldest of the sisters whom the reader has met
somewhat prominently in an apostolic incident in
Canada, out of which much of the early history of
the British mission very directly grew.

Mary was of good family, well educated, and
piously raised, being originally a Methodist, and a
devoted admirer of the character of John Wesley.
Indeed the family of the Fieldings and their con-

nections were semi-apostolic even before their iden-
tification with the Church of Latter-day Saints.

In 1834 Mary emigrated to Canada. Here she
joined her youngest brother, Joseph, and her sister,
Mercy Rachel (born in England in 1807), who had
preceded her to America in 1832. As we have seen,
this brother and his two sisters were living near
Toronto, Upper Canada, at the time when Parley P.
Pratt arrived there on his mission, and they immediately embraced the faith. This was in May, 1836.

In the following spring the Fieldings gathered to
Kirtland. Soon the youngest of the sisters, Mercy
Rachel, was married by the prophet to Elder Robert
B. Thompson, one of the literati of the Church,
who was appointed on a mission to Canada with his
wife. At the same time Joseph Fielding was appointed on mission to England, to assist the apostles
in that land. But Mary remained in Kirtland, and
on the 24th of December, 1837, she was married to
Hyrum Smith.

Here something deserves to be told of the Fielding family in amplification of the incidental men-
tionings already made.

The Rev. James Fielding (of Preston, England),
Mary's brother, was quite a religious reformer, and
of sufficient ministerial reputation and force to
become the founder and head of a Congregational
Methodist Church. Originally he was a minister of
the regular body of that powerful sect, but becoming
convinced that modern Methodists had departed
from their primitive faith, and that their church no
longer enjoyed the Holy Ghost and its gifts, which
measurably attended their illustrious founder and

his early disciples, the Rev. Mr. Fielding inaugurated
a religious reform in the direction intimated. It
was an attempt to revive in his ministerial sphere
the spiritual power of the Wesleyan movement;
nor did he stop at this, but sought to convince his
disciples of the necessity of "contending earnestly
for the faith once delivered to the saints."

Other branches of the family also became prominent in the religious reforms of England that arose
about the time of the establishing of the Church of
Latter-day Saints in America. One of the Fielding
sisters married no less a personage than the Rev.
Timothy R. Matthews, who figured nearly as con-
spicuously as the Rev. James Fielding in the early
history of the British mission. This Rev. Timothy
Matthews was at first minister of the Church of England, and is said to have been a very able and learned
man. With the famous Robert Aitken, whom he
called his "son," he attempted reformation even in
the established Church; or rather, these innovative
divines denounced the "apostasy" of that Church,
and prosecuted a semi-apostolic mission. It was
eminently successful, Robert Aitken and himself
raising up large congregations of disciples in Preston, Liverpool, Bedford, Northampton and London.
These disciples were popularly called Aitkenites
and Matthewites. Quite relevant is all this to the
history of the Latter-day Saints in England, for the
congregations of the Rev. James Fielding, Rev.
Timothy R. Matthews, and Rev. John Richards
(father of Jennetta), gave to the apostles their first
disciples abroad, and these ministers themselves were
their instruments in establishing the British mission.

But the name of Fielding, after those of the apostles, was principal in accomplishing these results. The sisters Mary and Mercy, with Joseph, half converted by their letters, the congregation of their reverend brother in Preston, before the advent there of the apostles. In their Brother James' chapel the first apostolic sermon in foreign lands was preached by Heber C. Kimball, and it was one of the Fielding sisters (Mrs. Watson), who gave to the elders the first money for the "gospel's sake" donated to the church abroad.

But to return to Kirtland. Hyrum Smith was a widower at the date of Mary Fielding's arrival there from Canada. And this means that his *only* wife was dead; for polygamy was unknown in the Church at that time. It will therefore, be seen how pertinent is the often-repeated remark of the sisters that the saints were not driven and persecuted because of polygamy, but because of their belief in "new and continued revelation." In becoming Hyrum's wife, Mary assumed the responsible situation of step-mother to his five children, the task of which she performed with unwavering fidelity, taking care of them for years after the martyrdom of her husband, and taking the place of both father and mother to them in the exodus of the Church to the Rocky Mountains. And Mary was well trained for this latter task during her husband's lifetime, besides being matured in years and character before her marriage.

From Kirtland, with her husband and family, she removed to Far West, Mo., where, on the first day of November, 1838, her husband and his brother, the prophet, with others, were betrayed by the Mormon Colonel Hinkle into the hands of the armed mob under General Clark, in the execution of Gov. Boggs' exterminating order. On the following day Hyrum was marched, at the point of the bayonet, to his house, by a strong guard, who with hideous oaths and threats commanded Mary to take her last farewell of her husband, for, " His die was cast, and his doom was sealed," and she need never think she would see him again; allowing her only a moment, as it were, for that terrible parting, and to provide a change of clothes for the final separation. In the then critical condition of her health this heart-rending scene came nigh ending her life; but the natural vigor of her mind sustained her in the terrible trial. Twelve days afterwards she gave birth to her first born, a son; but she remained prostrate on a bed of affliction and suffering for several months. In January, 1839, she was taken in a wagon, with her infant, on her sick bed, to Liberty, Clay county, Mo., where she was granted the privilege of visiting her husband in jail, where he was confined by the mob, without trial or conviction, because, forsooth, he was a " Mormon."

While in this condition of health, with her husband immured in a dungeon and surrounded by fiends in human form, thirsting for his life, a company of armed men, led by the notorious Methodist priest, Bogart, entered her poor abode and searched it, breaking open a trunk and carrying away papers and valuables belonging to her husband. In this helpless condition also she was forced from what shelter she had, in the worst season of the year, to cross the bleak prairies of Missouri, expelled from the State, to seek protection among strangers in the more hospitable State of Illinois. Here is the story that her sister Mercy tells of those days and scenes:

"In 1838 I traveled in company with Hyrum "Smith and family to Far West. To describe in a "brief sketch the scenes I witnessed and the suffer- "ings I endured would be impossible. An incident "or two, however, I will relate.

"My husband, with many of the brethren, being "threatened and pursued by a mob, fled into the "wilderness in November, leaving me with an infant "not five months old. Three months of distressing "suspense I endured before I could get any intelli- "gence from him, during which time I staid with my "sister, wife of Hyrum Smith, who, having given "birth to a son while her husband was in prison, on "the 13th of November took a severe cold and was "unable to attend to her domestic duties for four "months. This caused much of the care of her "family, which was very large, to fall on me. Mobs "were continually threatening to massacre the in- "habitants of the city, and at times I feared to lay "my babe down lest they should slay me and leave "it to suffer worse than immediate death. About "the 1st of February, 1839, by the request of her "husband, my sister was placed on a bed in a wagon "and taken a journey of forty miles, to visit him in "the prison. Her infant son, Joseph F., being then "but about eleven weeks old, I had to accompany "her, taking my own babe, then near eight months "old. The weather was extremely cold, and we "suffered much on the journey. This circumstance

"I always reflect upon with peculiar pleasure, not-
"withstanding the extreme anxiety I endured from
"having the care of my sick sister and the two
"babes. The remembrance of having had the honor
"of spending a night in prison, in company with the
"prophet and patriarch, produces a feeling I cannot
"express.

"Shortly after our return to Far West we had to
"abandon our homes and start, in lumber wagons,
"for Illinois; my sister being again placed on a bed,
"in an afflicted state. This was about the middle
"of February, and the weather was extremely cold.
"I still had the care of both babes. We arrived at
"Quincy about the end of the month."

The following interesting letter, from Mary to
her brother Joseph in England, will fitly close for
the present the sketch of these sisters:

"COMMERCE, Ill., North America,
"June, 1839.

"MY VERY DEAR BROTHER:

"As the elders are expecting shortly to take their
leave of us again to preach the gospel in my native
land, I feel as though I would not let the opportunity of writing you pass unimproved. I believe it will
give you pleasure to hear from us by our own hand;
notwithstanding you will see the brethren face to
face, and have an opportunity of hearing all particulars respecting us and our families.

"As it respects myself, it is now so long since I
wrote to you, and so many important things have
transpired, and so great have been my affliction,
etc., that I know not where to begin; but I can say,
hitherto has the Lord preserved me, and I am still
among the living to praise him, as I do to-day. I

have, to be sure, been called to drink deep of the
bitter cup; but you know, my beloved brother,
this makes the sweet sweeter.

" You have, I suppose, heard of the imprisonment
of my dear husband, with his brother Joseph, Elder
Rigdon, and others, who were kept from us nearly
six months; and I suppose no one felt the painful
effects of their confinement more than myself.   I
was left in a way that called for the exercise of all
the courage and grace I possessed.   My husband
was taken from me by an armed force, at a time
when I needed, in a particular manner, the kindest
care and attention of such a friend, instead of which,
the care of a large family was suddenly and unexpectedly left upon myself, and, in a few days after,
my dear little Joseph F. was added to the number.
Shortly after his birth I took a severe cold, which
brought on chills and fever; this, together with the
anxiety of mind I had to endure, threatened to
bring me to the gates of death.   I was at least four
months entirely unable to take any care either of
myself or child; but the Lord was merciful in so
ordering things that my dear sister could be with me.
Her child was five months old when mine was born;
so she had strength given her to nurse them both.

" You will also have heard of our being driven,
as a people, from the State, and from our homes;
this happened during my sickness, and I had to be
removed more than two hundred miles, chiefly on
my bed.   I suffered much on my journey; but in
three or four weeks after we arrived in Illinois, I
began to amend, and my health is now as good as
ever.   It is now little more than a month since the
Lord, in his marvelous power, returned my dear
husband, with the rest of the brethren, to their
families, in tolerable health.   We are now living in
Commerce, on the bank of the great Mississippi
river.   The situation is very pleasant; you would
be much pleased to see it.   How long we may be

permitted to enjoy it I know not; but the Lord knows what is best for us. I feel but little concerned about where I am, if I can keep my mind staid upon God; for, you know in this there is perfect peace. I believe the Lord is overruling all things for our good. I suppose our enemies look upon us with astonishment and disappointment.

"I greatly desire to see you, and I think you would be pleased to see our little ones; will you pray for us, that we may have grace to train them up in the way they should go, so that they may be a blessing to us and the world? I have a hope that our brothers and sisters will also embrace the fullness of the gospel, and come into the new and everlasting covenant; I trust their prejudices will give way to the power of truth. I would gladly have them with us here, even though they might have to endure all kind of tribulation and affliction with us and the rest of the children of God, in these last days, so that they might share in the glories of the celestial kingdom. As to myself, I can truly say, that I would not give up the prospect of the latter-day glory for all that glitters in this world. O, my dear brother, I must tell you, for your comfort, that my hope is full, and it is a glorious hope; and though I have been left for near six months in widowhood, in the time of great affliction, and was called to take, joyfully or otherwise, the spoiling of almost all our goods, in the absence of my husband, and all unlawfully, just for the gospel's sake (for the judge himself declared that he was kept in prison for no other reason than because he was a friend to his brother), yet I do not feel in the least discouraged; no, though my sister and I are here together in a strange land, we have been enabled to rejoice, in the midst of our privations and persecutions, that we were counted worthy to suffer these things, so that we may, with the ancient saints who suffered in like manner, inherit the same glorious reward. If it had not been for this hope, I should have sunk before this ; but, blessed be the God and rock of my salvation, here I am, and am perfectly satisfied and happy, having not the smallest desire to go one step backward.

" Your last letter to Elder Kimball gave us great pleasure ; we thank you for your expression of kindness, and pray God to bless you according to your desires for us.

" The more I see of the dealings of our Heavenly Father with us as a people, the more I am constrained to rejoice that I was ever made acquainted with the everlasting covenant. O may the Lord keep me faithful till my change comes ! O, my dear brother, why is it that our friends should stand out against the truth, and look on those that would show it to them as enemies ? The work here is prospering much ; several men of respectability and intelligence, who have been acquainted with all our difficulties, are coming into the work.

" My husband joins me in love to you. I remain, my dear brother and sister, your affectionate sister,

"MARY SMITH."

CHAPTER XXVI.

THE QUORUM OF THE APOSTLES GO ON MISSION TO
ENGLAND—THEIR LANDING IN GREAT BRITAIN—
THEY HOLD A CONFERENCE—A HOLIDAY FESTI-
VAL—MOTHER MOON AND FAMILY—SUMMARY OF
A YEAR'S LABORS — CROWNING PERIOD OF THE
BRITISH MISSION.

Scarcely had the saints made their exodus from
Missouri—while many of them were still domiciled
in tents on the banks of the Mississippi, and Nauvoo
could only boast of a few rude houses to prophesy
the glory of a "second Zion"—ere nine of the quorum of the apostles were abroad, working their
missionary wonders in foreign lands. From that
period to the present (1877), the history of the
Latter-day Church, with its emigrations, has quite
one-half belonged to the European mission, which
has given to America one hundred thousand emigrants.

Early in the year 1840 (January 11th), apostles
Wilford Woodruff and John Taylor, with Elder
Theodore Turley, landed on the shores of England.
They chose their several fields of labor and soon
were actively engaged in the ministry.

On the 19th of March of the same year Brigham

Young, Heber C. Kimball, George A. Smith, Parley
P. Pratt, Orson Pratt, and Reuben Hedlock sailed
from New York on board the *Patrick Henry*. A
number of the saints came down to the wharf to
bid them farewell. When the elders got into the
small-boat to go out to the ship, the saints on shore
sang " The Gallant Ship is Under Way," etc., in
which song the elders joined until their voices were
separated by the distance.

Liverpool was reached by these apostles on the
6th of April. It was the anniversary of the organization of the Church, just ten years before. The
next day they found Elder Taylor and John Moon,
with about thirty saints who had just received the
work in that place, and on the day following they
went to Preston by railroad.

In Preston, the cradle of the British mission, the
apostles were met by a multitude of saints, who
rejoiced exceedingly at the event of the arrival of
the twelve in that land.

Willard Richards immediately hastened to Preston and gave an account of the churches in the
British isles, over which he had been presiding
during the interval from the return of Heber C.
Kimball and Orson Hyde to America. The president of the twelve at once commenced to grapple
with the work in foreign lands, convened a conference, and wrote to Wilford Woodruff to attend.

It was on the 14th of April, 1840, that the first
council of the twelve apostles, in a foreign land,
was held at Preston. There were present Brigham
Young, Heber C. Kimball, Parley P Pratt, Orson
Pratt, John Taylor, Wilford Woodruff, and George

A. Smith. These proceeded to ordain Willard Richards to their quorum, and then Brigham Young was chosen, by a unanimous vote, the standing president of the twelve.

Then followed, during the next two days, " A " General Conference of the Church of Jesus Christ " of Latter-day Saints," held in the Temperance Hall at Preston, with Heber C. Kimball presiding, and William Clayton clerk. There were represented at this time, one thousand six hundred and seventy-one members, thirty-four elders, fifty-two priests, thirty-eight teachers, and eight deacons.

The conference over, the apostles kept the old Christian holiday of Good Friday, to regale their spirits after their long journey, which had so quickly followed the many vicissitudes of persecution in their native land, and before separating again on their arduous mission.

The place chosen to spend their holiday was the village of Penwortham, two miles from Preston. That day Mother Moon made a feast for the apostles at her house. From her treasury of "fat things" she brought forth a bottle of wine which she had kept for forty years. This the elders blessed and then partook of it. That bottle of wine is spoken of to this day. The family of Mother Moon has also a history. Here is their page, from Heber's journal of his first mission abroad:

" Having an appointment to preach in the village " of Wrightington, while on the way I stopped at " the house of Brother Francis Moon, when I was " informed that the family of Matthias Moon had " sent a request by him for me to visit them, that

"they might have the privilege of conversing with
"me on the subject of the gospel. Accordingly
"Brother Amos Fielding and I paid them a visit
"that evening. We were very kindly received by
"the family, and had considerable conversation on
"the subject of my mission to England, and the
"great work of the Lord in the last days. They
"listened with attention to my statements, but at
"the same time they appeared to be prejudiced
"against them. We remained in conversation until
"a late hour, and then returned home. On our way
"Brother Fielding observed that he thought our
"visit had been in vain, as the family seemed to have
"considerable prejudice. I answered, be not faith-
"less but believing; we shall yet see great effects
"from this visit, for I know that some of the family
"have received the testimony, and will shortly
"manifest the same; at which remark he seemed
"surprised.

"The next morning I continued my journey to
"Wrightington and Hunter's Hill. After spending
"two or three days in that vicinity, preaching, I bap-
"tized seven of the family of Benson, and others,
"and organized a branch.

"I returned by the way of Brother Fielding's, with
"whom I again tarried for the night. The next
"morning I started for Preston, but when I got
"opposite the lane leading to Mr. Moon's, I was
"forcibly led by the spirit of the Lord to call and
"see them again. I therefore directed my steps to
"the house. On my arrival I knocked at the door.
"Mrs. Moon exclaimed: 'Come in! come in! You
"are welcome here! I and the lasses (meaning her

" daughters) have just been calling on the Lord, and
" praying that he would send you this way.' She
" then informed me of her state of mind since I was
" there, and said she at first rejected my testimony,
" and endeavored to think lightly on the things I
" had advanced, but on trying to pray, the heavens
" seemed like brass over her head, and it was like
" iron under her feet. She did not know what was
" the matter, saying, ' Certainly the man has not be-
" witched me, has he ?' And upon inquiring she
" found it was the same with the lasses. They then
" began to reflect on the things I told them, and
" thinking it possible that I had told them the truth,
" they resolved to lay the case before the Lord, and
" beseech him to give them a testimony concerning
" the things I had testified of. She then observed
" that as soon as they did so light broke in upon
" their minds ; they were convinced that I was a
" messenger of salvation ; that it was the work of
" the Lord, and they had resolved to obey the gos-
" pel. That evening I baptized Mr. Moon and his
" wife, and four of his daughters. * * * I visited
" Mr. Moon again, and baptized the remainder of
" his family, consisting of thirteen souls, the youngest
" of whom was over twenty years of age. They
" received the gospel as little children, and rejoiced
" exceedingly in its blessings. The sons were very
" good musicians and the daughters excellent sing-
" ers. When they united their instruments and
" voices in the songs of Zion the effect was truly
" transporting. Before I left England there were
" about thirty of that family and connections bap-
" tized, five of whom—Hugh, John, Francis, William

"and Thomas Moon—were ordained to be fellow-
"laborers with us in the vineyard, and I left them
" rejoicing in the truths they had embraced."

After their short rest in Preston, refreshed and
inspired by the communion of so many of their
quorum, these apostles rose like giants to their
work. Brigham Young and Willard Richards went
with Wilford Woodruff into Herefordshire, where
Brigham obtained money to publish the Book of
Mormon; Heber C. Kimball visited the disciples
whom he had brought into the Church during his
first mission; Orson Pratt went into Scotland,
George A. Smith went into Staffordshire, John
Taylor continued his labors at Liverpool, where he
raised up a conference, and Parley P. Pratt repaired
to Manchester to publish the *Millennial Star*.

A year passed. Here is the summary of its history, from Brigham Young's journal:

" It was with a heart full of thanksgiving and
" gratitude to God, my Heavenly Father, that I
" reflected upon his dealings with me and my breth-
" ren of the twelve during the past year of my life,
" which was spent in England. It truly seems a
" miracle to look upon the contrast between our
" landing and departing from Liverpool. We landed
" in the spring of 1840, as strangers in a strange
" land, and penniless, but through the mercy of God
" we have gained many friends, established churches
" in almost every noted town and city of Great
" Britain, baptized between seven and eight thou-
" sand souls, printed five thousand Books of Mor-
" mon, three thousand hymn-books, two thousand
" five hundred volumes of the *Millennial Star*, and

"fifty thousand tracts; emigrated to Zion one thou-
"sand souls, establishing a permanent shipping
"agency, which will be a great blessing to the saints,
"and have left sown in the hearts of many thousands
"the seed of eternal life, which shall bring forth
"fruit to the honor and glory of God; and yet we
"have lacked nothing to eat, drink or wear; in all
"these things I acknowledge the hand of God."

But even this was eclipsed by the results of the
next ten years.   Besides the thousands who had emigrated, the British mission, at the culmination of this
third period, numbered nearly forty thousand souls.
The *Millennial Star* reached a weekly circulation of
twenty-two thousand; and there were half a million
of Orson Pratt's tracts in circulation throughout the
land.   This crowning period was during the presiden-
cies of Orson Spencer, Orson Pratt, and Franklin
and Samuel Richards.

Too vast this missionary work abroad, and too
crowded its events, for us to follow the historic
details; but we shall, however, frequently hereafter
meet representative women from Europe, and read
in their sketches many episodes of the saints in
foreign lands.

CHAPTER XXVII.

And what the part of the sisterhood in this great
work outlined in foreign lands?

The sisters were side by side with the most potent
missionaries the Latter-day Church found. They
made nearly as many converts to Mormonism as the
elders. They were, often times, the direct instruments which brought disciples into the Church.
The elders riveted the anchor of faith by good gospel logic, and their eloquent preachers enchanted
the half-inspired mind with well-described millennial
views, but the sisters, as a rule, by the nicest evangelical diplomacy brought the results about. They
agitated the very atmosphere with their magical
faith in the new dispensation; they breathed the
spirit of their own beautiful enthusiasm into their
neighborhoods; they met the first brunt of persecution and conquered it by their zeal; they
transformed unbelief into belief by their personal

testimonies, which aroused curiosity, or made their relatives and neighbors sleepless with active thoughts of the new, and inspired doubts of the old; they enticed the people to hear their elders preach, and did more to disturb the peace of the town than could have done the town-crier; they crowded their halls with an audience when without their sisterly devising those halls had remained often empty and cold.

In the British mission—in England, Scotland and Wales—the sisters had much better missionary opportunities than in America. The vast extent of country over which the American people were sparsely scattered, forty to fifty years ago, and the almost immediate gatherings of the disciples to a centre place, or a local Zion, necessarily confined the missionary movement at home nearly exclusively to the apostles and their aids, the "Seventies;" and thus as soon as the disciples "gathered out of "Babylon," American society lost even the little leaven which the elders had inspired in its midst.

But in England, Scotland and Wales, and at a later period in Scandinavia, it was very different. Not merely one local Zion and a score of branches scattered over a score of States, but in the British mission at its zenith of progress there were over five hundred branches, fifty conferences, and about a dozen pastorates—the latter very like Mormon provinces or bishoprics. There the sisters had grand missionary opportunities. From village to town, and from town to city, they helped the elders push their work until this vast church superstructure was reared. With such a leaven as the Mor-

mon sisterhood in Great Britain, converts were
made so fast that it was nearly twenty years before
even the immense yearly emigration of the saints
to America began visibly to tell in weakening missionary operations in that prolific land.

It has often been a matter of wonder how it
happened that Mormonism was such a mighty proselyting power in England compared with what it
had been in America. The two views presented
suggest the exact reason; and in addition to the
gathering genius of the Mormons, the very "tidal
wave" of the country has swept migrating peoples
westward. Three hundred Mormon cities have
sprung up on the Pacific slope, just as five hundred
branches did in Great Britain, which has required
all the gathering energies of the Church for over
a quarter of a century to deplete her of these
proselyting saints. It was Great Britain that gave
to the sisters their grand missionary opportunities.

Here another view of the sisters presents itself.
Much of the success of "Mormonism" in foreign
lands is due to the fact that the elders, like Christ
and his apostles of old, went about preaching the
gospel "without purse or scrip."

This apostolic custom captivated woman at once.
Her sympathies were charmed. She admired the
heroic devotion and self-abnegation of such ministers of Christ. Their examples directly appealed to
her, so like were they to her own faith. The disinter-
ested aims and efforts of these men for human good
so accorded with her own divine aspirations, that
she leapt with a glorious enthusiasm to their side.

For once woman had found the opportunity to exercise her own methods of apostleship.

She saw these elders upon the altar of sacrifice for a Christian cause. Out in the wilderness of society were they, during the best years of youth, preaching without purse or scrip, trusting in Providence for their daily bread as truly as do the sparrows whom the Great Father feeds. Wandering through the world were these devoted men, often with blood in their well-worn shoes, preaching the glad tidings of a new dispensation which the angels had opened to bring immortality to mortals, and establish the order of heaven on earth. Such were the examples which the elders presented in their ministry, and such examples woman loved.

Though they bore the title of elders, these missionaries, especially the native ones, were generally young men from the age of twenty to thirty. Scarcely were they converted ere they were sent out to mission the land. The prophet Joseph had well cogitated on the saying of Christ, " The harvest is great but the laborers are few;" and it was at once a bold and happy stroke of genius on his part to leave the beaten track of choosing only matured and experienced divines, calling instead a multitude of youths and striplings to aid him in evangelizing the world. This was much like Mohammed's choosing of the youthful enthusiast Ali to be his lieutenant in his religious empire-founding mission. And so at one time might have been found in Europe nearly a thousand of these young men, out in the ministry, bearing the title of elders. Strange example! Elders at twenty; veterans at twenty-five, who had built up their conferences! This pleased woman. It was unique. The example touched her heart and stimulated her faith through her very sympathy for and admiration of the heroic.

Into the villages of England, Scotland and Wales these youths made their way, with hymn-book and Bible in hand, but with no ministerial recommendation except a forceful, innovative intellectuality, and souls inspired with the glories of a new and conquering faith.

Alone, at eventide, they would uncover their heads, on some green bit of common, or, if on the Sabbath day, would daringly near the old village church, which well might tremble at such sacrilege, as did they literally in those bold missionary attempts, that never had been made but for youth's rich unconsciousness of inability. Then would ring out the hymn of the Latter-day Saints:

> " Go, ye messengers of glory,
> Run, ye legates of the skies,
> Go and tell the pleasing story,
> That a glorious angel flies;
> Great and mighty,
> With a message from on high !"

Or perchance it would be this instead :

> " The morning breaks, the shadows flee;
> Lo, Zion's standard is unfurled;
> The dawning of a brighter day
> Majestic rises on the world."

And many a village has been startled with this tremendous proclamation, from the lips of young men :

> " Jehovah speaks ! Let Earth give ear!
> And gentile nations turn and live ! "

First the woman would come out to listen, on the threshold of her cottage, after supper; then she would draw near, and wonder about this boy-preacher—to her eyes so much like her own boy, who, perhaps, is playing at some evening game with his companions, near by. Next comes her husband, and after awhile the boys themselves leave their games, and with their sisters, gather to listen. And so are also gathered other family groups of the village to swell the impromptu congregation. This is a truthful picture, for the author is describing a literal experience.

Now comes the supplemental story of this boy-elder, that he is out in the world preaching the gospel without purse or scrip, that he has eaten nothing that day since breakfast, that he has journeyed miles and is tired out, and that he has no place in which to lay his head that night.

The mother and her daughters whisper. They have conceived an idea that will exactly fit that poor boy's case. Father is approached. At first he will not listen to the proposition; but at last he yields. What else could he do? When did woman fail if her sympathies were enlisted? To their home the boy-missionary is taken. A supper is gleaned from the humble peasant's leavings. Water is furnished to bathe the sore and blood-stained feet. The woman is half converted by the sight of so much youthful heroism. Mother and daughters dream of the boy-missionary that night.

'Tis a simple story; but from that house Mormonism is destined to spread through all the village, until the aged clergyman, educated at college, in his pulpit which he has occupied for a quarter of a century, fears that boy as much as a second Goliah might have feared the stripling David.

And thus Mormonism ran from village to town, and from town to city; carried, of course, to the larger places by the "veterans;" but in all cases very similar. How much the sisters—mothers and daughters—had to do in this work may be seen at a glance.

But the most salient view to be taken of Mormonism abroad is, as the great spiritual movement of the age. The reader may be assured that it was the beautiful themes of a new dispensation—themes such as angels might have accompanied with their hosannas—that charmed disciples into the Mormon Church. Spiritual themes and the gifts of the Holy Ghost were what converted the tens of thousands in Great Britain; not a cold materialism, much less a sensual gospel. Even to the simplest, who scarcely knew the meaning of idealities, the spiritual and the ideal of Mormonism were its principal charms. Indeed, it is to the fact that Mormonism was, in its missionary history, such a unique and extraordinary spiritual, and yet matter-of-fact, movement, that it owes its principal and rare successes.

In America, the splendid ambitions of empire-founding, the worldly opportunities presented by a migrating people and a growing commonwealth, sometimes charmed the dominating mind; but in the foreign missions, especially in Great Britain, where it received its highest intellectual interpretation from elders who championed it on the public platform against the best orthodox disputants in the land, it was Mormonism as a great spiritual work that captivated most, and above all it was this aspect of it that most captivated the sisterhood. In this view, and in this view only, can the explanation be found of how it took such a deep and lasting hold upon the female portion of society.

In the early rise of the Church abroad the disciples knew nothing of the society-founding successes of Brigham Young, which to-day make Mormonism quite potent in America and a periodical sensation to the American Congress. Nothing of this; but much of the divine, much of the spiritual, much of the angels' coming to reign with them in a millennium, with Christ on earth.

Such was Mormonism abroad. Such has it ever been, with the sisters, at home. Its success in making converts among women, both old and young, has no parallel in the history of churches. Its all-potent influence on the heart and brain of woman was miraculous. She received it in as great faith as was that of the woman who laid hold of the skirt of Christ's garment and was healed. She exulted in its unspeakably beautiful themes; she reveled in its angelic experiences; she multiplied its disciples.

In some respects Mormonism, in its history and manifestations abroad, compares strikingly with the more recent history of spiritualism in America. Their geniuses are undoubtedly very different, but their potency over society has been similar. The one was apostolic and Hebraic, with a God as the source of its inspirations, a priesthood linking the heavens and the earth as its controlling powers, and another Catholic or Universal Church as the aim of

18

its ministry. The other has pulled down what it has dared to call the idols of Deity, makes war on priesthood, and on the Hebrew Jehovah, whom the Mormons serve, and disintegrates all churches. Yet the themes of both have been themes of the angels' coming to visit the earth again; "new revelations to suit the age;" another great spiritual dispensation for the world.

Mormonism abroad, then, was supremely an apostolic spiritual work. Paul's famous epistle to the Corinthians, upon spiritual gifts, presents an exact view of what Mormonism has been; and as it was a chapter often read to the saints—the subject of a thousand sermons—it may here be fitly quoted to illustrate the view. The apostle says:

"Now concerning spiritual gifts, brethren, I would not have you ignorant.   *   *   *   *

"Now there are diversities of gifts, but the same spirit.

"And there are differences of administration, but the same Lord.

"And there are diversities of operations, but it is the same God which worketh all in all.

"But the manifestation of the spirit is given to every man to profit withal.

"For to one is given by the spirit the word of wisdom; to another the word of knowledge by the same spirit;

"To another faith by the same spirit; to another the gifts of healing by the same spirit;

"To another the working of miracles; to another prophesy; to another discerning of spirits; to another divers kinds of tongues; to another the interpretation of tongues;

"But all these worketh that one and the self-same spirit, dividing to every man severally as he will.

"For as the body is one, and hath many members, and all the members of that one body, being many, are one body: so also is Christ.

"For by one spirit are we all baptized into one body, whether we be Jews or Gentiles, whether we be bond or free; and have been all made to drink into one spirit. *   *   *   *

"And God hath set some in the church, first, apostles; secondarily, prophets; thirdly, teachers; after that miracles; then gifts of healings, helps, governments, diversities of tongues.

"Are all apostles? Are all prophets? Are all teachers? Are all workers of miracles?

"Have all the gifts of healing? Do all speak with tongues? Do all interpret?

"But covet earnestly the best gifts; and yet shew I unto you a more excellent way."

In another chapter of Paul's epistle to the Corinthians, he presents another famous spiritual view:

"How is it, then, brethren? When ye come together, every one of you hath a psalm, hath a doctrine hath a tongue, hath a revelation, hath an interpretation. Let all things be done unto edifying.

"If any man speak in an unknown tongue, let it be by two, or at the most by three, and that by course; and let one interpret.

"But if there be no interpreter, let him keep silence in the church; and let him speak to himself, and to God.

"Let the prophets speak two or three, and let the other judge.

"If anything be revealed to another that sitteth by, let the first hold his peace.

"For ye may all prophesy one by one, that all may learn, and all may be comforted.

"And the spirits of the prophets are subject to the prophets.

" For God is not the author of confusion, but of peace, as in all churches of the saints."

This is a very exact picture of the Latter-day Saints' testimony meetings. It is indeed a striking illustration of the gospel and its manifestations, as familiar to them as their own faces.

It was this spiritual gospel that the sisters promulgated in Great Britain, and it was this that made the tens of thousands of converts. Had not Mormonism been of this kind, and had not such been its manifestations, woman never would have received it and become its apostle; nor would it have made such a stir in the world.

The sisters also missioned the land by the distribution of tracts. This made them to be preachers, in a way; and they carried their sermons to the homes of rich and poor, to be read at the fireside by those who, but for this, never would have gone to hear an elder preach.

In all the towns and cities of her Majesty's kingdom the saints organized tract societies. In London, where many branches flourished, these tract organizations were numerous; the same was measurably the case with Birmingham, Manchester, Liverpool, Sheffield, and the principal cities of Scotland and Wales. These tract distributers were numbered by the thousand. They held their monthly meetings, mapped out their districts and brought in their regular reports. At one time, as before stated, they had in circulation half a million of Orson Pratt's tracts. It is scarcely necessary to say that the sisters principally did this work, to which should be added that they were assisted by the young men of each branch. In short, the sisters, in the work abroad, were a great missionary power.

And here it may be observed that all evangelical history proves that woman is ever the most potent evangelist. She permeates society with the influence of her church, makes converts in the homes of her neighbors, where her pastor could never reach without her help, and inspires the very faith by which miracles are wrought.

Woman has many striking examples of her influence and acts in the history of religious empire-founding. Miriam charmed the congregation of Israel with her songs, and strengthened her brother Moses' power by her prophesies; Esther rendered the captivity of her people lighter by her mediation; Judith delivered her nation from the Assyrian captain; the two Marys and Martha seemed to have understood Jesus better than did his apostles even, and they saw first their risen Lord; St. Helena did much to make her son, Constantine, the imperial champion of Christianity; perchance had there been no Cadijah the world would never have known a Mohammed; the Catholic Church has been more potent through the sisters of its various orders; and the examples which the Mormon sisterhood have given are almost as striking as those of the sisters of that church.

These are some of the views which may be presented of the sisters in their great missionary work abroad, and they are also fit illustrations of the spiritual movement, which they represent, in the age.

CHAPTER XXVIII.

MORMONISM AND THE QUEEN OF ENGLAND—PRESEN-
TATION OF THE BOOK OF MORMON TO THE QUEEN
AND PRINCE ALBERT—ELIZA R. SNOW'S POEM ON
THAT EVENT—"ZION'S NURSING MOTHER"—HEBER
C. KIMBALL BLESSES VICTORIA.

Here an interesting story is to be told of Mormonism and the Queen of England.

It will be remembered that Victoria ascended the throne of Great Britain just three days before Heber C. Kimball, Orson Hyde and Willard Richards arrived in her realm to preach the gospel of Messiah's coming.

There was something poetic in this. Victoria became connected in some way with the new dispensation. She alone of all the monarchs of the earth was prophetically cast in its *dramatis personæ*. Poetry and prophesy both were pregnant with much of subject and promise that concerned Victoria of England. She may not be aware of it, but there is quite a romance of the British Queen in Mormon history, to which the presentation of the Book of Mormon to herself and the late Prince consort gives pictorial display.

Before leaving England, President Brigham Young,

who had succeeded in raising means to publish the Book of Mormon, gave directions for copies to be specially prepared and richly bound for presentation to her Majesty and the Prince consort. The honor of this devolved on Lorenzo Snow, who was at that period President of the London Conference. The presentation was made in 1842, through the politeness of Sir Henry Wheatley; and it is said her Majesty condescended to be pleased with the gift. Whether she ever read the Book of Mormon is not known, although, if the presentation has not altogether faded from her memory, Mormonism has been since that date sensational enough to provoke even a monarch to read the book, if for nothing better than curiosity; so, not unlikely Queen Victoria has read some portions at least of the Book of Mormon. The unique circumstance called forth from the pen of Eliza R. Snow the following poem, entitled " Queen Victoria :"

> " Of all the monarchs of the earth
>   That wear the robes of royalty,
> She has inherited by birth
>   The broadest wreath of majesty.
>
> From her wide territorial wing
>   The sun does not withdraw its light,
> While earth's diurnal motions bring
>   To other nations day and night.
>
> All earthly thrones are tott'ring things,
>   Where lights and shadows intervene;
> And regal honor often brings
>   The scaffold or the guillotine.
>
> But still her sceptre is approved—
>   All nations deck the wreath she wears;
> Yet, like the youth whom Jesus loved,
>   One thing is lacking even there.

But lo! a prize possessing more
  Of worth than gems with honor rife—
A herald of salvation bore
  To her the words of endless life.

That gift, however fools deride,
  Is worthy of her royal care;
She'd better lay her crown aside
  Than spurn the light reflected there.

O would she now her influence lend—
  The influence of royalty,
Messiah's kingdom to extend,
  And Zion's 'nursing Mother' be;

She, with the glory of her name
  Inscribed on Zion's lofty spire,
Would win a wreath of endless fame,
  To last when other wreaths expire.

Though over millions called to reign—
  Herself a powerful nation's boast,
'Twould be her everlasting gain
  To serve the King, the Lord of Hosts.

For there are crowns and thrones on high,
  And kingdoms there to be conferred;
There honors wait that never die,
  There fame's immortal trump is heard.

Truth speaks—it is Jehovah's word;
  Let kings and queens and princes hear:
In distant isles the sound is heard—
  Ye heavens, rejoice; O earth, give ear.

The time, the time is now at hand
  To give a glorious period birth—
The Son of God will take command,
  And rule the nations of the earth."

It will be seen that our Hebraic poetess has suggested for Victoria of England the title of "Zion's Nursing Mother." The reference is to Isaiah's glorious song of Zion. He, according to the universally accepted interpretation, foresaw the rise of Messiah's kingdom on the earth in the last days.

" And they shall call thee the City of the Lord, the Zion of the Holy One of Israel.

" And the Gentiles shall come to thy light, and kings to the brightness of thy rising.

" And kings shall be thy nursing fathers, and their queens thy nursing mothers.

" Thou shalt also be a crown of glory in the hand of the Lord, and a royal diadem in the hand of thy God.

" Behold, thy salvation cometh; behold, his reward is with him and his work before him."

This is the subject of which the gorgeous Isaiah sang; and the prophesy of Joseph and the poetry of Eliza have applied it principally to America as Zion, and conditionally, to Queen Victoria as her " Nursing Mother."

Many earthly thrones were about to totter. Soon France—from the days of Charlemagne styled "The Eldest Daughter of the Church"—saw her crown trampled in the very gutter, by the rabble of Paris, and a few years later the scepter of Rome was wrested from the hands of the " successor of St. Peter " by Victor Emanuel; yet of Victoria of England, Zion's poetess sings:

" But still *her* sceptre is approved."

Mark the poetic and prophetic significance between America as Zion, and Great Britain, represented in Victoria. A new age is born. Victoria is its imperial star; while from America—the land that owns no earthly sovereign—come these apostles to her realm just three days after the sceptre is placed in her hands. The prophet of America sends them to proclaim to Great Britain the rising of a

star superior to her own.   It is the star of Messiah's
kingdom.   She is called to her mission as its Nursing Mother.

Seeing that Joseph was the prophet of America,
and that the British mission has given to the Mormon Zion over a hundred thousand of her children
already gathered to build up her cities and rear her
temples, it is not strange that the burden of this
prophesy should have been claimed and shared between the two great English speaking nations.

But there is a personal romance as well, which
centres in Victoria.   At the time Sister Eliza wrote
the poem to her name, Victoria of England was
quite a theme in the Mormon Church.   Not only
in her own realm, among her own subjects, but in
Zion also she was preached about, prophesied about,
dreamed about, and seen in visions.   Brigham, as
we have seen, caused special copies of the Book of
Mormon to be prepared for her and Prince Albert;
Lorenzo Snow presented them through the courtesy
of a state personage, and his sister immortalized
the circumstance in verse.   The story is told, also,
that Heber C. Kimball, while in London, blessed
Victoria, as she passed, by the power and authority
of his apostleship; and what Heber did was done
with the spirit and with the understanding also.
Queen Victoria has been remarkably successful, and
unrivalled in the glory of her reign.

CHAPTER XXIX.

LITERAL APPLICATION OF CHRIST'S COMMAND—THE
SAINTS LEAVE FATHER AND MOTHER, HOME AND
FRIENDS, TO GATHER TO ZION—MRS. WILLIAM
STAINES—HER EARLY LIFE AND EXPERIENCE—A
MIDNIGHT BAPTISM IN MIDWINTER — FAREWELL
TO HOME AND EVERY FRIEND—INCIDENTS OF THE
JOURNEY TO NAUVOO.

How characteristic the following gospel passages!
How well and literally have they been applied in
the history and experience of the Latter-day Saints:

" He that loveth father or mother more than me,
is not worthy of me; and he that loveth son or
daughter more than me, is not worthy of me.

" And he that taketh not his cross, and followeth
after me, is not worthy of me.

" He that findeth his life shall lose it ; and he that
loseth his life for my sake, shall find it.

" And every one that has forsaken houses, or
brethren, or sisters, or father, or mother, or wife, or
children, or lands, for my name's sake, shall receive
a hundred fold, and shall inherit everlasting life."

This gospel was preached by the Mormon elders
with nothing of the " spiritual " sense so acceptable
to fashionable churches. Nothing of the idealistic
glamour was given to it. Most literal, indeed almost
cruelly Christian, was Mormonism here.

But it was not until the "gathering" was preached to the disciples in Great Britain, that the full significance of such a gospel was realized. True it was made as severe to the saints in America, through their persecutions; especially when at length they were driven from the borders of civilization. To the British mission, however, in the early days, we must go for striking illustrations. A "gathering dispensation" preached to Europe before the age of emigration had set in! At first it startled, aye, almost appalled the disciples in Great Britain. In those days the common people of England scarcely ever strayed ten miles from the churchyards where had slept their kindred from generation to generation. True the mechanic traveled in search of employment from one manufacturing city to another, passed along by the helping hand of trade societies; but families, as a rule, never moved. Migration was to them an incomprehensible law, to be wondered at even in the example of the birds who were forced by climate to migrate as the season changed. Migrating peoples could only be understood in the examples of the Jews or Gipseys, both of whom were looked upon as being "under the curse." "Going to London" was the crowning event of a lifetime to even the well-to-do townsman, a hundred miles distant from the metropolis; going to America was like an imagined flight to the moon. At best emigration was transportation from fatherland, and the emigration of tens of thousands of England-loving saints was a transportation to the common people without parallel for cruelty.

It was long before English society forgave the

American elders for preaching emigration in England. It looked upon them absolutely as the betrayers of a confiding religious people who had already been too much betrayed by an American delusion.

And as observed, the doctrine of emigration from native land to America—the new world; another world in seeming—and that, too, as a necessity to salvation, or at least to the obedience of heaven's commands, appalled at first the very "elect." Nothing but the Holy Ghost could dissipate the terrors of emigration.

Sister Staines shall be first chosen to personally illustrate this subject, because of the peculiarity of her experience, and for the reason that she is the wife of William C. Staines, himself an early Mormon emigrant to Nauvoo, and to-day the general emigration agent of the Church, and who, during the past fifteen years, has emigrated, under the direction of President Young, about fifty thousand souls from Europe. Others of the sisters will follow in this peculiar line of Mormon history.

Priscilla Mogridge Staines was born in Widbrook, Wiltshire, England, March 11th, 1823.

"My parents," she says, "were both English. "My father's name was John Mogridge, and my "mother's maiden name was Mary Crook.

"I was brought up in the Episcopal faith from "my earliest childhood, my parents being members "of the Episcopal Church. But as my mind became "matured, and I thought more about religion, I "became dissatisfied with the doctrines taught by "that Church, and I prayed to God my Heavenly

"Father to direct me aright, that I might know the
"true religion.

"Shortly after being thus concerned about my
"salvation, I heard Mormonism and believed it.
"God had sent the true gospel to me in answer to
"my prayer.

"It was a great trial for a young maiden (I was
"only nineteen years of age) to forsake all for the
"gospel—father, mother, brothers and sisters—and
"to leave my childhood's home and native land,
"never expecting to see it again. This was the
"prospect before me. The saints were already
"leaving fatherland, in obedience to the doctrine of
"gathering, which was preached at this time with
"great plainness by the elders as an imperative
"command of God. We looked upon the gathering
"as necessary to our salvation. Nothing of our
"duty in this respect was concealed, and we were
"called upon to emigrate to America as soon as the
"way should open, to share the fate of the saints,
"whatever might come. Young as I was and alone
"of all my family in the faith, I was called to take
"up my cross and lay my earthly all upon the altar;
"yet so well satisfied was I with my new religion
"that I was willing to make every sacrifice for it in
"order to gain my salvation and prove myself not
"unworthy of the saints' reward.

"Having determined to be baptized, I resolved
"to at once obey the gospel, although it was mid-
"winter, and the weather bitterly cold.

"It is proper to here state that baptism was a
"trial to the converts in England in those days.
"They had to steal away, even unknown to their

"friends oftentimes, and scarcely daring to tell the
"saints themselves that they were about to take up
"the cross; and not until the ordinance had been
"administered, and the Holy Ghost gave them
"boldness, could they bring themselves to proclaim
"openly that they had cast in their lot with the
"despised Mormons. Nor was this all, for generally
"the elders had to administer baptism when the
"village was wrapt in sleep, lest persecutors should
"gather a mob to disturb the solemn scene with
"gibes and curses, accompanied with stones or clods
"of earth torn from the river bank and hurled at
"the disciple and minister during the performance
"of the ceremony.

"On the evening of a bitterly cold day in mid-
"winter, as before stated, I walked four miles to the
"house of a local elder for baptism. Arriving at his
"house, we waited until midnight, in order that the
"neighbors might not disturb us, and then repaired
"to a stream of water a quarter of a mile away.
"Here we found the water, as we anticipated, frozen
"over, and the elder had to chop a hole in the ice
"large enough for the purpose of baptism. It was
"a scene and an occasion I shall never forget.
"Memory to-day brings back the emotions and
"sweet awe of that moment. None but God and
"his angels, and the few witnesses who stood on the
"bank with us, heard my covenant; but in the
"solemnity of that midnight hour it seemed as
"though all nature were listening, and the recording
"angel writing our words in the book of the Lord.
"Is it strange that such a scene, occurring in the life
"of a latter-day saint, should make an everlasting
"impression, as this did on mine?

"Having been thus baptized, I returned to the "house in my wet and freezing garments.

"Up to this hour, as intimated, my heart's best "affection had been centred on home, and my "greatest mental struggle in obeying the gospel "had been over the thought of soon leaving that "home; but no sooner had I emerged from the "water, on that night of baptism, and received my "confirmation at the water's edge, than I became "filled with an irresistible desire to join the saints "who were gathering to America. The usual con-"firmation words, pronounced upon my head, 'Re-"ceive ye the gift of the Holy Ghost,' were, indeed, "potent. They changed the current of my life. This "remarkable and sudden change of mind and the "now all-absorbing desire to emigrate with the "saints was my first testimony to the truth and "power of the gospel.

"Shortly thereafter (December 27th, 1843), I left "the home of my birth to gather to Nauvoo. I was "alone. It was a dreary winter day on which I went "to Liverpool. The company with which I was to "sail were all strangers to me. When I arrived at "Liverpool and saw the ocean that would soon roll "between me and all I loved, my heart almost failed "me. But I had laid my idols all upon the altar. "There was no turning back. I remembered the "words of the Saviour: 'He that leaveth not father "and mother, brother and sister, for my sake, is not "worthy of me,' and I believed his promise to those "who forsook all for his sake; so I thus alone set "out for the reward of everlasting life, trusting in "God.

" In company with two hundred and fifty saints I
" embarked on the sailing vessel *Fanny*, and after a
" tedious passage of six weeks' duration, we arrived
" in New Orleans. There an unexpected difficulty
" met us. The steamer *Maid of Iowa*, belonging to
" the prophet Joseph, and on which the company of
" saints had expected to ascend the Mississippi to
" Nauvoo, was embargoed and lashed to the wharf.
" But Providence came to our aid. A lady of for-
" tune was in the company—a Mrs. Bennett—and
" out of her private purse she not only lifted the
" embargo, but also fitted out the steamer with all
" necessary provisions, fuel, etc., and soon the com-
" pany were again on their way.

" The journey up the river was a tedious and
" eventful one, consuming five weeks of time. At
" nearly every stopping place the emigrants were
" shamefully insulted and persecuted by the citizens.
" At Memphis some villain placed a half consumed
" cigar under a straw mattress and other bedding
" that had been laid out, aft of the ladies' cabin, to
" air. When we steamed out into the river the draft,
" created by the motion of the boat, soon fanned the
" fire into a quick flame. Fortunately I myself dis-
" covered the fire and gave the alarm in time to
" have it extinguished before it had consumed more
" than a portion of the adjoining woodwork. Per-
" haps one minute more of delay in its discovery,
" and that company of two hundred and fifty souls
" would have been subjected to all the horrors and
" perils incident to a panic and fire on shipboard.

" At another place the pilot decided to tie up the
" boat at a landing and wait for the subsiding of a

"furious gale that was blowing. This he accord-
"ingly did, and let off steam, thinking to remain
"there over night. In the meantime a mob gath-
"ered. We were Mormons. Too often had mobs
"shown that the property of Mormons might be
"destroyed with impunity, in the most lawless man-
"ner, and their lives taken by the most horrible
"means. Had that boat been consumed by fire,
"'twould have been but a pleasing sensation, seeing
"that it belonged to the Mormon prophet; and the
"two hundred and fifty men, women and children,
"if consumed, would have been, in the eyes of their
"persecutors, only so many Mormons well disposed
"of. Thus, doubtless, would have thought the mob
"who gathered at that landing-place and cut the
"boat adrift. The *Maid of Iowa* was now submitted
"to the triple peril of being adrift without steam,
"at the mercy of a treacherous current, and in the
"midst of a hurricane. The captain, however, suc-
"ceeded in raising the steam, and the boat was
"brought under sufficient control to enable her to
"be brought to, under shelter of a heavy forest,
"where she was tied up to the trees and weathered
"the gale.

"At another landing a mob collected and began
"throwing stones through the cabin windows, smash-
"ing the glass and sash, and jeopardizing the lives
"of the passengers. This was a little too much for
"human forbearance. The boat was in command of
"the famous Mormon captain, Dan Jones; his
"Welsh blood was now thoroughly warm; he knew
"what mobs meant. Mustering the brethren, with
"determined wrath he ordered them to parade with

" loaded muskets on the side of the boat assailed.
" Then he informed the mob that if they did not
" instantly desist, he would shoot them down like so
" many dogs; and like so many dogs they slunk
" away.

" As the *Maid of Iowa* had made slow progress,
" and had been frequently passed by more swift-
" going steamers, her progress was well known by
" the friends of Nauvoo. So on the day of our
" arrival the saints were out *en masse* to welcome us.
" I had never before seen any of those assembled,
" yet I felt certain, as the boat drew near, that I
" should be able to pick out the prophet Joseph at
" first sight.   This belief I communicated to Mrs.
" Bennett, whose acquaintance I had made on the
" voyage.   She wondered at it; but I felt impressed
" by the spirit that I should know him. As we
" neared the pier the prophet was standing among
" the crowd.   At the moment, however, I recognized
" him according to the impression, and pointed him
" out to Mrs. Bennett, with whom I was standing
" alone on the hurricane deck.

" Scarcely had the boat touched the pier when,
" singularly enough, Joseph sprang on board, and,
" without speaking with any one, made his way direct
" to where we were standing, and addressing Mrs.
" Bennett by name, thanked her kindly for lifting
" the embargo from his boat, and blessed her for so
" materially aiding the saints."

CHAPTER XXX.

RISE OF NAUVOO — INTRODUCTION OF POLYGAMY—
MARTYRDOM OF JOSEPH AND HYRUM—CONTINU-
ATION OF ELIZA R. SNOW'S NARRATIVE—HER AC-
CEPTANCE OF POLYGAMY, AND MARRIAGE TO
THE PROPHET—GOVERNOR CARLIN'S TREACHERY—
HER SCATHING REVIEW OF THE MARTYRDOM—
MOTHER LUCY'S STORY OF HER MURDERED SONS.

Meanwhile, since the reader has been called to
drop the historical thread of the saints in America
for a view of the rise of Mormonism in foreign lands,
Nauvoo, whose name signifies "the beautiful city,"
has grown into an importance worthy her romantic
name and character as the second Zion. Nauvoo
was bidding fair to become the queen of the West;
and had she been allowed to continue her career for
a quarter of a century, inspired by the gorgeous
genius of her prophet, although she would not have
rivaled Chicago or St. Louis as a commercial city,
yet would she have become the veritable New Jerusalem of America—in the eyes of the "Gentiles"
scarcely less than in the faith of our modern Israel.

Polygamy, also, by this time has been introduced
into the Church, and the examples of the patriarchs
Abraham and Jacob, and of kings David and Solo-

mon, have begun to prevail. That the "peculiar institution" was the cross of the sisterhood in those days, it would be heartless to attempt to conceal, for, as already seen, the first wives of the founders of Mormondom were nearly all daughters of New England, whose monogamic training was of the severest kind, and whose monogamic conceptions were of the most exacting nature.

Polygamy was undoubtedly introduced by Joseph himself, at Nauvoo, between 1840 and 1844. Years afterwards, however, a monogamic rival church, under the leadership of young Joseph Smith, the first born of the prophet, arose, denying that the founder of Mormondom was the author of polygamy, and affirming that its origin was in Brigham Young, subsequent to the martyrdom of the prophet and his brother Hyrum. This, with the fact that nearly the whole historic weight of polygamy rests with Utah, renders it expedient that we should barely touch the subject at Nauvoo, and wait for its stupendous sensation after its publication to the world by Brigham Young—a sensation that Congress has swelled into a national noise, and that General Grant has made the hobgoblin of his dreams.

Nor can we deal largely with the history of Nauvoo. It is not the representative period of the sisters. They only come in with dramatic force in their awful lamentation over the martyrdom, which was not equaled in Jerusalem at the crucifixion. The great historic period of the women of Mormondom is during the exodus of the Church and its removal to the Rocky Mountains, when they figured quite as strongly as did the women of ancient Israel in the exodus from Egypt. We can scarcely hope to do full justice to that period, but hasten to some of its salient views. And here the historic thread shall be principally continued by Eliza R. Snow. She, touching the city of the saints, and then slightly on the introduction of polygamy, says:

" The location of the city of Nauvoo was beautiful, but the climate was so unhealthy that none but Latter-day Saints, full of faith, and trusting in the power of God, could have established that city. Chills and fever was the prevailing disease. Notwithstanding we had this to contend with, through the blessing of God on the indefatigable exertions of the saints, it was not long before Nauvoo prompted the envy and jealousy of many of the adjacent inhabitants, and, as the ' accuser of the brethren' never sleeps, we had many difficulties to meet, which ultimately culminated in the most bitter persecutions.

" To narrate what transpired within the seven years in which we built and occupied Nauvoo, the beautiful, would fill many volumes. That is a history that never will, and never can, repeat itself. Some of the most important events of my life transpired within that brief term, in which I was married, and in which my husband, Joseph Smith, the prophet of God, sealed his testimony with his blood.

" Although in my youth I had considered marriage to have been ordained of God, I had remained single; and to-day I acknowledge the kind overruling providences of God in that circumstance as fully as in any other of my life; for I have not known of one of my former suitors having received the truth; by which it is manifest that I was singularly preserved from the bondage of a marriage tie which would, in all probability, have prevented my receiving, or enjoying the free exercise of, that religion which has been, and is now, dearer to me than life.

"In Nauvoo I had the first intimation, or at least the first understanding, that the practice of a plurality of wives would be introduced into the Church. The thought was very repugnant to my feelings, and in direct opposition to my educational prepossessions; but when I reflected that this was the dispensation of the fullness of times, embracing all other dispensations, it was plain that plural marriage must be included; and I consoled myself with the idea that it was a long way in the distance, beyond the period of my mortal existence, and that, of course, I should not have it to meet. However, it was announced to me that the 'set time' had come—that God had commanded his servants to establish the order, by taking additional wives.

"It seemed for awhile as though all the traditions, prejudices, and superstitions of my ancestry, for many generations, accumulated before me in one immense mass; but God, who had kept silence for centuries, was speaking; I knew it, and had covenanted in the waters of baptism to live by every word of his, and my heart was still firmly set to do his bidding.

"I was sealed to the prophet, Joseph Smith, for time and eternity, in accordance with the celestial law of marriage which God had revealed, the ceremony being performed by a servant of the Most High—authorized to officiate in sacred ordinances.

This, one of the most important events of my life, I have never had cause to regret. The more I comprehend the pure and ennobling principle of plural marriage, the more I appreciate it. It is a necessity in the salvation of the human family—a necessity in redeeming woman from the curse, and the world from its corruptions.

"When I entered into it, my knowledge of what it was designed to accomplish was very limited; had I then understood what I now understand, I think I should have hailed its introduction with joy, in consideration of the great good to be accomplished. As it was, I received it because I knew that God required it.

"When in March, 1842, the prophet, Joseph Smith, assisted by some of the leading elders in the church, organized the Female Relief Society (now the great female organization of Utah), I was present, and was appointed secretary of that society, of which I shall say more hereafter. In the summer of 1842 I accompanied Mrs. Emma Smith, the president of the society, to Quincy, Ill., with a petition signed by several hundred members of the society, praying his Excellency, Governor Carlin, for protection from illegal suits then pending against Joseph Smith. We met with a very cordial reception, and presented the petition, whereupon the governor pledged his word and honor that he would use his influence to protect Mr. Smith, whose innocence he acknowledged. But, soon after our return, we learned that at the time of our visit and while making protestations of friendship, Governor Carlin was secretly conniving with the basest of men to destroy our

leader. He was even combining with minions of
the great adversary of truth in the State of Missouri,
who were vigilant in stirring up their colleagues in
Illinois, to bring about the terrible crisis.

" The awful tragedy of the 27th of June, 1844, is
a livid, burning, scathing stain on our national
escutcheon. To look upon the noble, lifeless forms
of those brothers, Joseph and Hyrum Smith, as
they lay side by side in their burial clothes, having
been brought home from Carthage, where they had .
been slaughtered in their manhood and in their innocence, was a sight that might well appal the heart
of a true American citizen; but what it was for
loving wives and children, the heart may feel, but
the tongue can never tell.

" This scene occurred in America, ' the land of the
free and the home of the brave,' to which our ancestors fled for religious freedom—where the ' dear
old flag yet waves,' and under which not one effort
has been made to bring to justice the perpetrators
of that foul deed."

To the aged mother of the prophet and patriarch
of the Mormon Church shall be given the personal
presentation of the subject of the martyrdom; for
although the mother's heartrending description cannot be considered as a sufficiently great historical
word-picture of the scene, yet there is much of
tragic force in it. She says:

" On the morning of the 24th of June, 1844,
" Joseph and Hyrum were arrested for treason, by a
" warrant founded upon the oaths of A. O. Norton
" and Augustine Spencer.

" I will not dwell upon the awful scene which suc-

"ceeded. My heart is thrilled with grief and indig-
"nation, and my blood curdles in my veins whenever
"I speak of it.

"My sons were thrown into jail, where they re-
"mained three days, in company with Brothers
"Richards, Taylor, and Markham. At the end of
"this time, the governor disbanded most of the men,
"but left a guard of eight of our bitterest enemies
"over the jail, and sixty more of the same character
"about a hundred yards distant. He then came into
"Nauvoo with a guard of fifty or sixty men, made
"a short speech, and returned immediately. During
"his absence from Carthage, the guard rushed
"Brother Markham out of the place at the point of
"the bayonet. Soon after this, two hundred of
"those discharged in the morning rushed into Car-
"thage, armed, and painted black, red and yellow,
"and in ten minutes fled again, leaving my sons
"murdered and mangled corpses!

"In leaving the place, a few of them found Samuel
"coming into Carthage alone, on horseback, and
"finding that he was one of our family, they at-
"tempted to shoot him, but he escaped out of their
"hands, although they pursued him at the top of
"their speed for more than two hours. He suc-
"ceeded the next day in getting to Nauvoo in season
"to go out and meet the procession with the bodies
"of Hyrum and Joseph, as the mob had the kind-
"ness to allow us the privilege of bringing them
"home, and burying them in Nauvoo, notwithstand-
"ing the immense reward which was offered by the
"Missourians for Joseph's head.

"Their bodies were attended home by only two

"persons, save those who went from this place.
"These were Brother Willard Richards, and a Mr.
"Hamilton; Brother John Taylor having been shot
"in prison, and nearly killed, he could not be moved
"until sometime afterwards.

"After the corpses were washed, and dressed in
"their burial clothes, we were allowed to see them.
"I had for a long time braced every nerve, roused
"every energy of my soul, and called upon God to
"strengthen me; but when I entered the room, and
"saw my murdered sons extended both at once be-
"fore my eyes, and heard the sobs and groans of
"my family, and the cries of 'Father! husband!
"brothers!' from the lips of their wives, children,
"brother, and sisters, it was too much; I sank back,
"crying to the Lord, in the agony of my soul,
"'My God, my God, why hast thou forsaken this
"family!' A voice replied, 'I have taken them to
"myself, that they might have rest.' Emma was
"carried back to her room almost in a state of in-
"sensibility. Her oldest son approached the corpse,
"and dropped upon his knees, and laying his cheek
"against his father's and kissing him, exclaimed,
"'Oh! my father! my father!' As for myself, I was
"swallowed up in the depth of my afflictions; and
"though my soul was filled with horror past imagi-
"nation, yet I was dumb, until I arose again to
"contemplate the spectacle before me. Oh! at that
"moment how my mind flew through every scene of
"sorrow and distress which we had passed together,
"in which they had shown the innocence and sym-
"pathy which filled their guileless hearts. As I
"looked upon their peaceful, smiling countenances,

" I seemed almost to hear them say, 'Mother, weep
"not for us, we have overcome the world by love;
"we carried to them the gospel, that their souls
"might be saved; they slew us for our testimony,
"and thus placed us beyond their power; their as-
"cendency is for a moment, ours is an eternal
"triumph.'

" I then thought upon the promise which I had
"received in Missouri, that in five years Joseph
"should have power over all his enemies. The
"time had elapsed, and the promise was fulfilled.

" I left the scene and returned to my room, to
"ponder upon the calamities of my family. Soon
"after this Samuel said: 'Mother, I have had a
"dreadful distress in my side ever since I was chased
"by the mob, and I think I have received some
"injury which is going to make me sick.' And in-
"deed he was then not able to sit up, as he had
"been broken of his rest, besides being dreadfully
"fatigued in the chase, which, joined to the shock
"occasioned by the death of his brothers, brought
"on a disease that never was removed.

" On the following day the funeral rites of the
"murdered ones were attended to, in the midst of
"terror and alarm, for the mob had made their ar-
"rangements to burn the city that night, but by the
"diligence of the brethren, they were kept at bay
"until they became discouraged, and returned to
"their homes.

" In a short time Samuel, who continued unwell,
"was confined to his bed, and lingering till the 30th
"of July, his spirit forsook its earthly tabernacle,
"and went to join his brothers, and the ancient
"martyrs, in the paradise of God."

CHAPTER XXXI.

The heroism of the Mormon women rose to more
than tragic splendor in the exodus. Only two circumstances after the martyrdom connect them
strongly with their beloved city. These attach to
their consecrations in, and adieus to, the temple,
and the defence of Nauvoo by the remnant of the
saints in a three days' battle with the enemy. Then
came the evacuation of the city several months
after the majority of the twelve, with the body of
the Church, had taken up their march towards the
Rocky Mountains.

Early in February, 1846, the saints began to cross
the Mississippi in flat-boats, old lighters, and a
number of skiffs, forming quite a fleet, which was
at work night and day under the direction of the
police.

On the 15th of the same month, Brigham Young,
with his family, and others, crossed the Mississippi
from Nauvoo, and proceeded to the " Camps of

Israel," as they were styled by the saints, which waited on the west side of the river, a few miles on the way, for the coming of their leader. These were to form the vanguard of the migrating saints, who were to follow from the various States where they were located, or had organized themselves into flourishing branches and conferences; and soon after this period also began to pour across the Atlantic that tide of emigration from Europe, which has since swelled to the number of about one hundred thousand souls.

In Nauvoo the saints had heard the magic cry, "To your tents, O Israel!" And in sublime faith and trust, such as history scarcely gives an example of, they had obeyed, ready to follow their leader whithersoever he might direct their pilgrim feet.

The Mormons were setting out, under their leader, from the borders of civilization, with their wives and their children, in broad daylight, before the eyes of ten thousand of their enemies, who would have preferred their utter destruction to their "flight," notwithstanding they had enforced it by treaties outrageous beyond description, inasmuch as the exiles were nearly all American born, many of them tracing their ancestors to the very founders of the nation. They had to make a journey of fifteen hundred miles over trackless prairies, sandy deserts and rocky mountains, through bands of warlike Indians, who had been driven, exasperated, towards the West; and at last to seek out and build up their Zion in valleys then unfruitful, in a solitary region where the foot of the white man had scarcely trod. These, too, were to be followed by the aged,

the halt, the sick and the blind, the poor, who were
to be helped by their little less destitute brethren,
and the delicate young mother with her new-born
babe at her breast, and still worse, for they were not
only threatened with the extermination of the poor
remnant at Nauvoo, but news had arrived that the
parent government designed to pursue their pioneers with troops, take from them their arms, and
scatter them, that they might perish by the way,
and leave their bones bleaching in the wilderness.

At about noon, on the 1st of March, 1846, the
" Camp of Israel" began to move, and at four o'clock
nearly four hundred wagons were on the way, traveling in a north-westerly direction. At night they
camped again on Sugar Creek, having advanced
five miles. Scraping away the snow they pitched
their tents upon the frozen ground; and, after building large fires in front, they made themselves as
comfortable as possible under the circumstances.
Indeed, it is questionable whether any other people
in the world could have cozened themselves into a
happy state of mind amid such surroundings, with
such a past fresh and bleeding in their memories,
and with such a prospect as was before both themselves and the remnant of their brethren left in
Nauvoo to the tender mercies of the mob. In his
diary, Apostle Orson Pratt wrote that night: " Notwithstanding our sufferings, hardships and privations, we are cheerful, and rejoice that we have the
privilege of passing through tribulation for the
truth's sake."

These Mormon pilgrims, who took much consolation on their journey in likening themselves to the

Pilgrim fathers and mothers of this nation, whose
descendants many of them, as we have seen, actually
were, that night made their beds upon the frozen
earth. "After bowing before our great Creator,"
wrote Apostle Pratt, "and offering up praise and
thanksgiving to him, and imploring his protection,
we resigned ourselves to the slumbers of the night."

But the weather was more moderate that night
than it had been for several weeks previous. At
their first encampment the thermometer at one time
fell twenty degrees below zero, freezing over the
great Mississippi. The survivors of that journey
will tell you they never suffered so much from the
cold in their lives as they did on Sugar Creek.

And what of the Mormon women? Around them
circles almost a tragic romance. Fancy may find
abundant subject for graphic story of the devotion,
the suffering, the matchless heroism of the sisters,
in the telling incident that nine children were born
to them the first night they camped out on Sugar
Creek, February 5th, 1846. That day they wept
their farewells over their beloved city, or in the
sanctuary of the temple, in which they had hoped
to worship till the end of life, but which they left
never to see again; that night suffering nature administered to them the mixed cup of woman's
supremest joy and pain.

But it was not prayer alone that sustained these
pilgrims. The practical philosophy of their great
leader, daily and hourly applied to the exigencies of
their case, did almost as much as their own matchless faith to sustain them from the commencement
to the end of their journey. With that leader had

very properly come to the " Camp of Israel" several of the twelve and the chief bishops of the Church, but he also brought with him a quorum, humble in pretensions, yet useful as high priests to the saints in those spirit-saddening days. It was Captain Pitt's brass band. That night the president had the brethren and sisters out in the dance, and the music was as glad as at a merry-making. Several gentlemen from Iowa gathered to witness the strange, interesting scene. They could scarcely believe their own senses when they were told that these were Mormons in their "flight from civilization," bound they knew not whither, except where God should lead them "by the hand of his servant."

Thus in the song and the dance the saints praised the Lord. When the night was fine, and supper, which consisted of the most primitive fare, was over, some of the men would clear away the snow, while others bore large logs to the camp-fires in anticipation of the jubilee of the evening. Soon, in a sheltered place, the blazing fires would roar, and fifty couples, old and young, would join, in the merriest spirit, to the music of the band, or the rival revelry of the solitary fiddle. As they journeyed along, too, strangers constantly visited their camps, and great was their wonderment to see the order, unity and good feeling that prevailed in the midst of the people. By the camp-fires they would linger, listening to the music and song; and they fain had taken part in the merriment had not those scenes been as sacred worship in the exodus of a God-fearing people. To fully understand the incidents here narrated, the reader must couple in his mind the idea of an exodus with the idea of an Israelitish jubilee; for it was a jubilee to the Mormons to be delivered from their enemies at any price.

At one point on their journey the citizens of a town near by came over to camp to invite the "Nauvoo Band," under Captain Pitt, to come to their village for a concert. There was some music left in the brethren. They had not forgotten how to sing the "songs of Zion," so they made the good folks of the village merry, and for a time forgot their own sorrows.

These incidents of travel were varied by an occasional birth in camp. There was also the death of a lamented lady early on the journey. She was a gentle wife of a famous Mormon missionary, Orson Spencer, once a Baptist minister of excellent standing. She had requested the brethren to take her with them. She would not be left behind. Life was too far exhausted by the persecutions to survive the exodus, but she could yet have the honor of dying in that immortal circumstance of her people. Several others of the sisters also died at the very starting. Ah, who shall fitly picture the lofty heroism of the Mormon women!

CHAPTER XXXII.

CONTINUATION OF ELIZA R. SNOW'S NARRATIVE—AD-
VENT OF A LITTLE STRANGER UNDER ADVERSE
CIRCUMSTANCES—DORMITORY, SITTING-ROOM, OF-
FICE, ETC., IN A BUGGY—"THE CAMP"—INTER-
ESTING EPISODES OF THE JOURNEY—GRAPHIC DE-
SCRIPTION OF THE METHOD OF PROCEDURE—
MOUNT PISGAH—WINTER QUARTERS.

The subject and action of the exodus thus opened,
we shall let the sisters chiefly tell their own stories
of that extraordinary historic period. Eliza R.
Snow, continuing her narrative, says:

"We had been preceded by thousands, and I was
informed that on the first night of the encampment
nine children were born into the world, and from
that time, as we journeyed onward, mothers gave
birth to offspring under almost every variety of circumstances imaginable, except those to which they
had been accustomed; some in tents, others in
wagons—in rain-storms and in snow-storms. I heard
of one birth which occurred under the rude shelter
of a hut, the sides of which were formed of blankets
fastened to poles stuck in the ground, with a bark
roof through which the rain was dripping. Kind
sisters stood holding dishes to catch the water as it

fell, thus protecting the new-comer and its mother
from a shower-bath as the little innocent first entered on the stage of human life; and through faith
in the great ruler of events, no harm resulted to
either.

"Let it be remembered that the mothers of these
wilderness-born babes were not savages, accustomed
to roam the forest and brave the storm and tempest—
those who had never known the comforts and deli-
cacies of civilization and refinement. They were
not those who, in the wilds of nature, nursed their
offspring amid reeds and rushes, or in the recesses
of rocky caverns; most of them were born and
educated in the Eastern States—had there embraced
the gospel as taught by Jesus and his apostles, and,
for the sake of their religion, had gathered with the
saints, and under trying circumstances had assisted,
by their faith, patience and energies, in making
Nauvoo what its name indicates, 'the beautiful.'
There they had lovely homes, decorated with flowers
and enriched with choice fruit trees, just beginning
to yield plentifully.

"To these homes, without lease or sale, they had
just bade a final adieu, and with what little of their
substance could be packed into one, two, and in
some instances, three wagons, had started out,
desertward, for—where? To this question the only
response at that time was, God knows.

"From the 13th to the 18th we had several snow-
storms and very freezing weather, which bridged the
Mississippi sufficiently for crossing heavily loaded
wagons on the ice. We were on timbered land, had
plenty of wood for fuel, and the men rolled heavy

logs together, and kept large fires burning, around the bright blaze of which, when not necessarily otherwise engaged, they warmed themselves. The women, when the duties of cooking and its *et ceteras* did not prompt them out, huddled with their children into wagons and carriages for protection from the chilling breezes.

"My dormitory, sitting-room, writing-office, and frequently dining-room, was the buggy in which Sister Markham, her little son David, and I, rode. One of my brother's wives had one of the old-fashioned foot-stoves, which proved very useful. She frequently brought it to me, filled with live coals from one of those mammoth fires—a kindness which I remember with gratitude; but withal, I frosted my feet enough to occasion inconvenience for weeks afterwards.

"When all who designed traveling in one camp, which numbered about five thousand, had crossed the river, the organization of the whole into hundreds, fifties, and tens, commenced, and afterwards was completed for the order of traveling; with pioneers, commissaries, and superintendents to each hundred, and captains over fifties and tens. It was impossible for us to move in a body; and one company filed off after another; and, on the first of March we broke camp and moved out four or five miles and put up for the night, where at first view the prospect was dreary enough. It was nearly sunset—very cold, and the ground covered with snow to the depth of four or five inches; but with brave hearts and strong hands, and a supply of spades and shovels, the men removed the snow, and suddenly transformed the bleak desert scene into a living town, with cloth houses, log-heap fires, and a multitude of cheerful inhabitants. The next day, with weather moderated, the remainder of the original camp arrived with the Nauvoo band, and tented on the bluff, which overlooked our cozy dell, and at night stirring strains of music filled the atmosphere, on which they were wafted abroad, and re-echoed on the responsive breezes.

> " Lo! a mighty host of people,
>   Tented on the western shore
> Of the noble Mississippi,
>   They, for weeks, were crossing o'er.
> At the last day's dawn of winter,
>   Bound with frost and wrapped with snow,
> Hark! the sound is, ' Up, and onward!
> Camp of Zion, rise and go.'

> " All, at once, is life and motion—
>   Trunks and beds and baggage fly;
> Oxen yoked and horses harnessed—
>   Tents, rolled up, are passing by.
> Soon the carriage wheels are rolling
>   Onward to a woodland dell,
> Where, at sunset, all are quartered—
>   Camp of Israel, all is well.

> " Soon the tents are thickly clustered—
>   Neighboring smokes together blend—
> Supper served—the hymns are chanted,
>   And the evening prayers ascend.
> Last of all, the guards are stationed;
>   Heavens! must guards be serving here?
> Who would harm the homeless exiles?
>   Camp of Zion, never fear.

> " Where is freedom?   Where is justice?
>   Both have from the nation fled,
> And the blood of martyred prophets
>   Must be answered on its head.
> Therefore, ' To your tents, O, Israel,'
>   Like your Father Abram dwell;
> God will execute his purpose—
>   Camp of Zion, all is well.

"From time to time, companies of men either volunteered or were detailed from the journeying camps, and, by going off the route, obtained jobs of work for which they received food in payment, to meet the necessities of those who were only partially supplied, and also grain for the teams.

"As we passed through a town on the Des Moines river, the inhabitants manifested as much curiosity as though they were viewing a traveling menagerie of wild animals. Their levity and apparent heartlessness was, to me, proof of profound ignorance. How little did those people comprehend our movement, and the results the Almighty had in view.

"On the 2d of March we again moved forward—and here I will transcribe from my journal: 'March 3d—Our encampment this night may truly be recorded as a miracle, performed on natural, and yet peculiar principles—a city reared in a few hours, and everything in operation that actual living required, and many additional things, which, if not extravagancies, were certainly convenient. The next day, great numbers of the people of the adjacent country were to be seen patrolling the nameless streets of our anonymous city, with astonishment visible in their countenances. In the evening, Sister Markham and I took a stroll abroad, and in the absence of names to the streets, and numbers to the tents, we lost our way, and had to procure a guide to pilot us home.'

"At this point Brother Markham exchanged our buggy for a lumber wagon, and in performing an act of generosity to others, so filled it as to give Sister M. and me barely room to sit in front. And when we started again, Sister M. and I were seated on a chest with brass-kettle and soap-box for our footstools, and were happy in being as comfortably situated as we were; and well we might be, for many of our sisters walked all day, rain or shine, and at night prepared suppers for their families, with no sheltering tents; and then made their beds in and under wagons that contained their earthly all. How frequently, with intense sympathy and admiration, I watched the mother, when, forgetful of her own fatigue and destitution, she took unwearied pains to fix up, in the most palatable form, the allotted portion of food, and as she dealt it out was cheering the hearts of her homeless children, while, as I truly believed, her own was lifted to God in fervent prayer that their lives might be preserved, and, above all, that they might honor him in the religion for which she was an exile from the home once sacred to her, for the sake of those precious ones that God had committed to her care. We were living on rations— our leaders having counseled that arrangement, to prevent an improvident use of provision that would result in extreme destitution.

"We were traveling in the season significantly termed 'between hay and grass,' and the teams, feeding mostly on browse, wasted in flesh, and had but little strength; and it was painful, at times, to see the poor creatures straining every joint and ligature, doing their utmost, and looking the very picture of discouragement. When crossing the low lands, where spring rains had soaked the mellow soil, they frequently stalled on level ground, and we could move only by coupling teams, which made

very slow progress. From the effects of chills and
fever, I had not strength to walk much, or I should
not have been guilty of riding after those half-fam-
ished animals. It would require a painter's pencil
and skill to represent our encampment when we
stopped, as we frequently did, to give the jaded
teams a chance to recuperate, and us a chance to
straighten up matters and things generally. Here
is a bit from my journal:

"'Our town of yesterday has grown to a city. It
is laid out in a half hollow square, fronting east and
south on a beautiful level—with, on one side, an
almost perpendicular, and on the other, a gradual
descent into a deep ravine, which defines it on the
west and north. At nine o'clock this morning I
noticed a blacksmith's shop in operation, and everything, everywhere, indicating real life and local industry. Only the sick are idle; not a stove or
cooking utensil but is called into requisition; while
tubs, washboards, etc., are one-half mile distant,
where washing is being done by the side of a stream
of water beneath the shade of waving branches. I
join Sister M. in the washing department, and
get a buggy ride to the scene of action, where the
boys have the fire in waiting—while others of our
mess stop in the city and do the general work of
housekeeping; and for our dinner send us a generous
portion of their immense pot-pie, designed to satisfy
the hunger of about thirty stomachs. It is made
of rabbits, squirrels, quails, prairie chickens, etc.,
trophies of the success of our hunters, of whom
each division has its quota. Thus from time to
time we are supplied with fresh meat, which does

much in lengthening out our flour. Occasionally our jobbers take bacon in payment, but what I have seen of that article is so rancid that nothing short of prospective starvation would tempt me to eat it.'

"On the 20th of April we arrived at the head waters of the Grand River, where it was decided to make a farming establishment, to be a resting and recruiting place for the saints who should follow us. Elders Bent, Benson and Fullmer were appointed to preside over it.

"The first of June found us in a small grove on the middle fork of Grand River. This place, over which Elders Rich and Huntington were called to preside, was named Pisgah; and from this point most of the divisions filed off, one after another. Colonel Markham appropriated all of his teams and one wagon to assist the twelve and others to pursue the journey westward, while he returned to the States for a fresh supply. Before he left, we were in a house made of logs laid up 'cob fashion,' with from three to eight inches open space between them—roofed by stretching a tent cloth over the ridgepole and fastening it at the bottom, on the outside, which, with blankets and carpets put up on the north end, as a shield from the cold wind, made us as comfortable as possible.

"Companies were constantly arriving and others departing; while those who intended stopping till the next spring were busily engaged in making gardens, and otherwise preparing for winter—sheltering themselves in rude log huts for temporary residence.

"The camps were strung along several hundred

miles in length from front to rear, when, about the
last of June, one of the most remarkably unreason-
able requisitions came officially to President Young,
from the United States government, demanding five
hundred efficient men to be drawn from our traveling camps, to enter the United States military
service, and march immediate to California and
assist in the war with Mexico. Upon the receipt
of this demand, President Young and Heber C.
Kimball, with due loyalty to an unprotective government, under which we had been exiled from our
homes, started immediately from their respective
divisions, on horseback, calling for volunteers, from
one extremity of our line to the other; and in an
almost incredibly short time the five hundred men,
who constituted the celebrated 'Mormon Battalion,'
were under marching orders, commanded by Col.
Allen, of the United States Infantry. It was our
'country's call,' and the question, 'Can we spare five
hundred of our most able-bodied men?' was not
asked. But it was a heavy tax—a cruel draft—one
which imposed accumulated burdens on those who
remained, especially our women, who were under
the necessity of driving their own teams from the
several points from which their husbands and sons
left, to the Salt Lake Valley; and some of them
walked the whole of that tedious distance.

On the 2d of August Brother Markham arrived
from the East with teams; and on the 19th we bade
good-bye to Mount Pisgah. Brother M. was minus
one teamster, and as Mrs. M. and I were to constitute the occupants of one wagon, with a gentle yoke
of oxen, she proposed to drive. But, soon after we

started, she was taken sick, and, of course, the driving fell to me. Had it been a horse-team I should have been amply qualified, but driving oxen was entirely a new business; however, I took the whip and very soon learned to ' haw and gee,' and acquitted myself, as teamster, quite honorably, driving most of the way to winter quarters. The cattle were so well trained that I could sit and drive. At best, however, it was fatiguing—the family being all sick by turns, and at times I had to cook, as well as nurse the sick; all of which I was thankful for strength to perform.

"On the 27th we crossed the Missouri at Council Bluffs, and the next day came up with the general camp at winter quarters. From exposure and hardship I was taken sick soon after with a slow fever, that terminated in chills and fever, and as I lay sick in my wagon, where my bed was exposed to heavy autumnal rains, and sometimes wet nearly from head to foot, I realized that I was near the gate of death; but my trust was in God, and his power preserved me. Many were sick around us, and no one could be properly cared for under the circumstances. Although, as before stated, I was exposed to the heavy rains while in the wagon, worse was yet to come.

"On the 28th a company, starting out for supplies, required the wagon that Sister M. and I had occupied; and the log house we moved into was but partly chinked and mudded, leaving large crevices for the wind—then cold and blustering. This hastily-erected hut was roofed on one side, with a tent-cloth thrown over the other, and, withal, was minus a chimney. A fire, which was built on one side, filled the house with smoke until it became unendurable. Sister Markham had partially recovered from her illness, but was quite feeble. I was not able to sit up much, and, under those circumstances, not at all, for the fire had to be dispensed with. Our cooking was done out of doors until after the middle of November, when a chimney was made, the house enclosed, and other improvements added, which we were prepared to appreciate.

"About the last of December I received the sad news of the death of my mother. She had lived to a good age, and had been a patient participator in the scenes of suffering consequent on the persecutions of the saints. She sleeps in peace; and her grave, and that of my father, whose death preceded hers less than a year, are side by side, in Walnut Grove, Knox county, Ill.

"At winter quarters our extensive encampment was divided into wards, and so organized that meetings for worship were attended in the several wards. A general order was established and cheerfully carried out, that each able-bodied man should either give the labor of each tenth day, or contribute an equivalent, for the support of the destitute, and to aid those families whose men were in the battalion, and those who were widows indeed.

"Our exposures and privations caused much sickness, and sickness increased destitution; but in the midst of all this, we enjoyed a great portion of the spirit of God, and many seasons of refreshing from his presence, with rich manifestations of the gifts and power of the gospel. My life, as well as the lives of many others, was preserved by the power of God, through faith in him, and not on natural principles as comprehended by man."

CHAPTER XXXIII.

BATHSHEBA W. SMITH'S STORY OF THE LAST DAYS OF
NAUVOO—SHE RECEIVES CELESTIAL MARRIAGE AND
GIVES HER HUSBAND FIVE "HONORABLE YOUNG
WOMEN" AS WIVES — HER DESCRIPTION OF THE
EXODUS AND JOURNEY TO WINTER QUARTERS—
DEATH OF ONE OF THE WIVES—SISTER HORNE
AGAIN.

Sister Bathsheba W. Smith's story of the last
days of Nauvoo, and the introduction of polygamy,
and also her graphic detail of the exodus, will be of
interest at this point.   She says:

"Immediately after my marriage, my husband, as
"one of the apostles of the Church, started on a mis-
"sion to some of the Eastern States.

"In the year 1840 he was in England, and again
"went East on mission in 1843, going as far as Bos-
"ton, Mass., preaching and attending conferences
"by the way.   He returned in the fall; soon after
"which, we were blessed by receiving our endow-
"ments, and were sealed under the holy law of
"celestial marriage.   I heard the prophet Joseph
"charge the twelve with the duty and responsibility
"of administering the ordinances of endowments
"and sealing for the living and the dead.   I met

"many times with Brother Joseph and others who
"had received their endowments, in company with
"my husband, in an upper room dedicated for that
"purpose, and prayed with them repeatedly in those
"meetings. I heard the prophet give instructions
"concerning plural marriage; he counseled the sis-
"ters not to trouble themselves in consequence of
"it, that all would be right, and the result would be
"for their glory and exaltation.

"On the 5th of May, 1844, my husband again
"started on mission, and, after he left, a terrible per-
"secution was commenced in the city of Nauvoo,
"which brought about the barbarous murder of our
"beloved prophet, and his brother, the patriarch.
"The death of these men of God caused a general
"mourning which I cannot describe. My husband
"returned about the first of August, and soon the
"rest of the twelve returned. The times were very
"exciting, but under the wise counsels of the twelve,
"and others, the excitement abated. The temple
"was so far finished in the fall of 1845, that thou-
"sands received their endowments. I officiated for
"some time as priestess.

"Being thoroughly convinced, as well as my hus-
"band, that the doctrine of plurality of wives was
"from God, and having a fixed determination to
"attain to celestial glory, I felt to embrace the whole
"gospel, and believing that it was for my husband's
"exaltation that he should obey the revelation on
"celestial marriage, that he might attain to king-
"doms, thrones, principalities and powers, firmly
"believing that I should participate with him in all
"his blessings, glory and honor; accordingly, within

" the last year, like Sarah of old, I had given to my
" husband five wives, good, virtuous, honorable young
" women.   They all had their home with us ; I being
" proud of my husband, and loving him very much,
" knowing him to be a man of God, and believing
" he would not love them less because he loved me
" more for doing this.   I had joy in having a testi-
" mony that what I had done was acceptable to my
" Father in Heaven.

  " The fall of 1845 found Nauvoo, as it were, one
" vast mechanic shop, as nearly every family was
" engaged in making wagons.   Our parlor was used
" as a paint-shop in which to paint wagons.   All
" were making preparations to leave the ensuing
" winter.   On the 9th of February, 1846, in com-
" pany with many others, my husband took me and
" my two children, and some of the other members
" of his family (the remainder to follow as soon as
" the weather would permit), and we crossed the
" Mississippi, to seek a home in the wilderness.
" Thus we left a comfortable home, the accumula-
" tion and labor of four years, taking with us but a
" few things, such as clothing, bedding and provi-
" sions, leaving everything else for our enemies.
" We were obliged to stay in camp for a few weeks,
" on Sugar Creek, because of the weather being very
" cold.   The Mississippi froze over so that hundreds
" of families crossed on the ice.   As soon as the
" weather permitted, we moved on West.   I will not
" try to describe how we traveled through storms of
" snow, wind and rain—how roads had to be made,
" bridges built, and rafts constructed—how our poor
" animals had to drag on, day after day, with scanty

" feed—nor how our camps suffered from poverty,
" sickness and death. We were consoled in the
" midst of these hardships by seeing the power of
" God manifested through the laying on of the hands
" of the elders, causing the sick to be healed and
" the lame to walk. The Lord was with us, and his
" power was made manifest daily. At the head of a
" slough where we camped several days, we were
" visited by the Mus-Quaw-ke band of Indians, headed
" by Pow-Sheek, a stately looking man, wearing a
" necklace of bear's claws. They were fierce look-
" ing men, decorated as they were for war; but they
" manifested a friendly spirit, and traded with us.
" The next move of our camp was to the Missouri
" river bank. The cattle were made to swim, and
" our wagons were taken over on a flat-boat that our
" people had built. We made two encampments
" after we crossed the river, when we found it too
" late to proceed farther that year. The last en-
" campment was named Cutler's Park. The camps
" contained about one thousand wagons. Our men
" went to work cutting and stacking the coarse
" prairie grass for hay. The site for our winter
" quarters was selected and surveyed, and during
" the fall and winter some seven hundred log-cabins
" were built; also about one hundred and fifty dug-
" outs or caves, which are cabins half under ground.
" This was on the Missouri river, about six miles
" above the present city of Omaha. My husband
" built four cabins and a dug-out. Our chimnies
" were made of sod, cut with a spade in the form of
" a brick; clay was pounded in to make our fire-
" places and hearths. In our travels the winds had

"literally blown our tent to pieces, so that we
" were glad to get into cabins. The most of the
" roofs were made of timber, covered with clay.
" The floors were split and hewed puncheon; the
" doors were generally made of the same material,
" of cottonwood and linn. Many houses were cov-
" ered with oak-shakes, fastened on with weight-
" poles. A few were covered with shingles. A log
" meeting-house was built, about twenty-four by
" forty feet, and the hewn floor was frequently used
" for dancing. A grist-mill was built and run by
" water-power, and in addition to this, several horse-
" mills and hand-mills were used to grind corn.

" Our scanty and only supply of bread, consisting
" generally of corn, was mostly brought from Mis-
" souri, a distance of some one hundred and fifty
" miles, where it fortunately was plentiful and cheap.
" The camp having been deprived of vegetable food
" the past year, many were attacked with scurvy.
" The exposure, together with the want of necessary
" comforts, caused fevers and ague, and affections of
" the lungs. Our own family were not exempt.
" Nancy Clement, one of my husband's wives, died;
" also her child. She was a woman of excellent dis-
" position, and died in full faith in the gospel."

An incident or two of Sister Horne's story may
very properly accompany the foregoing. She says:

" I took my last look, on earth, of Joseph and
" Hyrum Smith. May I never experience another
" day similar to that! I do not wish to recall the
" scene but for a moment. That terrible martyrdom
" deeply scarred the hearts and bewildered the senses
" of all our people. We could scarcely realize the

"awful event, except in the agony of our feelings;
"nor comprehend the dark hour, beyond the solemn
"loneliness which, pervaded the city and made the
"void in our stricken hearts still more terrible to
"bear.   For the moment the sun of our life had set.
"The majority of the apostles were far from home,
"and we could do no more than wake the indigna-
"tion of heaven against the murderers by our lamen-
"tations, and weep and pray for divine support in
"that awful hour.

   "Two years had not passed away after the mar-
"tyrdom, before the saints were forced by their
"enemies to hasten their flight from Nauvoo."

   With the Camp of Israel, Sister Horne and family
journeyed to winter quarters, sharing the common
experience of the saints, so well described by those
who have preceded her.

CHAPTER XXXIV.

" It was June 27th, 1844," writes Zina D. Young
(one of the Huntington sisters, with whom the
reader is familiar), " and it was rumored that Joseph
"was expected in from Carthage. I did not know
"to the contrary until I saw the Governor and his
"guards descending the hill by the temple, a short
"distance from my house. Their swords glistened
"in the sun, and their appearance startled me, though
"I knew not what it foreboded. I exclaimed to a
"neighbor who was with me, ' What is the trouble!
"It seems to me that the trees and the grass are in
"mourning!' A fearful silence pervaded the city,
"and after the shades of night gathered around us
"it was thick darkness. The lightnings flashed, the
"cattle bellowed, the dogs barked, and the elements
"wailed. What a terrible night that was to the
"saints, yet we knew nothing of the dark tragedy
"which had been enacted by the assassins at Car-
"thage.

" The morning dawned; the sad news came; but
"as yet I had not heard of the terrible event. I
"started to go to Mother Smith's, on an errand.
"As I approached I saw men gathered around the
"door of the mansion. A few rods from the house
"I met Jesse P. Harmon. 'Have you heard the
"news?' he asked. 'What news?' I inquired.
"'Joseph and Hyrum are dead!' Had I believed
"it, I could not have walked any farther. I has-
"tened to my brother Dimick. He was sitting in
"his house, mourning and weeping aloud as only
"strong men can weep. All was confirmed in a
"moment. My pen cannot utter my grief nor de-
"scribe my horror. But after awhile a change came,
"as though the released spirits of the departed
"sought to comfort us in that hour of dreadful
"bereavement.

> " 'The healer was there, pouring balm on my heart,
>   And wiping the tears from my eyes;
> He was binding the chain that was broken in twain,
>   And fastening it firm in the skies.'

" Never can it be told in words what the saints
"suffered in those days of trial; but the sweet spirit—
"the comforter—did not forsake them; and when
"the twelve returned, the mantle of Joseph fell upon
"Brigham.

" When I approached the stand (on the occasion
"when Sidney Rigdon was striving for the guardian-
"ship of the Church), President Young was speak-
"ing. It was the voice of Joseph Smith—not that
"of Brigham Young. His very person was changed.
"The mantle was truly given to another. There
"was no doubting this in the minds of that vast

" assembly. All witnessed the transfiguration, and
" even to-day thousands bear testimony thereof. I
" closed my eyes. I could have exclaimed, I know
" that is Joseph Smith's voice! Yet I knew he had
" gone. But the same spirit was with the people;
" the comforter remained.

" The building of, the temple was hurried on.
" The saints did not slacken their energies. They
" had a work to do in that temple for their dead,
" and blessings to obtain for themselves. They had
" learned from the prophet Joseph the meaning of
" Paul's words, ' Why then are ye baptized for the
" dead, if the dead rise not at all?'

" Passing on to the exodus. My family were
" informed that we were to leave with the first com-
" pany. So on the 9th of February, 1846, on a clear
" cold day, we left our home at Nauvoo. All that
" we possessed was now in our wagon. Many of
" our things remained in the house, unsold, for most
" of our neighbors were, like ourselves, on the wing.

" Arrived at Sugar Creek, we there first saw who
" were the brave, the good, the self-sacrificing. Here
" we had now openly the first examples of noble-
" minded, virtuous women, bravely commencing to
" live in the newly-revealed order of celestial mar-
" riage.

" ' Women ; this is my husband's wife !'

" Here, at length, we could give this introduction,
" without fear of reproach, or violation of man-made
" laws, seeing we were bound for the refuge of the
" Rocky Mountains, where no Gentile society ex-
" isted, to ask of Israel, ' What doest thou?'

" President Young arrived on Sugar Creek, and at

"once commenced to organize the camp. George
" A. Smith was the captain of our company of fifty.·

" I will pass over the tedious journey to the
"Chariton river, in the face of the fierce winds of
"departing winter, and amid rains that fairly inun-
"dated the land. By day we literally waded through
"mud and water, and at night camped in anything
"but pleasant places.

" On the bank of the Chariton an incident oc-
"curred ever eventful in the life of woman. I had
"been told in the temple that I should acknowledge·
"God even in a miracle in my deliverance in
"woman's hour of trouble, which hour had now
"come. We had traveled one morning about five
"miles, when I called for a halt in our march. There
"was but one person with me—Mother Lyman, the
"aunt of George A. Smith; and there on the bank
"of the Chariton I was delivered of a fine son. On
"the morning of the 23d, Mother Lyman gave me
"a cup of coffee and a biscuit. What a luxury for
"special remembrance! Occasionally the wagon
"had to be stopped, that I might take breath. Thus
"I journeyed on. But I did not mind the hardship
"of my situation, for my life had been preserved,
"and my babe seemed so beautiful.

" We reached Mount Pisgah in May. I was now
"with my father, who had been appointed to preside
"over this temporary settlement of the saints. But
"an unlooked for event soon came. One evening
"Parley P. Pratt arrived, bringing the word from
"headquarters that the Mormon battalion must be
"raised in compliance with the requisition of the ·
"government upon our people. And what did this

"news personally amount to, to me? That I had
"only my father to look after me now; for I had
"parted from my husband; my eldest brother,
"Dimick Huntington, with his family, had gone into
"the battalion, and every man who could be spared
"was also enlisted. It was impossible for me to go
"on to winter quarters, so I tarried at Mount Pisgah
"with my father.

"But, alas! a still greater trial awaited me! The
"call for the battalion had left many destitute.
"They had to live in wagons. But worse than des-
"titution stared us in the face. Sickness came upon
"us and death invaded our camp. Sickness was so
"prevalent and deaths so frequent that enough help
"could not be had to make coffins, and many of the
"dead were wrapped in their grave-clothes and
"buried with split logs at the bottom of the grave
"and brush at the sides, that being all that could
"be done for them by their mourning friends. Too
"soon it became my turn to mourn. My father was
"taken sick, and in eighteen days he died. Just
"before he left us for his better home he raised him-
"self upon his elbow, and said: 'Man is like the
"flower or the grass—cut down in an hour! Father,
"unto thee do I commend my spirit!' This said,
"he sweetly went to rest with the just, a martyr for
"the truth; for, like my dear mother, who died in
"the expulsion from Missouri, he died in the expul-
"sion from Nauvoo. Sad was my heart. I alone
"of all his children was there to mourn.

"It was a sad day at Mount Pisgah, when my
"father was buried. The poor and needy had lost
"a friend—the kingdom of God a faithful ser-

"vant. There upon the hillside was his resting
"place. The graveyard was so near that I could
"hear the wolves howling as they visited the spot;
"those hungry monsters, who fain would have un-
"sepulchred those sacred bones!

"Those days of trial and grief were succeeded by
"my journey to winter quarters, where in due time
"I arrived, and was welcomed by President Young
"into his family."

CHAPTER XXXV.

THE PIONEERS—THE PIONEER COMPANIES THAT FOL-
LOWED—METHOD OF THE MARCH—MRS. HORNE
ON THE PLAINS—THE EMIGRANT'S POST-OFFICE—
PENTECOSTS BY THE WAY—DEATH AS THEY JOUR-
NEYED—A FEAST IN THE DESERT—"AUNT LOUISA"
AGAIN.

Very properly President Young and a chosen
cohort of apostles and elders formed the band of
pioneers who bore the standard of their people to
the Rocky Mountains. On the 7th of April, 1847,
that famous company left winter quarters in search
of another Zion and gathering place. Three women
only went with them. These must be honored with
a lasting record. They were Clara Decker, one of
the wives of Brigham Young; her mother, and Ellen
Sanders, one of the wives of H. C. Kimball.

Yet the sisters as a mass were scarcely less the
co-pioneers of that apostolic band, for they followed
in companies close upon its track. It was with
them faith, not sight. They continued their pil-
grimage to the West early in June. On the 12th,
Captain Jedediah M. Grant's company moved out
in the advance.

"After we started out from winter quarters," says

Sister Eliza Snow, "three or four days were consumed in maneuvering and making a good ready, and then, at an appointed place for rendezvous, a general meeting was held around a liberty-pole erected for the purpose, and an organization effected, similar to that entered into after leaving Nauvoo.

" As we moved forward, one division after another, sometimes in fifties, sometimes in tens, but seldom traveling in hundreds, we passed and repassed each other, but at night kept as nearly compact as circumstances would admit, especially when in the Indian country. East of Fort Laramie many of the Sioux Nation mixed with our traveling camps, on their way to the fort, where a national council was in session. We had no other trouble with them than the loss of a few cooking utensils, which, when unobserved, they lightly fingered; except in one instance, when our ten had been left in the rear to repair a broken wagon, until late in the evening. It was bright moonlight, and as we were passing one of their encampments, they formed in a line closely by the roadside, and when our teams passed, they simultaneously shook their blankets vigorously on purpose to frighten the teams and cause a stampede, probably with the same object in view as white robbers have in ditching railroad trains. However, no serious injury occurred, although the animals were dreadfully frightened."

Sister Horne thus relates some incidents of the journey:

" Apostle John Taylor traveled in the company " that my family was with, Bishop Hunter being cap- " tain of the company of one hundred, and Bishop

"Foutz and my husband being captains of fifties.
"The officers proposed, for safety in traveling
"through the Indian country, that the two fifties
"travel side by side, which was agreed to, Bishop
"Foutz's fifty taking the north side. For some days
"the wind blew from the south with considerable
"force, covering the fifty on the north with dust
"from our wagons. This continued for two weeks;
"it was then agreed that the two companies should
"shift positions in order to give us our fair propor-
"tion of the dust; but in a day or two afterwards
"the wind shifted to the north, thus driving the dust
"on to the same company as before. After having
"some good natured badinage over the circumstance,
"our company changed with the unfortunates and
"took its share of the dust.

"One day a company of Indians met us and mani-
"fested a desire to trade, which we were glad to do;
"but as the brethren were exchanging corn for buf-
"falo robes, the squaws were quietly stealing every-
"thing they could lay hands upon. Many bake-
"kettles, skillets and frying-pans were missing when
"we halted that night.

"As our wagons were standing while the trading
"was going on, one Indian took a great fancy to my
"little girl, who was sitting on my knee, and wanted
"to buy her, offering me a pony. I told him 'no
"trade.' He then brought another pony, and still
"another, but I told him no; so he brought the
"fourth, and gave me to understand that they were
"all good, and that the last one was especially good
"for chasing buffalo. The situation was becoming
"decidedly embarrassing, when several more wagons

"drew near, dispersing the crowd of Indians that
"had gathered around me, and attracting the atten-
"tion of my persistent patron."

The emigrant's post-offices are thus spoken of by
Sister Eliza:

"Much of the time we were on an untrodden
way; but when we came on the track of the pioneers, as we occasionally did, and read the date of
their presence, with an 'all well' accompaniment, on
a bleached buffalo skull, we had a general time of
rejoicing."

For years those bleached buffalo skulls were made
the news agents of the Mormon emigrations. The
morning newspaper of to-day is not read with so
much eagerness as were those dry bones on the
plains, telling of family and friends gone before.

It was a long, tedious journey to those pioneer
sisters, yet they had pentecosts even on their pil-
grimage. Again quoting from Sister Eliza:

"Many were the moon and starlight evenings
when, as we circled around the blazing fire, and sang
our hymns of devotion, and songs of praise to him
who knows the secrets of all hearts, the sound of
our united voices reverberated from hill to hill, and
echoing through the silent expanse, seemed to fill
the vast concave above, while the glory of God
seemed to rest on all around. Even now while I
write, the remembrance of those sacredly romantic
and vivifying scenes calls them up afresh, and arouses
a feeling of response that language is inadequate to
express."

But there were dark days also. The story changes
to sickness in the wagons and death by the wayside:

"Death," says Sister Eliza, "made occasional inroads among us. Nursing the sick in tents and wagons was a laborious service; but the patient faithfulness with which it was performed is, no doubt, registered in the archives above, as an unfading memento of brotherly and sisterly love. The burial of the dead by the wayside was a sad office. For husbands, wives and children to consign the cherished remains of loved ones to a lone, desert grave, was enough to try the firmest heartstrings.

"Although every care and kindness possible under the circumstances were extended to her, the delicate constitution of Mrs. Jedediah M. Grant was not sufficient for the hardships of the journey. I was with her much, previous to her death, which occurred so near to Salt Lake Valley, that by forced drives, night and day, her remains were brought through for interment. Not so, however, with her beautiful babe of eight or ten months, whose death preceded her's about two weeks; it was buried in the desert."

The companies now began to hear of the pioneers and the location of "Great Salt Lake City." On the 4th of August several of the Mormon battalion were met returning from the Mexican war. They were husbands and sons of women in this division. There was joy indeed in the meeting. Next came an express from the valley, and finally the main body of the pioneers, returning to winter quarters. On the Sweetwater, Apostle Taylor made for them a royal feast, spoken of to this day. Sisters Taylor, Horne, and others of our leading pioneer women, sustained the honors of that occasion.

Early in October the companies, one after another, reached the valley.

The next year many of the pioneers made their second journey to the mountains, and with them now came Daniel H. Wells, the story of whose wife, Louisa, shall close these journeys of the pioneers.

Although exceedingly desirous of crossing the plains with the first company of that year, her father was unable to do more than barely provide the two wagons necessary to carry his family and provisions, and the requisite number of oxen to draw them. The luxury of an extra teamster to care for the second wagon was out of the question; and so Louisa, although but twenty-two years of age, and although she had never driven an ox in her life, heroically undertook the task of driving one of the outfits, and caring for a younger brother and sister.

The picture of her starting is somewhat amusing. After seeing that her allotment of baggage and provisions, along with her little brother and sister, had been stowed in the wagon; with a capacious old-fashioned sun-bonnet on her head, a parasol in one hand and an ox-whip in the other, she placed herself by the side of her leading yoke of oxen and bravely set her face westward. Matters went well enough for a short distance, considering her inexperience with oxen; but the rain began to pour, and shortly her parasol was found to be utterly inadequate, so in disgust she threw it into the wagon, and traveled on in the wet grass amid the pouring rain. Presently the paste-board stiffeners of her sun-bonnet began to succumb to the persuasive moisture, and before night, draggled and muddy, and thoroughly wet to the skin, her appearance was fully as forlorn as her condition was pitiable.

This was truly a discouraging start, but nothing daunted she pressed on with the company, and never allowed her spirits to flag. Arrived at the Sweetwater, her best yoke of oxen died from drinking the alkali water, and for a substitute she was obliged to yoke up a couple of cows. Then came the tug of war; for so irregular a proceeding was not to be tolerated for a moment by the cows, except under extreme compulsion. More unwilling and refractory laborers were probably never found, and from that point onward Louisa proceeded only by dint of the constant and vigorous persuasions of her whip.

During the journey a Mrs. McCarthy was confined; and it was considered necessary that Louisa should nurse her. But it was impossible for her to leave her team during the day; so it was arranged that she should attend the sick woman at night. For three weeks she dropped her whip each night when the column halted, and leaving her team to be cared for by the brethren, repaired to Mrs. McCarthy's wagon, nursing her through the night, and then seizing her whip again as the company moved forward in the morning.

However, she maintained good health throughout the journey, and safely piloted her heterodox outfit into the valley along with the rest of the company.

On the journey, after wearing out the three pairs of shoes with which she was provided, she was obliged to sew rags on her feet for protection. But each day these would soon wear through, and often she left bloody tracks on the cruel stones.

It was on this journey that she first became acquainted with Gen. Wells, to whom she was married shortly after they reached the valley. As the senior wife of that distinguished gentleman, "Aunt Louisa" is well known throughout Utah; and as a most unselfish and unostentatious dispenser of charity, and an ever-ready friend and helper of the sick and needy, her name is indellibly engraved on the hearts of thousands.

CHAPTER XXXVI.

BATHSHEBA W. SMITH'S STORY CONTINUED—THE PIO-
NEERS RETURN TO WINTER QUARTERS—A NEW
PRESIDENCY CHOSEN—OLIVER COWDERY RETURNS
TO THE CHURCH—GATHERING THE REMNANT FROM
WINTER QUARTERS—DESCRIPTION OF HER HOUSE
ON WHEELS.

Continuing her narration of affairs at winter
quarters, Sister Bathsheba W. Smith says:

" As soon as the weather became warm, and the
" gardens began to produce early vegetables, the
" sick began to recover. We felt considerable anx-
" iety for the safety of the pioneers, and for their
" success in finding us a home. About the first of
" December, to our great joy, a number of them
" returned. They had found a place in the heart of
" the Great Basin, beyond the Rocky Mountains, so
" barren, dry, desolate and isolated that we thought
" even the cupidity of religious bigots would not be
" excited by it. The pioneers had laid out a city,
" and had commenced a fort ; and some seven hun-
" dred wagons and about two thousand of our people
" had by this time arrived there. The country was
" so very dry that nothing could be made to grow
" without irrigation.

"After the location of winter quarters a great
"number of our people made encampments on the
"east side of the river, on parts of the Pottawat-
"omie lands. The camps, thus scattered, spread
"over a large tract. On one occasion my husband
"and I visited Hyde Park, one of these settlements,
"in company with the twelve apostles. They there
"held a council in a log-cabin, and a great manifes-
"tation of the holy spirit was poured out upon those
"present. At this council it was unanimously
"decided to organize the First Presidency of the
"Church according to the pattern laid down in the
"Book of Covenants. Soon after, a general confer-
"ence was held in the log tabernacle at Kanesville
"(now Council Bluffs), at which the saints acknowl-
"edged Brigham Young President of the Church,
"and Heber C. Kimball and Willard Richards his
"councilors.

"Shortly after this conference our family moved
"to the Iowa side of the river. My husband bought
"two log-cabins, and built two more, which made us
"quite comfortable. The winter was very cold, but
"wood was plentiful, and we used it freely. The
"situation was a romantic one, surrounded as we
"were on three sides by hills. We were favored
"with an abundance of wild plums and raspberries.
"We called the place Car-bun-ca, after an Indian
"brave who had been buried there.

"In May, 1848, about five hundred wagons fol-
"lowed President Young on his return to Salt Lake.
"In June some two hundred wagons followed Dr.
"Willard Richards. When Dr. Richards left, all
"the saints that could not go with him were com-

"pelled by the United States authorities to vacate
"winter quarters. They recrossed into Iowa, and
"had to build cabins again. This was a piece of
"oppression which was needless and ill-timed, as
"many of the families which had to move were
"those of the men who had gone in the Mormon
"battalion. This compulsory move was prompted
"by the same spirit of persecution that had caused
"the murder of so many of our people, and had
"forced us all to leave our homes and go into the
"wilderness.

"On the Iowa side of the river we raised wheat,
"Indian corn, buckwheat, potatoes, and other vege-
"tables; and we gathered from the woods hazel and
"hickory nuts, white and black walnuts, and in ad-
"dition to the wild plums and raspberries before
"mentioned, we gathered elderberries, and made
"elderberry and raspberry wine. We also preserved
"plums and berries. By these supplies we were
"better furnished than we had been since leaving
"our homes. The vegetables and fruits caused the
"scurvy to pretty much disappear.

"In September, 1848, a conference was held in a
"grove on Mosquito Creek, about two thousand of
"the saints being present. Oliver Cowdery, one of
"the witnesses of the Book of Mormon, was there.
"He had been ten years away from the Church, and
"had become a lawyer of some prominence in North-
"ern Ohio and Wisconsin. At this conference I
"heard him bear his testimony to the truth of the
"Book of Mormon, in the same manner as is re-
"corded in the testimony of the three witnesses in
"that book.

" In May, 1849, about four hundred wagons were
" organized and started West.

" In the latter part of June following, our family
" left our encampment. We started on our journey
" to the valley in a company of two hundred and
" eighteen wagons. These were organized into
" three companies, which were subdivided into com-
" panies of ten, each company properly officered.
" Each company also had its blacksmith and wagon-
" maker, equipped with proper tools for attending
" to their work of setting tires, shoeing animals, and
" repairing wagons.

" Twenty-four of the wagons of our company be-
" longed to the Welch saints, who had been led
" from Wales by Elder Dan Jones. They did not
" understand driving oxen. It was very amusing to
" see them yoke their cattle; two would have an
" animal by the horns, one by the tail, and one or
" two others would do their best to put on the yoke,
" whilst the apparently astonished ox, not at all en-
" lightened by the gutteral sounds of the Welch
" tongue, seemed perfectly at a loss what to do, or
" to know what was wanted of him. But these
" saints amply made up for their lack of skill in
" driving cattle by their excellent singing, which
" afforded us great assistance in our public meetings,
" and helped to enliven our evenings.

" On this journey my wagon was provided with
" projections, of about eight inches wide, on each
" side of the top of the box. The cover, which was
" high enough for us to stand erect, was widened by
" these projections. A frame was laid across the
" back part of our wagon, and was corded as a bed-

"stead; this made our sleeping very comfortable.
"Under our beds we stowed our heaviest articles.
"We had a door in one side of the wagon cover, and
"on the opposite side a window. A step-ladder was
"used to ascend to our door, which was between the
"wheels. Our cover was of 'osnaburg,' lined with
"blue drilling. Our door and window could be
"opened and closed at pleasure. I had, hanging
"up on the inside, a looking-glass, candlestick, pin-
"cushion, etc. In the centre of our wagon we had
"room for four chairs, in which we and our two chil-
"dren sat and rode when we chose. The floor of
"our traveling house was carpeted, and we made
"ourselves as comfortable as we could under the
"circumstances.

"After having experienced the common vicissi-
"tudes of that strange journey, having encountered
"terrible storms and endured extreme hardships, we
"arrived at our destination on the 5th of November,
"one hundred and five days after leaving the Mis-
"souri river. Having been homeless and wandering
"up to this time, I was prepared to appreciate a
"home."

CHAPTER XXXVII.

"I will beat you to the valley, and ask no help
"from you either!"

―――――

The exodus called out the women of Mormondom in all their Spartan strength of character.
They showed themselves State-founders indeed.
We are reading examples of them as pioneers un-
surpassed even by the examples of the immortal
band of pioneer apostles and elders who led them
to the "chambers of the mountains." The following story of the widow of Hyrum Smith will finely
illustrate this point:

At the death of the patriarch the care of the
family fell upon his widow, Mary Smith. Besides
the children there were several helpless and infirm

people, whom for various charitable reasons the patriarch had maintained; and these also she cared for, and brought through to the valley the major part of them, under unusually trying circumstances.

Passing over the incidents of her journey to winter quarters, after the expulsion from Nauvoo, we come at once to her heroic effort from winter quarters westward. In the spring of 1848 a tremendous effort was made by the saints to emigrate to the valley on a grand scale. No one was more anxious than Widow Smith; but to accomplish it seemed an impossibility, for although a portion of her household had emigrated in 1847, she still had a large and, comparatively, helpless family—her sons John and Joseph, mere boys, being her only support. Without teams sufficient to draw the number of wagons necessary to haul provisions and outfit for the family, and without means to purchase, or friends who were in circumstances to assist, she determined to make the attempt, and trust in the Lord for the issue. Accordingly every nerve was strained, and every available object was brought into requisition. Cows and calves were yoked up, two wagons lashed together, and a team barely sufficient to draw one was hitched on to them, and in this manner they rolled out from winter quarters some time in May. After a series of the most amusing and trying circumstances, such as sticking in the mud, doubling teams up all the little hills, and crashing at ungovernable speed down the opposite sides, breaking wagon-tongues and reaches, upsetting, and vainly trying to control wild steers, heifers, and unbroken cows, they finally succeeded in reaching the Elk

Horn, where the companies were being organized for the plains.

Here Widow Smith reported herself to President Kimball as having "started for the valley." Meantime, she had left no stone unturned or problem untried, which promised assistance in effecting the necessary preparations for the journey. She had done to her utmost, and still the way looked dark and impossible.

President Kimball consigned her to Captain ——'s fifty. The captain was present. Said he :

"Widow Smith, how many wagons have you ?"

" Seven."

" How many yokes of oxen have you ?"

" Four," and so many cows and calves.

" Well," said the captain, "it is folly for you to "start in this manner; you never can make the "journey, and if you try it you will be a burden "upon the company the whole way. My advice to "you is, to go back to winter quarters and wait till "you can get help."

Widow Smith calmly replied : " Father ——" (he was an aged man), " I will beat you to the valley, "and will ask no help from you either !"

This seemed to nettle the old gentleman, and it doubtless influenced his conduct toward her during the journey.

While lying at Elk Horn she sent back and succeeded in buying on credit, and hiring for the journey, several yoke of oxen from brethren who were not able to emigrate that year, and when the companies were ready to start she and her family were somewhat better prepared for the journey, and rolled out with lighter hearts and better prospects than favored their egress from winter quarters.

As they journeyed on the captain lost no opportunity to vent his spleen on the widow and her family; but she prayerfully maintained her integrity of purpose, and pushed vigorously on, despite several discouraging circumstances.

One day, as they were moving slowly through the hot sand and dust, in the neighborhood of the Sweetwater, the sun pouring down with excessive heat, towards noon, one of Widow Smith's best oxen laid down in the yoke, rolled over on his side, and stiffened out his legs spasmodically, evidently in the throes of death. The unanimous opinion was that he was poisoned. All the hindmost teams of course stopped, the people coming forward to know what was the matter. In a short time the captain, who was in advance of the company, perceiving that something was wrong, came to the spot. Probably no one supposed for a moment that the ox would recover, and the captain's first words on seeing him were :

" He is dead, there is no use working with him; " we'll have to fix up some way to take the widow " along; I told her she would be a burden upon the " company."

Meantime Widow Smith had been searching for a bottle of consecrated oil in one of the wagons, and now came forward with it, and asked her brother, Joseph Fielding, and the other brethren, to administer to the ox, thinking that the Lord would raise him up. They did so, pouring a portion of oil on the top of his head, between and back of the horns, and all laid hands upon him, and one prayed, administering the ordinance as they would have done to a human being that was sick. In a moment he gathered up his legs, and at the first word arose to his feet, and traveled right off as well as ever. He was not even unyoked from his mate.

On the 22d of September the company crossed over " Big Mountain," when they had the first glimpse of Salt Lake Valley. Every heart rejoiced, and with lingering fondness they gazed upon the goal of their wearisome journey. The descent of the western side of " Big Mountain " was precipitous and abrupt, and they were obliged to rough-lock the hind wheels of the wagons, and, as they were not needed, the forward cattle were turned loose to be driven to camp, the "wheelers" only being retained on the wagons. Desirous of shortening the next day's journey as much as possible, they drove on till a late hour in the night, and finally camped near the eastern foot of the " Little Mountain." During this night's drive several of Widow Smith's cows, that had been turned loose from the teams, were lost in the brush. Early next morning her son John returned to hunt for them, their service in the teams being necessary to proceed.

At an earlier hour than usual the captain gave orders for the company to start, knowing well the circumstances of the widow, and that she would be obliged to remain till John returned with the lost cattle. Accordingly the company rolled out, leaving her and her family alone. Hours passed by ere John returned with the lost cattle, and the company could be seen toiling along far up the mountain.

And to human ken it seemed probable that the widow's prediction would ingloriously fail. But as the company were nearing the summit of the mountain a cloud burst over their heads, sending down the rain in torrents, and throwing them into utter confusion. The cattle refused to pull, and to save the wagons from crashing down the mountain side, they were obliged to unhitch, and block the wheels. While the teamsters sought shelter, the storm drove the cattle in every direction, so that when it subsided it was a day's work to find them and get them together. Meantime, as noted, John had returned with the stray cattle, and they were hitched up, and the widow and family rolled up the mountain, passing the company and continuing on to the valley, where she arrived fully twenty hours in advance of the captain. And thus was her prophesy fulfilled.

She kept her husband's family together after her arrival in the valley, and her prosperity was unparalleled. At her death, which occurred September 21st, 1852, she left them comfortably provided for, and in possession of every educational endowment that the facilities of the times would permit.

CHAPTER XXXVIII.

The early days in the valley are thus described
by Eliza R. Snow:

"Our first winter in the mountains was delight-
ful; the ground froze but little; our coldest weather
was three or four days in November, after which
the men plowed and sowed, built houses, etc. The
weather seemed to have been particularly ordered
to meet our very peculiar circumstances. Every
labor, such as cultivating the ground, procuring fuel
and timber from the canyons, etc., was a matter of
experiment. Most of us were houseless; and what
the result would have been, had that winter been
like the succeeding ones, may well be conjectured.

"President Young had kindly made arrangements
for me to live with his wife, Clara Decker, who came
with the pioneers, and was living in a log-house
about eighteen feet square, which constituted a
portion of the east side of our fort. This hut, like
most of those built the first year, was roofed with
willows and earth, the roof having but little pitch,

the first-comers having adopted the idea that the valley was subject to little if any rain, and our roofs were nearly flat. We suffered no inconvenience from this fact until about the middle of March, when a long storm of snow, sleet and rain occurred, and for several days the sun did not make its appearance. The roof of our dwelling was covered deeper with earth than the adjoining ones, consequently it did not leak so soon, and some of my neighbors huddled in for shelter; but one evening, when several were socially sitting around, the water commenced dripping in one place, and then in another; they dodged it for awhile, but it increased so rapidly that they finally concluded they might as well go to their own wet houses. After they had gone I spread my umbrella over my head and shoulders as I ensconced myself in bed, the lower part of which, not shielded by the umbrella, was wet enough before morning. The earth overhead was thoroughly saturated, and after it commenced to drip the storm was much worse indoors than out.

" The small amount of breadstuff brought over the plains was sparingly dealt out; and our beef, made of cows and oxen which had constituted our teams, was, before it had time to fatten on the dry mountain grass, very inferior. Those to whom it yielded sufficient fat to grease their griddles, were considered particularly fortunate. But we were happy in the rich blessings of peace, which, in the spirit of brotherly and sisterly union, we mutually enjoyed in our wild mountain home.

" Before we left winter quarters, a committee, appointed for the purpose, inspected the provisions of each family, in order to ascertain that all were provided with at least a moderate competency of flour, etc. The amount of flour calculated to be necessary was apportioned at the rate of three-quarters of a pound for adults and one-half pound per day for children. A portion of the battalion having been disbanded on the Pacific coast, destitute of pay for their services, joined us before spring, and we cheerfully divided our rations of flour with them, which put us on still shorter allowance.

"Soon after our arrival in the valley, a tall liberty-pole was erected, and from its summit (although planted in Mexican soil), the stars and stripes seemed to float with even more significance, if possible, than they were wont to do on Eastern breezes.

> " I love that flag. When in my childish glee—
> A prattling girl, upon my grandsire's knee—
> I heard him tell strange tales, with valor rife,
> How that same flag was bought with blood and life.

> " And his tall form seemed taller when he said, '
> ' Child, for that flag thy grandsire fought and bled.'
> My young heart felt that every scar he wore,
> Caused him to prize that banner more and more.

> " I caught the fire, and as in years I grew,
> I loved the flag; I loved my country too.
>   *   *   *   *   *   *

> " There came a time that I remember well—
> Beneath the stars and stripes we could not dwell!
> We had to flee; but in our hasty flight
> We grasped the flag with more than mortal might;

> " And vowed, although our foes should us bereave
> Of all things else, the flag we would not leave.
> We took the flag; and journeying to the West,
> We wore its motto graven on each breast."

The personal narrative, up to the period of the Utah war, is thus continued by Bathsheba W. Smith:

" In 1856 my husband was sent as delegate to " Washington, by vote of the people of the Territory, " to ask for the admission of Utah as a State. In " May, 1857, he returned. Congress would not admit " Utah into the Union. On his journey East his " horse failed, and he had to walk about five hundred " miles on the plains. This made him very foot-sore, " as he was a heavy man.

" On the 24th of July, 1857, I was in company " with my husband and a goodly number of others " at the Big Cottonwood Lake, near the head of Big " Cottonwood Canyon, where we were celebrating " the anniversary of the arrival of the pioneers in " Salt Lake Valley, when word was brought to us " that the United States mail for Utah was stopped, " and that President James Buchanan was sending " out an army to exterminate us. We turned to " hear what President Young would say. In effect " he said: 'If they ever get in, it will be because we " will permit them to do so.'

" In September my husband went out into the " mountains and stayed about four weeks, assisting " in conducting the correspondence with the leaders " of the invading army. Fear came upon the army, " and they dared not come face to face with our peo- " ple ; so they stayed out in the mountains, while our " people came home, excepting a few who remained " to watch them.

" Soon after my husband's return, he married Sis- " ter Susan Elizabeth West, and brought her home.

23

"About this time I was having a new house built.
"One day, in the forenoon, I had been watching the
"men plastering it, and had been indulging in the
"pleasant thoughts that would naturally occur on
"such an occasion, when my husband came home
"and said it had been determined in council that all
"of our people were to leave their homes and go
"south, as it was thought wiser to do this than to
"fight the army. Accordingly, on the last day of
"March, 1858, Sister Susan, myself, and son and
"daughter, started south, bidding farewell to our
"home with much the same feelings that I had ex-
"perienced at leaving Nauvoo.

"Peace having subsequently been restored, we
"returned to Salt Lake City on the third of July
"following. Instead of flowers, I found weeds as
"high as my head all around the house. When we
"entered the city it was near sunset; all was quiet;
"every door was shut and every window boarded
"up. I could see but two chimneys from which
"smoke was issuing. We were nearly the first that
"had returned. Being thus restored to my home
"again, I was happy and contented, although I had
"but few of the necessaries of life."

CHAPTER XXXIX.

THE WOMEN OF MORMONDOM IN THE PERIOD OF THE
UTAH WAR—THEIR HEROIC RESOLVE TO DESOLATE
THE LAND—THE SECOND EXODUS—MRS. CARRING-
TON—GOVERNOR CUMMING'S WIFE—A NATION OF
HEROES.

For an example of the heroism of woman excelling
all other examples of history—at least of modern
times—let us turn to that of the Mormon women
during the Utah war.

In the expulsions from Missouri, first from county
to county, and then *en masse* from the State, undoubtedly the Mormons yielded to the compulsion
of a lawless mob, coupled with the militia of the
State, executing the exterminating order of Governor Boggs. It was an example of suffering and
martyrdom rather than of spontaneous heroism.
Something of the same was illustrated in the expulsion from Illinois. It was at the outset nothing
of choice, but all of compulsion. True, after the
movement of the community, inspired by the apostolic forcefulness of Brigham Young and his compeers, swelled into a grand Israelitish exodus, then
the example towered like a very pyramid of heroism ;
and in that immortal circumstance who can doubt
that the heroic culminated in the women ?

But what shall be said of their example during the Utah war? Here were women who chose and resolved to give an example to the civilized world such as it had never seen. The proposed exodus from Utah was not in the spirit of submission, but an exhibition of an invincible spirit finding a method of conquest through an exodus. This was not weakness, but strength. It was as though the accumulated might and concentrated purposes of their lives were brought into a supreme action. The example of the Utah war was in fact all their own. The Mormons were not subdued. Had the issue come, they would have left Utah as conquerors.

"Tell the government that the troops now on the "march for Utah shall not enter the Great Salt "Lake Valley. Tell the people of the United "States that should those troops force an entrance "they will find Utah a desert, every house burned "to the ground, every tree cut down, and every field "laid waste. We will apply the torch to our own "dwellings,· cut down those richly-laden orchards "with our own hands, turn the fruitful field again " into a desert, and desolate our cities, with accla-"mations."

Such was the tenor of the communication carried by Captain Van Vliet to the government. And he had seen the whole people lift up their hands in their tabernacle to manifest their absolute resolution to the nation, and heard those acclamations in anticipation of their act.

The very nature of the case brought the women of Mormondom into supreme prominence. *Their* hands would have applied the torches to their homes; they would have been the desolaters of the fast-growing cities of Utah. The grandeur of the action was in these unconquerable women, who would have maintained their religion and their sacred institutions in the face of all the world.

The example of the wife of Albert Carrington will, perchance, be often recalled, generations hence. Capt. Van Vliet, of the United States Army, had arrived in Salt Lake City in the midst of the troubles out of which grew the "war." He was received most cordially by the authorities, but at the same time was given to understand that the people were a unit, and that they had fully determined upon a programme. The sisters took him into their gardens, and showed him the paradise that their woman-hands would destroy if the invading army came. He was awed by the prospect—his ordinary judgment confounded by such extraordinary examples. To the lady above-mentioned, in whose garden he was one day walking, in conversation with the governor and others, he exclaimed:

"What, madam! would you consent to see this "beautiful home in ashes and this fruitful orchard "destroyed?"

"Yes!" answered Sister Carrington, with heroic resolution, "I would not only consent to it, but I "would set fire to my home with my own hands, "and cut down every tree, and root up every plant!"

Coupled with this will be repeated the dramatic incident of Governor Cumming's wife weeping over the scene of the deserted city after the community had partly executed their resolution.

The saints had all gone south, with their leader,

when Governor Cumming, with his wife, returned
from Camp Scott. They proceeded to the residence
of Elder Staines, whom they found in waiting. His
family had gone south, and in his garden were significantly heaped several loads of straw.

The governor's wife inquired their meaning, and
the cause of the silence that pervaded the city.
Elder Staines informed her of their resolve to burn
the town in case the army attempted to occupy it

" How terrible!" she exclaimed. "What a sight
"this is! I shall never forget it! it has the appear-
"ance of a city that has been afflicted with plague.
"Every house looks like a tomb of the dead! For
"two miles I have seen but one man in it. Poor
"creatures! And so all have left their hard-earned
"homes?"

Here she burst into tears.

"Oh! Alfred (to her husband), something must
"be done to bring them back! Do not permit the
"army to stay in the city! Can't you do something
"for them?"

"Yes, madam," said he, "I shall do all I can, rest
"assured."

Mrs. Cumming wept for woman! But the women
of Mormondom gloried in their sublime action as
they had never done before. They felt at that moment that their example was indeed worthy of a
modern Israel.

It thus struck the admiration of journalists both
in America and Europe. The Mormons were pronounced "A nation of heroes!" Those heroes were
twice ten thousand women, who could justly claim
the tribute equally with their husbands, their brethren and their sons.

CHAPTER XL.

The death-bed of a latter-day saint !

It was in the house of Heber C. Kimball, in the
little town of Mendon, N. Y., on the 8th of September, 1832. Principal around that glorious death-bed
were Brigham Young, Heber C. Kimball, and Vilate,
his wife.

The dying saint was Miriam Works, first wife of
Brigham Young—a man of destiny, but then unknown in the great world. " In her expiring mo-
" ments," he says, " she clapped her hands and
" praised the Lord, and called upon Brother Kimball
" and all around to also praise the Lord !"

———

On the 8th of June, 1803, in Seneca, Ontario
county, N. Y., was born Mary Ann Angell, now for

forty-five years the wife of Brigham Young, the mother of his eldest sons, and the faithful step-mother of the daughters of Miriam Works.

Her parents early leaving her birthplace, Mary was brought up in Providence, R. I. She was what in those days was denominated a pious maiden, for her family was strictly of the old Puritan stock of the country. She early became a Sunday-school teacher, and united with the Free-Will Baptists. The study of the prophesies quite engrossed her mind, and she was confidently looking for their fulfillment. Her semi-ministerial duties as a Sunday-school teacher toned and strengthened her early womanhood; and hence she resolved never to marry until she met "a man of God" to whom her heart should go out, to unite with him in the active duties of a Christian life. Thus it came about that she remained a maiden until nearly thirty years of age. But the providence that watched over her had chosen for her a husband.

It was during the year 1830 that Thomas B. Marsh came to Providence, bringing with him the Book of Mormon. From him Mary obtained a copy, and having prayerfully read it, became convinced that it was a work of inspiration. After this she went to Southern New York, where her parents were visiting, and there she and her parents were baptized by John P. Greene—Brigham's brother-in-law. It was about this time that the Youngs, the Greenes and the Kimballs came into the Church.

Alone, Mary set out for Kirtland, which had just become the gathering place of the saints; and there she remained a year before Brigham and Heber gathered with their families. Vilate Kimball was still acting the part of a mother to the little daughters of Miriam. Through hearing Brigham preach in Kirtland, Mary Angell became acquainted with him. She had found her mate; he had found a mother indeed to his little motherless Elizabeth and Vilate.

At the period of the famous march of the elders from Ohio to Missouri, in 1834, to "redeem Zion" in Jackson county, Mary, now for over a year the wife of Brigham Young, became the mother of his first son, Joseph A., who was born October 14, 1834, just at the return of her husband, after the disbanding of Zion's Camp. Thus during the most trying period of her first year of marriage, was she left alone in the struggle of life, providing for herself, and caring for her husband's motherless girls.

But a still more trying period came to this excellent woman, after her husband became a member of the quorum of the twelve, and when the rebellion against Joseph arose in Kirtland. First the prophet and Sidney Rigdon had to flee for their lives, and next Brigham Young had to escape from Kirtland. Then came her severest struggle. She now had five children to care and provide for—the two daughters of Miriam, her Joseph A., and Brigham, Jr., with his twin sister, Mary Ann. Those were dark days of persecution and want. The apostates and anti-Mormons frequently searched her house for her husband, and the faithful in Kirtland all had enough to do to sustain themselves, in the absence of their shepherds, who were now refugees in Far West. At length, with the five children, she reached her husband; but not long to rest, for quickly came the expulsion from Missouri, in which period she broke up her home many times before finally settling in Montrose, on the opposite side of the river from Nauvoo.

Scarcely had Brigham and the twelve effected the exodus of the saints from Missouri to Illinois, ere Joseph, having escaped from prison, sent the twelve with its president to England, on mission.

On each side of the Mississippi, in cabins and tents, the Mormon people lay, exhausted by their many expulsions; the multitude sick, many dying, the vigor of life scarcely left even in their strong-willed leaders. Thus lying on the river-side at Commerce and Montrose, they presented a spectacle no longer suggestive of irresistible empire-founders. Joseph was sick; Brigham was sick; the twelve were all sick; the prophet's house and door-yard was a hospital. It was then that the prophet, knowing that power must be invoked or the people would perish, leaped from his sick bed, and entering first the tents and cabins of the apostles, and bidding them arise and follow him, went like an arch-angel through the midst of his disciples, and "healed "the multitude." It is a grand picture in the memory of the saints, being called "The Day of "God's Power." Reverse that picture, and there is seen the exact condition of Mary Angell Young and the other apostles' wives when the president and his quorum started on mission to England, leaving them to the care of the Lord, and their brethren. It was a period quite as trying to these apostolic sisters as that of the exodus, afterwards.

And to none more so than to Mary, who had now the burden of six children to sustain during her husband's absence in a foreign land.

The following entries in the president's journal embody a most graphic story, easily seized by the imagination:

"We arrived in Commerce on the 18th (May, "1839), and called upon Brother Joseph and his "family. Joseph had commenced laying out the "city plot.

"23d—I crossed the Mississippi with my family, "and took up my residence in a room in the old mil- "itary barracks, in company with Brother Woodruff "and his family.

"September 14, 1839—I started from Montrose "on my mission to England. My health was so "poor that I was unable to go thirty rods, to the "river, without assistance. After I had crossed the "river I got Israel Barlow to carry me on his horse "behind him, to Heber C. Kimball's, where I re- "mained sick 'till the 18th. I left my wife sick, with "a babe only ten days old, and all my children sick "and unable to wait upon each other.

"17th—My wife crossed the river, and got a boy "with a wagon to bring her up about a mile, to "Brother Kimball's, to see me. I remained until "the 18th at Brother Kimball's, when we started, "leaving his family also sick."

Continue the picture, with the husband's absence, and the wife's noble, every-day struggle to maintain and guard his children, and we have her history well described for the next two years.

Taking up the thread again in September, 1841:

"On my return from England," says Brigham, in his diary, "I found my family living in a small unfin-"ished log-cabin, situated on a low, wet lot, so "swampy that when the first attempt was made to "plough it the oxen mired; but after the city was "drained it became a very valuable garden spot."

The scene, a year later, is that of President Young at "death's door," and the wife battling with death to save her husband. He was suddenly attacked with a slight fit of apoplexy. This was followed by a severe fever. For eighteen days he lay upon his back, and was not turned upon his side during that period.

"When the fever left me, on the eighteenth day," he says, "I was bolstered up in my chair, but was so "near gone that I could not close my eyes, which "were set in my head; my chin dropped down, and "my breath stopped. My wife, seeing my situation, "threw some cold water in my face and eyes, which "I did not feel in the least; neither did I move a "muscle. She then held my nostrils between her "thumb and finger, and placing her mouth directly "over mine, blew into my lungs until she filled them "with air. This set my lungs in motion, and I again "began to breathe. While this was going on I was "perfectly conscious of all that was passing around "me; my spirit was as vivid as it ever was in my "life; but I had no feeling in my body."

Mary, by the help of God, had thus saved the life of President Young!

It was about this time that polygamy, or "celes-"tial marriage," was introduced into the Church. To say that it was no cross to these Mormon wives—daughters of the strictest Puritan parentage—would be to mock their experience. It was thus, also, with their husbands, in Nauvoo, in 1842. President Young himself tells of the occasion when he stood by the grave of one of the brethren and wished that the lot of the departed was his own. The burden of polygamy seemed heavier than the hand of death. It was nothing less than the potency of the " Thus saith the Lord," and the faith of the saints as a community, that sustained them— both the brethren and the sisters. Mary Angell gave to her husband other wives, and the testimony which she gives to-day is that it has been the "Thus "saith the Lord" unto her, from the time of its introduction to the present.

Scarcely necessary is it to observe that she was in the exodus. Seven children were now under her care. Alice, Luna, and John W. were born in Montrose and Nauvoo, while the twin sister of Brigham, Jr., had died. With these she remained at winter quarters while the president led the pioneers to the Rocky Mountains. Her benevolence to the poor at winter quarters (and who of them were then rich!) is spoken of to this day. Indeed, benevolence has ever been a marked trait in her life.

Then came the hut in the valley. The "heat and "burden of the day" had not passed. Full twenty years of struggle, self-sacrifice, and devotion as a wife, uncommon in its examples, filled up the pages of " Sister Young's history," as a latter-day saint, before the days of social prominence came.

The hut in the valley, where she lived in 1849, is a good pioneer picture. It stood on the spot where now stands her residence—the "White House;" and some ten rods north-west of that location stood a row of log-cabins where dwelt President Young's other wives, with their children.

Since then the days of grandeur, befitting her station, have come; but "Mother Young"—a name honored in her bearing—has lived most in the public mind as the faithful wife, the exemplary mother, and a latter-day saint in whose heart benevolence and native goodness have abounded. She is now seventy-four years of age—closing a marked and worthy life; and her latest expressed desire is that a strong testimony should be borne of her faith in Mormonism, and the righteousness of her husband in carrying out the revelation, given through Joseph Smith, on polygamy, as the word and will of the Lord to his people.

CHAPTER XLI.

It was nearly twenty-three years after the establishment of the Church of Jesus Christ of Latter-day
Saints, that the revelation on celestial marriage
was published to the world. On the 6th of April,
1830, the Church was founded on the 14th of September, 1852, the *Deseret News* published an extra,
containing the said revelation, the origin thus dated:
"Given to Joseph Smith, Nauvoo, July 12, 1843;"
and in the *Millennial Star*, January 1st, 1853, it was
published to the saints of the British mission.

No need here for a review of that document on
plural marriage, nor a sociological discussion of this
now world-noised institution of the Mormons; but
as some persons have ascribed that institution to
President Young, and denied that Joseph Smith
was its revelator, the word of sisters who have been
with the Church from the beginning shall be offered
as a finality upon the question of its origin.

Eliza R. Snow has already testified on the subject
of her marriage to the prophet Joseph, not by
proxy, but personally, during his lifetime; and all

the Church know her as Joseph's wife. The daughters of Bishop Partridge, and others, were also sealed to him in person, in the order of celestial marriage.

A very proper one to speak here is Mother Whitney, for it was her husband, Bishop Whitney, who preserved the revelation on polygamy. Speaking of the time when her husband kept store for Joseph (1842–3), she says: "It was "during this time that Joseph received the revelation "concerning celestial marriage; also concerning the "ordinances of the house of the Lord. He had been "strictly charged, by the angel who committed these "precious things into his keeping, that he should "only reveal them to such ones as were pure, and full "of integrity to the truth, and worthy and capable of "being entrusted with divine messages; that to spread "them abroad would only be like casting pearls be- "fore swine; and that the most profound secresy was "to be maintained, until the Lord saw fit to make it "known publicly through his servants. Joseph had "the most implicit confidence in my husband's up- "rightness and integrity of character, and so he "confided to him the principles set forth in that rev- "elation, and also gave him the privilege of reading "and making a copy of it, believing it would be per- "fectly safe with him. It is this same copy that was "preserved in the providence of God; for Emma "(Joseph's wife), afterwards becoming indignant, "burned the original, thinking she had destroyed the "only written document upon the subject in existence. "My husband revealed these things to me. We had "always been united, and had the utmost faith and "confidence in each other. We pondered upon the

"matter continually, and our prayers were unceasing
"that the Lord would grant us some special manifes-
"tation concerning this new and strange doctrine.
"The Lord was very merciful to us, revealing unto
"us his power and glory. We were seemingly wrapt
"in a heavenly vision; a halo of light encircled us,
"and we were convinced in our own bosoms that God
"heard and approved our prayers and intercedings
"before him. Our hearts were comforted, and our
"faith made so perfect that we were willing to give
"our eldest daughter, then seventeen years of age,
"to Joseph, in the order of plural marriage. Laying
"aside all our traditions and former notions in regard
"to marriage, we gave her with our mutual consent.
"She was the first woman given in plural marriage
"with the consent of both parents. Of course these
"things had to be kept an inviolate secret; and as
"some were false to their vows and pledges of secresy,
"persecution arose, and caused grievous sorrow to
"those who had obeyed, in all purity and sincerity,
"the requirements of this celestial order of marriage.
"The Lord commanded his servants; they themselves
"did not comprehend what the ultimate course of
"action would be, but were waiting further develop-
"ments from heaven. Meantime, the ordinances of
"the house of the Lord were given, to bless and
"strengthen us in our future endeavors to promulgate
"the principles of divine light and intelligence; but
"coming in contact with all preconceived notions
"and principles heretofore taught as the articles of
"religious faith, it was not strange that many could
"not receive it. Others doubted; and only a few
"remained firm and immovable."

24

On the publication of the revelation on polygamy, the theological writers of the Church issued pamphlets, promulgating and defending the "peculiar institution," as the Gentiles styled it. Orson Spencer issued *Patriarchal Marriage;* Parley P. Pratt issued *Marriage and Morals in Utah;* and Orson Pratt was sent to Washington to proclaim, at the seat of government, the great social innovation. This was the origin of the *Seer*, a periodical there issued by him. Among the various writings of the times, upon the subject, was a tract entitled *Defence of Polygamy by a Lady of Utah, in a Letter to her Sister in New Hampshire.* The following are extracts from it, in which is strikingly made manifest the fact that the sisterhood accepted polygamy upon the examples of the Hebrew Bible, rather than upon any portion of the Book of Mormon :

"SALT LAKE CITY, January 12, 1854.

" DEAR SISTER:

"Your letter of October 2d was received yesterday. * * * It seems, my dear sister, that we are no nearer together in our religious views than formerly. Why is this ? Are we not all bound to leave this world, with all we possess therein, and reap the reward of our doings here in a neverending hereafter? If so, do we not desire to be undeceived, and to know and to do the truth ? Do we not all wish in our hearts to be sincere with ourselves, and to be honest and frank with each other? If so, you will bear with me patiently, while I give a few of my reasons for embracing, and holding sacred, that particular point in the doctrine of the Church of the Saints, to which you, my dear sister, together with a large majority of Christendom, so decidedly object—I mean a 'plurality of wives.'

"I have a Bible which I have been taught from my infancy to hold sacred. In this Bible I read of a holy man named Abraham, who is represented as the friend of God, a faithful man in all things, a man who kept the commandments of God, and who is called in the New Testament the 'father of the faithful.' I find this man had a plurality of wives, some of whom were called concubines. I also find his grandson, Jacob, possessed of four wives, twelve sons and a daughter. These wives are spoken very highly of by the sacred writers, as honorable and virtuous women. 'These,' say the Scriptures, 'did build the house of Israel.' Jacob himself was also a man of God, and the Lord blessed him and his house, and commanded him to be fruitful and multiply. I find also that the twelve sons of Jacob, by these four wives, became princes, heads of tribes, patriarchs, whose names are had in everlasting remembrance to all generations.

"Now God talked with Abraham, Isaac and Jacob, frequently; and his angels also visited and talked with them, and blessed them and their wives and children. He also reproved the sins of some of the sons of Jacob for hating and selling their brother, and for adultery. But in all his communications with them, he never condemned their family organization; but on the contrary, always approved of it, and blessed them in this respect. He even told Abraham that he would make him the father of many nations, and that in him and his seed all the nations and kindreds of the earth should be blessed. In later years I find the plurality of wives perpetuated, sanctioned, and provided for in the law of Moses.

"David, the psalmist, not only had a plurality of wives, but the Lord spoke by the mouth of Nathan the prophet and told David that he (the Lord) had given his master's wives into his bosom; but because he had committed adultery with the wife of

Uriah, and caused his murder, he would take his wives and give them to a neighbor of his, etc.

" Here, then, we have the word of the Lord, not only sanctioning polygamy, but actually giving to King David the wives of his master (Saul), and afterward taking the wives of David from him, and giving them to another man. Here we have a sample of severe reproof and punishment for adultery and murder, while polygamy is authorized and approved by the word of God.

" But to come to the New Testament. I find Jesus Christ speaks very highly of Abraham and his family. He says: ' Many shall come from the east, and from the west, and from the north, and from the south, and shall sit down with Abraham, Isaac and Jacob, in the kingdom of God.' Again he said: ' If ye were Abraham's seed, ye would do the works of Abraham.'

" Paul the apostle wrote to the saints of his day, and informed them as follows: ' As many of you as have been baptized into Christ have put on Christ; and if ye are Christ's then are ye Abraham's seed, and heirs according to the promise.' He also sets forth Abraham and Sarah as patterns of faith and good works, and as the father and mother of faithful Christians, who should, by faith and good works, aspire to be counted the sons of Abraham and daughters of Sarah.

" Now let us look at some of the works of Sarah, for which she is so highly commended by the apostles, and by them held up as a pattern for Christian ladies to imitate.

" ' Now Sarah, Abram's wife, bare him no children; and she had an hand-maid, an Egyptian, whose name was Hagar. And Sarah said unto Abram, Behold now, the Lord hath restrained me from bearing; I pray thee go in unto my maid; it may be that I may obtain children by her. And Abram harkened unto the voice of Sarah. And Sarah, Abram's wife, took Hagar her maid, the Egyptian, after Abram had dwelt ten years in the land of Canaan, and gave her to her husband, Abram, to be his wife.' (Gen. xvi.; 1, 2, 3).

" According to Jesus Christ and the apostles,

then, the only way to be saved, is to be adopted into the great family of polygamists, by the gospel, and then strictly follow their examples. Again, John the Revelator describes the holy city of the Heavenly Jerusalem, with the names of the twelve sons of Jacob inscribed on the gates.

"To sum up the whole, then, I find that polygamists were the friends of God; that the family and lineage of a polygamist was selected, in which all nations should be blessed; that a polygamist is named in the New Testament as the father of the faithful Christians of after ages, and cited as a pattern for all generations. That the wife of a polygamist, who encouraged her husband in the practice of the same, and even urged him into it, and officiated in giving him another wife, is named as an honorable and virtuous woman, a pattern for Christian ladies, and the very mother of all holy women in the Christian Church, whose aspiration it should be to be called her daughters.

"That Jesus has declared that the great fathers of the polygamic family stand at the head in the kingdom of God; in short, that all the saved of after generations should be saved by becoming members of a polygamic family; that all those who do not become members of it, are strangers and aliens to the covenant of promise, the commonwealth of Israel, and not heirs according to the promise made to Abraham.

"That all people from the east, west, north and south, who enter into the kingdom, enter into the society of polygamists, and under their patriarchal rule and covenant.

"Indeed no one can approach the gates of heaven without beholding the names of twelve polygamists (the sons of four different women by one man), engraven in everlasting glory upon the pearly gates.

"My dear sister, with the Scriptures before me, I could never find it in my heart to reject the heavenly vision which has restored to man the fullness of the gospel, or the latter-day prophets and apostles, merely because in this restoration is included the ancient law of matrimony and of family organization and government, preparatory to the restoration of all Israel.

    *   *   *   *   *   *

" Your affectionate sister,
" BELINDA MARDEN PRATT.
" Mrs. Lydia Kimball, Nashua, N. H."

CHAPTER XLII.

Next after the revelation on celestial marriage,
through Joseph the prophet, the Bible of the Hebrews, and not the sacred record of the ancients of
this continent, must be charged with the authority,
the examples, and, consequently, the practice of
polygamy in the Latter-day Church. The examples
of Abraham, Jacob, Solomon, and the ancients of
Israel generally, and not the examples of Nephi,
Mormon, and their people, whose civilization is now
extinct, have been those accepted by our modern
Israel—examples of such divine potency that the
women of England and America, with all their
monogamic training and prejudice, have dared not
reject nor make war against in woman's name.

Ever and everywhere is the genius of Mormonism so strikingly in the Abrahamic likeness and
image, that one could almost fancy the patriarchs
of ancient Israel inspiring a modern Israel to perpetuate their name, their faith and their institutions.
Who shall say that this is not the fact? Surely

this patriarchal genius of the Mormons is the most extraordinary test of a modern Israel. Jerusalem, not Rome, has brought forth the Mormons and their peculiar commonwealth.

And here it should be emphasized that polygamy had nought to do with the expulsions of the Mormons from Missouri and Illinois. The primitive "crime" of the Mormons was their belief in new revelation. Fifty years ago that was a monstrous crime in the eyes of sectarian Christendom. The present generation can scarcely comprehend how blasphemous the doctrine of modern revelation seemed to this very nation of America, which now boasts of ten to twelve millions of believers in revelation from some source or other. Thus wonderful has been the change in fifty years!

Viewed as a cause of their persecutions in the past, next to this faith of the Mormons in Jehovah's speaking, was their rapid growth as a gathered and organized people, who bid fair to hold the balance of political power in several States. A prominent grievance with Missouri and Illinois was exactly that urged against the growth of the ancient Christians—"if we let them alone they will take away our name and nation!"

Following down the record until the period of the Utah war, it is still the fact that polygamy was not the cause of the anti-Mormon crusade. It was not even the excuse of that period, as given by President Buchanan and Congress. It was merely an Israelitish trouble in the world.

Soon after this, however, polygamy did become the excuse, both to Congress and the dominant political party of the country, to take action against the Mormons and their Israelitish institutions. In framing the Chicago platform, the Republican party, just rising to supremacy, made slavery one of its planks, and polygamy another. Upon these "twin relics" they rode into the administration of the government of the country.

Then came the anti-polygamic law of 1862, especially framed against the Mormons. But it was found to be inoperative. Lincoln, who had known many of them in the early days, let the Mormons alone.

The civil war was over. The South had succumbed. The work of reconstruction was fairly in progress. The conquerer Grant, and his administration, resolved to grapple with "polygamic theocracy," as they styled it—if need be by the action and issues of another Mormon war.

First came Colfax to Zion, to "spy out the land." To the polygamic saints he administered the gentle warning of a soft tongue, which, however, concealed a serpent's sting. Returning east, after his famous tour across the continent, he opened a theological assault upon Mormon polygamy in the *New York Independent*, and soon became engaged in a regular battle with apostle John Taylor. Returning to Zion, on his second visit, the Vice-President actually preached an anti-polygamic sermon to the Mormons, one evening, in front of the Townsend House, in Salt Lake City, in which he quoted what he interpreted as anti-polygamic passages from the Book of Mormon.

The scene changes to Washington. Colfax, Cullom, Grant and Dr. Newman are in travail with the Cullom bill and anti-Mormon crusade.

The Cullom bill passed the House and went to the Senate. President Grant had resolved to execute it, by force of arms, should the courts fail. Vice-President Colfax, while in Utah, had propounded the serious question, "Will Brigham Young fight?"

Congress and the nation thought that now the doom of Mormon polygamy had come.

Suddenly, like a wall of salvation, fifty thousand women of Mormondom threw themselves around their patriarchs and their institutions! A wonderful people, these Mormons! More wonderful these women!

CHAPTER XLIII.

GRAND MASS MEETING OF THE WOMEN OF UTAH
ON POLYGAMY AND THE CULLOM BILL—THEIR
NOBLE REMONSTRANCE—SPEECHES OF APOSTOLIC
WOMEN—THEIR RESOLUTIONS—WOMAN'S RIGHTS
OR WOMAN'S REVOLUTION.

Probably the most remarkable woman's rights
demonstration of the age, was that of the women
of Mormondom, in their grand mass-meetings, held
throughout Utah, in all its principal cities and settlements, in January of 1870. And it was the more
singular and complex, because Utah is the land of
polygamy—the only land in all Christendom where
that institution has been established—and that, too,
chiefly by an Anglo-Saxon people—the last race in
the world that the sociologist might have supposed
would have received the system of plural marriage!
Hence, they have lifted it to a plane that, perhaps,
no other race could have done—above mere sexual
considerations, and, in its theories, altogether incompatible with the serfdom of woman ; for the tens
of thousands of the women of Utah not only held
their grand mass-meetings to confirm and maintain
polygamy, but they did it at the very moment of
the passage of their female suffrage bill ; so that in

their vast assemblages they were virtually exercising their vote.

On the 13th of January, 1870, "notwithstanding the inclemency of the weather, the old tabernacle," says the *Deseret News*, "was densely packed with "ladies of all ages, and, as that building will com-"fortably seat five thousand persons, there could "not have been fewer than between five and six "thousand present on the occasion."

It was announced in the programme that there were to be none present but ladies. Several re-porters of the press, however, obtained admittance, among whom was Colonel Finley Anderson, special correspondent of the *New York Herald*.

The meeting was opened with a very impressive prayer from Mrs. Zina D. Young; and then, on mo-tion of Eliza R. Snow, Mrs. Sarah M. Kimball was elected president. Mrs. Lydia Alder was chosen secretary, and Mrs. M. T. Smoot, Mrs. M. N. Hyde, Isabella Horn, Mary Leaver, Priscilla Staines and Rachel Grant, were appointed a committee to draft resolutions. This was done with executive dis-patch ; for many present had for years been leaders of women's organizations. The president arose and addressed a few pithy remarks to the vast assemblage. She said :

"We are to speak in relation to the government "and institutions under which we live. She would "ask, Have we transgressed any law of the United "States ? [Loud " no " from the audience.] Then "why are we here to-day? We have been driven "from place to place, and wherefore ? Simply for "believing and practicing the counsels of God, as

"contained in the gospel of heaven.   The object of
"this meeting is to consider the justice of a bill now
"before the Congress of the United States.   We
"are not here to advocate woman's rights, but man's
"rights.   The bill in question would not only de-
"prive our fathers, husbands and brothers, of enjoy-
"ing the privileges bequeathed to citizens of the
"United States, but it would deprive us, as women,
"of the privilege of selecting our husbands; and
"against this we unqualifiedly protest."

During the absence of the committee on resolutions, the following speech was delivered by Bathsheba W. Smith :

" *Beloved Sisters and Friends:* It is with no ordi-
"nary feelings that I meet with you on the present
"occasion.   From my early youth I have been iden-
"tified with the Latter-day Saints; hence, I have
"been an eye and ear witness to many of the wrongs
"that have been inflicted upon our people by a spirit
"of intolerant persecution.

" I watched by the bedside of the first apostle,
" David W. Patten, who fell a martyr in the Church.
" He was a noble soul.   He was shot by a mob
" while defending the saints in the State of Missouri.
" As Brother Patten's life-blood oozed away, I stood
" by and heard his dying testimony to the truth of
" our holy religion—declaring himself to be a friend
" to all mankind.   His last words, addressed to his
" wife, were: 'Whatever you do, oh! do not deny
" the faith.'   This circumstance made a lasting im-
"pression on my youthful mind.

" I was intimately acquainted with the life and
" ministry of our beloved prophet Joseph, and our

"patriarch Hyrum Smith. I know that they were
"pure men, who labored for the redemption of the
"human family. For six years I heard their public
"and private teachings. It was from their lips that
"I heard taught the principle of celestial marriage;
"and when I saw their mangled forms cold in death,
"having been slain for the testimony of Jesus, by
"the hands of cruel bigots, in defiance of law, jus-
"tice and executive pledges; and although this was
"a scene of barbarous cruelty, which can never be
"erased from the memory of those who witnessed
"the heartrending cries of widows and orphans, and
"mingled their tears with those of thousands of
"witnesses of the mournful occasion—the memories
"of which I hardly feel willing to awaken—yet I
"realized that they had sealed their ministry with
"their blood, and that their testimony was in force.

"On the 9th day of February, 1846—the middle
"of a cold and bleak winter—my husband, just
"rising from a bed of sickness, and I, in company
"with thousands of saints, were driven again from
"our comfortable home—the accumulation of six
"years' industry and prudence—and, with the little
"children, commenced a long and weary journey
"through a wilderness, to seek another home; for
"a wicked mob had decreed we must leave. Gov-
"ernor Ford, of Illinois, said the laws were power-
"less to protect us. Exposed to the cold of winter
"and the storms of spring, we continued our jour-
"ney, amid want and exposure, burying by the
"wayside a dead mother, a son, and many kind
"friends and relatives.

"We reached the Missouri river in July. Here

" our country thought proper to make a requisition
" upon us for a battalion to defend our national flag
" in the war pending with Mexico. We responded
" promptly, many of our kindred stepping forward
" and performing a journey characterized by their
" commanding officer as ' unparalleled in history.'
" With most of our youths and middle-aged men
" gone, we could not proceed; hence, we were com-
" pelled to make another home, which, though hum-
" ble, approaching winter made very desirable. In
" 1847-8, all who were able, through selling their
" surplus property, proceeded; we who remained
" were told, by an unfeeling Indian department, we
" must vacate our houses and re-cross the Missouri
" river, as the laws would not permit us to remain
" on Indian lands! We obeyed, and again made a
" new home, though only a few miles distant. The
" latter home we abandoned in 1849, for the purpose
" of joining our co-religionists in the then far-off
" region, denominated on the map ' the Great Amer-
" ican Desert,' and by some later geographies as
" ' Eastern Upper California.'

" In this isolated country we made new homes,
" and, for a time, contended with the crickets for a
" scanty subsistence. The rude, ignorant, and almost
" nude Indians were a heavy tax upon us, while
" struggling again to make comfortable homes and
" improvements; yet we bore it all without com-
" plaint, for we were buoyed up with the happy
" reflections that we were so distant from the States,
" and had found an asylum in such an undesirable
" country, as to strengthen us in the hope that our
" homes would not be coveted; and that should we,

"through the blessing of God, succeed in planting
"our own vine and fig tree, no one could feel heart-
"less enough to withhold from us that religious
"liberty which we had sought in vain amongst our
"former neighbors.

"Without recapitulating our recent history, the
"development of a people whose industry and
"morality have extorted eulogy from their bitter
"traducers, I cannot but express my surprise, min-
"gled with regret and indignation, at the recent
"efforts of ignorant, bigoted, and unfeeling men—
"headed by the Vice-President—to aid intolerant
"sectarians and reckless speculators, who seek for
"proscription and plunder, and who feel willing to
"rob the inhabitants of these valleys of their hard-
"earned possessions, and, what is dearer, the consti-
"tutional boon of religious liberty."

Sister Smith was followed by Mrs. Levi Riter, in
a few appropriate remarks, and then the committee
on resolutions reported the following:

"*Resolved*, That we, the ladies of Salt Lake City,
in mass-meeting assembled, do manifest our indignation, and protest against the bill before Congress,
known as 'the Cullom bill,' also the one known as
'the Cragin bill,' and all similar bills, expressions
and manifestoes.

"*Resolved*, That we consider the above-named
bills foul blots on our national escutcheon—absurd
documents—atrocious insults to the honorable executive of the United States Government, and
malicious attempts to subvert the rights of civil and
religious liberty.

"*Resolved*, That we do hold sacred the constitution bequeathed us by our forefathers, and ignore,

with laudable womanly jealousy, every act of those men to whom the responsibilities of government have been entrusted, which is calculated to destroy its efficiency.

" *Resolved*, That we unitedly exercise every moral power and every right which we inherit as the daughters of American citizens, to prevent the passage of such bills, knowing that they would inevitably cast a stigma on our republican government by jeopardizing the liberty and lives of its most loyal and peaceful citizens.

" *Resolved*, That, in our candid opinion, the presentation of the aforesaid bills indicates a manifest degeneracy of the great men of our nation; and their adoption would presage a speedy downfall and ultimate extinction of the glorious pedestal of freedom, protection, and equal rights, established by our noble ancestors.

" *Resolved*, That we acknowledge the institutions of the Church of Jesus Christ of Latter-day Saints as the only reliable safeguard of female virtue and innocence; and the only sure protection against the fearful sin of prostitution, and its attendant evils, now prevalent abroad, and as such, we are and shall be united with our brethren in sustaining them against each and every encroachment.

" *Resolved*, That we consider the originators of the aforesaid bills disloyal to the constitution, and unworthy of any position of trust in any office which involves the interests of our nation.

" *Resolved*, That, in case the bills in question should pass both Houses of Congress, and become a law, by which we shall be disfranchised as a Territory, we, the ladies of Salt Lake City, shall exert all our power and influence to aid in the support of our own State government."

These resolutions were greeted with loud cheers

25

from nearly six thousand women, and carried unanimously; after which, Sister Warren Smith, a relict of one of the martyrs of Haun's Mill, arose, and with deep feeling, said :

"*Sisters :* As I sat upon my seat, listening, it "seemed as though, if I held my peace, the stones "of the streets would cry out. With your prayers "aiding me, I will try and make a few remarks. [See chapter on Haun's Mill massacre, in which Sister Smith substantially covers the same ground.] "We are here to-day to say, if such scenes shall be "again enacted in our midst. I say to you, my sis-"ters, you are American citizens; let us stand by "the truth, if we die for it."

Mrs. Wilmarth East then said : "It is with feel-"ings of pleasure, mingled with indignation and "disgust, that I appear before my sisters, to express "my feelings in regard to the Cullom bill, now be-"fore the Congress of this once happy republican "government. The constitution for which our fore-"fathers fought and bled and died, bequeaths to us "the right of religious liberty—the right to worship "God according to the dictates of our own con-"sciences ! Does the Cullom bill give us this right ? "Compare it with the constitution, if you please, "and see what a disgrace has come upon this once "happy and republican government ! Where, O, "where, is that liberty, bequeathed to us by our "forefathers—the richest boon ever given to man "or woman, except eternal life, or the gospel of the "Son of God ? I am an American citizen by birth. "Having lived under the laws of the land, I claim "the right to worship God according to the dictates

"of my conscience, and the commandments that
"God shall give unto me. Our constitution guar-
"antees life, liberty, and the pursuit of happiness, to
"all who live beneath it. What is life to me, if I
"see the galling yoke of oppression placed on the
"necks of my husband, sons and brothers, as Mr.
"Cullom would have it? I am proud to say to you
"that I am not only a citizen of the United States
"of America, but a citizen of the kingdom of God,
"and the laws of this kingdom I am willing to sus-
"tain and defend both by example and precept. I
"am thankful to-day that I have the honored priv-
"ilege of being the happy recipient of one of the
"greatest principles ever revealed to man for his
"redemption and exaltation in the kingdom of
"God—namely, plurality of wives; and I am thank-
"ful to-day that I know that God is at the helm, and
"will defend his people."

A veteran sister, Mrs. McMinn, could not refrain
from expressing herself in unison with her sisters,
in indignation at the bill. She was an American
citizen; her father had fought through the revolution with General Washington; and she claimed the
exercise of the liberty for which he had fought. She
was proud of being a latter-day saint.

In answer to an inquiry, she stated that she was
nearly eighty-five years of age.

Sister Eliza R. Snow then addressed the meeting,
as follows :

"*My Sisters:* In addressing you at this time, I
"realize that the occasion is a peculiar and interest-
"ing one. We are living in a land of freedom, under
"a constitution that guarantees civil and religious

"liberty to all—black and white, Christians, Jews,
"Mohammedans and Pagans; and how strange it is
"that such considerations should exist as those which
"have called us together this afternoon.

"Under the proud banner which now waves from
"ocean to ocean, strange as it may seem, we, who
"have ever been loyal citizens, have been persecuted
"from time to time and driven from place to place,
"until at last, beyond the bounds of civilization,
"under the guidance of President Young, we found
"an asylum of peace in the midst of these mountains.

"There are, at times, small and apparently trivial
"events in the lives of individuals, with which every
"other event naturally associates. There are cir-
"cumstances in the history of nations, which serve
"as centres around which everything else revolves.

"The entrance of our brave pioneers, and the
"settlement of the latter-day saints in these moun-
"tain vales, which then were only barren, savage
"wilds, are events with which not only our own fu-
"ture, but the future of the whole world, is deeply
"associated.

"Here they struggled, with more than mortal
"energy, for their hearts and hands were nerved by
"the spirit of the Most High, and through his bless-
"ing they succeeded in drawing sustenance from the
"arid soil; here they erected the standard on which
"the 'star spangled banner' waved its salutation of
"welcome to the nations of the earth; and here it
"will be bequeathed, unsullied, to future generations.
"Yes, that 'dear old flag' which in my girlhood I
"always contemplated with joyous pride, and to
"which the patriotic strains of my earliest muse were

" chanted, here floats triumphantly on the mountain
" breeze.

" Our numbers, small at first, have increased, until
" now we number one hundred and fifty thousand;
" and yet we are allowed only a territorial govern-
" ment. Year after year we have petitioned Con-
" gress for that which is our inalienable right to
" claim—a State government; and, year after year,
" our petitions have been treated with contempt.
" Such treatment as we have received from our rulers,
" has no precedent in the annals of history.

" And now, instead of granting us our rights as
" American citizens, bills are being presented to Con-
" gress, which are a disgrace to men in responsible
" stations, professing the least claim to honor and
" magnanimity; bills which, if carried into effect,
" would utterly annihilate us as a people. But this
" will never be. There is too much virtue yet exist-
" ing in the nation, and above all there is a God in
" heaven whose protecting care is over us, and who
" takes cognizance of the acts of men.

" My sisters, we have met to-day to manifest our
" views and feelings concerning the oppressive policy
" exercised towards us by our republican government.
" Aside from all local and personal feelings, to me it
" is a source of deep regret that the standard of
" American liberty should have been so far swayed
" from its original position, as to have given rise to
" circumstances which not only render such a meet-
" ing opportune, but absolutely necessary.

" Heretofore, while detraction and ridicule have
" been poured forth in almost every form that malice
" could invent, while we have been misrepresented

"by speech and press, and exhibited in every shade
"but our true light, the ladies of Utah have remained
"comparatively silent. Had not our aims been of
"the most noble and exalted character, and had we
"not known that we occupied a standpoint far above
"our traducers, we might have returned volley for
"volley; but we have all the time realized that to
"contradict such egregious absurdities, would be a
"great stoop of condescension—far beneath the dig-
"nity of those who profess to be saints of the living
"God; and we very unassumingly applied to our-
"selves a saying of an ancient apostle, in writing to
"the Corinthians, 'Ye suffer fools, gladly, seeing that
"yourselves are wise.'

" But there is a point at which silence is no longer
"a virtue. In my humble opinion, we have arrived
"at that point. Shall we—ought we—to be silent,
"when every right of citizenship, every vestige of
"civil and religious liberty, is at stake? When our
"husbands and sons, our fathers and brothers, are
"threatened with being either restrained in their
"obedience to the commands of God, or incarcer-
"ated, year after year, in the dreary confines of a
"prison, will it be thought presumptuous? Ladies,
"this subject as deeply interests us as them. In the
"kingdom of God, woman has no interests separate
"from those of man—all are mutual.

" Our enemies pretend that, in Utah, woman is
"held in a state of vassalage—that she does not act
"from choice, but by coercion—that we would even
"prefer life elsewhere, were it possible for us to
"make our escape. What nonsense! We all know
"that if we wished we could leave at any time—

"either to go singly, or to rise *en masse*, and there
"is no power here that could, or would wish to, pre-
"vent us.

"I will now ask this assemblage of intelligent
"ladies, do you know of any place on the face of the
"earth, where woman has more liberty, and where
"she enjoys such high and glorious privileges as she
"does here, as a latter-day saint? No! The very
"idea of woman here in a state of slavery is a bur-
"lesque on good common sense. The history of
"this people, with a very little reflection, would in-
"struct outsiders on this point. It would show, at
"once, that the part which woman has acted in it,
"could never have been performed against her will.
"Amid the many distressing scenes through which
"we have passed, the privations and hardships con-
"sequent upon our expulsion from State to State,
"and our location in an isolated, barren wilderness,
"the women in this Church have performed and
"suffered what could never have been borne and
"accomplished by slaves.

"And now, after all that has transpired, can our
"opponents expect us to look on with silent indif-
"ference and see every vestige of that liberty for
"which many of our patriotic grandsires fought and
"bled, that they might bequeath to us, their children,
"the precious boon of national freedom, wrested
"from our grasp? They must be very dull in esti-
"mating the energy of female character, who can
"persuade themselves that women who for the sake
"of their religion left their homes, crossed the plains
"with handcarts, or as many had previously done,
"drove ox, mule and horse-teams from Nauvoo

"and from other points, when their husbands and
"sons went, at their country's call, to fight her bat-
"tles in Mexico; yes, that very country which had
"refused us protection, and from which we were
"then struggling to make our escape—I say those
"who think that such women and the daughters of
"such women do not possess too much energy of
"character to remain passive and mute under exist-
"ing circumstances, are 'reckoning without their
"host.' To suppose that we should not be aroused
"when our brethren are threatened with fines and
"imprisonment, for their faith in, and obedience to,
"the laws of God, is an insult to our womanly na-
"tures.

"Were we the stupid, degraded, heartbroken
"beings that we have been represented, silence
"might better become us; but as women of God,
"women filling high and responsible positions, per-
"forming sacred duties—women who stand not as
"dictators, but as counselors to their husbands, and
"who, in the purest, noblest sense of refined wo-
"manhood, are truly their helpmates—we not only
"speak because we have the right, but justice and
"humanity demand that we should.'

"My sisters, let us, inasmuch as we are free to do
"all that love and duty prompt, be brave and unfal-
"tering in sustaining our brethren. Woman's faith
"can accomplish wonders. Let us, like the devout
"and steadfast Miriam, assist our brothers in up-
"holding the hands of Moses. Like the loving
"Josephine, whose firm and gentle influence both
"animated and soothed the heart of Napoleon, we
"will encourage and assist the servants of God in

" establishing righteousness; but unlike Josephine,
" never will political inducements, threats or perse-
" cutions, prevail on us to relinquish our matrimo-
" nial ties.   They were performed by the authority
" of the holy priesthood, the efficiency of which
" extends into eternity.

" But to the law and to the testimony.   Those
" obnoxious, fratricidal bills—I feel indignant at the
" thought that such documents should disgrace our
" national legislature.   The same spirit prompted
" Herod to seek the life of Jesus—the same that
" drove our Pilgrim fathers to this continent, and the
" same that urged the English government to the
" system of unrepresented taxation, which resulted
" in the independence of the American colonies, is
" conspicuous in those bills.   If such measures are
" persisted in they will produce similar results.   They
" not only threaten extirpation to us, but they augur
" destruction to the government.   The authors of
" those bills would tear the constitution to shreds;
" they are sapping the foundation of American free-
" dom—they would obliterate every vestige of the
" dearest right of man—liberty of conscience—and
" reduce our once happy country to a state of
" anarchy.

" Our trust is in God.   He who led Israel from
" the land of Egypt—who preserved Shadrach, Mes-
" hach and Abednego in the fiery furnace—who
" rescued Daniel from the jaws of hungry lions, and
" who directed Brigham Young to these mountain
" vales, lives, and overrules the destinies of men and
" nations.   He will make the wrath of man praise
" him; and his kingdom will move steadily forward,

"until wickedness shall be swept from the earth,
"and truth, love and righteousness reign triumph-
"antly."

Next came a concise, powerful speech from Harriet Cook Young. She said:

"In rising to address this meeting, delicacy
"prompts me to explain the chief motives which
"have dictated our present action. We, the ladies
"of Salt Lake City, have assembled here to-day,
"not for the purpose of assuming any particular
"political power, nor to claim any special preroga-
"tive which may or may not belong to our sex; but
"to express our indignation at the unhallowed
"efforts of men, who, regardless of every principle
"of manhood, justice, and constitutional liberty,
"would force upon a religious community, by a direct
"issue, either the course of apostacy, or the bitter
"alternative of fire and sword. Surely the instinct
"of self-preservation, the love of liberty and happi-
"ness, and the right to worship God, are dear to
"our sex as well as to the other; and when these
"most sacred of all rights are thus wickedly assail-
"ed, it becomes absolutely our duty to defend
"them.

"The mission of the Latter-day Saints is to re-
"form abuses which have for ages corrupted the
"world, and to establish an era of peace and right-
"eousness. The Most High is the founder of this
"mission, and in order to its establishment, his
"providences have so shaped the world's history,
"that, on this continent, blest above all other lands,
"a free and enlightened government has been insti-
"tuted, guaranteeing to all social, political, and

"religious liberty. The constitution of our country
"is therefore hallowed to us, and we view with a
"jealous eye every infringement upon its great
"principles, and demand, in the sacred name of
"liberty, that the miscreant who would trample it
"under his feet by depriving a hundred thousand
"American citizens of every vestige of liberty,
"should be anathematized throughout the length
"and breadth of the land, as a traitor to God and
"his country.

"It is not strange that, among the bigoted and
"corrupt, such a man and such a measure should
"have originated; but it will be strange indeed if
"such a measure find favor with the honorable and
"high-minded men who wield the destinies of the
"nation. Let this seal of ruin be attached to the
"archives of our country, and terrible must be the
"results. Woe will wait upon her steps, and war
"and desolation will stalk through the land; peace
"and liberty will seek another clime, while anarchy,
"lawlessness and bloody strife hold high carnival
"amid the general wreck. God forbid that wicked
"men be permitted to force such an issue upon the
"nation!

"It is true that a corrupt press, and an equally
"corrupt priestcraft, are leagued against us—that
"they have pandered to the ignorance of the masses,
"and vilified our institutions, to that degree that
"it has become popular to believe that the latter-
"day saints are unworthy to live; but it is also true
"that there are many, very many, right-thinking
"men who are not without influence in the nation;
"and to such do we now most solemnly and earn-

"estly appeal. Let the united force of this assem-
"bly give the lie to the popular clamor that the
"women of Utah are oppressed and held in bond-
"age. Let the world know that the women of Utah
"prefer virtue to vice, and the home of an honora-
"ble wife to the gilded pageantry of fashionable
"temples of sin. Transitory allurements, glaring
"the senses, as is the flame to the moth, short-lived
"and cruel in their results, possess no charms for
"us. Every woman in Utah may have her hus-
"band—the husband of her choice. Here we are
"taught not to destroy our children, but to preserve
"them, for they, reared in the path of virtue and
"trained to righteousness, constitute our true glory.

"It is with no wish to accuse our sisters who are
"not of our faith that we so speak ; but we are deal-
"ing with facts as they exist. Wherever monogamy
"reigns, adultery, prostitution and fœticide, directly
"or indirectly, are its concomitants. It is not enough
"to say that the virtuous and high-minded frown
"upon these evils. We believe they do. But frown-
"ing upon them does not cure them; it does not
"even check their rapid growth ; either the remedy
"is too weak, or the disease is too strong. The
"women of Utah comprehend this ; and they see, in
"the principle of plurality of wives, the only safe-
"guard against adultery, prostitution, and the reck-
"less waste of pre-natal life, practiced throughout
"the land.

"It is as co-workers in the great mission of uni-
"versal reform, not only in our own behalf, but also,
"by precept and example, to aid in the emancipa-
"tion of our sex generally, that we accept in our

"heart of hearts what we know to be a divine com-
"mandment: and here, and now, boldly and pub-
"licly, we do assert our right, not only to believe in
"this holy commandment, but to practice what we
"believe.

"While these are our views, every attempt to
"force that obnoxious measure upon us must of ne-
"cessity be an attempt to coerce us in our religious
"and moral convictions, against which did we not
"most solemnly protest, we would be unworthy the
"name of American women."

Mrs. Hannah T. King followed with a stinging
address to General Cullom himself. She said:

"*My Dear Sisters:* I wish I had the language I
"feel to need, at the present moment, to truly repre-
"sent the indignant feelings of my heart and brain
"on reading, as I did last evening, a string of thirty
"'sections,' headed by the words, 'A Bill in aid of
"the Execution of the Laws in the Territory of
"Utah, and for other purposes.' The 'other pur-
"poses' contain the pith of the matter, and the ada-
"mantine chains that the author of the said bill seeks
"to bind this people with, exceed anything that the
"feudal times of England, or the serfdom of Russia,
"ever laid upon human beings. My sisters, are we
"really in America—the world-renowned land of
"liberty, freedom, and equal rights?—the land of
"which I dreamed, in my youth, as being almost an
"earthly elysium, where freedom of thought and re-
"ligious liberty were open to all!—the land that
"Columbus wore his noble life out to discover!—
"the land that God himself helped him to exhume,
"and to aid which endeavor Isabella, a queen, a

"woman, declared she would pawn her jewels and
"crown of Castile, to give him the outfit that he
"needed!—the land of Washington, the Father of
"his Country, and a host of noble spirits, too nu-
"merous to mention!—the land to which the *May-*
"*flower* bore the pilgrim fathers, who rose up and
"left their homes, and bade their native home 'good
"night,' simply that they might worship God by a
"purer and holier faith, in a land of freedom and
"liberty, of which the name America has long been
"synonymous! Yes, my sisters, this is America·
"but oh! how are the mighty fallen!

 "Who, or what, is the creature who framed this
"incomparable document? Is he an Esquimaux or
"a chimpanzee? What isolated land or spot pro-
"duced him? What ideas he must have of women!
"Had he ever a mother, a wife, or a sister? In
"what academy was he tutored, or to what school
"does he belong, that he so coolly and systematic-
"ally commands the women of this people to turn
"traitors to their husbands, their brothers, and their
"sons? Short-sighted man of 'sections' and 'the
"bill!' Let us, the women of this people—the sis-
"terhood of Utah—rise *en masse*, and tell this non-
"descript to defer 'the bill' until he has studied the
"character of woman, such as God intended she
"should be; then he will discover that devotion,
"veneration and faithfulness are her peculiar attri-
"butes; that God is her refuge, and his servants her
"oracles; and that, especially, the women of Utah
"have paid too high a price for their present posi-
"tion, their present light and knowledge, and their
"noble future, to succumb to so mean and foul a

"thing as Baskin, Cullom & Co.'s bill. Let him
"learn that they are one in heart, hand and brain,
"with the brotherhood of Utah—that God is their
"father and their friend—that into his hands they
"commit their cause—and on their pure and simple
"banner they have emblazoned their motto, 'God,
"and my right!'"

The next who spoke was Phœbe Woodruff, who
said :

"*Ladies of Utah:* As I have been called upon to
"express my views upon the important subject which
"has called us together, I will say that I am happy
"to be one of your number in this association. I am
"proud that I am a citizen of Utah, and a member
"of the Church of Jesus Christ of Latter-day Saints.
"I have been a member of this church for thirty-six
"years, and had the privilege of living in the days
"of the prophet Joseph, and heard his teaching for
"many years. He ever counseled us to honor, obey
"and maintain the principles of our noble constitu-
"tion, for which our fathers fought, and which many
"of them sacrificed their lives to establish. Presi-
"dent Brigham Young has always taught the same
"principle. This glorious legacy of our fathers, the
"constitution of the United States, guarantees unto
"all the citizens of this great republic the right to
"worship God according to the dictates of their own
"consciences, as it expressly says, 'Congress shall
"make no laws respecting an establishment of reli-
"gion, or prohibiting the free exercise thereof.'
"Cullom's bill is in direct violation of this declara-
"tion of the constitution, and I think it is our duty
"to do all in our power, by our voices and influence,

"to thwart the passage of this bill, which commits a
"violent outrage upon our rights, and the rights of
"our fathers, husbands and sons; and whatever may
"be the final result of the action of Congress in
"passing or enforcing oppressive laws, for the sake
"of our religion, upon the noble men who have sub-
"dued these deserts, it is our duty to stand by them
"and support them by our faith, prayers and works,
"through every dark hour, unto the end, and trust
"in the God of Abraham, Isaac and Jacob to defend
"us and all who are called to suffer for keeping the
"commandments of God. Shall we, as wives and
"mothers, sit still and see our husbands and sons,
"whom we know are obeying the highest behest of
"heaven, suffer for their religion, without exerting
"ourselves to the extent of our power for their de-
"liverance? No; verily no! God has revealed
"unto us the law of the patriarchal order of mar-
"riage, and commanded us to obey it. We are
"sealed to our husbands for time and eternity, that
"we may dwell with them and our children in the
"world to come; which guarantees unto us the
"greatest blessing for which we are created. If the
"rulers of the nation will so far depart from the spirit
"and letter of our glorious constitution as to de-
"prive our prophets, apostles and elders of citizen-
"ship, and imprison them for obeying this law, let
"them grant this, our last request, to make their
"prisons large enough to hold their wives, for where
"they go we will go also."

Sisters M. I. Horne and Eleanor M. Pratt followed
with appropriate words, and then Sister Eliza R.
Snow made the following remarks:

My remarks in conclusion will be brief. I heard
"the prophet Joseph Smith say, if the people rose
"and mobbed us and the authorities countenanced
"it, they would have mobs to their hearts' content.
"I heard him say that the time would come when
"this nation would so far depart from its original
"purity, its glory, and its love of freedom and pro-
"tection of civil and religious rights, that the con-
"stitution of our country would hang as it were by
"a thread. He said, also, that this people, the sons
"of Zion, would rise up and save the constitution,
"and bear it off triumphantly.

"The spirit of freedom and liberty we should
"always cultivate, and it is what mothers should
"inspire in the breasts of their sons, that they may
"grow up brave and noble, and defenders of that
"glorious constitution which has been bequeathed
"unto us. Let mothers cultivate that spirit in
"their own bosoms. Let them manifest their own
"bravery, and cherish a spirit of encountering diffi-
"culties, because they have to be met, more or
"less, in every situation of life. If fortitude and
"nobility of soul be cultivated in your own bosoms,
"you will transmit them to your children; your
"sons will grow up noble defenders of truth and
"righteousness, and heralds of salvation to the na-
"tions of the earth. They will be prepared to fill
"high and responsible religious, judicial, civil and
"executive positions. I consider it most important,
"my sisters, that we should struggle to preserve
"the sacred constitution of our country—one of
"the blessings of the Almighty, for the same spirit
"that inspired Joseph Smith, inspired the framers

"of the constitution; and we should ever hold it "sacred, and bear it off triumphantly."

Mrs. Zina D. Young then moved that the meeting adjourn *sine die*, which was carried, and Mrs. Phœbe Woodruff pronounced the benediction.

CHAPTER XLIV.

WIVES OF THE APOSTLES—MRS. ORSON HYDE—INCI-
DENTS OF THE EARLY DAYS—THE PROPHET—
MARY ANN PRATT'S LIFE STORY—WIFE OF GEN.
CHARLES C. RICH—MRS. FRANKLIN D. RICHARDS—
PHŒBE WOODRUFF—LEONORA TAYLOR—MARIAN
ROSS PRATT—THE WIFE OF DELEGATE CANNON—
VILATE KIMBALL AGAIN.

The life of Mrs. Orson Hyde is replete with incidents of the early days, including the shameful
occurrence of the tarring and feathering of the
prophet, which took place while he was at her
father's house.

Her maiden name was Marinda M. Johnson, she
being the daughter of John and Elsa Johnson, a
family well known among the pioneer converts of
Ohio. She was born in Pomfret, Windsor county,
Vermont, June 28, 1815.

"In February of 1818," she says, "my father, in
"company with several families from the same place,
"emigrated to Hiram, Portage county, Ohio. In
"the winter of 1831, Ezra Booth, a Methodist min-
"ister, procured a copy of the Book of Mormon
"and brought it to my father's house. They sat up
"all night reading it, and were very much exercised

"over it. As soon as they heard that Joseph Smith
"had arrived in Kirtland, Mr. Booth and wife and
"my father and mother went immediately to see
"him. They were convinced and baptized before
"they returned. They invited the prophet and
"Elder Rigdon to accompany them home, which
"they did, and preached several times to crowded
"congregations, baptizing quite a number. I was
"baptized in April following. The next fall Joseph
"came with his family to live at my father's house.
"He was at that time translating the Bible, and
"Elder Rigdon was acting as scribe. The following
"spring, a mob, disguising themselves as black men,
"gathered and burst into his sleeping apartment one
"night, and dragged him from the bed where he was
"nursing a sick child. They also went to the house
"of Elder Rigdon, and took him out with Joseph
"into an orchard, where, after choking and beating
"them, they tarred and feathered them, and left
"them nearly dead. My father, at the first onset,
"started to the rescue, but was knocked down, and
"lay senseless for some time. Here I feel like bear-
"ing my testimony that during the whole year that
"Joseph was an inmate of my father's house I never
"saw aught in his daily life or conversation to make
"me doubt his divine mission.

"In 1833 we moved to Kirtland, and in 1834 I
"was married to Orson Hyde, and became fully
"initiated into the cares and duties of a missionary's
"wife, my husband in common with most of the
"elders giving his time and energies to the work of
"the ministry.

"In the summer of 1837, leaving me with a three-

"weeks old babe, he, in company with Heber C.
" Kimball and others, went on their first mission to
" England. Shortly after his return, in the summer
"of 1838, we, in company with several other fami-
" lies, went to Missouri, where we remained till the
" next spring. We then went to Nauvoo. In the
"spring of 1840 Mr. Hyde went on his mission to
" Palestine; going in the apostolic style, without
" purse or scrip, preaching his way, and when all
"other channels were closed, teaching the English
" language in Europe, till he gained sufficient money
" to take him to the Holy Land, where he offered
"up his prayer on the Mount of Olives, and dedi-
"cated Jerusalem to the gathering of the Jews in
"this dispensation. Having accomplished a three-
"years mission, he returned, and shortly after, in
" accordance with the revelation on celestial mar-
"riage, and with my full consent, married two more
"wives. At last we were forced to flee from Nau-
" voo, and in the spring of 1846, we made our way
"to Council Bluffs, where our husband left us to go
"again on mission to England. On his return, in
"the fall of 1847, he was appointed to take charge
"of the saints in the States, and to send off the
" emigration as fast as it arrived in a suitable con-
"dition on the frontiers; also to edit a paper in the
"church interest, the name of which was *Frontier*
" *Guardian.*

" In the summer of 1852 we brought our family
"safely through to Salt Lake City, where we have
"had peace and safety ever since.

" In 1868 I was chosen to preside over the branch
"of the Female Relief Society of the ward in

"which I reside, the duties of which position I have
"prayerfully attempted to perform."

––––––––

Mary Ann Pratt deserves mention next. It will
be remembered that the apostle Parley P. Pratt lost
his first wife at the birth of his eldest son. He
afterwards married the subject of this sketch, and
she becomes historically important from the fact
that she was one of the first of those self-subduing
women who united with their husbands in establishing the law of celestial marriage, or the "Patriarchal Order." *She gave to her husband other wives.*
Taking up the story of her life with her career as a
Latter-day Saint, she says :

"I was baptized into the Church of Jesus Christ
"of Latter-day Saints in the spring of 1835, being
"convinced of the truthfulness of its doctrines by
"the first sermon I heard; and I said in my heart,
"if there are only three who hold firm to the faith,
"I will be one of that number; and through all the
"persecution I have had to endure I have ever felt
"the same; my heart has never swerved from that
"resolve.

"I was married to Parley P. Pratt in the spring
"of 1837, and moving to Missouri, endured with
"him the persecution of the saints, so often recorded
"in history. When my husband was taken by a
"mob, in the city of Far West, Mo., and carried to
"prison, I was confined to my bed with raging fever,
"and not able to help myself at all, with a babe
"three months old and my little girl of five years;

"but I cried mightily to the Lord for strength to
" endure, and he in mercy heard my prayer and car-
" ried me safely through. In a few days word came
" to me that my husband was in prison and in chains.
" As soon as my health was sufficiently restored I
"took my children and went to him. I found him
"released from his chains, an . was permitted to
"remain with him. I shared his dungeon, which
"was a damp, dark, filthy place, without ventilation,
"merely having a small grating on one side. In
" this we were obliged to sleep.

" About the middle of March I bid adieu to my
" beloved companion, and returned to Far West to
" make preparations for leaving the State. Through
" the kind assistance of Brother David W. Rogers
" (now an aged resident of Provo), I removed to
" Quincy, Ill., where I remained until the arrival of
" Mr. Pratt, after his fortunate escape from prison,
" where he had been confined eight months without
" any just cause.

" Passing briefly over the intervening years, in
" which I accompanied my husband on various mis-
" sions, first to New York, and thence to England,
" where I remained two years; and, returning to
" Nauvoo, our sojourn in that beautiful city a few
" years, and our final expulsion, and the final weary
"gathering to Utah; I hasten to bear my testi-
" mony to the world that this is the church and
" people of God, and I pray that I may be found
" worthy of a place in his celestial kingdom."

The tragedy of the close of the mortal career of
Parley P. Pratt is still fresh in the public mind. It
is one of the terrible chapters of Mormon his-

tory which the pen of his wife has not dared to touch.

———

Another of these " first wives " is presented in the person of Sister Rich.

Sarah D. P. Rich, wife of Gen. Chas. C. Rich, and daughter of John and Elizabeth Pea, was born September 23d, 1814, in St. Clair county, Ill. In December, 1835, she became a member of the Church of Latter-day Saints, and had the pleasure shortly after of seeing her father's family, with a single exception, converted to the same faith. In 1837 they removed to Far West, Mo., where the saints were at that time gathering. At this place she for the first time met Mr. Rich, to whom she was married on the 11th of February, 1838. During the autumn of 1838, the mob having driven many of the saints from their homes in the vicinity, she received into her house and sheltered no less than seven families of the homeless outcasts. Among the number was the family of Apostle Page, and it was during her sojourn with Mrs. Rich that Apostle Page's wife died. Mrs. R. stood in her door and saw the infamous mob-leader and Methodist preacher, Bogard, shoot at her husband as he was returning from the mob camp under a flag of truce. That night Mr. Rich was compelled to flee for his life, and she did not see him again until she joined him three months later, on the bank of the Mississippi, opposite Quincy. They made the crossing in a canoe, the river being so full of ice that the regular ferry-boat could not be used. From this place they removed

to Nauvoo, where she remained during all the succeeding persecutions and trials of the church, until
February, 1846, when they were forced to leave,
which they did, with her three small children, crossing the Mississippi on the ice. Journeying westward to Mount Pisgah, Iowa, they remained during
the following season, and planted and harvested a
crop of corn. In the spring of 1847 they removed
to winter quarters, and six weeks afterwards started
out on the weary journey across the plains. She
arrived in Salt Lake Valley on the 2d of October,
1847, with the second company of emigrants, of
which her husband was the leadet.

Since that time she has resided continually in
Salt Lake City, with the exception of a short sojourn in Bear Lake Valley, and has endured without
complaint all of the trials, privations and hardships
incident to the settlement of Utah. She is the
mother of nine children, and is well known as the
friend of the poor, the nurse of the sick, and the
counselor of the friendless and oppressed among
the people; and it is needless to add that she has
passed her life in the advocacy and practice of the
principles of that gospel which she embraced in the
days of her youth.

———

Mrs. Jane S. Richards, wife of the distinguished
apostle, Franklin D. Richards, and daughter of Isaac
and Louisa Snyder, was born January 31st, 1823, in
Pamelia, Jefferson county, N. Y. The prophet and
pilot of her father's house into the church was
Elder John E. Page, who brought to them the gos-

pel in 1837, while they were living near Kingston, Canada. The family started thence for Far West, Mo., in 1839, but were compelled by sickness to stop at La Porte, Indiana. Here, through the faithful ministrations of her brother Robert, she was restored from the effects of a paralytic stroke, and immediately embraced the faith. In the autumn following (1840) she first saw young Elder Richards, then on his first mission. In 1842, after her father's family had moved to Nauvoo, she was married to Mr. Richards. In the journey of the saints into the wilderness, after their expulsion from Nauvoo, she drank to the bitter dregs the cup of hardship and affliction, her husband being absent on mission and she being repeatedly prostrated with sickness. At winter quarters President Young said to her, "It may truly be said, if any have come up through great tribulation from Nauvoo, you have." There her little daughter died, and was the first to be interred in that memorable burying ground of the saints. Here also her husband's wife, Elizabeth, died, despite the faithful efforts of friends, and had it not been for their unwearied attentions, Jane also would have sunk under her load of affliction and sorrow.

In 1848, Mr. Richards having returned from mission, they gathered to the valley. In 1849 she gave her only sister to her husband in marriage. From that time forth until their removal to Ogden, in 1869, hers was the fortune of a missionary's wife, her husband being almost constantly on mission. In 1872 she accepted the presidency of the Ogden Relief Society, which she has since very acceptably filled. Among the noteworthy items of interest connected with her presidency of this society, was the organization of the young ladies of Ogden into a branch society for the purpose of retrenchment and economy in dress, moral, mental and spiritual improvement, etc., which has been most successfully continued, and is now collaterally supported by many branch societies in the county. But her labors have not been confined to Ogden alone. She has been appointed to preside over the societies of Weber county; and, as a sample of her efforts, we may instance that she has established the manufacture of home-made straw bonnets and hats, which industry has furnished employment to many. Her heart and home have ever been open to the wants of the needy; and the sick and afflicted have been the objects of her continual care.

The closing words of the wife of Apostle Woodruff, at the grand mass-meeting of the women of Utah, have in them a ring strongly suggestive of what must have been the style of speech of those women of America who urged their husbands and sons to resist the tyranny of George III.; throw off the yoke of colonial servitude, and prove themselves worthy of national independence.

Phœbe W. Carter was born in Scarboro, in the State of Maine, March 8th, 1807. Her father was of English descent, connecting with America at about the close of the seventeenth century. Her mother, Sarah Fabyan, was of the same place, and three generations from England. The name of Fabyan was one of the noblest names of Rome, ere England was a nation, and that lofty tone and strength of character so marked in the wife of Apostle Woodruff was doubtless derived from the Fabyans, Phœbe being of her mother's stamp.

In the year 1834 she embraced the gospel, and, about a year after, left her parents and kindred and journeyed to Kirtland, a distance of one thousand miles—a lone maid, sustained only by a lofty faith and trust in Israel's God. In her characteristic Puritan language she says :

' My friends marveled at my course, as did I, but " something within impelled me on. My mother's " grief at my leaving home was almost more than I " could bear; and had it not been for the spirit " within I should have faltered at the last. My " mother told me she would rather see me buried " than going thus alone out into the heartless world. " ' Phœbe,' she said, impressively, 'will you come " back to me if you find Mormonism false ?' I " answered, 'yes, mother; I will, thrice.' These were " my words, and she knew I would keep my promise. " My answer relieved her trouble ; but it cost us all " much sorrow to part. When the time came for " my departure I dared not trust myself to say fare- " well ; so I wrote my good-byes to each, and leav- " ing them on my table, ran down stairs and jumped " into the carriage. Thus I left the beloved home " of my childhood to link my life with the saints of " God.

" When I arrived in Kirtland I became acquainted " with the prophet, Joseph Smith, and received more

" evidence of his divine mission. There in Kirtland
" I formed the acquaintance of Elder Wilford Wood-
" ruff, to whom I was married in 1836. With him I
" went to the 'islands of the sea,' and to England,
" on missions.

" When the principle of polygamy was first taught
" I thought it the most wicked thing I ever heard of;
" consequently I opposed it to the best of my abil-
" ity, until I became sick and wretched. As soon,
" however, as I became convinced that it originated
" as a revelation from God through Joseph, and
" knowing him to be a prophet, I wrestled with my
" Heavenly Father in fervent prayer, to be guided
" aright at that all-important moment of my life.
" The answer came. Peace was given to my mind.
" I knew it was the will of God; and from that time
" to the present I have sought to faithfully honor
" the patriarchal law.

" Of Joseph, my testimony is that he was one of
" the greatest prophets the Lord ever called; that
" he lived for the redemption of mankind, and died
" a martyr for the truth. The love of the saints for
" him will never die.

" It was after the martyrdom of Joseph that I
" accompanied my husband to England, in 1845.
" On our return the advance companies of the saints
" had just left Nauvoo under President Young and
" others of the twelve. We followed immediately
" and journeyed to winter quarters.

" The next year Wilford went with the pioneers
" to the mountains, while the care of the family de-
" volved on me. After his return, and the reorgan-
" ization of the first presidency, I accompanied my

" husband on his mission to the Eastern States. In
" 1850 we arrived in the valley, and since that time
" Salt Lake City has been my home.

" Of my husband I can truly say, I have found
" him a worthy man, with scarcely his equal on earth.
" He has built up a branch wherever he has labored.
" He has been faithful to God and his family every
" day of his life. My respect for him has increased
" with our years, and my desire for an eternal union
" with him will be the last wish of my mortal life."

Sister Phœbe is one of the noblest of her sex—a
mother in Israel. And in her strength of character,
consistency, devotion, and apostolic cast, she is second to none.

———

A most worthy peer of sister Woodruff was Leonora, the wife of Apostle John Taylor. She was the
daughter of Capt. Cannon, of the Isle of Man, England, and sister of the father of George Q. Cannon.
She left England for Canada, as a companion to the
wife of the secretary of the colony, but with the intention of returning. While in Canada, however, she met
Elder Taylor, then a Methodist minister, whose wife
she afterwards became. They were married in 1833.
She was a God-fearing woman, and, as we have seen,
was the first to receive Parley P. Pratt into her
house when on his mission to Canada. In the spring
of 1838 she gathered with her husband and two
children to Kirtland. Thence they journeyed to
Far West. She was in the expulsion from Missouri;
bore the burden of her family in Nauvoo, as a missionary's wife, while her husband was in England;

felt the stroke of the martyrdom, in which her husband was terribly wounded; was in the exodus; was then left at winter quarters while her husband went on his second mission to England; but he returned in time for them to start with the first companies that followed the pioneers. Sister Leonora was therefore among the earliest women of Utah.

When the prospect came, at the period of the Utah war, that the saints would have to leave American soil, and her husband delivered those grand patriotic discourses to his people that will ever live in Mormon history, Sister Taylor nobly supported his determination with the rest of the saints to put the torch to their homes, rather than submit to invasion and the renunciation of their liberties. She died in the month of December, 1867. Hers was a faithful example, and she has left an honored memory among her people.

Marian Ross, wife of Apostle Orson Pratt, is a native of Scotland, and was reared among the Highlands. When about seventeen years of age she visited her relatives in Edinburgh, where Mormonism was first brought to her attention. She was shortly afterwards baptized near the harbor of Leith, on the 27th of August, 1847. A singular feature of Mrs. Pratt's experience was that in a dream she was distinctly shown her future husband, then on his mission to Scotland. When she saw him she at once recognized him. She made her home at Apostle Pratt's house in Liverpool, for a short time, and then emigrated to America, in 1851. After being in Salt Lake City a few months she was married to Mr. Pratt. She testifies, " I have been in polygamy " twenty-five years, and have never seen the hour " when I have regretted that I was in it. I would " not change my position for anything earthly, no " matter how grand and gorgeous it might be ; even " were it for the throne of a queen. For a surety do " I know that my Redeemer liveth, and that he is a " prayer-hearing and prayer-answering God."

Another of these apostolic women, who with their husbands founded Utah, is the wife of Albert Carrington. She was also in the valley in 1847. Her grand example and words to Captain Van Vliet, when the saints were resolving on another exodus, have been already recorded. A volume written could not make her name more imperishable.

Nor must Artimisa, the first wife of Erastus Snow, who is so conspicuous among the founders of St. George, be forgotten. She is one of the honorable women of Utah, and the part she has sustained, with her husband, in building up the southern country, has been that of self-sacrifice, endurance, and noble example.

Mention should also be made of Elizabeth, daughter of the late Bishop Hoagland, and first wife of

George Q. Cannon. She has borne the burden of the day as a missionary's wife, and has also accompanied her husband on mission to England; but her most noteworthy example was in her truly noble conduct in standing by her husband in those infamous persecutions of the politicians, over the question of polygamy, in their efforts to prevent him taking his seat in Congress.

———

Here let us also speak of the death of Sister Vilate Kimball, whose history has been given somewhat at length in previous chapters. After sharing with her husband and the saints the perils and hardships of the exodus, and the journey across the plains, and after many years of usefulness to her family and friends, she died Oct. 22d, 1867. She was mourned by none more sincerely than by her husband, who, according to his words spoken over her remains, was "not long after her."

CHAPTER XLV.

The heroic conduct of the Mormon women, in
their eventful history, is not strange, nor their
trained sentiments of religious liberty exaggerated
in the action of their lives ; for it must not be forgotten that many a sister among the Latter-day
Saints had lived in the time of the Revolution, and
had shown examples not unworthy of Martha
Washington herself. Of course those women of
the Revolution are now sleeping with the just, for
nearly fifty years have passed since the rise of the
church, but there are still left those who can remember the father of their country, and the mothers
who inspired the war of independence. We have
such an one to present in the person of Aunt Rhoda
Richards, the sister of Willard, the apostle, and first
cousin of Brigham Young.

Scarcely had the British evacuated New York,
and Washington returned to his home at Mount
Vernon, when Rhoda Richards was born. She was
the sister of Phineas, Levi, and Willard Richards—
three of illustrious memory in the Mormon Church

—was born August 8th, 1784, at Hopkington, Mass.,
and now, at the advanced age of ninety-three, thus
speaks of her life and works. She says :

" During the early years of my life I was much
" afflicted with sickness, but, through the mercies
" and blessings of my Heavenly Father, at the ad-
" vanced age of nearly ninety-three, I live, and am
" privileged to bear my individual testimony, that
" for myself I know that Joseph Smith was a true
" prophet of the living God ; and that the work
" which he, as an humble instrument in the hands of
" God, commenced in this, the evening of time, will
" not be cut short, save as the Lord himself, accord-
" ing to his promise, shall cut short his work in right-
" eousness.

" My first knowledge of the Mormons was gained
" through my cousin, Joseph Young, though I had
" previously heard many strange things concerning
" them. I lay on a bed of sickness, unable to sit up,
" when Cousin Joseph came to visit at my father's
" house. I remember distinctly how cautiously my
" mother broached the subject of the new religion
" to him. Said she, ' Joseph, I have heard that some
" of the children of my sister, Abigail Young, have
" joined the Mormons. How is it ?' Joseph replied,
" ' It is true, Aunt Richards, and I am one of them !'
" It was Sabbath day, and in the morning Cousin
" Joseph attended church with my parents ; but in
" the afternoon he chose to remain with my brother
" William, and myself, at home. He remarked that
" he could not enjoy the meeting, and in reply I said,
" ' I do not see why we might not have a meeting
" here.' My cousin was upon his feet in an instant,

" and stood and preached to us—my brother and
" myself—for about half an hour, finishing his dis-
" course with, ' There, Cousin Rhoda, I don't know
" but I have tired you out !' When he sat down I
" remarked that meetings usually closed with prayer.
" In an instant he was on his knees, offering up a
" prayer. That was the first Mormon sermon and
" the first Mormon prayer I ever listened to. I
" weighed his words and sentences well. It was
" enough. My soul was convinced of the truth.
" But I waited a year before being baptized. Dur-
" ing that time I read the books of the church, and
" also saw and heard other elders, among whom was
" my cousin, Brigham Young, and my brothers,
" Phineas, Levi, and Willard ; all of which served to
" strengthen my faith and brighten my understand-
" ing.

   " A short time after I was baptized and confirmed
" I was greatly afflicted with the raging of a cancer,
" about to break out in my face. I knew too well
" the symptoms, having had one removed previously.
" The agony of such an operation, only those who
" have passed through a like experience can ever
" imagine. The idea of again passing through a
" like physical suffering seemed almost more than
" humanity could endure. One Sabbath, after the
" close of the morning service, I spoke to the presid-
" ing elder, and acquainted him with my situation,
" requesting that I might be administered to, accord-
" ing to the pattern that God had given, that the
" cancer might be rebuked and my body healed.
" The elder called upon the sisters present to unite
" their faith and prayers in my behalf, and upon the

" brethren to come forward and lay their hands upon
" me, and bless me in the name of the' Lord Jesus
" Christ, according to my desire. It was done, and
" I went home completely healed, and rejoicing in
" the God of my salvation. Many times have I
" since been healed by the same power, when, appar-
" ently, death had actually seized me as his prey. I
" would not have it understood, however, that I have
" been a weakly, sickly, useless individual all my
" life. Those who have known me can say quite to
" the contrary. Some of our ambitious little girls
" and working women would doubtless be interested
" in a simple sketch of some few things which I
" have accomplished by manual labor. When my-
" self and my sisters were only small girls, our ex-
" cellent mother taught us how to work, and in such
" a wise manner did she conduct our home educa-
" tion that we always loved to work, and were never
" so happy as when we were most usefully employed.
" We knit our own and our brothers' stockings, made
" our own clothes, braided and sewed straw hats and
" bonnets, carded, spun, wove, kept house, and did
" everything that girls and women of a self-sustain-
" ing community would need to do. The day that
" I was thirteen years old I wove thirteen yards of
" cloth ; and in twenty months, during which time I
" celebrated my eightieth birthday, I carded twenty
" weight of cotton, spun two hundred and fifteen
" balls of candlewicking, and two hundred run of
" yarn, prepared for the weaver's loom ; besides do-
" ing my housework, knitting socks, and making
" shirts for ' my boys ' (some of the sons of my bro-
" thers). I merely make mention of these things as

" samples of what my life-work has been. I never
" was an idler, but have tried to be useful in my
" humble way, 'doing what my hands found to do
" with my might.' I now begin to feel the weight of
" years upon me, and can no longer do as I have
" done in former years for those around me; but,
" through the boundless mercies of God, I am still
" able to wash and iron my own clothes, do up my
" lace caps, and write my own letters. My memory
" is good, and as a general thing I feel well in body
" and mind. I have witnessed the death of many
" near and dear friends, both old and young. In my
" young days I buried my first and only love, and
" true to that affiance, I have passed companionless
" through life ; but am sure of having my proper
" place and standing in the resurrection, having been
" sealed to the prophet Joseph, according to the ce-
" lestial law, by his own request, under the inspira-
" tion of divine revelation."

A very beautiful incident is this latter—the
memory of her early love, for whose sake she kept
sacred her maiden life. The passage is exquisite in
sentiment, although emanating from a heart that
has known the joys and sorrows of nearly a hundred years.

———

Lydia Partridge, the aged relict of the first bishop
of the Mormon Church, may well accompany the
venerable sister of Willard Richards.

She was born September 26, 1793, in the town of
Marlboro, Mass., her parents' names being Joseph
Clisbee and Merriam Howe. The course of events

finally brought her to Ohio, where she made the acquaintance of, and married, Edward Partridge. Her husband and herself were proselyted into the Campbellite persuasion by Sidney Rigdon ; but they soon afterwards became converts to Mormonism, and Mr. Partridge thereupon commenced his career as a laborer in the ministry of the church. They were among the first families to locate in Missouri, and also among the first to feel the sting of persecution in that State. Removing finally to Nauvoo, her husband there died. In the after-wanderings of the saints in search of a home in the wilderness she accompanied them. It may be briefly said of her that now, after forty-five years in the church, she is as firm and steadfast as ever in her faith, and is one of the staunchest advocates of polygamy.

Next comes Margaret T. M. Smoot, wife of Bishop Smoot, with the testimony of her life.

She was born in Chester District, South Carolina, April 16th, 1809. Her father, Anthony McMeans, was a Scotchman by birth, emigrating to America at an early age, and settling in South Carolina, where he resided at the breaking out of the Revolutionary war. Fired with patriotic zeal, he immediately enlisted in the ranks, and continued fighting in the cause of liberty until the close of the war, when he returned to his home, where he remained until his death. Her mother was a Hunter, being of Irish extraction. Her grandfather Hunter also served in the Revolutionary war, being an intimate friend of Gen. Washington. For these reasons Mrs. Smoot is justly proud of her lineage. Her husband, the bishop, being also of revolutionary descent, they as a family well exemplify the claim made elsewhere, that the Mormons were originally of the most honored and patriotic extraction.

She embraced the Mormon faith in 1834, and was married to Mr. Smoot the following year, in the State of Kentucky. In 1837 they went to Far West, Mo., and their history thence to Utah is the oft-told story of outrage and persecution. It is proper to remark, however, that their son, William, was one of the original pioneers, and that their family was among the first company that entered the valley.

Sister Smoot is known in the church as one of the most illustrious examples of the "first wives" who accepted and gave a true Israelitish character and sanctity to the "patriarchal order of marriage;" while the long-sustained position of her husband as Mayor of Salt Lake City, enhances the effect of her social example.

———

A few incidents from the life of Sister Hendricks, whose husband was wounded in "Crooked River battle," where the apostle David Patten fell, may properly be here preserved.

Of that mournful incident, she says: "A neighbor "stopped at the gate and alighted from his horse; "I saw him wipe his eyes, and knew that he was "weeping; he came to the door and said, 'Mr. Hen-"dricks wishes you to come to him at the Widow

" Metcalf's.   He is shot.'   I rode to the place, four
" miles away, and there saw nine of the brethren,
" pale and weak from their wounds, being assisted
" into the wagons that were to take them to their
" homes.   In the house was my husband, and also
" David Patten, who was dying.   My husband was
" wounded in the neck in such a manner as to injure
" the spinal column, which paralyzed his extremities.
" Although he could speak, he could not move any
" more than if he were dead."

Mr Hendricks lived until 1870, being an almost
helpless invalid up to that time.   Their son William
was a member of the famous battalion.   Mrs. H.
still survives, and is the happy progenitress of five
children, sixty-three grandchildren, and twenty-three
great-grandchildren.

———

The wife of Bishop McRae deserves remembrance
in connection with an incident of the battle of
Nauvoo.   When it was determined to surrender
that city, the fugitive saints were naturally anxious
to take with them in their flight whatever of property, etc., they could, that would be necessary to
them in their sojourn in the wilderness.   It will be
seen at once that nothing could have been of more
service to them than their rifles and ammunition.
Hence, with a refinement of cruelty, the mobbers
determined to rob them of these necessaries.   They
accordingly demanded the arms and ammunition of
all who left the city, and searched their wagons to
see that none were secreted.   Mrs. McRae was determined to save a keg of powder, however, and so

she ensconced herself in her wagon with the powder keg as a seat, covering it with the folds of her dress. Soon a squad of the enemy came to her wagon, and making as if to search it, asked her to surrender whatever arms and ammunition she might have on hand. She quietly kept her seat, however, and coolly asked them, "How many more times are you going to search this wagon to-day?" This question giving them the impression that they had already searched the wagon, they moved on, and Mrs. McRae saved her powder.

She still lives, and is at present a much respected resident of Salt Lake City.

———

Mrs. Mary M. Luce, a venerable sister, now in her seventy-seventh year, and a resident of Salt Lake City, deserves a passing mention from the fact that her religion has caused her to traverse the entire breadth of the continent, in order to be gathered with the saints. She was a convert of Wilford Woodruff, who visited her native place while on mission to the "Islands of the Sea" (Fox Islands, off the Coast of Maine). In 1838, with her family, she journeyed by private conveyance from Maine to Illinois, joining the saints at Nauvoo. This was, in those days, a very long and tedious journey, consuming several months' time. During the persecutions of Nauvoo, she was reduced to extreme poverty; but, after many vicissitudes, was enabled to reach Salt Lake City the first year after the pioneers, where she has since continued to reside. In her experience she has received many tests and manifestations of the divine origin of the latter-day work, and testifies that "these are the happiest days" of her life.

Elizabeth H., wife of William Hyde, for whom "Hyde Park," Utah, was named, was born in Holliston, Middlesex county, Mass., October 2d, 1813. She was the daughter of Joel and Lucretia Bullard, and a descendant, on the maternal side, from the Goddards. Her mother and herself were baptized into the Mormon faith in 1838, and they moved to Nauvoo in 1841, where Elizabeth was married to Elder Hyde, in 1842. He was on mission most of the time up to 1846, when they left Nauvoo, in the exodus of the church. Her husband joined the Mormon battalion in July following, returning home in the last month of 1847. In the spring of 1849, with their three surviving children, they journeyed to Salt Lake Valley, where they resided until about seventeen years ago, when they removed to Cache Valley, and founded the settlement which bears their name. Mr. Hyde died in 1872, leaving five wives and twenty-two children. "It is my greatest "desire," says sister Hyde, "that I may so live as to "be accounted worthy to dwell with those who have "overcome, and have the promise of eternal lives, "which is the greatest gift of God."

Nor should we forget to mention "Mother Sessions," another of the last-century women who have gathered to Zion. Her maiden name was Patty Bartlett, and she was born February 4th, 1795, in the town of Bethel, Oxford county, Maine. She was married to David Sessions in 1812, and survives both him and a second husband. Herself and husband joined the church in 1834, moved to Nauvoo in 1840, and left there with the exiled saints in 1846. In the summer of 1847 they crossed the plains to the valley, Mrs. Sessions, although in her fifty-third year, driving a four-ox team the entire distance.

Mother Sessions is a model of zeal, frugality, industry and benevolence. When she entered the valley she had but five cents, which she had found on the road; now, after having given many hundreds of dollars to the perpetual emigration fund, tithing fund, etc., and performing unnumbered deeds of private charity, she is a stockholder in the "Z. C. M. I." to the amount of some twelve or thirteen thousand dollars, and is also possessed of a competence for the remainder of her days; all of which is a result of her own untiring efforts and honorable business sagacity. As a testimony of her life she says, "I am now eighty-two years of age. I drink "no tea nor coffee, nor spirituous liquors; neither do "I smoke nor take snuff. To all my posterity and "friends I say, do as I have done, and as much "better as you can, and the Lord will bless you as "he has me."

———

Mrs. R. A. Holden, of Provo, is another of the

revolutionary descendants. Her grandfather, Clement Bishop, was an officer in the revolutionary war, was wounded, and drew a pension until his death. Mrs. H., whose maiden name was Bliss, was born in 1815, in Livingston county, N. Y., and after marrying Mr. Holden, in 1833, moved to Illinois, where, in 1840, they embraced the gospel. Their efforts to reach the valley and gather with the church form an exceptional chapter of hardship and disappointment. Nevertheless, they arrived at Provo in 1852, where they have since resided; Mrs. Holden being, since 1867, the president of the Relief Society of the Fourth Ward of that city.

Sister Diantha Morley Billings is another of the aged and respected citizens of Provo. She was born August 23d, 1795, at Montague, Mass. About the year 1815 she moved to Kirtland, Ohio, and there was married to Titus Billings. Herself and husband and Isaac Morley, her brother, were among the first baptized in Kirtland. They were also among the first to remove to Missouri, whence they were driven, and plundered of all they possessed, by the mobs that arose, in that State, against the saints. Her husband was in Crooked River battle, standing by Apostle Patten when he fell.

They reached Utah in 1848, and were soon thereafter called to go and start settlements in San Pete. They returned to Provo in 1864, and in 1866 Mr. Billings died.

While living in Nauvoo, after the expulsion from

Missouri, Mrs. Billings was ordained and set apart by the prophet Joseph to be a nurse, in which calling she has ever since been very skillful.

Mrs. Amanda Wimley, although but eight years a resident of Utah, was converted to Mormonism in Philadelphia, in the year 1839, under the preaching of Joseph the prophet, being baptized shortly afterward. For thirty years the circumstances of her life were such that it was not expedient for her to gather with the church ; she nevertheless maintained her faith, and was endowed to a remarkable degree with the gift of healing, which she exercised many times with wonderful effect in her own family. Journeying to Salt Lake City some eight years since, on a visit merely, she has now fully determined to permanently remain, as the representative of her father's house, to " do a work for her ancestry and posterity."

Polly Sawyer Atwood, who died in Salt Lake City, Oct. 16th, 1876, is worthy of a passing notice, because of her many good deeds in the service of God. She was another of the last century women, being born in 1790, in Windham, Conn. Her parents were Asahel and Elizabeth Sawyer. Herself and husband, Dan Atwood, first heard the gospel in 1839, and were straightway convinced of its truth. They journeyed to Salt Lake in 1850. Here she displayed in a remarkable manner the works and gifts of faith, and was much sought after by the sick and afflicted, up to the day of her death, which occurred in her 86th year. It is worthy of mention that she was the mother of three men of distinction in the church—Millen Atwood, who was one of the pioneers, a missionary to England, captain of the first successful handcart company, and a member of the high council; Miner Atwood, who was a missionary to South Africa, and also a member of the high council; and Samuel Atwood, who is one of the presiding bishops of the Territory.

In connection with Mother Atwood may also properly be mentioned her daughter-in-law, Relief C. Atwood, the wife of Millen, who received the gospel in New Hampshire, in 1843, and in 1845 emigrated to Nauvoo. This was just before the expulsion of the church from that city, and in a few months she found herself in the wilderness. At winter quarters, after the return of the pioneers, she married Mr. Atwood, one of their number, and with him in 1848 journeyed to the valley. Their trials were at first nigh overwhelming, but in a moment of prayer, when they were about to give up in despair, the spirit of the Lord rested upon Mr. A., and he spoke in tongues, and at the same time the gift of interpretation rested upon her. It was an exhortation to renewed hope and trust, which so strengthened them that they were able to overcome every difficulty. Her family has also received many striking manifestations of the gift of healing—so much so that she now bears testimony that " God is their great physician, in whom she can safely trust."

———

Sister Sarah B. Fiske, who was born in Potsdam, St. Lawrence Co., N. Y., in 1819, is another of revolutionary ancestry; her grandfathers, on both paternal and maternal side, having served in the revolutionary war.   In 1837 she was married to Ezra H. Allen.   Shortly thereafter they were both converted to Mormonism, and in 1842 moved to Nauvoo.   In the spring of '43 they joined the settlement which was attempted at à place called Shockoquan, about twenty-five miles north of Nauvoo.   Journeying with the saints on the exodus, she stopped at Mount Pisgah, while her husband went forward in the battalion.   Nearly two years passed, and word came that the brethren of the battalion were coming back. With the most intense anxiety she gathered every word of news concerning their return, and at last was informed that they were at a ferry not far away. She hastened to make herself ready and was about to go out to meet him when the word was brought that her husband had been murdered by Indians in the California mountains.   She was handed her husband's purse, which had been left by the Indians, and which contained his wages and savings.   This enabled her to procure an outfit, and in 1852 she journeyed to the valley.

———

Here let us mention another octogenarian sister

in the person of Jane Neyman, daughter of David and Mary Harper, who was born in Westmoreland Co., Pa., in 1792. She embraced the gospel in 1838, and became at once endowed with the gift of healing, which enabled her to work many marvelous cures, among which may be mentioned the raising of two infants from apparent death, they each having been laid out for burial. Herself and family received an unstinted share of the persecutions of the saints, in Missouri, and afterwards in Nauvoo, in which latter place her husband died. Her daughter, Mary Ann Nickerson, then residing on the opposite side of the river from Nauvoo, on the occasion of the troubles resulting in the battle of Nauvoo, made cartridges at her home, and alone in her little skiff passed back and forth across the Mississippi (one mile wide at that point), delivering the cartridges, without discovery. While the battle was raging she also took seven persons, including her mother, on a flat-boat, and by her unaided exertions ferried them across the river. This heroic lady is now living in Beaver, Utah.

Mrs. Neyman, now in her 85th year, testifies concerning the truth of the gospel as revealed through Joseph Smith: "I know it is the work of God, by the unerring witness of the Holy Ghost."

Malvina Harvey Snow, daughter of Joel Harvey, was born in the State of Vermont, in 1811. She was brought into the church under the ministry of Orson Pratt, in 1833, he being then on mission in that section. Her nearest neighbor was Levi Snow, father of Apostle Erastus Snow. The Snow family mostly joined the new faith, and Malvina and her sister Susan journeyed with them to Missouri. At Far West she was married to Willard Snow, in 1837, and in about two years afterward they were driven from the State. They settled at Montrose, but, while her husband was on mission to England, she moved across the river to Nauvoo, the mob having signified their intention to burn her house over her head. In 1847 they started for Utah, from Council Bluffs, in the wake of the pioneers, arriving in the valley in the fall of that year. Says Sister Malvina, " My faithful sister, Susan, was with me " from the time I left our father's house in Vermont, "and when we arrived in Utah my husband took her " to wife. She bore him a daughter, but lost her life " at its birth. I took the infant to my bosom, and " never felt any difference between her and my own " children. She is now a married woman. In 1850 " my husband was called on mission to Denmark, " from which he never returned. He was buried in " the Atlantic, being the only missionary from Utah " that was ever laid in the sea. I raised my five chil- " dren to manhood and womanhood, and have now " lived a widow twenty-six years. Hoping to finally " meet my beloved husband and family, never again " to part, I am patiently waiting the hour of reunion. " May the Lord Jesus Christ help me to be faithful " to the end."

Sister Caroline Tippits, whose maiden name was

Pew, deserves to be mentioned as one of the earlier members of the church, having embraced the gospel in 1831. Shortly afterwards she joined the saints in Jackson county, Mo., and during the persecutions that ensued, endured perhaps the most trying hardships that were meted out to any of the sisters. Driven out into the midst of a prairie, by the mob, in the month of January, with a babe and two-years-old child, she was compelled to sleep on the ground with only one thin quilt to cover them, and the snow frequently falling three or four inches in a night. She came to Utah with the first companies, and is reckoned among the most faithful of the saints.

———

Julia Budge, first wife of Bishop William Budge, may be presented as one of the women who have made polygamy honorable. She was born in Essex, England, where she was baptized by Chas. W. Penrose, one of the most distinguished of the English elders, who afterwards married her sister—a lady of the same excellent disposition. The bishop is to-day the husband of three wives, whose children have grown up as one family, and the wives have lived together "like sisters." No stranger, with preconceived notions, would guess that they sustained the very tender relation of sister-wives. Their happy polygamic example is a sort of "household word" in the various settlements over which the bishop has presided.

———

Sister Nancy A. Clark, daughter of Sanford Por-

ter, now a resident of Farmington, Utah, has had a
most remarkable personal experience as a servant
of God. When a little girl, less than eight years of
age, residing with her parents in Missouri, she, in
answer to prayer, received the gift of tongues, and
became a great object of interest among the saints.
During and succeeding the persecutions in that
State, and while her father's family were being
driven from place to place, her oft-repeated spiritual
experiences were the stay and comfort of all around
her. Her many visions and experiences would fill a
volume. It is needless to say that she is among the
most faithful and devoted of the sisterhood.

A pretty little instance of faith and works is
related by Martha Granger, the wife of Bishop William G. Young, which is worthy of record. In September, 1872, the bishop was riding down Silver
Creek Canyon, on his way to Weber river, when he
became sunstruck, and fell back in his wagon, insen-
sible. His horses, as if guided by an invisible hand,
kept steadily on, and finally turned into a farmer's
barnyard. The farmer, who was at work in the
yard, thinking some team had strayed away, went
up to catch them, when he discovered the bishop (a
stranger to him) in the wagon. He thought at first
that the stranger was intoxicated, and so hitched
the team, thinking to let him lay and sleep it off.
But upon a closer examination, failing to detect the
fumes of liquor, he concluded the man was sick, and
calling assistance, took him into the shade of a hay-

stack, and cared for him. Still the bishop remained unconscious, and the sun went down, and night came on.

Forty miles away, the bishop's good wife at home had called her little seven-years-old child to her knee, to say the usual prayer before retiring. As the little child had finished the mother observed a far-off look in its eyes, and then came the strange and unusual request: "Mother, may I pray, in my own words, for pa? he's sick." "Yes, my child," said the mother, wonderingly. "Oh Lord, heal up pa, that he may live and not die, and come home," was the faltering prayer; and in that same moment the bishop, in that far-off farmer's yard, arose and spoke; and in a few moments was himself praising God for the succor that he knew not had been invoked by his own dear child.

CHAPTER XLVI.

Harriet A., wife of Lorenzo Snow, was born in
Aurora, Portage Co., Ohio, Sept. 13, 1819. Her honorable lineage is best established by reference to the
fact that her parents were natives of New England,
that one of her grandfathers served in the Revolutionary war, and that her progenitors came to America in the *Mayflower*.

At twenty-five years of age she embraced the
gospel, and in 1846 gathered with the church at
Nauvoo. In January, '47, she was married to Elder
Snow, and in the February following, with her husband and his three other wives, crossed the Mississippi and joined the encampment of the saints who
had preceded them.

Thence to Salt Lake Valley her story is not dis-
similar to that of the majority of the saints, except

in personal incident and circumstance. A praise-
worthy act of hers, during the trip across the plains,
deserves historical record, however. A woman had
died on the way, leaving three little children—one
of them a helpless infant. Sister Snow was so
wrought upon by the pitiful condition of the infant,
that she weaned her own child and nursed the
motherless babe. By a stupid blunder of her teamster, also, she was one night left behind, alone, with
two little children on the prairie. Luckily for her,
a wagon had broken down and had been abandoned
by the company. Depositing the babes in the
wagon-box, she made search, and found that some
flour and a hand-bell had been left in the wreck, and
with this scanty outfit she set about making supper.
She first took the clapper out of the bell, then stopped up the hole where it had been fastened in.
This now served her for a water-pitcher. Filling it
at a brook some distance away, she wet up some of
the flour; then, with some matches that she had
with her, started a fire, and baked the flour-cakes,
herself and thirteen-months-old child making their
supper upon them. She then ensconced herself in
the wagon with her babes, and slept till early morning, when her husband found her and complimented
her highly for her ingenuity and bravery.

From the valley Apostle Snow was sent to Italy
on mission, where he remained three years. An il-
lustrative incident of his experience on his return,
is worth telling. His return had been announced,
and his children, born after his departure, were as
jubilant over his coming as the others; but one little
girl, although in raptures about her father before he

came, on his arrival felt somewhat dubious as to whether he was her father or not, and refused to approach him for some time, and no persuasion could entice her. At length she entered the room where he was sitting, and after enquiring of each of the other children, " Is that my favvy?" and receiving an affirmative response, she placed herself directly in front of her father, and looking him full in the face, said, " Is you my favvy?" " Yes," said he, " I am your father." The little doubter, being satisfied, replied, " well, if you is my favvy, I will kiss you." And she most affectionately fulfilled the promise, being now satisfied that her caresses were not being lavished on a false claimant.

Sister Snow, as will be perceived, was among the first to enter polygamy, and her testimony now is, after thirty years' experience, that " It is a pure and sacred principle, and calculated to exalt and ennoble all who honor and live it as revealed by Joseph Smith."

Mrs. Elmira Tufts, of Salt Lake City, was born in Maine, in the year 1812. Her parents were both natives of New England, and her mother, Betsy Bradford, was a descendant of William Bradford, who came to America on the *Mayflower*, in 1620, and, after the death of Governor Carver, was elected governor of the Little Plymouth Colony, which position he held for over thirty years. Her father, Nathan Pinkham, also served in the Revolution.

With her husband, Mrs. Tufts gathered to Nauvoo in 1842. With the body of the church they shared the vicissitudes of the exodus, and finally the gathering to the valley. Here Mr. Tufts died in 1850.

Mrs. T. had the pleasure of visiting the recent centennial exhibition, and declares that this is the' height and acme of America's grandeur. "The "grand display," she says, "which all nations were "invited to witness, is like the bankrupt's grand ball, "just before the crash of ruin."

Vienna Jacques was born in the vicinity of Boston, in 1788. She went to Kirtland in 1833, being a single lady and very wealthy. When she arrived in Kirtland she donated all of her property to the church. She is one of the few women mentioned in the Book of Doctrine and Covenants. Her lineage is very direct to the martyr John Rogers. She is still living and retains all of her faculties.

The three women who came to the valley with the pioneers are deserving of mention in connection with that event.

Mrs. Harriet Page Wheeler Young, the eldest of the three above mentioned, was born in Hillsborough, N. H., September 7th, 1803. She was baptized into the Mormon connection in February, 1836, at New Portage, Ohio; went with the saints to Missouri, and was expelled from that State in 1839; went from there to Nauvoo, and in the spring of 1844 was married to Lorenzo Dow Young, brother

of President Young. She was with her husband in
the exodus; and, on the 7th of April, 1847, in company with Helen Saunders, wife of Heber C. Kimball, and Clara Decker, wife of President Young,
accompanied the pioneers on their famous journey
to the valley of the Great Salt Lake.

They arrived in the valley on the 24th of July,
1847, and camped near what is now Main street,
Salt Lake City. Plowing and planting was immediately commenced, and houses were soon reared in
what was afterwards called the " Old Fort." On
the 24th of September, following, she presented to
her husband a son, the first white male child born
in the valley.

In the early days, as is well known, the new settlers of Salt Lake were considerably troubled with
Indian depredations. One day, when " Uncle Lorenzo " was gone from home, and his wife was alone,
an Indian came and asked for biscuit. She gave
him all she could spare, but he demanded more, and
when she refused, he drew his bow and arrow and
said he would kill her. But she outwitted him. In
the adjoining room was a large dog, which fact the
Indian did not know, and Sister Young, feigning
great fear, asked the Indian to wait a moment, while
she made as if to go into the other room for more
food. She quickly untied the dog, and, opening
the door, gave him the word. In an instant the
Indian was overpowered and begging for mercy.
She called off the dog, and bound up the Indian's
wounds and let him go, and she was never troubled
by Indians again. Her dying testimony to her husband, just before she expired, December 22d, 1871,

was that she had never known any difference in her feelings and love for the children born to him by his young wives, and her own.

Sister Helen Saunders Kimball remained in the valley with her husband and reared a family. She died November 22d, 1871.

Clara Decker Young is still living, and has an interesting family.

Here may very properly be mentioned the first daughter of "Deseret;" or, more strictly speaking, the first female child born in Utah. Mrs. James Stopley, now a resident of Kanarrah, Kane county, Utah, and the mother of five fine children, is the daughter of John and Catherine Steele, who were in the famous Mormon battalion. Just after their discharge from the United States service they reached the site of Salt Lake City (then occupied by the pioneers), and on the 9th of August, 1847, their little daughter was born. This being a proper historical incident, inasmuch as she was the first white child born in the valley, it may be interesting to note that the event occurred on the east side of what is now known as Temple Block, at 4 o'clock A. M., of the day mentioned. In honor of President Brigham Young, she was named Young Elizabeth. Her father writes of her at that time as being "a stout, healthy child, and of a most amiable disposition."

Among the veteran sisters whose names should

be preserved to history, are Mrs. Mary Snow Gates, Mrs. Charlotte Alvord, and Mrs. Diana Drake. They are uniques of Mormon history, being the three women who, with "Zion's Camp," went up from Kirtland to Missouri, "to redeem Zion." Their lives have been singularly eventful, and they rank among the early disciples of the church and the founders of Utah.

———

And here let us make a lasting and honorable record of the women of the battalion:

Mrs. James Brown,	Mrs. O. Adams,
" Albina Williams,	" J. Chase,
" —— Tubbs,	" —— Sharp,
" D. Wilkin,	" J. Hess,
" Fanny Huntington,	" John Steele,
" J. Harmon, and	" C. Stillman,
daughter,	" —— Smith,
" U. Higgins,	" M. Ballom,
" E. Hanks,	" W. Smithson,
" Melissa Corey,	" A. Smithson.

These are the noble Mormon women who accepted the uncertain fortunes of war, in the service of their country. Be their names imperishable in American history.

CHAPTER XLVII.

ONE OF THE FOUNDERS OF CALIFORNIA—A WOMAN
MISSIONARY TO THE SOCIETY ISLANDS—HER LIFE
AMONG THE NATIVES—THE ONLY MORMON WOMAN
SENT ON MISSION WITHOUT HER HUSBAND—A
MORMON WOMAN IN WASHINGTON—A SISTER FROM
THE EAST INDIES—A SISTER FROM TEXAS.

The Mormons were not only the founders of
Utah, but they were also the first American emigrants to California. Fremont and his volunteers,
and the American navy, had, it is true, effected the
coup de main of taking possession of California, and
the American flag was hoisted in the bay of San
Francisco at the very moment of the arrival of the
ship *Brooklyn* with its company of Mormon emigrants, but to that company belongs the honor of
first settlers. The wife of Col. Jackson thus nar-
rates:

" In the month of February, 1846, I left home
" and friends and sailed in the ship *Brooklyn* for Cal-
" ifornia. Before starting I visited my parents in
" New Hampshire. I told them of my determination
" to follow God's people, who had already been noti-
" fied to leave the United States; that our destination
" was the Pacific coast, and that we should take ma-

" terials to plant a colony. When the hour came for
" parting my father could not speak, and my mother
" cried out in despair, 'When shall we see you again,
" my child?' 'When there is a railroad across the
" continent,' I answered.

" Selling all my household goods, I took my child
" in my arms and went on board ship. Of all the
" memories of my life not one is so bitter as that
" dreary six months' voyage, in an emigrant ship,
" around the Horn.

" When we entered the harbor of San Francisco,
" an officer came on board and said, 'Ladies and
" gentlemen, I have the honor to inform you that
" you are in the United States.' Three cheers from
" all on board answered the announcement.

" Unlike the California of to-day, we found the
" country barren and dreary; but we trusted in God
" and he heard our prayers; and when I soaked the
" mouldy ship-bread, purchased from the whale-ships
" lying in the harbor, and fried it in the tallow taken
" from the raw hides lying on the beach, God made
" it sweet to me, and to my child, for on this food I
" weaned her. It made me think of Hagar and her
" babe, and of the God who watched over her."

Passing over the hardships endured by these emigrants, which were greatly augmented by the fact
that war was then raging between the United States
and the Spanish residents of California, we deem it
proper to here incorporate, as matter of history,
some statements of Mrs. Jackson, made to the California journals, concerning the early days of San
Francisco. She says:

" From many statements made by persons who

" have lately adopted California as their home, I am
" led to believe it is the general impression that no
" American civilized beings inhabited this region
" prior to the discovery of gold; and that the news
" of this discovery reaching home, brought the first
" adventurers. As yet I have nowhere seen re-
" corded the fact that in July, 1846, the ship *Brook-*
" *lyn* landed on the shore of San Francisco bay two
" hundred and fifty passengers, among whom were
" upwards of seventy females ; it being the first emi-
" gration to this place *via* Cape Horn.

" In October previous a company had arrived
" overland, most of whom had been detained at
" Sacramento fort, being forbidden by the governor
" to proceed further. Upon arriving in Yerba Buena,
" in '46, we found two of these families, some half
" dozen American gentlemen, three or four old Cal-
" ifornians with their families, the officers and ma-
" rines of the sloop of war *Portsmouth*, and about
" one hundred Indians, occupying the place now
" called San Francisco.

" The ship *Brooklyn* left us on the rocks at the
" foot of what is now Broadway. From this point
" we directed our steps to the old adobe on (now)
" Dupont street. It was the first to shelter us from
" the chilling winds. A little further on (toward
" Jackson street), stood the adobe of old 'English
" Jack,' who kept a sort of depot for the milk woman,
" who came in daily, with a dozen bottles of milk
" hung to an old horse, and which they retailed at a
" real (twelve and a half cents) per bottle. At this
" time, where now are Jackson and Stockton streets
" were the outer boundaries of the town. Back of

"the home of 'English Jack' stood a cottage built
"by an American who escaped from a whale-ship
"and married a Californian woman. Attached to
"this house was a windmill and a shop. In this
"house I lived during the winter of '46, and the
"principal room was used by Dr. Poet, of the navy,
"as a hospital. Here were brought the few who
"were saved of the unfortunate 'Donner party,'
"whose sad fate will never be forgotten. One of
"the Donner children, a girl of nine years, related
"to me that her father was the first of that party to
"fall a victim to the cold and hunger. Her mother
"then came on with the children, 'till the babe grew
"sick and she was unable to carry it further. She
"told the children to go on with the company, and
"if the babe died, or she got stronger, she would
"come to them, but they saw her no more. After
"this, two of her little brothers died, and she told
"me, with tears running down her face, that she saw
"them cooked, and had to eat them; but added, as
"though fearful of having committed a crime, 'I
"could not help it; I had eaten nothing for days,
"and I was afraid to die.' The poor child's feet
"were so badly frozen that her toes had dropped
"off."

———

Very dramatic and picturesque have often been
the situations of the Mormon sisters. Here is the
story of one of them, among the natives of the Society Islands. She says:

"I am the wife of the late Elder Addison Pratt,
"who was the first missionary to the Society Islands,

"he having been set apart by the prophet for this
"mission in 1843. My husband went on his mis-
"sion, but I, with my children, was left to journey
"afterwards with the body of the church to the
"Rocky Mountains.

"We reached the valley in the fall of 1848, and
"had been there but a week when Elder Pratt ar-
"rived, coming by the northern route with soldiers
"from the Mexican war. He had been absent five
"years and four months. Only one of his children
"recognized him, which affected him deeply. One
"year passed away in comparative comfort and
"pleasure, when again Mr. Pratt was called to go
"and leave his family, and again I was left to my
"own resources. However, six months afterwards
"several elders were called to join Elder Pratt in
"the Pacific Isles, and myself and family were per-
"mitted to accompany them. Making the journey
"by ox-team to San Francisco, on the 15th of Sep-
"tember, 1850, we embarked for Tahiti. Sailing to
"the southwest of that island three hundred and
"sixty miles we made the Island of Tupuai, where
"Mr. Pratt had formerly labored, and where we ex-
"pected to find him, but to our chagrin found that
"he was a prisoner under the French governor at
"Tahiti. After counseling upon the matter we de-
"cided to land on Tupuai and petition the governor
"of Tahiti for Mr. Pratt's release, which we did,
"aided by the native king, who promised to be
"responsible for Mr. Pratt's conduct. The petition
"was granted by the governor, and in due course
"Mr. Pratt joined us at Tupuai. It was a day of
"great rejoicing among the natives when he arrived,

"they all being much attached to him, and it was
"also a great day for our children.

"A volume might be written in attempting to
"describe the beauties of nature on that little speck
"in the midst of the great ocean; but I must hasten
"to speak of the people. Simple and uncultivated
"as the natives are, they are nevertheless a most
"loveable and interesting race. Their piety is deep
"and sincere and their faith unbounded.

"Within a year I became a complete master of
"their language, and addressed them publicly in the
"*fere-bure-ra* (prayer-house), frequently. My daily
"employment. was teaching in the various depart-
"ments of domestic industry, such as needle-work,
"knitting, etc., and my pupils, old and young, were
"both industrious and apt."

Elder Addison Pratt died in 1872, but his respected missionary wife is living in Utah to-day,
resting from her labors and waiting for the reward
of the faithful.

———

A somewhat similar experience to the above is
that of Sister Mildred E. Randall, who went with
her husband, at a later date, to labor in the Sandwich Islands. Her first mission lasted about
eighteen months, and her second one three years.
On her third mission to the islands, she was called
to go without her husband; thus making her to be
the only woman, in the history of the church, who
has been called to go on foreign mission independently of her husband.

———

In this connection will also suitably appear Sister Elizabeth Drake Davis, who served her people well while in the Treasury department at Washington.

She was born in the town of Axminster, Devonshire, England, and was an only child. Having lost her father when she was but ten years of age, and not being particularly attached to her mother, her life became markedly lonely and desolate. In her extremity she sought the Lord in prayer, when a remarkable vision was shown her, which was repeated at two subsequent times, making a permanent impression on her life, and, in connection with other similar experiences, leading her to connect herself with the Church of Latter-day Saints.

After being widowed in her native land she crossed the Atlantic and resided for two years in Philadelphia. In May, 1859, with a company of Philadelphian saints, she gathered to Florence, for the purpose of going thence to Utah. An incident there occurred that will be of interest to the reader. She says:

"We reached Florence late one evening; it was "quite dark and raining; we were helped from the "wagons and put in one of the vacant houses— "myself, my two little daughters and Sister Sarah "White. Early next morning we were aroused by "some one knocking at the door; on opening it we "found a little girl with a cup of milk in her hand; "she asked if there was 'a little woman there with "two little children.' 'Yes,' said Sister White, 'come "in.' She entered, saying to me, 'If you please my "ma wants to see you; she has sent this milk to "your little girls.' Her mother's name was strange to

" me, but I went, thinking to find some one that I had
" known.   She met me at the door with both hands
" extended in welcome.   ' Good morning, Sister
" Elizabeth,' said she.   I told her she had the ad-
" vantage of me, as I did not remember ever seeing
" her before.   ' No,' said she, ' and I never saw you
" before.   I am Hyrum Smith's daughter (Lovina
" Walker); my father appeared to me three times
" last night, and told me that you were the child of
" God, that you was without money, provisions or
" friends, and that I must help you.'   It is needless
" to add that this excellent lady and myself were
" ever thereafter firm friends, until her death, which
" occurred in 1876.   I will add that previous to her
" last illness I had not seen her in thirteen years;
" that one night her father appeared to me, and
" making himself known, said his daughter was in
" sore need; I found the message was too true.
" Yet it will ever be a source of gratitude to think I
" was at last able to return her generous kindness
" to me when we were strangers."

Mrs. Davis' husband (she having married a second
time) enlisted in the United States Army in March,
1863.   Shortly thereafter she received an appointment as clerk in the Treasury department at Washington, which position she held until November,
1869, when she resigned in order to prosecute, un-
hampered, a design which she had formed to memorialize Congress against the Cullom bill.   In this
laudable endeavor she was singularly successful;
and it is proper to add that by dint of pure pluck, as
against extremely discouraging circumstances, she
secured the co-operation of Gen. Butler, and Mr.

Sumner, the great Senator from Massachusetts. It is entirely just to say that her efforts were largely instrumental in modifying the course of Congress upon the Mormon question, at that time.

Sister Davis is at present one of the active women of Utah, and will doubtless figure prominently in the future movements of the sisterhood.

The story of Sister Hannah Booth is best told by herself. She says:

" I was born in Chumar, India. My father was a
" native of Portugal, and my mother was from Man-
" illa. My husband was an officer in the English
" army in India, as were also my father and grand-
" father. We lived in affluent circumstances, keep-
" ing nine servants, a carriage, etc., and I gave my
" attention to the profession of obstetrics.

" When the gospel was introduced into India, my
" son Charles, who was civil engineer in the army,
" met the elders traveling by sea, and was converted.
" He brought to me the gospel, which I embraced
" with joy, and from that time was eager to leave
" possessions, friends, children and country, to unite
" with this people. My son George, a surgeon in
" the army, remained behind, although he had em-
" braced the gospel. My sister, a widow, and my
" son Charles and his wife—daughter of Lieutenant
" Kent, son of Sir Robert Kent, of England—and
" their infant daughter, came with me. Reaching
" San Francisco, we proceeded thence to San Ber-
" nardino, arriving there in 1855. Having, in India,

" had no occasion to perform housework, we found
" ourselves greatly distressed in our new home, by
" our lack of such needful knowledge. We bought
" a stove, and I tried first to make a fire. I made
" the fire in the first place that opened (the oven),
" and was greatly perplexed by its smoking and not
" drawing. We were too mortified to let our ignor-
" ance be known, and our bread was so badly made,
" and all our cooking so wretchedly done, that we
" often ate fruit and milk rather than the food we
" had just prepared. We also bought a cow, and not
" knowing how to milk her, had great trouble. Four
" of us surrounded her ; my son tied her head to the
" fence, her legs to a post, her tail to another; and
" while he stood by to protect me, my sister and
" daughter-in-law to suggest and advise, I proceeded
" to milk—on the wrong side, as I afterwards learned.
" After a while, however, some good sisters kindly
" taught us how to work.

" Just as we had become settled in our own new
" house the saints prepared to leave San Bernardino
" —in the winter of '56–7. We sold our home at
" great sacrifice, and, six of us in one wagon, with
" two yoke of Spanish oxen, started for Utah. On
" the desert our oxen grew weak and our supplies
" began to give out. We, who at home in India had
" servants at every turn, now had to walk many
" weary miles, through desert sands, and in climbing
" mountains. My sister and I would, in the morn-
" ing, bind our cashmere scarfs around our waists,
" take each a staff, and with a small piece of bread
" each, we would walk ahead of the train. At noon
" we would rest, ask a blessing upon the bread, and

" go on.   Weary, footsore and hungry, we never re-
" gretted leaving our luxurious homes, nor longed to
" return.   We were thankful for the knowledge that
" had led us away, and trusted God to sustain us in
" our trials and lead us to a resting-place among the
" saints.   After our journey ended, we began anew
" to build a home.

" I am, after twenty years among this people,
" willing to finish my days with them, whatever their
" lot and trials may be, and I pray God for his holy
" spirit to continue with me to the end."

Nor should we omit to mention Mrs. Willmirth
East, now in her 64th year, who was converted to
Mormonism while residing with her father's family
in Texas, in 1853.   Her ancestors fought in the
Revolutionary war, and her father, Nathaniel H.
Greer, was a member of the legislature of Georgia,
and also a member of the legislature of Texas, after
his removal to that State.   She has long resided in
Utah, is a living witness of many miracles of healing, and has often manifested in her own person the
remarkable gifts of this dispensation.   She may be
accounted one of the most enthusiastic and steadfast of the saints.

CHAPTER XLVIII.

A LEADER FROM ENGLAND—MRS HANNAH T. KING—
A MACDONALD FROM SCOTLAND—THE "WELSH
QUEEN"—A REPRESENTATIVE WOMAN FROM IRE-
LAND—SISTER HOWARD—A GALAXY OF THE SIS-
TERHOOD, FROM "MANY NATIONS AND TONGUES"—
INCIDENTS AND TESTIMONIALS.

Here the reader meets an illustration of women
from many nations baptized into one spirit, and
bearing the same testimony.

Mrs. Hannah T. King, a leader from England,
shall now speak. She says:

"In 1849, while living in my home in Dernford
"Dale, Cambridgeshire, England, my attention was
"first brought to the serious consideration of Mor-
"monism by my seamstress. She was a simple-
"minded girl, but her tact and respectful ingenuity
"in presenting the subject won my attention, and I
"listened, not thinking or even dreaming that her
"words were about to revolutionize my life.

"I need not follow up the thread of my thoughts
"thereafter; how I struggled against the conviction
"that had seized my mind; how my parents and
"friends marveled at the prospect of my leaving the
"respectable church associations of a life-time and

"uniting with 'such a low set'; how I tried to be
"content with my former belief, and cast the new
"out of mind, but all to no purpose. Suffice it to
"say I embraced the gospel, forsook the aristocratic
"associations of the 'High Church' congregation
"with which I had long been united, and became an
"associate with the poor and meek of the earth.

"I was baptized Nov. 4th, 1850, as was also my
"beloved daughter. My good husband, although not
"persuaded to join the church, consented to emi-
"grate with us to Utah, which we did in the year
"1853, bringing quite a little company with us at
"Mr. King's expense."

Since her arrival in the valley, Mrs. King has been
constantly prominent among the women of Utah.
Her name is also familiar as a poetess, there having
emanated from her pen some very creditable poems.

Scotland comes next with a representative woman
in the person of Elizabeth G. MacDonald. She
says:

"I was born in the city of Perth, Perthshire,
"Scotland, on the 12th of January, 1831, and am
"the fifth of ten daughters born to my parents, John
"and Christina Graham.

"My attention was first brought to the church of
"Latter-day Saints in 1846, and in 1847 I was bap-
"tized and confirmed, being the second person bap-
"tized into the church in Perth. This course
"brought down upon me so much persecution, from
"which I was not exempt in my own father's house,

"that I soon left home and went to Edinburgh.
" There I was kindly received by a Sister Gibson
" and welcomed into her house. After two years
" had passed my father came to me and, manifesting
" a better spirit than when I saw him last, prevailed
" upon me to return with him. He had in the mean-
" time become partially paralyzed, and had to use a
" crutch. Two weeks after my return he consented
" to be baptized. While being baptized the afflic-
"tion left him, and he walked home without his
" crutch, to the astonishment of all who knew him.
" This was the signal for a great work, and the
" Perth branch, which previously had numbered but
" two, soon grew to over one hundred and fifty
" members.

    " In May, '51, I was married to Alexander Mac-
" Donald, then an elder in the church. He went
" immediately on mission to the Highlands ; but in
" 1852 he was called to take charge of the Liverpool
" conference, whither I went with him, and there we
" made our first home together.

    " In May, '53, I fell down stairs, which so seri-
" ously injured me that I remained bedridden until
" the following marvelous occurrence: One Satur-
" day afternoon as I was feeling especially depressed
" and sorrowful, and while my neighbor, Mrs. Kent,
" who had just been in, was gone to her home for
" some little luxury for me, as I turned in my bed I
" was astonished to behold an aged man standing at
" the foot. As I somewhat recovered from my natu-
" ral timidity he came towards the head of the bed
" and laid his hands upon me, saying, ' I lay my
" hands upon thy head and bless thee in the name

"of the God of Abraham, Isaac and Jacob. The
" Lord hath seen the integrity of thine heart. In
" tears and sorrow thou hast bowed before the Lord,
" asking for children; this blessing is about to be
" granted unto thee. Thou shalt be blessed with
" children from this hour. Thou shalt be gathered
" to the valleys of the mountains, and there thou
" shalt see thy children raised as tender plants by
" thy side. Thy children and household shall call
" thee blessed. At present thy husband is better
" than many children. Be comforted. These bless-
" ings I seal upon thee, in the name of Jesus.
" Amen.' At this moment Sister Kent came in, and
" I saw no more of this personage. His presence
" was so impressed upon me that I can to this day
" minutely describe his clothing and countenance.

"The next conference, after this visitation,
" brought the word that Brother MacDonald was re-
" leased to go to the valley, being succeeded by Elder
" Spicer W. Crandall. We started from Liverpool
" in March, '54, and after the usual vicissitudes of
" sea and river navigation, finally went into camp
" near Kansas Village on the Missouri. From there
" we started for Utah in Capt. Daniel Carns' com-
" pany, reaching Salt Lake City on the 30th of Sep-
" tember.

" In 1872 my husband was appointed to settle in
" St. George, where we arrived about the middle of
" November. Here we have since remained, and I
" have taken great pleasure in this southern country,
" especially in having my family around me, in the
" midst of good influences. The people here are
" sociable and kind, and we have no outside influ-

" ences to contend with.   All are busy and industri-
" ous and striving to live their religion."

————

The wife of the famous Captain Dan Jones, the
founder of the Welsh mission, is chosen to represent her people.   She thus sketches her life to the
period of her arrival in Zion:

" I was born April 2d, 1812, in Claddy, South
" Wales.   My parents were members of the Baptist
" Church, which organization I joined when fifteen
" years of age.   In 1846, several years after my
" marriage, while keeping tavern, a stranger stopped
" with us for refreshments, and while there unfolded
" to me some of the principles of the, then entirely
" new to me, Church of Latter-day Saints.   His
" words made a profound impression upon my mind,
" which impression was greatly heightened by a
" dream which I had shortly thereafter; but it was
" some time before I could learn more of the new
" doctrine.   I made diligent inquiry, however, and
" was finally, by accident, privileged to hear an elder
" preach.   In a conversation with him afterwards I
" became thoroughly convinced of the truth of Mor-
" monism, and was accordingly baptized into the
" church.   This was in 1847.   After this my house
" became a resort for the elders, and I was the spe-
" cial subject of persecution by my neighbors.

" In 1848 I began making preparations to leave
" my home and start for the valley.   Everything was
" sold, including a valuable estate, and I determined
" to lay it all upon the altar in an endeavor to aid

"my poorer friends in the church to emigrate also.
"In 1849 I bade farewell to home, country and
"friends, and with my six children set out for the
"far-off Zion. After a voyage, embodying the.
"usual hardships, from Liverpool to New Orleans,
"thence up the Mississippi and Missouri rivers to
"Council Bluffs, some fifty fellow-passengers dying
"with cholera on the way, in the early summer I
"started across the plains. I had paid the passage
"of forty persons across the ocean and up to Coun-
"cil Bluffs, and from there I provided for and paid
"the expenses of thirty-two to Salt Lake City.
"Having every comfort that could be obtained, we
"perhaps made the trip under as favorable circum-
"stances as any company that has ever accom-
"plished the journey."

For her magnanimous conduct in thus largely
helping the emigration of the Welsh saints, coupled
with her social standing in her native country, she
was honored with the title of " The Welsh Queen."
The title is still familiar in connection with her
name. Since her arrival in Zion she has known
many trials, but is still firm in the faith of the
Latter-day work.

———

The following is a brief personal sketch of Mrs.
Howard, an Irish lady, of popularity and prominence in Utah :

" Presuming there are many persons who believe
"there are no Irish among the Mormons, I wish to
"refute the belief, as there are many in our various
"towns, most staunch and faithful.

"My parents, Robert and Lucretia Anderson, re-
"sided in Carlow, County Carlow, Ireland, where,
"on the 12th of July, 1823, I was born. In 1841
"my beloved mother died, and in the same year I
"married, and went to reside in Belfast with my
"husband.

" My father, who was a thorough reformer in his
"method of thought, originally suggested several
"governmental and social innovations that were
"afterwards adopted by the government and the
"people. He died in 1849.

" My parents were Presbyterians, in which faith I
" was strictly brought up; but I early came to the
"conclusion that my father was right when he said,
"as I heard him one day: 'The true religion is yet
"to come.' After my marriage I attended the
"Methodist Church mostly, led a moral life, tried
"to be honest in deal, and 'did' (as well as circum-
"stances would allow) 'unto others as I would they
"should do to me.' I thus went on quietly, until
"the 'true religion' was presented to me by a Mr.
"and Mrs. Daniel M. Bell, of Ballygrot. My rea-
"son was satisfied, and I embraced the truth with
"avidity.

" In February, 1858, my husband, myself and our
"six children left Ireland on the steamship *City of*
"*Glasgow*, and in due time arrived at Council
"Bluffs. Starting across the plains, the first day
"out I sustained a severe accident by being thrown
"from my carriage, but this did not deter us, and
"we arrived all safe and well in Salt Lake City on
"the 25th of September.

" In 1868 I went with my husband on a mission

" to England; had a pleasant, interesting time, and
" astonished many who thought 'no good thing
" could come out of Utah.' While there I was the
" subject of no little curious questioning, and there-
" fore had many opportunities of explaining the
" principles of the gospel. There was one principle
" I gloried in telling them about—the principle of
" plural marriage; and I spared no pains in speak-
" ing of the refining, exalting influence that was
" carried with the doctrine, wherever entered into in
" a proper manner."

Sister Howard has not exaggerated in claiming
that the Irish nation has been fairly represented in
the Mormon Church. Some of its most talented
members have been directly of that descent, though
it is true that Mormonism never took deep root in
Ireland; but that is no more than a restatement of
the fact that Protestantism of any kind has never
flourished in that Catholic country.

Of the esteemed lady in question it may be added
that she is one of the most prominent of the women
of Utah, one of the councilors of Mrs. President
Horne, and a leader generally, in those vast female
organizations and movements inspired by Eliza R.
Snow, in the solution of President Young's peculiar
society problems.

Scandinavia shall be next represented among the
nationalities in the church. The Scandinavian mission has been scarcely less important than the British
mission. It is not as old, but to-day it is the most
vigorous, and for the last quarter of a century it has

been pouring its emigrations into Utah by the thousands. Indeed a very large portion of the population of Utah has been gathered from the Scandinavian peoples. The mission was opened by Apostle Erastus Snow, in the year 1850. One of the first converts of this apostle, Anna Nilson, afterwards became his wife. Here is the brief notice which she gives of herself:

" I am the daughter of Hans and Caroline Nilson, "and was born on the 1st of April, 1825, in a little "village called Dalby, in the Province of Skaana, in "the kingdom of Sweden. At the age of seventeen "I removed to Copenhagen, Denmark. There, in "1850, when the elders from Zion arrived, I gladly "received the good news, and was the first woman "baptized into the Church of Latter-day Saints in "that kingdom. The baptism took place on the "12th of August, 1850; there were fifteen of us; "the ordinance was performed by Elder Erastus "Snow. Some time after this we hired a hall for "our meetings, which called public attention to us "in some degree, whereupon we became the subjects "of rowdyism and violent persecution. One even-"ing in particular, I recollect that I was at a meet-"ing in a village some eight miles out from Copen-'hagen ; as we started to go home we were assailed "by a mob which followed and drove us for several "miles. Some of the brethren were thrown into "ditches and trampled upon, and the sisters also "were roughly handled. Finding myself in the "hands of ruffians, I called on my heavenly Father, "and they dropped me like a hot iron. They pelted "us with stones and mud, tore our clothes, and

" abused us in every way they could.   These perse-
" cutions continued some weeks, until finally stop-
" ped by the military.

" In 1852, one week before Christmas, I left Co-
" penhagen, in the first large company, in charge of
" Elder Forssgren.   We encountered a terrible storm
" at the outset, but were brought safely through to
" Salt Lake City, where I have since resided."

A Norwegian sister, Mrs. Sarah A. Peterson, the
wife of a well-known missionary, has remembrance
next.   She says :

" I was born in the town of Murray, Orleans
" county, N. Y., February 16, 1827.   My parents,
" Cornelius and Carrie Nelson, were among the first
" Norwegians who emigrated to America.   They
" left Norway on account of having joined the Qua-
" kers, who, at that time, were subject to much
" persecution in that country.   In the neighborhood
" was quite a number of that sect, and they con-
" cluded to emigrate to America in a body.   As
" there was no direct line of emigration between
" Norway and America, they purchased a sloop, in
" which they performed the voyage.   Having been
" raised on the coast, they were all used to the duties
" of seamen, and found no trouble in navigating
" their vessel.   They also brought a small cargo of
" iron with them, which, together with the vessel,
" they sold in New York, and then moved to the
" northwestern portion of that State, and settled on
" a wild tract of woodland.   Eight years afterwards

30

"my father died. I was at that time six years old.
"When I was nine years old my uncle went to Illi-
"nois, whence he returned with the most glowing
"accounts of the fertility of the soil, with plenty of
"land for sale at government price. The company
"disposed of their farms at the rate of fifty dollars
"per acre, and again moved from their homes, set-
"tling on the Fox River, near Ottawa, Ill. Here,
"when fourteen years of age, I first heard the gos-
"pel, and at once believed in the divine mission of
"the prophet Joseph; but on account of the oppo-
"sition of relatives, was prevented joining the
"church until four years later.

"In the spring of 1849 I left mother and home
"and joined a company who were preparing to leave
"for the valley. On our way to Council Bluffs I
"was attacked with cholera. But there was a young
"gentleman in the company by the name of Canute
"Peterson, who, after a season of secret prayer in
"my behalf, came and placed his hands upon my
"head, and I was instantly healed. Two weeks
"after our arrival at the Bluffs I was married to
"him. We joined Ezra T. Benson's company, and
"arrived in Salt Lake City on the 25th of October,
"and spent the winter following in the 'Old Fort.'
"In 1851 we removed to Dry Creek, afterwards
"called Lehi. My husband was among the very
"first to survey land and take up claims there. In
"1852 he was sent on mission to Norway. During
"the four years he was absent I supported myself
"and the two children. In 1856 he returned, much
"broken in health because of his arduous labor and
"exposure in the rigorous climate of that country.

" In the fall of 1857 my husband added another
" wife to his family ; but I can truly say that he did
" not do so without my consent, nor with any other
" motive than to serve his God. I felt it our duty
" to obey the commandment revealed through the
" prophet Joseph, hence, although I felt it to be
" quite a sacrifice, I encouraged him in so doing.
" Although not so very well supplied with house-
" room, the second wife and I lived together in har-
" mony and peace. I felt it a pleasure to be in her
" company, and even to nurse and take care of her
" children, and she felt the same way toward me and
" my children. A few years afterwards my husband
" married another wife, but also with the consent
" and encouragement of his family. This did not
" disturb the peaceful relations of our home, but the
" same kind feelings were entertained by each mem-
" ber of the family to one another. We have now
" lived in polygamy twenty years, have eaten at the
" same table and raised our children together, and
" have never been separated, nor have we ever wished
" to be."

Mrs. Peterson is the present very efficient President of the Relief Society at Ephraim, which up to
date has disbursed over eleven thousand dollars.

Here will also properly appear a short sketch of
Bishop Hickenlooper's wife Ann, who made her way
to Zion with the famous hand-cart company, under
Captain Edmund Ellsworth. She had left home and
friends in England in 1856, coming to Council

Bluffs with the regular emigration of that year, and continuing her journey with the hand-cart company, as before stated. From her journal we quote:

"After traveling fourteen weeks we arrived in "the near vicinity of Salt Lake City, where Presi-"dent Young and other church leaders, with a brass "band and a company of military, met and escorted "us into the city. As we entered, and passed on to "the public square in the 16th Ward, the streets "were thronged with thousands of people gazing "upon the scene. President Young called on the "bishops and people to bring us food. In a short "time we could see loads of provisions coming to "our encampment. After partaking of refreshments "our company began to melt away, by being taken "to the homes of friends who had provided for them. "I began to feel very lonely, not knowing a single "person in the country, and having no relatives to "welcome me. I felt indeed that I was a stranger "in a strange land. Presently, however, it was ar-"ranged that I should go to live with Mr. Hicken-"looper's people, he being bishop of the 6th Ward. "After becoming acquainted with the family, to "whom I became much attached, his first wife invited "me to come into the family as the bishop's third "wife, which invitation, after mature consideration, "I accepted.

"I am now the mother of five children, and for "twenty years have lived in the same house with "the rest of the family, and have eaten at the same "table. My husband was in Nauvoo in the days of "the prophet Joseph, and moved with the saints "from winter quarters to this city, where he has been

" bishop of the 6th Ward twenty-nine years, and of
" the 5th and 6th Wards fifteen years."

Several of the sisters who first received the gospel in England and emigrated to Nauvoo during
the lifetime of the prophet, claim historic mention.
Ruth Moon, wife of William Clayton (who during
the last days of Joseph became famous as his scribe),
was among the first fruits of the British mission.
With her husband she sailed in the first organized
company of emigrant saints on board the *North
America*.   Here are a few items worth preserving,
from her diary of that voyage :

" Friday, Sept. 4, 1840.—Bid good-bye to Penwortham, and all started by rail to Liverpool, where
we arrived about 5 o'clock, and immediately went
on board the packet-ship *North America*, Captain
Loeber, then lying in Prince's dock.

" Tuesday, Sept. 8.—At eight o'clock the ship left
the dock ; was towed out into the river Mersey, and
set sail for New York.   On getting into the English
Channel we were met by strong head-winds, which
soon increased to a gale, compelling the ship to
change her course and sail around the north coast
of Ireland.   The decks were battened down three
days and nights.   During the gale four of the principal sails were blown away, and the ship otherwise
roughly used.

" Saturday, Sept. 12.—The storm having abated,
we had a very pleasant view of the north part of
Ireland, farms and houses being in plain sight.

" Tuesday, Sept. 22.—About eleven o'clock the
company was startled by the ominous cry of the
chief mate, ' All hands on deck, and buckets with

water.' The ship had taken fire under the cook's galley. The deck was burned through, fire dropping on the berths underneath. It was soon extinguished without serious damage having been done.

"Sunday, Oct. 11.—Arrived in New York."

They journeyed thence by steamer up the Hudson river to Albany; by canal from Albany to Buffalo; by steamer thence to Chicago; and by flat-boat down the Rock river to Nauvoo, where they arrived Nov. 24th.

———

Elizabeth Birch, who was born in Lancashire, England, in 1810, was a widow with four children when she first heard the gospel, which was brought to Preston, by the American elders, in 1837. The new religion created great excitement in that section, and people often walked ten miles and more to hear the elders preach. She was baptized at Preston, on the 24th of Dec., 1838. In 1841 she sailed in the ship *Sheffield* for New Orleans, and thence up the Mississippi river in the second company of saints that sailed for America. In the fall of that year she was married to Mr. Birch. Her husband being one of those designated to help finish the temple at Nauvoo they were in the city during the famous battle of Nauvoo. Her recollections of that perilous event are very vivid. During the fight one of the sisters brought into her house a cannon-ball which she had picked up, just from the enemy's battery. It was too hot to be handled. They reached the valley in 1850.

Concerning polygamy, she says: "In 1858, my

" husband having become convinced that the doc-
" trine of celestial marriage and plurality of wives
" was true, instructed me in regard to it ; and be-
" coming entirely.satisfied that the principle is not
" only true, but that it is commanded, I gave my
" consent to his taking another wife, by whom he had
" one daughter ; and again in 1860 I consented to his
" taking another one, by whom he had a large family
" of children. These children we have raised to-
" gether, and I love them as if they were my own.
" Our husband has been dead two years, but we still
" live together in peace, and each contributes to the
" utmost for the support of the family."

Lucy Clayton, wife of Elder Thomas Bullock,
was the first of the saints to enter Carthage jail
after the martyrdom of Joseph and Hyrum. She
tells a graphic tale of the excitement of the people
of Carthage on that occasion—how they fled, panic-
stricken, from their homes, led by Governor Ford,
thinking that the people of Nauvoo would wreak
vengeance upon them for the murder that had been
committed in their midst. She was also among the
remnant of the sick and dying saints on the banks
of the Mississippi, after the expulsion, when they
were miraculously fed by quails that alighted in
their midst. This is an often-told wonder, and is
classed with the immortal episode of the children of
Israel, fed by quails in the wilderness.

The wife of Thomas Smith is also entitled to

historic mention. Her husband, in the early days
of the British mission, made a great stir in England,
as a Mormon elder, and she was with him in his
ministry. He bore the euphonious epithet of
"Rough Tom." Having both the genius and fame
of an iconoclast, he disputed, on the platform, with
the same sectarian champions who met the great
infidels Holyoke, Barker and Bradlaugh. His career
as a Mormon elder was quite a romance, and in all
its scenes his wife, Sister Sarah, was a participant,
though she was as gentle in spirit as he was bold
and innovative. A famous career was theirs, and
the spiritual power and signs that followed them
were astonishing. He was full of prophesy, and
she spake in tongues. He also cast out devils by
the legion. The spirits, good and bad, followed
him everywhere. It is of those thrilling scenes that
his widow now loves to speak, as a testimony of the
power of God, and of the signs following the believer. No sister from the old country could be
chosen as a better witness of the spiritual potency
of Mormonism than Sister Sarah Smith Wheeler.

Sister I. S. Winnerholm, from Denmark, was
brought into the church, in Copenhagen, through a
series of spiritual experiences of unusual power and
interest; and, throughout her entire life since, she
has been remarkably gifted with the power of healing, the interpretation of tongues, etc. Concerning
the gift of tongues, she testifies that at a ward

meeting in Salt Lake City she heard a lady manifest the gift by speaking in the dialect of Lapland, which she was fully competent to translate, being conversant with that dialect, and which the lady in question positively knew nothing about, as she had never seen a person from that country. Sister Winnerholm has been a resident of Salt Lake City since 1862, and a member of the church since 1853.

As a representative from Scotland, Sister Elizabeth Duncanson, who is one of "Zion's nurses," may be mentioned. A remarkable incident of her life is the fact that at about the identical moment of the martyrdom of Joseph and Hyrum Smith, she, in her home in Scotland, saw the entire tragedy in a dream. She told the dream to her husband at the time (both of them were members of the church), and they were much dispirited with their forebodings concerning it. In about six weeks, by due course of mail, the tidings reached them. Herself and husband reached Utah in 1855, and in that same year she was ordained, by President Young, to the office of nurse, which she has since most acceptably and skillfully filled.

Another sister from Scotland, Sister Mary Meiklejohn, since 1856 a resident of Tooele City, and also one of "Zion's nurses," shall here be mentioned. While residing in Bonhill, Scotland, herself and husband were baptized into the Mormon Church by Elder Robert Hamilton. Her husband at once became active in the work of spreading the gospel, and was soon the recipient of the benefits of the gift of healing, to a remarkable degree. By an accident one of his feet was crushed and terribly lacerated by being caught in a steam engine. The physicians determined that the foot must be amputated in order to save his life; but the elders thought differently, and after administering to him, they called a fast, for his benefit, among all the branches in the neighborhood, and the presiding elder prophesied that he should so completely recover the use of his foot as to dance on it many times in Zion. This has been literally fulfilled. Mrs. Meiklejohn is the very acceptable President of the Tooele Relief Society, which position she has held since its organization in 1870.

———

It is also noteworthy that among the sisters is Mrs. Josephine Ursenbach, once a Russian Countess. With the instincts of her rank, she took it upon her to officiate for many of her aristocratic compeers of Europe, in the beautiful ordinance of baptism for the dead. The Empress Josephine and Napoleon's wife, Louisa of Austria, were among the number. Also Elizabeth of England.

———

The reader will have noticed in the sketches of the sisters, both American and foreign, frequent mention of the "gift of tongues." This seems to have been markedly the woman's gift. One of the first who manifested it approvedly was Mother Whitney. She was commanded by the prophet Joseph to rise and sing in the gift of tongues in the early days of Kirtland. She did so, and Joseph pronounced it the "Adamic tongue," or the language spoken by Adam. Parley P. Pratt afterwards gave a written interpretation of it. It was a story, in verse, of Adam blessing his family in "Adam-Ondi-Ahman"—the Garden of Eden in America.

As an instance in which the gift of tongues proved of decidedly practical value, we transcribe the following incident, which occurred near Council Bluffs, in the history of a girl of seventeen by the name of Jane Grover (afterwards Mrs. Stewart), from her journal :

"One morning we thought we would go and " gather gooseberries. Father Tanner (as we famil-" iarly called the good, patriarchal Elder Nathan " Tanner), harnessed a span of horses to a light " wagon, and, with two sisters by the name of Lyman, " his little granddaughter, and me, started out. " When we reached the woods we told the old gen-" tleman to go to a house in sight and rest himself " while we picked the berries.

" It was not long before the little girl and I " strayed some distance from the rest, when sud-" denly we heard shouts. The little girl thought it " was her grandfather, and was about to answer, but " I restrained her, thinking it might be Indians. " We walked forward until within sight of Father " Tanner, when we saw he was running his team

"around. We thought nothing strange at first, but
"as we approached we saw Indians gathering around
"the wagon, whooping and yelling as others came
"and joined them. We got into the wagon to start
"when four of the Indians took hold of the wagon-
"wheels to stop the wagon, and two others held the
"horses by the bits, and another came to take me
"out of the wagon. I then began to be afraid as
"well as vexed, and asked Father Tanner to let me
"get out of the wagon and run for assistance. He
"said, 'No, poor child; it is too late!' I told him
"they should not take me alive. His face was as
"white as a sheet. The Indians had commenced to
"strip him—had taken his watch and handker-
"chief—and while stripping him, were trying to pull
"me out of the wagon. I began silently to appeal
"to my Heavenly Father. While praying and strug-
"gling, the spirit of the Almighty fell upon me and
"I arose with great power; and no tongue can tell
"my feelings. I was happy as I could be. A few
"moments before I saw worse than death staring me
"in the face, and now my hand was raised by the
"power of God, and I talked to those Indians in
"their own language. They let go the horses and
"wagon, and all stood in front of me while I talked
"to them by the power of God. They bowed their
"heads and answered 'Yes,' in a way that made me
"know what they meant. The little girl and Father
"Tanner looked on in speechless amazement. I
"realized our situation; their calculation was to kill
"Father Tanner, burn the wagon, and take us women
"prisoners. This was plainly shown me. When I
"stopped talking they shook hands with all three of

" us, and returned all they had taken from Father
" Tanner, who gave them back the handkerchief, and
" I gave them berries and crackers. By this time
" the other two women came up, and we hastened
" home.

" The Lord gave me a portion of the interpreta-
" tion of what I had said, which was as follows:

" 'I suppose you Indian warriors think you are
" going to kill us? Don't you know the Great
" Spirit is watching you and knows everything in
" your heart? We have come out here to gather
" some of our father's fruit. We have not come to
" injure you; and if you harm us, or injure one hair
" of our heads, the Great Spirit shall smite you to
" the earth, and you shall not have power to breathe
" another breath. We have been driven from our
" homes, and so have you; we have come out here
" to do you good, and not to injure you. We are
" the Lord's people and so are you; but you must
" cease your murders and wickedness; the Lord is
" displeased with it and will not prosper you if you
" continue in it. You think you own all this land,
" this timber, this water, all the horses: Why, you
" do not own one thing on earth, not even the air
" you breathe—it all belongs to the Great Spirit.'"

———

Of similar import, and fraught with similar incidents as the preceding, are the testimonies of Mercy
R. Thompson, sister of Mary Fielding; Mrs. Janet
Young, of South Cottonwood; Elizabeth S. Higgs,
of Salt Lake City; Ann Gillott Morgan, of Milk

Creek, originally from England; Zina Pugh Bishop, for twenty-eight years a member of the church; Anna Wilson, of Taylorsville, originally from Sweden; Mary C. Smith, a sister from Wales; Elizabeth Lane Hyde, a sister from South Wales; Sister M. Bingham, an aged saint from England; Sister Mary T. Bennson, of Taylorsville, for thirty-two years a member of the church; Mrs. Isabella Pratt Walton, of Mill Creek; Mrs. Margaret Pratt, from Scotland; and many more, concerning whom a faithful record might profitably be made.

CHAPTER XLIX.

THE MESSAGE TO JERUSALEM—THE ANCIENT TONES
OF MORMONISM—THE MORMON HIGH PRIESTESS
IN THE HOLY LAND—ON THE MOUNT OF OLIVES—
OFFICIATING FOR THE ROYAL HOUSE OF JUDAH.

"Comfort ye, comfort ye my people, saith your
God. Speak ye comfortably to Jerusalem, and cry
unto her, that her warfare is accomplished, that her
iniquity is pardoned ; for she hath received double
for all her sins. * * * O Zion, that bringest
glad tidings, get thee up into the high mountain; O
Jerusalem that bringest good tidings, lift up thy
voice with strength; lift it up, be not afraid; say
unto the cities of Judah, behold your God !"

Themes to this day not understood by the Gentiles ! Incomprehensible to the divines of Christendom !

The everlasting perpetuation of a chosen race—a
diviner monument in its dispersion and preserva-
tion than in its national antiquity. Its restoration
to more than its ancient empire, and the rebuilding
of Jerusalem, with Jehovah exalted in his chosen
people as the Lord God Omnipotent, is the vast
subject of the prophetic Hebrews.

It was such a theme that inspired the genius of
grand Isaiah, swelling into the exultation of millen-

nial jubilee for Israel, in his great declamatory of
"Comfort ye, comfort ye my people, saith your
God!"

Gentile Christendom has never been *en rapport*
with the Abrahamic subject. It has not incarnated
its genius. It is destitute of the very sense to appreciate the theme of Jerusalem rebuilt.

Israelitish Mormondom does understand that
subject. It has fully incarnated its genius. It has,
not only the prophetic sense to appreciate the theme
of Old Jerusalem rebuilt, but also the rising of the
New Jerusalem of the last days, whose interpreted symbol shall be, "The Lord God Omnipotent
reigneth!"

The divines of a Romish Christianity—Romish,
notwithstanding its sectarian protestantism—have
worn threadbare the New Testament; but the epic
soul of the old Hebrew Bible has never possessed
Gentile Christendom. To it, the prophesies and
sublimities of Isaiah, and the everlasting vastness
of the Abrahamic covenant and promise, are all, at
best, but as glorious echoes from the vaults of dead
and long buried ages.

Who has blown the trump of this Hebraic resurrection? One only—the prophet of Mormondom!

The Mormons are, as it were, clothing that soul
with flesh—giving the themes of that everlasting
epic forms and types. Their Israelitish action has
made the very age palpitate. They render the
"Comfort ye, comfort ye my people, saith your
God!" as literally as did they the command of their
prophet to preach the gospel to the British Isles,
and gather the saints from that land.

The thread of history leads us directly to a significant episode in the life of Eliza R. Snow, a prophetess and high priestess of Hebraic Mormondom, in which the "Comfort ye my people" became embodied in an actual mission to Jerusalem.

Very familiar to the Mormons is the fact that, at the period when Joseph sent the Twelve to foreign lands, two of their number, Orson Hyde and John E. Page, were appointed on mission to Jerusalem. The Apostle Page failed to fulfill his call, and ultimately apostatized; but Orson Hyde honored the voice that oracled the restoration of Israel, and the rebuilding of Jerusalem. He did not preach to Judah in the ordinary way, but on the Mount of Olives he reconsecrated the land, and uttered to the listening heavens a command for the Jews to gather and rebuild the waste places. It was as the refrain of the invisible fathers, concerning Israel's redemption, rising from the hearts of their Mormon children. And that mission of Orson Hyde was but a prophesy, to the sons of Judah, of coming events. Other missions were ordained, as it were, to psychologize the age into listening to the voice of Judah's comforter.

A few years since, the second mission to Jerusalem was accomplished. On the Mount of Olives this time stood also a woman—to take part in the second consecration! A woman's inspired voice to swell the divine command for Israel to gather and become again the favored nation—the crown of empires.

The journal of Sister Eliza thus opens this episode of her life:

31

"On the 26th of October, 1872, I started on the
"mission to Palestine. When I realized that I was
"indeed going to Jerusalem, in fulfillment of a pre-
"diction of the prophet Joseph that I should visit
"that antique city, uttered nearly thirty years before,
"and which had not only fled my anticipations, but
"had, for years, gone from memory, I was filled with
"astonishment."

The Jerusalem missionaries were President Geo.
A. Smith, Lorenzo Snow, his sister Eliza R. Snow,
and Paul A. Schettler, their secretary, accompanied
by several tourists. The following commission,
given to President Smith, stamps the apostolic
character of this peculiar mission, and connects it
with the former one, sent by the prophet Joseph, in
the person of Orson Hyde, thirty-two years before:

"SALT LAKE CITY, U. T.,
"October 15, 1872.

"PRESIDENT G. A. SMITH:

"*Dear Brother :* As you are about to start on an
extensive tour through Europe and Asia Minor,
where you will doubtless be brought in contact with
men of position and influence in society, we desire
that you closely observe what openings now exist,
or where they may be effected, for the introduction
of the gospel into the various countries you shall
visit.

"When you go to the land of Palestine, we wish
you to dedicate and consecrate that land to the
Lord, that it may be blessed with fruitfulness preparatory to the return of the Jews in fulfillment of
prophesy and the accomplishment of the purposes
of our Heavenly Father.

"We pray that you may be preserved to travel in
peace and safety; that you may be abundantly

blessed with words of wisdom and free utterance in all your conversations pertaining to the holy gospel, dispelling prejudice and sowing seeds of righteousness among the people.

"BRIGHAM YOUNG,
"DANIEL H. WELLS."

Joseph had also predicted that, ere his mortal career closed, "George A." should see the Holy Land. In the fulfillment of this he may therefore be considered as the proxy of his great cousin; while Sister Eliza, who, it will be remembered, was declared by the prophet to be of the royal seed of Judah, may be considered as a high priestess officiating for her sacred race.

Away to the East—the cradle of empires—to bless the land where Judah shall become again a nation, clothed with more than the splendor of the days of Solomon.

Uniting at New York, the company, on the 6th of November, sailed on board the steamer *Minnesota*. Arriving in London, they visited some of the historic places of that great city, and then embarked for Holland. From place to place on the continent they went, visiting the famous cities, stopping a day to view the battle-field of Waterloo, then resting a day or two at Paris. At Versailles they were received with honor by President Theirs, in their peculiar character as missionaries to Jerusalem. Thence back to Paris; from Paris to Marseilles; then to Nice, where they ate Christmas dinner; thence to San Reno, Italy; to Genoa, Turin, Milan, Venice, Florence, Rome. At Rome Sister Eliza passed her seventieth birthday, visiting the famous places of that classic city. On the 6th of February, 1873, the apostolic tourists reached Alexandria, Egypt; and at length they approached Jerusalem— the monument of the past, the prophesy of the future! They encamped in the "Valley of Hinnom." Here Sister Eliza writes:

"Sunday morning, March 2d, President Smith made arrangements with out dragoman, and had a tent, table, seats, and carpet taken up on the Mount of Olives, to which all the brethren of the company and myself repaired on horseback. After dismounting on the summit, and committing our animals to the care of servants, we visited the Church of Ascension, a small cathedral, said to stand on the spot from which Jesus ascended. By this time the tent was prepared, which we entered, and after an opening prayer by Brother Carrington, we united in the order of the holy priesthood, President Smith leading in humble, fervent supplications, dedicating the land of Palestine for the gathering of the Jews and the rebuilding of Jerusalem, and returned heartfelt thanks and gratitude to God for the fullness of the gospel and the blessings bestowed on the Latter-day Saints. Other brethren led in turn, and we had a very interesting season; to me it seemed the crowning point of the whole tour, realizing as I did that we were worshipping on the summit of the sacred mount, once the frequent resort of the Prince of Life."

This the literal record; but what the symbolical? A prophesy of Israel's restoration! A sign of the renewal of Jehovah's covenant to the ancient people! The "comfort ye" to Jerusalem! Zion, from the West, come to the Zion of the East, to ordain her with a present destiny! A New Jerusalem crying to the Old Jerusalem, " Lift up thy voice " with strength ; Lift it up, be not afraid ; say unto " the cities of Judah, behold your God !"

Woman on the Mount of Olives, in her character of prophetess and high priestess of the temple! A daughter of David officiating for her Father's house!

Surely the subject is unique, view this extraordinary scene as we may—either as a romantic episode of Mormonism, or as a real and beautiful prelude to Jerusalem redeemed.

At the Sea of Gallilee the Hebraic muse of Sister Eliza thus expressed the rapture awakened by the scenes of the sacred land:

> " I have stood on the shore of the beautiful sea—
> The renowned and immortalized Gallilee—
> When 'twas wrapped in repose, at eventide,
> Like a royal queen in her conscious pride.

> " No sound was astir—not a murmuring wave—
> Not a motion was seen, but the tremulous lave—
> A gentle heave of the water's crest—
> As the infant breathes on a mother's breast.

> " I thought of the past and present; it seemed
> That the silent sea with instruction teemed;
> For often, indeed, the heart can hear
> What never, in sound, has approached the ear.

> " There's a depth in the soul that's beyond the reach
> Of all earthly sound—of all human speech;
> A fiber, too pure and sacred, to chime
> With the cold, dull music of earth and time."

* * * * * * *

On their way home our tourists visited Athens. Everywhere, going and returning, they were honored. Even princes and prime ministers took a peculiar interest in this extraordinary embassy of Mormon Israel. Evidently all were struck by its unique character.

Recrossing the Atlantic, they returned to their mountain home; thus accomplishing one of the most singular and romantic religious missions on record.

CHAPTER L.

The Mormon women, as well as men, hold the
priesthood. To all that man attains, in celestial exaltation and glory, woman attains. She is his partner in estate and office.

John the Revelator thus tells the story of the
Church of the First Born, in the New Jerusalem,
which shall come down out of heaven:

"And they sang a new song, saying, Thou art
worthy to take the book and to open the seals
thereof: for thou wast slain, and hast redeemed us
unto God, by thy blood, out of every kindred and
tongue and nation:

"And hast made us unto our God kings and
priests: and we shall reign on the earth."

Joseph the Revelator has given a grand supple-
ment to this. He also saw that vast assembly of
the New Jerusalem, and heard that song. There
was the blessed woman-half of that redeemed

throng. The sisters sang unto the honor of the Lamb:

"And thou hast made us unto our God queens and priestesses: and we shall reign on the earth!"

"But this is lowering the theme," says the Gentile Christian; "the theme descends from man—the paragon of excellence—to woman. Enough that she should be implied—her identity and glory absorbed in man's august splendor! Enough, that, for man, woman was created.

Not so the grand economy of Mormonism. In the Mormon temple, woman is not merely implied, but well defined and named. There the theme of the song of the New Jerusalem is faithfully rendered in her personality. If man is anointed priest unto God, woman is anointed priestess; if symboled in his heavenly estate as king, she is also symboled as queen.

Gentile publishers, making a sensational convenience of apostate sisters, have turned this to the popular amusement; but to the faithful Mormon woman it is a very sacred and exalted subject.

But not presuming to more than cross the threshold of the temple, return we now to the Mormon woman in her social sphere and dignity. The grand organization of fifty thousand Mormon women, under the name of "Relief Societies," will sufficiently illustrate woman in the Mormon economy.

The Female Relief Society was organized by the prophet Joseph, at Nauvoo. Here is a minute from his own history:

"Thursday, March 24.—I attended by request the Female Relief Society, whose object is, the relief of the poor, the destitute, the widow, and the orphan, and for the exercise of all benevolent purposes. Its organization was completed this day.   Mrs. Emma Smith takes the presidential chair; Mrs. Elizabeth Ann Whitney and Mrs. Sarah M. Cleveland are her councilors; Miss Elvira Cole is treasuress, and our well-known and talented poetess, Miss Eliza R. Snow, secretary.   *   *   *   *   Our ladies have always been signalized for their acts of benevolence and kindness; but the cruel usage that they have received from the barbarians of Missouri, has hitherto prevented their extending the hand of charity in a conspicuous manner."

On another occasion he says:

" I met the members of the Female Relief Society, and after presiding at the admission of many new members, gave a lecture on the priesthood, showing how the sisters would come in possession of the privileges, blessings, and gifts of the priesthood, and that the signs should follow them, such as healing the sick, casting out devils, etc., and that they might attain unto these blessings by a virtuous life, and conversation, and diligence in keeping all the commandments."

But it is in Utah that we see the growth of this society to a vast woman's organization: an organization which will greatly influence the destiny of Utah, religiously, socially and politically, for the next century, and, presumably, for all time.

From 1846, the time of the exodus from Nauvoo, the Relief Society was inoperative until 1855, when it was re-organized in Salt Lake City.

It is a self-governing body, without a written constitution; but is thoroughly organized, and parliamentary in its proceedings. Each branch adopts

measures, makes arrangements, appointments, etc.,
independently of others. Because of these organizations, Utah has no " poor-houses." Under the
kind and sisterly policy of this society the worthy
poor feel much less humiliated, and are better supplied, than by any almshouse system extant. By an
admirable arrangement, under the form of visiting
committees, with well-defined duties, the deserving
subjects of charity are seldom, if ever, neglected or
overlooked.

Since its revival in Salt Lake City, the society
has extended, in branches, from ward to ward of the
cities, and from settlement to settlement, in the
country, until it numbers considerably over two
hundred branches; and, as new settlements are constantly being formed, the number of branches is
constantly increasing.

The funds of the society are mostly donations;
but many branches have started various industries,
from which they realize moderate incomes. Besides
stated business meetings each branch has set days
on which to work for the benefit of the poor. When
the society commenced its labors in Salt Lake City,
these industrial meetings would have reminded the
observer of the Israelites in Egypt, making "bricks
without straw "—the donations consisting of mate-
rials for patch-work quilts, rag-carpets, uncarded
wool for socks and stockings, etc. (In one well-
authenticated instance the hair from slaughtered
beeves was gathered, carded—by hand of course,
as there were no carding machines in the city at
that time—spun, and knit into socks and mittens.)
These industrial meetings, to this day, are very in-

teresting, from the varieties of work thus brought into close fellowship.

As fast as may be, the various branches are building for themselves places of meeting, workshops, etc. The first of these buildings was erected by the ladies of the Fifteenth Ward of Salt Lake City. They commenced their labors as above, their first capital stock being donations of pieces for patchwork quilts, carpet-rags, etc. By energy and perseverance, they have sustained their poor, and, in a few years, purchased land and built on it a commodious house.

It should be recorded, as unique in history, that the laying of the corner-stone of this building was performed by the ladies. This ceremony, being unostentatiously performed, was followed by appropriate speechmaking on the part of the presiding officer of the society, Mrs. S. M. Kimball, Eliza R. Snow, and others; each in turn mounting the corner-stone for a rostrum, and each winning deserved applause from the assembled thousands.

No greater tribute could be paid to the ladies of this organization, than the simple statement of the fact that, since its re-establishment, in 1855, the Relief Society has gathered and disbursed over one hundred thousand dollars!

———

Mrs. Sarah M. Kimball, who, as President of the Fifteenth Ward Society, sustained the honors of the above occasion, belonged to the original Relief Society in Nauvoo. As elsewhere recorded, she also presided at the grand mass-meeting of the sisters, in Salt Lake City, in 1870, and has repeatedly appeared as a speaker of talent, and as a leader among the women of Utah. Her favorite theme is female suffrage; but she abounds with other progressive ideas, and is a lady of decided character. Her history as a Mormon dates from the earliest rise of the church.

Mrs. Mary I. Horne, frequently mentioned elsewhere, is the President of the "General Retrenchment Society" of Salt Lake City. (It should be explained that these are auxiliary to the relief societies, and are more especially designed for the organization of the young ladies of Utah.) She is also President of the Fourteenth Ward Relief Society, where frequently the sisters hold something like general conventions of the societies of the city. She may be said to rank, as an organizer, next to President Eliza R. Snow.

Among those who have earned honorable mention, as presidents of relief societies, and leading officers in the more important movements of the sisters, may be mentioned Sisters Rachel Grant, Agnes Taylor Swartz, Maria Wilcox, Minerva, one of the wives of Erastus Snow, of Southern Utah; Agatha Pratt, Julia Pack, Anna Ivins, Sarah Church, Sister Barney, once a missionary to the Sandwich Islands, and now an active woman at home; Eliza-

beth Goddard, Hannah Pierce, Rebecca Jones, Jane
C. Richardson, Elmira Taylor, Leonora Snow Mor-
ley, sister to Lorenzo and Eliza R. Snow : she pre-
sided at Brigham City, until her recent death ; Mary
Ferguson, Sisters Evans, of Lehi; Sister Ezra Benson, Rebecca Wareham, Ruth Tyler, Sisters Hunter,
Hardy, and Burton, wives of the presiding bishops ;
Sister Chase, Sister Lever, Sarah Groo, Sister Lay-
ton, wife of Bishop Layton of the battalion ; Sister
Reed, Mary Ann, one of the wives of Apostle O.
Hyde ; Sarah Peterson, Ann Bringhurst, Ann Bry-
ant, Helena Madson, M. J. Atwood, Sister Wilde,
Caroline Callister, Emma Brown, wife of the man
who did the first plowing in the valley, Nancy Wall,
founder of Wallsburg; Elizabeth Stickney, Marga-
ret McCullough, Amy Bigler, Elizabeth Brown,
Ellen Whiton, P. S. Hart, Ann Tate, Anna Brown,
Martha Simons, Jane Simons, Margaret P. Young,
M. A. Hubbard, Agnes Douglas, Jane Cahoon, Mary
McAllister, Sister Albertson, Pres. in Bear River
City; Mary Dewey, M. A. Hardy, Ann Goldsbrough,
Mrs. Sarah Williams, and Miss Emily Williams, of
Canton, Ill.; Jane Bailey, Jane Bradley, Elizabeth
Boyes, Jane M. Howell, D. E. Dudley, Mary Ann
Hazon, Mahala Higgins, Jenet Sharp, Lulu Sharp,
Jane Price, Ann Daniels, Harriet Burnham, M. C.
Morrison, Nellie Hartley, M. A. P. Hyde, Elizabeth
Park, Margaret Randall, Elizabeth Wadoup, M. A.
Pritchett, M. A. P. Marshall, Sarah S. Taylor, Mary
Hutchins, Emily Shirtluff, A. E. H. Hanson, M. J.
Crosby, Cordelia Carter, Sarah B. Gibson, Harriet
Hardy, Isabella G. Martin, M. A. Boise, Louisa
Croshaw, Orissa A. Aldred, Julia Lindsay, C. Liljen-

quist, Harriet A. Shaw, Ann Lowe, Emma Porter,
Mary E. Hall, Lydia Remington, Ellen C. Fuller,
Harriet E. Laney, Rebecca Marcham, A. L. Cox,
Louisa Taylor, Agnes S. Armstrong, M. A. Hub-
bard, Mary A. Hunter, M. A. House, Mary Griffin,
Jane Godfrey, Lydia Rich, E. E. C. Francis, Lydia
Ann Wells, E. M. Merrill, Mary A. Bingham, Han-
nah Child, M. A. Hardy, Fannie Slaughter, Mary
Walker, Ann Hughes, Marian Petersom, Mary
Hanson, Aurelia S. Rogers, A. M. Frodsham, Sophro-
nia Martin.

Among the presidents and officers of the Young
Ladies' Retrenchment Societies, should be men-
tioned Mary Freeze, Melissa Lee, Mary Pierce,
Clara Stenhouse Young, Sarah Howard, Mary
Williams, Elizabeth Thomas, Cornelia Clayton,
Sarah Graham, Susannah E. Facer, Emily Richards,
Josephine West, Minnie Snow, May Wells, Emily
Wells, Annie E. Wells, Maggie J. Reese, Emily
Maddison, Hattie Higginson, Mattie Paul, Sarah
Russell, Alice M. Rich, Mary E. Manghan, Mar-
garet M. Spencer, Sarah Jane Bullock, Alice M.
Tucker, M. Josephine Mulet, M. J. Tanner, Sarah
Renshaw, Mary Ann Ward, Lizzie Hawkins, Mary
Leaver, Amy Adams, Rebecca Williams, Mary S.
Burnham, Emmarett Brown, Mary A. P. Marshall.

———

Mrs. Bathsheba Smith, whose name has appeared
elsewhere, is apostolic in the movements of the
sisterhood, and a priestess of the temple. Mrs.
Franklin D. Richards is the most prominent organ-

izer outside of the metropolis of Utah, having Ogden and Weber counties under her direction. Sister Smoot leads at Provo. The silk industries are under the direction of President Zina D. Young. Those sisters who have been most energetic in promoting this important branch of industry, which gives promise of becoming a financial success in Utah, have already earned historic laurels. Of these are Sisters Dunyan, Robison, Carter, Clark, Schettler, and Rockwood. Eliza R. Snow is president, and Priscilla M. Staines vice-president, of the woman's co-operative store, an enterprise designed to foster home manufactures. Thus are the women of Mormondom putting the inchoate State of Deseret under the most complete organization.

CHAPTER LI.

The women of Mormondom, and the marriage
question! Two of the greatest sensations of the
age united!

Here we meet the subject of woman, in two casts—
not less Gentile than Mormon.

Marriage is the great question of the age. It is
the woman's special subject. Monogamic, or polygamic, it is essentially one problem. Either phase
is good, or bad, just as people choose to consider
it, or just as they are educated to view it.

The Mormons have been, for a quarter of a century, openly affirming, upon the authority of a new
revelation and the establishment of a distinctive
institution, that Gentile monogamy is not good.
But more than this is in their history, their religion,
and their social examples. They have made marriage one of their greatest problems. And they
accept the patriarchal order of marriage, according
to the Bible examples, and the revelation of their
prophet, as a proper solution.

To Gentile Christians, monogamy is good, and polygamy barbarous. But it is the old story of likes and dislikes, in which people so widely differ.

That the Mormons have been strictly logical, and strictly righteous, in reviving the institutions of the Hebrew patriarchs, in their character of a modern Israel, may be seen at a glance, by any just mind. What sense in their claim to be the Israel of the last days had they not followed the types and examples of Israel? If they have incarnated the ancient Israelitish genius—and in that fact is the whole significance of Mormonism—then has the age simply seen that genius naturally manifested in the action of their lives.

A monstrous absurdity, indeed, for Christendom to hold that the Bible is divine and infallible, and at the same time to hold that a people is barbaric for adoption of its faith and examples! Enough this, surely, to justify the infidel in sweeping it away altogether. The Mormons and the Bible stand or fall together.

In view of this truth, it was a cunning move of the opposition to attempt to take polygamy out of its theologic cast and give it a purely sociologic solution, as in the effort of 1870, when it was proposed by Congressman Julian, of Indiana, to enfranchise the women of Utah. Brigham Young and the legislative body of Utah promptly accepted the proposition, and a bill giving suffrage to the women of Utah was passed by the Territorial Legislature, without a dissenting vote.

Here is a copy of that remarkable instrument:

AN ACT, *giving woman the elective franchise in the Territory of Utah.*

SEC. 1. Be it enacted by the Governor and the Legislative Assembly of the Territory of Utah, that every woman of the age of twenty-one years, who has resided in this territory six months next preceding any general or special election, born or naturalized in the United States, or who is the wife, or widow, or the daughter of a naturalized citizen of the United States, shall be entitled to vote at any election in this territory.

SEC. 2. All laws or parts of laws, conflicting with this act, are hereby repealed.

Approved Feb. 12, 1870.

It may be said by the anti-Mormon that this bill was intended by President Young to serve the purposes of his own mission rather than to benefit the newly enfranchised class; but, as the issue will prove, it was really an important step in the progress of reform. The women of Utah have now in their own hands the power to absolutely rule their own destiny; and this is more than can be said of the millions of their Gentile sisters.

The municipal election in Salt Lake City, which occurred but two days after the approval of this bill, for the first time in Mormon history presented a political home issue; but the new voting element was not brought largely into requisition. Only a few of the sisters claimed the honor of voting on that occasion. The first of these was Miss Seraph Young, a niece of President Young, who thus immortalized herself.

This grant of political power to the women of

Utah is a sign of the times. The fact cannot die that the Mormon people piloted the nation westward; and, under the inspiration of the great impulses of the age, they are destined to be the reformatory vanguard of the nation.

CHAPTER LII.

THE LIE OF THE ENEMY REFUTED—A VIEW OF THE
WOMEN IN COUNCIL OVER FEMALE SUFFRAGE—
THE SISTERS KNOW THEIR POLITICAL POWER.

It was charged, however, by the anti-Mormons,
that woman suffrage in Utah was only designed to
further enslave the Mormon women; that they took
no part in its passage, and have had no soul in its
exercise. Nearly the reverse of this is the case,
as the records, to follow, will show.

In the expositions of the Mormon religion, priesthood and genius, which have been given, it has
been seen that the women are, equally with their
prophets and apostles, the founders of their church
and the pillars of its institutions; the difference
being only that the man is first in the order, and
the woman is his helpmate; or, more perfectly expressed, "they twain are one," in the broadest and
most exalted sense. Hence, no sooner was suffrage
granted to the Mormon women, than they exercised
it as a part of their religion, or as the performance
of woman's life duties, marked out for her in the
economy of divine providence. In this apostolic
spirit, they took up the grant of political power.
Hence, also, in accordance with the fundamental

Mormon view of an essential partnership existing between the man and the woman, "in all things," both in this world and in the world to come, there grew up, as we have seen, in the days of Joseph the prophet, female organizations, set apart and blessed for woman's ministry in this life, to be extended into the "eternities." True, these women's organizations have been known by the name of relief societies, but their sphere extends to every department of woman's mission, and they may be viewed as female suffrage societies in a female suffrage movement, or society-mates of any masculine movement which might arise to shape or control human affairs, religious, social or political. It was this society that, as by the lifting of the finger, in a moment aroused fifty thousand women in Utah, simultaneously to hold their "indignation mass-meetings" throughout the territory, against the Cullom bill. At that very moment the female suffrage bill was passed by their Legislature, so that the exercise of their vote at the subsequent election was a direct expression of their will upon the most vital of all social questions—the marriage question. Here are the minutes of a general meeting of this great Female Relief Society, held in Salt Lake City, February 19, 1870— just seven days after the passage of their bill, and two days before the exercise of the female vote at the election :

MINUTES.—Most of the wards of the city were represented. Miss E. R. Snow was elected president, and Mrs. L. D. Alder secretary.

Meeting opened with singing; prayer by Mrs. Harriet Cook Young.

Miss Eliza R. Snow arose and said, to encourage the sisters in good works, she would read an account of our indignation meeting, as it appeared in the *Sacramento Union;* which account she thought a very fair one. She also stated that an expression of gratitude was due acting-Governor Mann, for signing the document granting woman suffrage in Utah, for we could not have had the right without his sanction, and said that Wyoming had passed a bill of this kind over its Governor's head, but we could not have done this.

The following names were unanimously selected to be a committee for said purpose: Eliza R. Snow, Bathsheba W. Smith, Sarah M. Kimball, M. T. Smoot, H. C. Young, N. D. Young, Phœbe Woodruff, M. I. Horne, M. N. Hyde, Eliza Cannon, Rachel Grant, Amanda Smith.

Mrs. Sarah M. Kimball said she had waited patiently a long time, and now that we were granted the right of suffrage, she would openly declare herself a woman's rights woman, and called upon those who would do so to back her up, whereupon many manifested their approval. She said her experience in life had been different from that of many. She had moved in all grades of society; had been both rich and poor; had always seen much good and intelligence in woman. The interests of man and woman cannot be separated; for the man is not without the woman nor the woman without the man in the Lord. She spoke of the foolish custom which deprived the mother of having control over her sons at a certain age; said she saw the foreshadowing of a brighter day in this respect in the future. She said she had entertained ideas that appeared wild, which she thought would yet be considered woman's rights; spoke of the remarks made by Brother Rockwood, lately, that women would have as much prejudice to overcome, in occupying certain positions, as men would in granting them, and concluded by declaring that woman was the helpmate of man in every department of life.

Mrs. Phœbe Woodruff said she was pleased with the reform, and was heart and hand with her sisters. She was thankful for the privilege that had been granted to women, but thought we must act in wisdom and not go too fast. She had looked for this day for years. God has opened the way for us. We have borne in patience, but the yoke on woman is partly removed. Now that God has moved upon our brethren to grant us the right of female suffrage, let us lay it by, and wait till the time comes to use it, and not run headlong and abuse the privilege. Great and blessed things are ahead. All is right and will come out right, and woman will receive her reward in blessing and honor. May God grant us strength to do right in his sight.

Mrs. Bathsheba W. Smith said she felt pleased to be engaged in the great work before them, and was heart and hand with her sisters. She never felt better in her life, yet never felt more her own weakness, in view of the greater responsibilities which now rested upon them, nor ever felt so much the necessity of wisdom and light; but she was determined to do her best. She believed that woman was coming up in the world. She encouraged her sisters with the faith that there was nothing required of them in the duties of life that they could not perform.

Mrs. Prescindia Kimball said: " I feel comforted and blessed this day. I am glad to be numbered in moving forward in this reform; feel to exercise double diligence and try to accomplish what is required at our hands. We must all put our shoulder to the wheel and go ahead. I am glad to see our daughters elevated with man, and the time come when our votes will assist our leaders, and redeem ourselves. Let us be humble, and triumph will be ours. The day is approaching when woman shall be redeemed from the curse placed upon Eve, and I have often thought that our daughters who are in polygamy will be the first redeemed. Then let us keep the commandments and attain to a fullness, and always bear in mind that our children born in the priesthood will be saviors on Mount Zion."

Mrs. Zina D. Young said she was glad to look upon such an assemblage of bright and happy faces, and was gratified to be numbered with the spirits who had taken tabernacles in this dispensation, and to know that we are associated with kings and priests of God; thought we do not realize our privileges. Be meek and humble and do not move one step aside, but gain power over ourselves. Angels will visit the earth, but are we, as handmaids of the Lord, prepared to meet them? We live in the day that has been looked down upon with great anxiety since the morn of creation.

Mrs. M. T. Smoot said: "We are engaged in a great work, and the principles that we have embraced are life and salvation unto us. Many principles are advanced on which we are slow to act. There are many more to be advanced. Woman's rights have been spoken of. I have never had any desire for more rights than I have. I have considered politics aside from the sphere of woman; but, as things progress, I feel it is right that we should vote, though the path may be fraught with difficulty."

Mrs. Wilmarth East said she would bear testimony to what had been said. She had found by experience that "obedience is better than sacrifice." I desire to be on the safe side and sustain those above us; but I cannot agree with Sister Smoot in regard to woman's rights. I have never felt that woman had her privileges. I always wanted a voice in the politics of the nation, as well as to rear a family. I was much impressed when I read the poem composed by Mrs. Emily Woodmanse—"Who Cares to Win a Woman's Thought." There is a bright day coming; but we need more wisdom and humility than ever before. My sisters, I am glad to be associated with you—those who have borne the heat and burden of the day, and ask God to pour blessings on your head.

Eliza R. Snow, in closing, observed, that there was a business item she wished to lay before the meeting, and suggested that Sister Bathsheba W. Smith be appointed on a mission to preach retrenchment all through the South, and woman's rights, if she wished.

The suggestion was acted upon, and the meeting adjourned with singing " Redeemer of Israel," and benediction by Mrs. M. N. Hyde.

Let the reader be further told that, though this was a sort of a convention of the great Relief Society of Utah, which can move fifty thousand women in a moment, it was not a woman's suffrage meeting. It was a gathering of the sisters for consideration of the retrenchment of the table, and general domestic economy, the retrenchment societies having been just inaugurated under the leadership of Sister Horne. But, it will be seen that the meeting was changed to a woman's feast of anticipations, and table-retrenchment met scarcely an incidental reference that day ; for the spirit of woman's future rested upon the sisters, spoke with its " still, small voice," and pointed to the bright looming star of woman's destiny.

That these women will move wisely, and in the fear of God, is very evident ; nor will they use the tremendous power which they are destined to hold to break up their church and destroy their faith in the revelation of the "new and everlasting covenant," given through the prophet Joseph Smith. Indeed, they will yet send their testimony through the world, with ten thousand voices, confirmed by the potency of the woman's vote, and flood the nation with their light.

Congress need not fear to trust the woman's supreme question into the safe keeping of fifty thousand God-fearing, self-sacrificing, reverent women. In vain will the anti-Mormons and pretentious " regenerators" look for these women to become revolutionary or impious. What they do will be done in the name and fear of the Lord; yet, mark the prophesy of one of their leaders: " The day is ap- " proaching when woman shall be redeemed from " the curse of Eve; and I have often thought that " our daughters who are in polygamy will be the " first redeemed."

Here is the curse: " In sorrow thou shalt bring " forth children ; and *thy desire shall be to thy hus-* " *band, and he shall rule over thee !*" Woman will be redeemed from that curse, as sure as the coming of to-morrow's sun. No more, after this generation, shall civilized man *rule* over his mate, but "they twain shall be one ;" and the sisters are looking for that millennial day. These are the " wise virgins " of the church; and their lamps are trimmed.

CHAPTER LIII.

But the enemies of the Mormons, at home and
abroad, who have sought to break up their religious
institutions and turn their sacred relations into un-
holy covenants, have, from the very hour of the grant
of woman's charter, also sought to take away from
them female suffrage. And perhaps they would
have done so ere now, had not a million American
women been on the side of the Mormons, in this.
Claggett of Montana, in his attack upon the people
of Utah, in the House of Representatives, January
29th, 1873, gave to Congress a touch of the anti-
Mormon opposition to female suffrage in Utah. He
said:

" My friend from Utah [Hooper] goes on to say
that Utah is a long way in advance of the age in
one respect; that female suffrage has been adopted
there. What was the reason for adopting that
measure ? Was it because the peculiar institution
of the territory recognizes in any degree whatever
the elevation, purity, and sanctity of women ? No,

sir. When the Union Pacific Railroad was completed, and when the influx of miners and other outsiders began to come into the territory, the chiefs of the Mormon hierarchy, fearing that power would pass from their hands by the gradual change of population, by adopting female suffrage trebled their voting power by a stroke of their pen; and I am credibly informed upon the authority of at least fifty men, that in practice in that territory any child or woman, from twelve years old and upwards, that can wear a yard of calico, exercises the prerogatives of a freeman, so far as voting is concerned."

The flippant remark of the delegate from Montana, that every Mormon woman could exercise the prerogative of a freeman, called forth a burst of laughter from the house; but it would have been more in keeping with the great theme of woman's rights, had a hearty "Thank God!" rang from the lips of those legislators who laughed in derision. Of course, the gentleman's statement was an exaggeration; but what a story he has unwittingly told of the power that has been committed to the hands of the Mormon women? What an epic prophesy he gave of woman's destiny, when he said, that from the age of twelve years they are trained in Utah to exercise the freeman's prerogative. If this be so— and it is near enough to the truth—and if the Mormon women have trebled the power of the men by the grant of female suffrage, then already do they hold not only their own destiny in their hands, but also the destiny of the men. Their very husbands are depending upon them for grace and salvation from their enemies, in spite of all their enemies' designs. Do legislators for a moment foolishly fear that the Mormon women will not discover this vast power which they hold, and discovering, wield it almost as a manifest destiny? They have discovered it; and their future movements will manifest it, to the astonishment of the whole civilized world. Fifty to a hundred thousand women, who are henceforth in one single State to be trained, from the age of twelve, to exercise the political power of "freemen," cannot but be free, and can have nothing less than a splendid future before them.

Mr. Claggett blasphemed against the truth, when he said that there was nothing in the Mormon religion that "recognized, in any degree whatever, the elevation, purity and sanctity of woman." This is a wicked outrage against the sisters, whose lives are stainless and matchless records of purity, devotion and heroism. That devotion of itself would elevate and enoble their characters; and, if Congress and the American people believe them to be martyrs to their religion, then their very martyrdom should sanctify them in the eyes of the nation.

Moreover, woman suffrage is a charter not incompatible with the genius of Mormonism, but in positive harmony therewith. The Mormon Church is originally based upon the woman as well as upon the man. She is with him a partner and priest, in all their religious institutions. The sisters have also exercised the vote in the church for the last forty-seven years, it being conferred with their membership. So female suffrage grows out of the very genius and institutions of their church.

Now the marriage question specially belongs to the women of the age, and not to Congress; and the

Mormon women must and will make the country practically confess as much. They will do it by a movement potent enough upon this question, if they have to stir all the women of America to the issue. They are forced to this by their supreme necessities—their honor, their duty, their love, their most sacred relations. Their brothers, their husbands and their sons are threatened with prisons, for that which their religion and the Bible sanction—that Bible which Christendom for nearly two thousand years has received as the word of God. If there be a radical fault, then is the fault in their too substantial faith in that word. Surely there can be no crime in a Bible faith, else Christendom had been under a condemnation that eternity itself would not outlive. But the damnation of Congress and the regenerators is to be visited upon the heads of the innocent—for the shaping of the case is making the sisters in the eye of the law dishonored women. The very spies and minions of the court enter their marriage chamber—sacred among even barbarians— to find the evidence for prosecution, or to drag them to the witness-box, to testify against their husbands, or disown them to screen them from punishment. Not in the history of civilization has there been such a monstrous example before. Claggett has said, in Congress, of their marriage, "That it tears " the crown jewel from the diadem of woman's purity, " and takes from her the holy bond which honors " her in all the nations of the earth; which has ele- " vated lechery to the dignity of a religious dogma, " and burns incense upon the altars of an unhallowed " lust; and above all, and as a crime against the fu-

"ture, which ages of forgiveness cannot condone nor
"the waters of ocean wash out, which yearly writes
"in letters that blister as they fall, the word 'bas-
"tard' across the branded brows of an army of little
"children. Such an institution is not entitled by
"any right, either human or divine, to hide the
"hideous deformity of its nakedness with the mantle
"of religion, nor seek shelter under the protecting
"ægis of the civil law." [Applause from Congress.]

The women of Mormondom must force Claggett
and Congress to take this back. It is such as he
who spoke, and they who applauded, who have
written "in letters that blister as they fall the word
"'bastard' across the branded brows of an army of
"little children," and the mothers of those dear little
branded ones must appeal to the wives and mothers
of America, to take that curse of "bastard" from
their innocent brows. They must ask those noble
women everywhere in America, who are earnestly
battling for their own rights, and especially the
supreme right of woman to settle the marriage
question; and the answer to their mighty prayer
shall come back to them from a million women,
throughout the land. The women of America, who
lead the van of the new civilization, shall cry to
Congress and the nation in behalf of their Mormon
sisters, with voices that will not be hushed, till justice be done. Indeed, already have they done this,
so far as the suffrage is concerned; and it is due to
them alone, under Providence, that the women of
Utah have not been disfranchised. This is best
brought home to the reader by reference to the following, from the report of the Pennsylvania Woman

Suffrage Association, read at the Opera House, Detroit, Mich., October 13, 1874:

"During the session of Congress we spent some time in the capital, proposing to work for the enfranchisement of the women of the District of Columbia and of the territories; but finding that Congress was more likely to disfranchise the women who already possessed this right, than to enfranchise others, our efforts were used, as far as possible, to prevent this backward step.

"Had we been a voter, we might have had less trouble to convince some of our friends in this affair.

"Several bills were introduced, any one of which, if it became a law, would have disfranchised the women of Utah.

"The McKee bill had been referred to the House Committee on Territories. While the subject was under discussion in the committee, by invitation of the members, on two occasions, we stated our views. One of the members, before the committee convened, gave his reason for favoring the passage of the bill.

"'The woman's vote sustains polygamy,' said he, 'and to destroy that, I would take the right of suffrage from every woman in the territory.'

"'Would it do that?' we inquired.

"'I think it would.'

"'Did polygamy exist in the territory before the women voted?'

"'Oh! yes.'

"'Have they ever had the privilege of voting against it?'

"'No; that has never been made an issue; but they voted to send a polygamist to Congress.'

"'Did any man vote for him?'

"'Yes, more than eleven thousand men, and ten thousand women.'

"'How many voted for the opposing candidate?'

"' Something less than two thousand men and women together.'

"' You intend to disfranchise the men who voted for this man ?' we asked.

"' Oh ! no.'

"' Then the polygamist can still come to Congress by a majority of five to one.' Though this was true, he seemed to think it very wrong to disfranchise the men

" How many of the committee reasoned as this one did, we are unable to say, but the majority wished to disfranchise the women, as they returned the bill to the House with the obnoxious sections unchanged. The friends of woman, by their honest work, prevented action being taken on the bill, and perhaps saved the country the disgrace of having done such a great wrong, which it could not soon have undone. There was something more vital to the well-being of the nation in this, than some of our legislators were willing to admit. Had they passed this act they would probably have laid the foundation for the ruin of the nation. If Congress has the power to disfranchise one class, it undoubtedly has the power to disfranchise another, and what freeman in such a case is secure in his rights ?

" Similar bills were before the Senate and House Judiciary Committees.

" The question came: Where shall we look for help among those in power? To the true, the trusted and the tried. To those of the grandest intellect and the purest heart. To the friends of the weak and the oppressed. Our appeal shall be made to the highest, to the honorable and most honored Charles Sumner. He cordially granted us a hearing. When we stated the object of our visit, he quietly remarked, 'You have come to the wrong person. I have no influence with these men.'

"After talking some time on the subject, he said, 'I should hesitate to take this right from any who now possess it. I will go farther; I would be willing to grant it to those who have it not.' He afterwards remarked, 'I shall investigate this matter thoroughly.'

"'The bill passed the Senate last year, and many good men voted for it,' we said.

" He kindly apologized for their action, in these words: 'They did not fully realize the nature of the bill; they had not examined it carefully.'

"'Had it deprived them, or any class of men, of the right to vote, would they have realized what it meant, and voted differently?' we inquired.

"'In that case they would doubtless have had sharp eyes to note all its defects,' he answered, with a smile. 'I did not vote on it. I was sick in bed at the time. Have you seen Mr. Frelinghuysen in reference to this?' was the next inquiry.

"'We have not. It seems useless. A man who would frame such a bill would not be likely to change it.'

" But we followed his advice, saw Mr. Frelinghuysen, Mr. Edmunds and others. Mr. Frelinghuysen declared he would not change his bill however much he might be abused.

" Two days after we again met Mr. Sumner and stated the results of our efforts.

" In closing this second interview Mr. Sumner said, 'I will present to the Senate any memorial or petition you may wish, and then refer it to the Judiciary Committee. That is the best way to do.'

" His farewell words were: 'Whether you succeed or not, I wish you all well.'

" Just three weeks from the day of our last conversation with Mr. Sumner, his work on earth ceased, and the cause of justice lost a grand friend. On the morning of February 20th we handed him a suffrage memorial, which he presented to the Senate, requesting that it be referred to the Judiciary Committee, which was almost his last official act."

The women of Utah were not disfranchised. Doubtless this was chiefly owing to the searching and logical editorials of the *Woman's Journal,* which placed the subject in its true light before the people, together with the action of the advocates of woman suffrage in New England, New York, Pennsylvania and other States. This was a grand victory for woman suffrage. Miss Mary F. Eastman, in her report to the New York Association, said: "When the bill, disfranchising the women of Utah, "came before Congress, our representatives were "promptly petitioned to use their influence against "the measure."

Thus it will be seen that the women of Mormondom and the women of America have a common cause, in this all-vital marriage question, which is destined to receive some very decided and peculiar solution before the end of the century. And it must be equally certain that fifty thousand God-fearing women, with the vote of "freemen"—as Mr. Claggett has it—coming fairly out upon the national platform, in the great issue, will give a toning to the marriage question, for which even orthodox Christians, now so much their enemies, will heartily thank God.

CHAPTER LIV.

WOMAN EXPOUNDS HER OWN SUBJECT—THE FALL—
HER REDEMPTION FROM THE CURSE—RETURNING
INTO THE PRESENCE OF HER FATHER—HER EX-
ALTATION.

The high priestess thus expounds the subject of
woman, from her Mormon standpoint:

In the Garden of Eden, before the act of disobe-
dience, through which Adam and Eve were shut out
from the presence of God, it is reasonable to suppose that Eve's position was not inferior to, but
equal with, that of Adam, and that the same law
was applicable to both. Moses says, " God created
man male and female." President Brigham Young
says, " Woman is man in the priesthood."

God not only foreknew, but he had a purpose to
accomplish through, the " fall;" for he had provided
a sacrifice; Jesus being spoken of as a " Lamb slain
from the foundation of the world."

It seems that woman took the lead in the great
drama. The curse followed, and she became subject to man; "and he shall rule over thee," which
presupposes a previous equality. But was that curse
to be perpetual? Were the daughters of Eve—
who was a willing instrument in effecting a grand

purpose, that shall ultimate in great good to the human family—to abide that curse forever? No. God had otherwise ordained. Through the atoning blood of Christ, and obedience to his gospel, a plan was devised to remove the curse and bring the sons and daughters of Adam and Eve, not only to their primeval standing in the presence of God, but to a far higher state of glory.

In the meridian of time, the Saviour came and introduced the gospel, "which before was preached unto Abraham," and which, after a lapse of nearly eighteen centuries—when men had "changed its ordinances, and broken the everlasting covenant"— when "the man of sin had been revealed, exalting himself above all that is called God"—after hireling priests had mutilated its form, discarded its powers, and rejected "the testimony of Jesus, which is the spirit of prophesy," the Lord restored it in fullness to the earth, with all its gifts, powers, blessings and ordinances.

For this purpose he raised up Joseph Smith, the great prophet of the last days, to whom the angel that John, when on the Isle of Patmos, saw "flying through the midst of heaven, having the everlasting gospel to preach to every nation, kindred, tongue and people, saying, fear God and give glory to him, for the hour of his judgment is come," etc., appeared, and announced the glorious news of the Dispensation of the Fullness of Times, and the restoration of the fullness of the gospel.

This gospel, and this only, will redeem woman from the curse primevally entailed. It is generally admitted that "Christianity" ameliorates the condition of woman; but the Christianity of the professing world, mutilated as it has been, can only ameliorate, it cannot redeem. Each religious denomination has fragments or portions of the true form, but no vestige of the vital power that was manifested by Jesus Christ, and restored through Joseph Smith. Nothing short of obedience to this gospel in its fullness will exalt woman to equality with man, and elevate mankind to a higher condition than we occupied in our pre-existent state.

Woman, in all enlightened countries, wields, directly or indirectly, the moving influence for good or for ill. It has been pertinently remarked : " Show " me the women of a nation, and I will describe that " nation." Let the pages of history decide if ever a nation became a wreck, so long as woman nobly honored her being by faithfully maintaining the principles of virtuous purity, and filled with grace and dignity her position as wife and mother.

Would God, the kind parent, the loving father, have permitted his children to sink into the fallen condition which characterizes humanity in its present degraded state, without instituting means by which great good would result? Would we, as intelligent beings in a former existence, have consented, as we did, to resign the remembrance and all recollection of that existence, and come down to earth and run our chances for good or evil, did we not know that, on reasonable conditions, and by means provided, we could work our way back to, at least, our original positions ? Emphatically, no ! It is only by that " spirit which searches all things, yea, even the deep things of God," that we can comprehend our own beings, and our missions on the earth, with the bearing of our pre-existence on our present lives, of which we only know what God reveals; and, as man, by his own wisdom cannot find out God, so man by reasoning cannot pry into the circumstances of his former life, nor extend his researches into the interminable eternities that lie beyond.

CHAPTER LV.

And the women of Zion have a press. More than up to their Gentile sisters are they in this respect. Few of the church organizations of Christendom can boast a woman's journal. There are but few of them in all the world, and they are mostly edited and supported by the heterodox rather than the orthodox element.

The *Woman's Exponent* is one of those few. It is published by the women of the Mormon Church, having a company organization, of which Eliza R. Snow is president. Mrs. Emeline B. Wells is the practical editor. It was established June 1st, 1872.

The *Woman's Exponent*, in a general sense, may be considered heterodox, seeing that it is an advocate of woman's rights on the marriage question and female suffrage, but it is also apostolic, and devoted to the Mormon mission. It represents the opinions and sentiments of the Mormon women. All of their organizations are fairly represented in its columns, and it is thus a means of intercommu nication between branches, bringing the remotest into close connection with the more central ones, and keeping all advised of the various society movements. Its editorial department is fully up to the standard of American journalism.

Mrs. Wells, the editor, like many prominent Mormon women previously mentioned, is of Puritan descent, being a native of New England, and of pure English extraction. Her family name was Woodward, and she was born in Petersham, Mass., February 29, 1828. At an early age she began to manifest a penchant for literature, and while in her teens produced many literary fragments that, as if by manifest destiny, pointed in the direction of her present profession. In 1842 she was baptized into the Mormon Church. It is needless to say that this was a cause of mortification to her many associates and friends, and especially so to a select few, whose appreciative kindness had pictured a glowing future for the young litterateur. Her mother, who was also a convert to the Mormon faith, fearing that the persuasions of friends might lead her into error, sent her to Nauvoo, in the spring of 1844, that she might be away from their influence. The people to whom her mother confided her, apostatized shortly after her arrival, but Emeline remained steadfast. Some time thereafter she became a plural wife. In the exodus, her mother, who had joined her the year before, succumbed under the accumulation of hardships that the saints had then to undergo, and, dying, joined the immortal company of martyrs who fell in those days of trial.

At winter quarters she was engaged in teaching,

until her journey to the valley in 1848. Here, since
the organization of relief societies, and more especially since the women of Utah obtained the right
of suffrage, she has employed a large portion of her
time in public labors, for the benefit and elevation
of woman. In addition to her present editorial
duties, she fills the responsible position of president
of the organization that, since November, 1876, has
been engaged in storing up grain against a day of
famine. Under the energetic management of this
organization, vast quantities of grain have been
stored in the various wards and settlements of
Utah.

Sister Emeline is also a poetess of no little merit.
As a set-off to the popular idea that the Mormon
women in polygamy have no sentiment towards
their husbands, the following exquisite production,
from her pen, entitled " The Wife to her Husband,"
is offered :

> It seems to me that should I die,
> And this poor body cold and lifeless lie,
> And thou shouldst touch my lips with thy warm breath,
>   The life-blood quicken'd in each sep'rate vein,
>   Would wildly, madly rushing back again,
> Bring the glad spirit from the isle of death.
>
> It seems to me that were I dead,
> And thou in sympathy shouldst o'er me shed
> Some tears of sorrow, or of sad regret,
>   That every pearly drop that fell in grief,
>   Would bud, or blossom, bursting into leaf,
> To prove immortal love could not forget.
>
> I do believe that round my grave,
> When the cool, fragrant, evening zephyrs wave,
> Shouldst thou in friendship linger near the spot,
>   And breathe some tender words in memory,
>   That this poor heart in grateful constancy,
> Would softly whisper back some loving thought.

I do believe that should I pass
Into the unknown land of happiness,
And thou shouldst wish to see my face once more,
That in my earnest longing after thee,
I would come forth in joyful ecstacy,
And once again gaze on thee as before.

I do believe my faith in thee,
Stronger than life, an anchor firm to be,
Planted in thy integrity and worth,
A perfect trust, implicit and secure;
That will all trials and all griefs endure,
And bless and comfort me while here on earth.

I do believe who love hath known,
Or sublime friendship's purest, highest tone,
Hath tasted of the cup of ripest bliss,
And drank the choicest wine life hath to give,
Hath known the truest joy it is to live;
What blessings rich or great compared to this?

I do believe true love to be,
An element that in its tendency,
Is elevating to the human mind;
An intuition which we recognize
As foretaste of immortal Paradise,
Through which the soul will be refined.

Among the more prominent contributors to the *Exponent* is Lu. Dalton, a lady in whose writings are manifested the true spirit and independence of the Mormon women. The vigor and vivacity of her poetic productions are suggestive of a future enviable fame.

Mrs. Hannah T. King, mentioned elsewhere, is a veteran poetess of well-sustained reputation. She ranked among the poetesses of England before joining the Mormon Church, being on intimate terms with the celebrated Eliza Cook.

Another of the sisters who has won distinction as a poetess of the church, is Emily Woodmansee. She is also a native of England, and began her poetic career when but a girl. Several of her poems have been reproduced in literary journals of the East, winning marked attention.

Miss Sarah Russell, who writes under the *nom de plume* of "Hope," is also a poetess of promise; but she is younger to fame than the before-mentioned.

Emily B. Spencer may also be mentioned in this connection.

Miss Mary E. Cook is an apostle of education, in the church. She is a professional graduate, and has held prominent positions in first-class schools of St. Louis and Chicago. Coming to Utah several years ago, Miss Cook, being a passionate student of ancient history, was attracted by a cursory glance at the Book of Mormon. On a careful perusal of it she was struck with the account therein given of the ancient inhabitants of this continent; and especially was she impressed with the harmony existing between that account and the works of Bancroft and others concerning the ancient races of America. She unhesitatingly pronounced the book genuine. Miss Cook has been instrumental in establishing the system of graded schools in Utah. Her success has been marked, in this capacity, and she is also a rising leader among the women of the church. With her should also be mentioned her sister, Miss Ida Cook, who is now one of the most prominent teachers of the territory. Nor should we omit to mention Orpha Everett, who is another prominent teacher.

The ladies are also represented in the historian's office of the church, in the person of a daughter of Apostle Orson Pratt, and Miss Joan M. Campbell.

Miss Campbell has been an *attache* of the historian's office since a mere child. She is a clerk of the Territorial Legislature, and a Notary Public.

Mrs. Romania B. Pratt, wife of Parley P. Pratt, Jr., is a medical professor. She is a graduate of the Woman's Medical College, Philadelphia, and is now connected, as a practitioner, with the celebrated water-cure establishment at Elmira, N. Y.

Sister Elise Shipp is another Mormon lady now under training for the medical profession in the Woman's Medical College, Pennsylvania.

Thus it will be seen that, in the educational and professional spheres, the Mormon women are making a creditable showing.

CHAPTER LVI.

RETROSPECTION—APOSTOLIC MISSION OF THE MORMON
WOMEN—HOW THEY HAVE USED THE SUFFRAGE—
THEIR PETITION TO MRS. GRANT—TWENTY-SEVEN
THOUSAND MORMON WOMEN MEMORIALIZE CON-
GRESS.

Ere this record be closed, let us review the later
acts of these extraordinary women, who have fairly
earned the position of apostles to the whole United
States.

They have pioneered the nation westward, where
Providence was directing its course of empire, and
now they are turning back upon the elder States of
the Union as pioneers of a new civilization.

The manifest prophesy of events is, that Utah, in
the near future, is going down from the mountains
of refuge to the very seat of government, with woman's mission to all America. Very consistently,
yet very significantly also, are the women of Utah
rising to power and importance in the nation, through
woman suffrage and the exercise of the constitutional right of petition.

Since the grant of woman suffrage they have
exercised the ballot repeatedly in their municipal
and territorial elections. Moreover, within that

time, they have voted upon the constitution for the
" State of Deseret," which will doubtless be substantially the one under which the territory will be
admitted into the Union.   Female suffrage was one
of the planks of that constitution.   It will become
a part of the organic act of the future State.   No
Congress will dare to expunge it, for such an attempt
would bring a million of the women of America into
an organized movement against the Congress that
should dare to array itself against this grand charter
of woman's freedom.   Though Wyoming was the
first to pass a woman suffrage bill, which met a veto
from its governor, and has experienced a somewhat
unhappy history since, the honor of having voted
for the greatest measures known in social and political economy rests with the women of Utah.
They have taken action upon the very foundation
of society-building.   Already, therefore, the women
of Utah lead the age in this supreme woman's issue;
and, if they carry their State into the Union first on
the woman suffrage plank, they will practically make
woman suffrage a dispensation in our national economy for all the States of the Federal Union.   And
it will be consistent to look for a female member of
Congress from Utah.   Let woman be once recognized as a power in the State, as well as in society
and the church, and her political rights can be extended according to the public mind.

The Mormon women have also fallen back upon
the original right of citizens to petition Congress.
Their first example of the kind was when they held
their grand mass-meetings throughout the territory
and memorialized Congress against the Cullom bill.

The second was the very remarkable petition to
Mrs. Grant. It is here reproduced as a historical
unique :

" MRS. PRESIDENT GRANT:

"*Honored Lady:* Deeming it proper for woman
to appeal to woman, we, Latter-day Saints, ladies of
Utah, take the liberty of preferring our humble and
earnest petition for your kindly and generous aid ;
not merely that you are the wife of the chief magistrate of this great nation, but we are also induced
to appeal to you because of your high personal
reputation for nobility and excellence of character.

" Believing that you, as all true women should
do (for in our estimation every wife should fill the
position of counselor to her husband), possess the
confidence of and have much influence with his
excellency, President Grant, we earnestly solicit
the exercise of that influence with him in behalf of
our husbands, fathers, sons and brothers, who are
now being exposed to the murderous policy of a
clique of federal officers, intent on the destruction
of our honest, happy, industrious and prosperous
people.

" We have broken no constitutional law ; violated
no obligation, either national or sectional ; we revere
the sacred constitution of our country, and have
ever been an order-loving, law-abiding people.

" We believe the institution of marriage to have
been ordained of God, and therefore subject to his
all-wise direction. It is a divine rite, and not a civil
contract, and hence no man, unauthorized of God,
can legally administer in this holy ordinance.

" We also believe in the Holy Bible, and that God
did anciently institute the order of plurality of wives,
and sanctioned and honored it in the advent of the
Saviour of the world, whose birth, on the mother's
side, was in that polygamous lineage, as he testified

to his servant John, on the Isle of Patmos, saying: 'I am the root and the offspring of David;' and we not only believe, but most assuredly know, that the Almighty has restored the fullness of the everlasting gospel, through the prophet Joseph Smith, and with it the plurality of wives. This we accept as a purely divine institution. With us it is a matter of conscience, knowing that God commanded its practice.

"Our territorial laws make adultery and licentiousness penal offences, the breach of which subjects offenders to fine and imprisonment. These laws are being basely subverted by our federal officers, who after unscrupulously wresting the territorial offices from their legitimate incumbents, in order to carry out suicidal schemes, are substituting licentiousness for the sacred order of marriage, and seeking by these measures to incarcerate the most moral and upright men of this territory, and thus destroy the peace and prosperity of this entire community. They evidently design to sever the conjugal, parental and paternal ties, which are dearer to us than our lives.

"We appreciate our husbands as highly as it is possible for you, honored madam, to appreciate yours. They have no interests but such as we share in common with them. If they are persecuted, we are persecuted also. If they are imprisoned, we and our children are left unprotected.

"As a community we love peace and promote it. Our leaders are peacemakers, and invariably stimulate the people to pacific measures, even when subjected to the grossest injustice. President Brigham Young and several of his associates, all noble and philanthropic gentlemen, are already under indictment to be arraigned, before a packed jury, mostly non-residents, for the crime of licentiousness, than which a more outrageous absurdity could not exist.

" Under these cruel and forbidding circumstances, dear madam, our most fervent petition to you is, that through the sympathy of your womanly heart you will persuade the President to remove these malicious disturbers of the peace, or at least that he will stop the disgraceful court proceedings, and send from Washington a committee of candid, intelligent, reliable men, who shall investigate matters which involve the rights of property, perhaps life, and more than all, the constitutional liberties of more than one hundred thousand citizens.

" By doing this you will be the honored instrument, in the hands of God, of preventing a foul disgrace to the present administration, and an eternal blot on our national escutcheon.

" And your petitioners will ever pray," etc.

It is believed that this petition had due weight in accomplishing the dismissal of Judge McKean, which afterward occurred.

The third example was still greater. It was a memorial to Congress, by the women of Utah, upon their marriage question, the grant of a homestead right to woman, and for the admission of Utah as a State. It was signed by twenty-six thousand six hundred and twenty-six women of Utah, and was duly presented to both houses of Congress.

And these are the acts and examples of enfranchised Mormon women; not the acts and promptings of President Young and the apostles, but of the leaders of the sisterhood. It may be stated, however, that President Young and the apostles approved and blessed their doings; but this confesses much to their honor.

How suggestive the question, What if the leading men of every State in the Union should do as much

for woman in her mission, instead of setting up bar-
riers in her way? Were such the case, in less than
a decade we should see female suffrage established
in every State of the federation.

CHAPTER LVII.

SARAH THE MOTHER OF THE COVENANT—IN HER THE
EXPOUNDING OF THE POLYGAMIC RELATIONS OF
THE MORMON WOMEN—FULFILMENT OF GOD'S
PROMISE TO HER—THE MORMON PARALLEL—SARAH
AND HAGAR DIVIDE THE RELIGIOUS DOMINATION
OF THE WORLD.

Meet we now Sarah the mother of the covenant.
In her is incarnated the very soul of patriarchal
marriage. In her is the expounding of the patriarchal relations of her Mormon daughters. Sarah,
who gave to her husband another wife, that the
covenant which the Lord made with him might be
fulfilled.

O woman, who shall measure thy love? And
thus to give thyself a sacrifice for thy love! Thus
on the altar ever!

It is thy soul-type in nature that makes nature
beneficent. Had not nature the soul of woman she
had been infinitely selfish; an infinite love had not
been born; there had been no Christ; no sacrifice
of self, that blessing and joy might come into the
world.

The story of Sarah is the more touchingly beautiful when we remember that it has its cross. It

would be a grievous wrong to Sarah's memory should we forget the sacrifice that her act necessitated, or underestimate that sacrifice. And let us not forget that it was not Abraham who bore that cross, great and good though he was.

The sacrifice in the initial of the covenant is a psalm to woman.

Keeping in mind the episode of Sarah and Hagar, let us continue the Abrahamic story:

" And God said unto Abraham, as for Sarai thy wife, thou shalt not call her name Sarai, but Sarah shall her name be.

" And I will bless her, and give thee a son also of her : yea, I will bless her, and she shall be a mother of nations; kings of people shall be of her.

*　　　*　　　*　　　*　　　*　　　*

" And the Lord visited Sarah as he had said, and the Lord did unto Sarah as he had spoken.

" For Sarah conceived, and bare Abraham a son in his old age, at the time of which God had spoken to him."

The divine story was once familiar; it is now almost forgotten. But it is the living word of God to the Mormon people.

Reincarnate in modern times the soul of this vast Abrahamic iliad. Breathe the breath of its genius into a young civilization. A civilization born not in the East, where once was the cradle of empires— where now are their crumbling tombs. A young civilization, born in the revirgined West—the West, where new empires are springing up on the very dust of empires which had expired when Egypt was but a maiden—ere Babylon was a mother—ere Rome was born.

Re-utter the word and will of that God who spake to the Hebrew sire on the plains of Mamre; utter it now in the birth and growth of a young Israel in the land of America. Comprehend him in his birth and in his growth. Consider his genius and his covenant.

In Abraham of old is the expounding and understanding of the renewed covenant with the latter-day Israel; and in Sarah of old is the expounding and understanding of patriarchal marriage among her Mormon daughters.

The Mormon woman is Sarah in the covenant, as she is Eve in the creation and fall. She has appropriated the text of the covenant. She claims her mother Sarah's rights. She invokes her mother Sarah's destiny: "She shall be a mother of nations; kings of people shall be of her."

Thus in the mind of the Mormon woman is patriarchal marriage established by her God. Be it confessed that woman was a listener to the Abrahamic promise in the days of Sarah; was she not also a listener in the days of Joseph the prophet? Could the heavens thus speak and woman fail to hear? Could such promises be made and motherhood fail to leap for joy?

If she dared to bear the patriarchal cross, was it not because she saw brightly looming in her destiny the patriarchal crown? In this life only the cross— in all the lives to come a crown of glory!

The Mormon woman knows nothing of "polygamy" as conceived by the Gentiles. She is constantly declaring this. There is no "many-wife system" in Mormondom. It is patriarchal marriage.

There is the destiny of a race in the Mormon woman's vision. For this came she into the world. In her is motherhood supremely exalted, and woman is redeemed from bondage to her husband.

Glance at the story of Sarah again. Mark its stupendous import to motherhood. Witness the introduction of polygamy into the Abrahamic family. And, if the wondrous sequel has any meaning, Isaac was the Lord's answering gift to Sarah's act, to fulfil the covenant.

And while remembering the sacrifice of Sarah and Hagar let us also remember the compensation. Those two mothers are without parallel in all history. Races and empires came of them. Sarah and Hagar, in their sons Isaac and Ishmael, have divided the world.

From Isaac's line was given to the world the Christ; from Ishmael came Mohammed, the prophet of hundreds of millions.

Weigh those two mothers, with their sons, their races, and their civilizations. What a weight of empire! What were Egypt and Babylon, compared with Sarah and Hagar?

The Abrahamic subject is the most stupendous of all history. That subject has been reincarnated in Mormonism. Its genius and covenants are with the Mormon people; the age is witnessing the results.

Patriarchal marriage is one of those results. Sarah is a live character of our times. She will fulfil her destiny.

From the courts above the Mormon woman shall look down upon an endless posterity. In the heavens and in the earth shall her generations be multiplied.

This is the faith of each Mormon Sarah—each mother of the covenant. This only is her polygamy.

CHAPTER LVIII.

WOMANHOOD THE REGENERATING INFLUENCE IN THE WORLD—FROM EVE, THE FIRST, TO MARY, THE SECOND EVE—GOD AND WOMAN THE HOPE OF MAN—WOMAN'S APOSTLESHIP—JOSEPH VS. PAUL—THE WOMAN NATURE A PREDICATE OF THE WORLD'S FUTURE.

In the beginning religion and nature dwelt together. The book of creation was gospel then. Creation was the only revelation.

Motherhood is the first grace of God, manifested through woman. The very name of all things is in the mother: "And Adam called his wife's name Eve; because she was the mother of all living."

See in what divine ordinance woman's mission on earth began. The theme of the initial psalm that ascended to the heavens, which listened to catch from earth the first notes of the everlasting harmonies: "I have gotten a man from the Lord!"

But the nature of the mother abounded not in Cain. Woman's soul was not manifested in her first-born. It was the strength, and the fierceness, and the selfishness of man that was first brought forth.

And Cain was very wroth because of his brother,

born with woman's nature, with his mother's gentleness manifested in him.   And he " rose up against
his brother and slew him."

Here is pre-epitomized the coming history of the
race.   In the savage strength of nature the world
began.   In the gentleness of woman, which at
length prevailed in her sons, civilization dawned.

Woman's apostleship as the minister of the " word
of God " commenced at the death of Abel.

Turn we now to Mary, the mother of Christ, to
see what kind of man she " hath gotten from the
Lord."   From the first Eve to the second Eve, to
find the grace of woman's nature spreading abroad
in her Jesus, for the salvation of the world.   Motherhood now in the regeneration.

" Hail thou that art highly favored, the Lord is
with thee: blessed art thou among women.

" And behold thou shalt conceive in thy womb,
and bring forth a son, and shalt call his name Jesus."

As also note the episode of her meeting with her
cousin Elizabeth, the mother of John the Baptist.

These mothers were conscious of the salvation to
be born of woman.   Elizabeth was filled with the
Holy Ghost, and blessed the greater mother; and
Mary magnified the Lord in psalm, and said: " Be-
" hold from henceforth all generations shall call me
" blessed."

We shall yet have to give to the gospel word
" regeneration " a very literal meaning.   The world

must be regenerated, in fact, before much salvation
can come unto it; regenerated through the divine
nature of woman endowing her sons; and regenerated in her apostolic ministry to the race; which in
this age is being so universally acknowledged.

The world must be born again. "Except a man
"be born again, he cannot enter into the kingdom
"of heaven." Except mankind be regenerated, no
Christ can reign with his saints on earth. There
is something more than mere figure of speech in
this gospel.

The generation of mankind began in Cain; the
regeneration of mankind began in Christ. The one
born with the club; the other endowed with all-
conquering love. The scepters of the two creations
typed in Cain and Jesus.

Jesus was not only the first fruits of the resurrection, but of the regeneration also. And motherhood
was (before fatherhood) first with God in this regeneration. Has egotistic man sufficiently cogitated over this fact? And does he fully comprehend
the equally significant fact that woman was the first
witness and testament of the resurrection?

And who began the regeneration of the race?
Whose human nature was manifested in the work?
The woman's!

God's nature in Christ needed no regeneration.
Nor did the woman's nature need regeneration, when
thus found pure, as in Mary. This is the great fact
embodied in the Christ example. As soon may
Christianity be wiped out as this fact!

What an astounding truth have we in this example—that God and woman have brought forth a

perfect creation and an infinite love, in Jesus their
Christ.

God was the father of Jesus. From him the
Holy Ghost. From him the wisdom of the eternities. From him the power to call a legion of angels
down to his help, had he so willed it. From him
the power to lay down his life and take it up again.
From him the power to conquer death and burst
the gates of hell.

The mother of Jesus—a virgin of the house of
David, and not a flaming goddess from the skies.

From woman, the love of Jesus for humanity.
From her his sympathies for the race. 'Twas she,
in her son, who forgave sin ; she who bade the sinner
go and sin no more; she who wept over Jerusalem
as a mother weepeth over her young And it was
woman, in her son, who died upon the cross for the
sins of the world !

It was not God the father who in Jesus died ; not
he who passed the dark hour of nature's struggle
in the garden; not God who prayed, " Take away
"this cup from me : nevertheless not what I will,
"but what thou wilt." 'Twas woman who was left
alone on the cross; she, in her son, who cried, " My
"God ! my God ! why hast thou forsaken me ?"

Love is of the woman. That is the great lesson
which the human nature of Jesus teaches; and it is
that element of her nature which shall save the
world.

Would we see what will be her teaching when her
apostleship comes to prevail in the earth, let us read
the sermon of her son on the Mount. Is not that
woman's own gospel ? Is it not also her philoso-

phy—" If thy brother smite thee on the one cheek
"turn unto him the other also ?"

And in this regeneration of the race, in nature
and spirit, God and woman are thus seen first alone.
Man came not to their help, but they came to the
help of man.   Here is groundwork indeed for the
reconstruction of society, and the remoulding of
philosophy !

In the past the apostleship of woman has not
been fairly granted to her, even among the most
civilized nations.   But it shall be ; and there is the
hope of the world.

Paul, in the egotism of man's apostleship, commanded, " Let the woman be silent in the church."
Yet the church is the type of woman.   If she be
silent, then will there be but little of saving gospel
in the world.   If woman's spiritual nature prevail
not in the church, then is the church dead.   If her
faith expires, then is there left but a wretched form
of godliness.

The prophet Joseph corrected Paul, and made
woman a voice in the church, and endowed her with
an apostolic ministry.

And in the regeneration is the entire significance
of Mormon patriarchal marriage.   First, woman in
her ever blessed office of motherhood ; next, in her
divine ministry.   Is not this according to the example ?

The chief faith of the Mormon women concerning themselves is that they are called with a holy
calling to raise up a righteous seed unto the Lord—
a holy nation—a people zealous of good works.

The Mormon women have a great truth here.

Woman must regenerate the race by endowing it with more of her own nature. She must bring forth a better type of man, to work out with her a better civilization.

It is blasphemy against the divine truth of the world's coming redemption, and of woman's mission in it, to scoff at the Mormon women for holding such a faith.

Woman shall leaven the earth with her own nature. She shall leaven it in her great office of maternity, and in her apostolic mission.

It shall be the lofty prophesy of the coming woman, " Behold from henceforth all nations call me " blessed !"

CHAPTER LIX.

Zion the joy of the whole earth ! She who cometh
down from heaven, with the anointing of salvation
upon her head.

The woman of the future, whom the Lord hath
chosen ! Her type is the church, with the divine
nature of the race restored.

Zion is coming down to be the spiritual mother
of the earth. She shall bruise the serpent's head,
in her seed and in her ministry. Now shall woman
be not only the mother of the individual Christ, but
she shall also be the mother of the universal Christ.

"Saviours shall come upon Mount Zion !"

The daughters of Zion shall multiply the seed of
Christ.

There was a beautiful consistency and a deep
mystical meaning in the words of the old Jewish
prophets when personifying Zion as the woman—
the woman of the Lord's choosing, for the earth's
joy.

They sang of Zion as the woman of the future :

" Oh that the salvation of Israel were come out of
" Zion !   When God bringeth back the captivity of
" his people, Jacob shall rejoice and Israel shall be
" glad."

True, Zion is sometimes spoken of as a city, but
always with a mixture of personification. As the
Hebrew poets rose to the height of their great subject they symbolized her as a veritable woman, with
a ministry in the earth ; and chiefly symbolized her
as the woman of the future.

David, the great psalmist, led the theme, for Zion
was his daughter; then glorious Isaiah swelled the
volume of earth's epic hymn. What a culmination
and personification is this : " For thy Maker is thy
" husband ; the Lord of Hosts is his name; and thy
" Redeemer the Holy One of Israel ; the God of
" the whole earth shall he be called."

This is the very subject of Mary the mother of
Jesus. But here enlarged. This is Zion, who shall
be mother of many Messiahs, for she shall bring
forth many sons, with the anointing of their Lord's
spirit upon them, to exalt his reign.

" Enlarge the place of thy tent, and let them
stretch forth the curtains of thy habitations ; for
thou shalt bring forth on the right hand and on the
left ; and thy seed shall inherit the Gentiles, and
make the desolate cities to be inhabited."

'Tis the divine mission of woman to the race,
oracled by lofty souls ; her holy apostleship on earth
pronounced. She is to be incarnated in a civilization on whose tables shall be written, " Thy Maker
is thine husband."

The mission of woman could not prevail in the barbaric periods of the race; 'twas man's work to chisel the rocks of the temple. Not even had her time come in the days of Christ, though no one has so distinctly foreshadowed it as he.

Paul is not to be unqualifiedly reproached for bidding woman be silent in the church. The time had not then come. Not as potent then as now the thought: " Show me the women of a nation and I " will tell thee its civilization." And there is still a deeper meaning in this than the popular thought. How beautifully has Jesus himself kept up the symbols of the coming woman. With him the woman— Zion—becomes the " Lamb's bride :"

" Then shall the kingdom of heaven be likened unto ten virgins, which took their lamps, and went forth to meet the bridegroom."

And this was to be in the age " when the Son of " Man shall come in his glory, and all the holy angels " with him."

At his first coming the kingdom of heaven was likened to twelve fishermen—not ten virgins—and he said unto them, " Take up your nets and follow " me and I will make you fishers of men."

But when the cry shall go forth, " Behold the bridegroom cometh," commotion is to be among the virgins of the earth—the virgins of Zion and the virgins of Babylon. Each will trim their lamps. Each will have their " five wise " and " five foolish." Every one will have her familiar spirit. But the God of Israel will send his spirit to inspire Zion, for her Maker is her husband. And the daughters of

35

Zion shall trim their lamps to go forth to meet the bridegroom, who is the Lamb of God.

The age of Messiah's coming is the woman's age! or there is no sense in the utterances of prophesy, nor meaning in the most beautiful parables of Christ.

And this is the woman's age! All humanity is proclaiming it!

The women of the age are obeying the impulses of the age. Do they know what those impulses mean? They have heard the cry, and have come forth. Do they comprehend what that cry has signified?—" Behold, the bridegroom cometh; go ye out to meet him!"

Unwittingly they are testing the Scriptures, and proving that the coming of Messiah is the crowning truth of the world. However, the five wise virgins of Zion are coming forth in faith. They are not unwittingly fulfilling their Lord's word. They have interpreted the cry, and are trimming their lamps.

Man may as well attempt to throw back the ocean with the hollow of his hand, or put out the sun with the breath of his command, as to attempt to defeat the oncoming of " woman's hour."

Let the God of humanity be praised for this; for did not the virgins come out at this eleventh hour, the fishermen might go again to their nets, and let the midnight pass, and earth take the consequence.

But how wondrously are the divine themes of earth's grace from God revealed. Down through the ages they came as echoes mellowed into more celestial tones.

Creation begins again! Zion—the New Jerusalem—is the Lamb's bride. She is the coming Eve.

"And I saw a new heaven and a new earth, for the first heaven and the first earth were passed away. * * *

"And I John saw the holy city, New Jerusalem, coming down from God out of heaven, prepared as a bride adorned for her husband.

"And there came unto me one of the seven angels * * * saying, come hither, I will shew thee the bride, the Lamb's wife.

"And I heard as it were the voice of a great multitude, and as the voice of many waters, and as the voice of many thunderings, saying Alleluia: for the Lord God Omnipotent reigneth.

"Let us be glad and rejoice, and give honor to him : for the marriage supper of the Lamb is come, and his wife hath made herself ready.

"And he saith unto me, write, Blessed are they which are called unto the marriage supper of the Lamb."

Surely there is a glorious prophesy and a sublime truth, hallelujahed from the ages down, in this proclamation of the woman's mission at the hour of the Lord's coming.

The lives of the Mormon women are as a testament to the age. The very character which their church has taken, as the literal Zion of the latter days, shall soon be recognized as the symbol of the hour.

And the virgins in every land shall hear the cry, "Behold, the bridegroom cometh; go ye out to meet him !"

CHAPTER LX.

TERRIBLE AS AN ARMY WITH BANNERS—FIFTY THOU-
SAND WOMEN WITH THE BALLOT—THEIR GRAND
MISSION TO THE NATION—A FORESHADOWING OF
THE FUTURE OF THE WOMEN OF MORMONDOM.

" Who is she that looketh forth as the morning,
" fair as the moon, clear as the sun, and terrible as
" an army with banners ?"

The Daughter of Zion!

Fifty thousand daughters of Zion! Each with
her banner!

Her banner, female suffrage!

It is the great battle of woman for woman's rights.
The Lord of Hosts is with her.

The rights of the women of Zion, and the rights
of the women of all nations.

Her battle-field: America first; the great world
next. And the God of Israel is in the controversy.

———

The chiefest right of woman is in the shaping
and settlement of the marriage question. The voice
of civilization well enunciates this supreme doctrine.
To commit this all-sacred matter to a congress of
politicians, or to leave it to the narrow exactitude

of the law-making department, is as barbaric as any monstrous thing the imagination can conceive. Not ruder was it in the warlike founders of Rome to seize the virgins as spoil, and make them wives to accomplish their empire-founding ambitions, than for a congress of American legislators to seize and prostitute the marriage question to their own political ends and popularity.

Can there be any doubt that the men of Washington have seized polygamy for their own ends? And are these men of the parliamentary Sodom of modern times the proper persons to decide the marriage question?

Will woman allow her sanctuary to be thus invaded and her supremest subject thus defiled?

If there is anything divine in human affairs it is marriage, or the relations between man and woman. Here love, not congressional law, must be the arbitrator. Here woman, not man, must give consent. It is the divine law of nature, illustrated in all civilized examples. What is not thus is barbaric.

Woman is chief in the consents of marriage. It is her right, under God her father and God her mother, to say to society what shall be the relations between man and woman—hers, in plain fact, to decide the marriage question.

The women of Mormondom have thus far decided on the marriage order of the patriarchs of Israel; for they have the Israelitish genius and conception of the object of man's creation. In the everlasting covenant of marriage they have considered and honored their God-father and God-mother.

In turn, the Gentile woman must decide the mar-

riage question for herself. The law of God and
nature is the same to her. The question still is the
woman's. She can decide with or without God, as
seemeth her best; but the Mormon woman has decided upon the experience and righteousness of her
Heavenly Father and her Heavenly Mother.

A certain manifest destiny has made the marriage
problem the supreme of Mormonism. How suggestive, in this view, is the fact that Congress, by
special legislation, has made polygamy the very
alpha and omega of the Mormon problem. The
Mormon women, therefore, must perforce of circumstances, by their faith and action greatly influence
the future destiny of Mormonism.

The enfranchisement of the Mormon women was
suggested by the country, to give them the power
to rule their own fate and to choose according to
their own free will. Nothing but their free will can
now prevail.

Their Legislature enfranchised them—gave them
the power absolute, not only to determine their own
lives, but to hold the very destiny of Utah.

If it was Brigham Young who gave to them that
unparalleled power, no matter what should be declared by the enemy as his motive, then has he done
more for woman than any man living. But Mormon apostles and representatives executed this
grand charter of woman's rights; and George Q.
Cannon's noble declaration at the time—that the
charter of female suffrage ought to be extended to
the entire republic—is deserving the acclamations
of the women of America.

New civilizations are the chiefest boons of humanity. Never was a new civilization more needed than now, for in the last century the world has rushed over the track-way of a thousand years. A train dashing forward at the rate of one hundred miles an hour would not be in more danger than will soon be society, unless a safety-valve—a new civilization—is opened.

This is the woman's age. The universal voice of society proclaims the fact. Woman must, therefore, lay the corner-stone of the new civilization. Her arm will be most potent in rearing the glorious structurē of the future. Man cannot prevent it, for in it is a divine intending.

There is a providence in the very attitude of the Mormon women. The prophesy is distinctly pronounced in the whole history of their lives, that they shall be apostolic to the age.

A new apostleship is ever innovative. The Mormon women have established an astounding innovation in polygamy It has been infinitely offensive. So much the better! For it has made a great noise in the world, and has shaken the old and rotten institutions of Christendom. That shaking was not only inevitable, but necessary, before a new civilization.

We have seen the daughters of Zion, with her sons, establish their institutions upon the foundation of new revelation. We have seen them rearing temples to the august name of the God of Israel. We have seen their matchless faith, their devotion, their heroism.

We have seen them, because of their fidelity to their religion, driven from city to city and from State to State.

We have seen them in the awful hour of martyrdom.

We have seen them in the exodus of modern Israel from Gentile civilization, following their Moses.

The daughters of Zion were going up to the chambers of the mountains, to hide from the oppressor till the day of their strength.

Their banners were then their pioneer whips. Their banner now is female suffrage—on it inscribed, "Woman's Rights! in the name of the God of Israel!"

Fifty thousand of the daughters of Zion! Each with her banner!

We have seen them on the cross, with their crown of thorns. We *shall* see them on their throne, with their crown of glory. In this is divine and everlasting justice.

They have sown in tears · they shall reap in gladness.

With their pioneer whips in their hands they came up to the chambers of refuge, as exiles.

With the scepter of woman's rights, they will go down as apostles to evangelize the nation.

"Who is she that looketh forth as the morning, "fair as the moon, clear as the sun, and terrible as "an army with banners?"

The Daughter of Zion!

Milton Keynes UK
Ingram Content Group UK Ltd.
UKHW041147231023
431175UK00001B/134